AF669216

RECENT RESEARCH ON LADAKH

6

RECENT RESEARCH ON LADAKH 6

Proceedings of the Sixth International Colloquium on Ladakh Leh 1993

Henry Osmaston & Nawang Tsering

(Editors)

MOTILAL BANARSIDASS PUBLISHERS
PRIVATE LIMITED • DELHI

First Asian Edition: 1997

ISBN: 81-208-1432-0

ASIAN EDITION : NOT FOR SALE IN EUROPE OR AMERICA

Also available at:

MOTILAL BANARSIDASS

41 U.A. Bungalow Road, Jawahar Nagar, Delhi 110 007
8, Mahalaxmi Chamber, Warden Road, Mumbai 400 026
120 Royapettah High Road, Mylapore, Chennai 600 004
Sanas Plaza, Subhash Nagar, Pune 411 002
16 St. Mark's Road, Bangalore 560 001
8 Camac Street, Calcutta 700 017
Ashok Rajpath, Patna 800 004
Chowk, Varanasi 221 001

Typeset in CGTimes by H. A. Osmaston
Tibetan set by Padma Lhadol & Lozang Jamspal

PRINTED IN INDIA

BY JAINENDRA PRAKASH JAIN AT SHRI JAINENDRA PRESS,
A-45 NARAINA, PHASE I, NEW DELHI 110 028
AND PUBLISHED BY NARENDRA PRAKASH JAIN FOR
MOTILAL BANARSIDASS PUBLISHERS PRIVATE LIMITED, BUNGA-
LOW ROAD, DELHI 110 007

CONTENTS

Papers in Ladakhi, all with English summary, three with English version (E) see above

PREFACE

For several years the International Association for Ladakh Studies (IALS) has wished to hold a colloquium in Ladakh itself; for several years this has been frustrated by political unrest. At last in 1993 the situation was favourable, and a local committee, assisted enthusiastically by many other people and groups in Ladakh, hosted an excellent and enjoyable meeting.

A notable feature was the high level of participation by Ladakhis, both in the presentation of formal and informal lectures and in the frequently vigorous and prolonged discussions, mostly in English but sometimes in Ladakhi. For some of them this was their first opportunity to take part in a meeting of this kind. Though most of the proceedings were recorded on tape we have sadly not had the resources to transcribe them, and many people were too modest to submit written contributions for publication.

However we have succeeded in collecting thirteen papers in English by Ladakhi's and six in Ladakhi. Three of each of these groups are actually duplicate versions (though not word-for-word translations) in both languages, which we hope may be useful both to Ladakhi students of English and to English-speaking students of Ladakhi. The other papers in Ladakhi have English summaries. Besides these, there are fifteen papers from non-Ladakhis.

We have supplied short biographical notes on each contributor, compiled from a variety of sources, not always the subject; we apologise for any errors.

Naturally the IALS does not necessarily support any views expressed in these papers.

We wish to thank many people who have helped in the publication of these proceedings: Sonam Wangchuk of SECMOL and his assistants Padma Lhadol and Rebecca Norman who typed most of the Ladakhi's papers on to disc; Francesca Merritt who did further valuable typing and editing of them; Lesley Rhodes, Maria Phylactou, Helena Norberg-Hodge, Neil Howard and John Crook who supplied important information; and Stephen Benning and Neil Howard who converted MAC discs to MS-DOS.

Finally we thank the University of Bristol Alumni Foundation for a generous loan to finance the printing of these proceedings.

Nawang Tsering
Henry Osmaston
Editors

PATRON'S MESSAGE TO THE COLLOQUIUM

EMBASSY OF INDIA
P.O. Box No. 691
ULAN BATOR, MONGOLIA

July 20, 1993.

I am very pleased to learn that the Sixth International Colloquium on Ladakh which was to be held in Leh much earlier, is now finally taking place from August 16-20, 1993 at Leh. I am grateful that the International Association for Ladakh Studies with whom I am connected in my capacity as its patron, is organising this colloquium. The Association had arranged similar meetings elsewhere in different countries which had greatly helped in understanding and in the propagation of Ladakh culture amongst people abroad.

As many of you have perhaps observed, Ladakh today has become a focal point for people everywhere for its peculiar but natural habitation and of co-existence. Although much has changed in the recent past, I am happy that people of Ladakh by and large, have been able to contain the erosion to their culture to a great extent and for this they owe much to our friends and well-wishers from abroad and in different parts of the country for their guidance and support. I would, in particular like to mention about the contribution made by various organisations such as Ladakh Ecological Development Group for their dual role - one for generating realisation among the people of Ladakh for a more ecologically sustainable development and two - for propagating this idea to the outside world which I am sure has helped many people in different parts of the world.

While Ladakh is known for its traditional culture and values, we have also faced situations in the recent past which even divided the people of this land into different groups and which caused much concern and anxiety among the people watching Ladakh. It may, however, be noted that this struggle of the people of Ladakh for a better future and to be master of their own destiny, had been going on for the past several decades but without much success. I am glad that today Ladakh is peaceful as in the past and the people of various communities are united again in their aspiration for a better future. Equally gratifying is the fact that our long and painful struggle is nearing its goal as I see favourable indications for an early settlement and meeting concerning our long standing demand for a genuine autonomy for Ladakh.

This is my fourth year in Mongolia as India's Ambassador.

Although this assignment has kept me away from my people for a substantial period of time, I am happy to note that due to close culture similarities, between Mongolia and Ladakh, I have also been able to contribute a little to the people of Mongolia who unlike us lost most of their traditions, culture and religion in the decades of communist rule. And if I may add, the people of Mongolia greatly admire the way Ladakhis have been able to preserve and develop their culture.

Today, although we see some progress in Ladakh, one feels sad to notice the effects of tourist money which is causing serious damage to our culture roots. We should be those who achieve success and prosperity without losing our own cultural values. A major responsibility therefore lies on the shoulders of Ladakhi youth whether they are Buddhist or Muslim to ensure that the cordial and friendly atmosphere which has been prevalent in Ladakh for centuries, is unhampered and undisturbed and that no external influence and interference be permitted which could cause damage to the peculiar Ladakhi way of life.

I hope that the participants of this colloquium are enjoying their stay in Ladakh. From here in distant Mongolia, I would like to welcome you all to Ladakh and offer my best wishes for a successful and a fruitful deliberation. I am equally grateful for your kind invitation to participate and inaugurate the colloquium, but have to express my regret for my inability to be present physically there.

Finally, my highest appreciation to Dr. Henry Osmaston, Honorary Secretary of the International Studies on Ladakh and to all other members and organisers of this colloquium for their contributions and for holding it this time in Ladakh.

Kushok Bakula

INAUGURAL SPEECH

Dr. Nawang Tsering
Chairman, IALS Ladakh Committee

Today on behalf of the members of local committee of the 6th Colloquium on Ladakh, I feel extremely happy to welcome you all at the Lion's Club Children's park, Leh. We extend our special welcome to those participants coming from Europe and America, as well as Ladakh and other parts of India.

Let me first introduce this association known as the International Association for Ladakh Studies (IALS). This association was formed at Herrnhut, Germany in 1987 with an international committee of distinguished scholars. Five colloquia on Ladakh have been held so far, at Konstanz (Switzerland) in 1981, at Pau (France) in 1985, at Herrnhut (Germany) in 1987, at Bristol (UK) in 1989, and at the School of Oriental and American studies in London in 1992.

In fact, the 5th colloquium on Ladakh was to have taken place at Leh in 1991 but the local committee for Leh colloquium preferred to postpone it to 1993. The most Ven. Kushok Bakula Rinpoche has been our patron, Prof. Mooniz Raza our President and Dr. Henry Osmaston our Honorary Secretary.

The main purpose of this association is to provide contact between all who are interested in the study of Ladakh, and to exchange information on Ladakh past and present. During the 12 years of its existence, Ladakh has been the focus of much attention by students in many discipline In a short time, since its opening it to tourism, Ladakh has emerged as a new field of research for scholars and students of different nationalities. Its resources remain inexhaustible, as its civilization has continued uninterrupted since the introduction of Buddhism before the 7th century AD. Keeping in mind Ladakh's past and present development, we have chosen as the theme for the 5th day of the colloquium 'The Cultural and Development aspects of Contemporary Ladakh'.

In the past Ladakhi drew their cultural and spiritual strength from Buddhist Kashmir and Tibet. Though our present form of cultural and religious traditions are a duplication of that of Tibet, nevertheless during almost 1800 years of its civilization, starting from the 2nd century AD., the Ladakhi themselves have contributed much in the field of different disciplines of traditional medicine, fine arts, logic, language and religion. Rinchen Zangpo was the foremost scholar and builder of temples, Spon Namkar Spalgon was the greatest Ladakhi painter. Lama Tsulkhrims Nyima and Lama Tashi Tamphel were the greatest reformers. What we see today in the monasteries, palaces and individuals homes are the legacy of these and other great scholars in the Ladakhi history.

As early as the 13th century, we had many well known visitors from different nations: the Rev Yashy, Rev.A.H. Francke, Henry Moorcroft and Csoma de Körös studied and learned the culture, religion, history, language and literature from the foremost Ladakhi scholars like Lama Zhadpa Dorje, Lama Kunga and Rev. Y.S. Gergan. Indeed the Ladakh gyalrabs Chimed Ster of Gergan has been the source book for all the subsequent historians up to Luciano Petech of Italy.

It is in the same tradition that the IALS has been making efforts to continue our research on Ladakh to learn more and know more about different aspects of development. *The Cultural Heritage of Ladakh* and *Ancient Futures — Learning from Ladakh* are the result of the painstaking work of Prof. Snellgrove and Helena Norberg Hodge.

In this 5 days colloquium, we have chosen a range of subjects under the headings of History, Culture, Religion, Health, Education, Anthropology, Tourism and Development. In conclusion on behalf of the Development Commissioner, Leh and the Ladakhi members of IALS under the guidance of Mr. Sonam Dawa, Director of LEDeG, I welcome you all once again.

A LETTER FROM LADAKH TO OUR FOREIGN VISITORS

Tsultim Gyatso
Reader in Buddhist Philosophy
C.I.B.S., Choglamsar, Leh.

Dear Friends,

Many foreign visitors come to Ladakh seeking the mystery of a by-gone era, and it is very clear that the wonderful mountains of Ladakh help you to conjure up a Ladakhi world outside our planet earth. Above all, when you go inside the Gompas with your guides, your belief in a mysterious Ladakh is reinforced. Many questions then crop up in your mind. When your guide is unable to explain the real, deeper meaning of things, you reluctantly come to the conclusion that all that happens in the monasteries belongs to the realm of sorcery and magic.

But the truth is that all that you see and find in the monasteries is very closely connected with how to free ourselves from suffering and attain true happiness. Some of the visitors who are really interested in such matters dismiss the monasteries as Tibetan Lamaism. Such misunderstandings are a result of ineffective communication. I am in no way thinking that I have the right answer to all your questions. What disappoints us the most is that established western writers write many things on Ladakh simply for the sake of creating sensational information. If this approach to the essentially philosophical culture of Ladakh continues, there is the real fear of feeding the readers on things which will not help them to understand truly Ladakh and its people.

In my own view, I believe that Ladakhi Buddhism has two sources — one from India and the other from Tibet. The tradition of Indian Buddhism that came to Ladakh through Kashmir has left nothing behind to recognise it. This tradition can be the Theravadic School of Buddhism. The living Buddhist culture that you still find in Ladakh is, of course, of Tibetan extraction which itself was introduced from India. Even though you do not find much material progress, people have taken their religious culture to a very high level of development. It will interest you all to know that the development of the Buddhist religion has been brought about without moving away from the original Buddhist teaching in India.

This is also the reason why His Holiness, the Dalai Lama, very proudly tells everyone that the complete form of Buddhism is still preserved in Tibetan. I am of the opinion that Buddhism is not simply a religion, it is also a science. We have to make a difference between life, religion and philosophy, and philosophy is the main agent of influence. When the philosophy is sound, the religion which believes in it is also sound. And then life based on such a religion is sound and purposeful. There are many people in Ladakh and other regions of the Himalaya who lead their lives according to their philosophical belief. They live their philosophy.

Now, we will talk about what we find in the monasteries. The first thing that you are attracted to in a Gompa is the wall paintings and the thangkas of the deities - some peaceful and others very terrifying. What they represent are the forces which assist us to attain to very high levels of spiritual attainment. We need not feel attached to the paintings of the peaceful deities and shun the wrathful-looking ones. It is also necessary that one should not covet the priceless old artifacts found in the Gompas. It is going to be a very vast field of study if we go in to the explanation of each and every statue, painting and thangka.

I feel it very important to explain that ultimately all the different gods, deities etc. represent the Buddha Sakyamuni, but it can not definitely be said that all the deities and Buddhisattvas are the Buddha himself. While discussing this subject we have to remember that the layman's approach and the approach by highly accomplished practitioners are vastly different. The Buddha Sakyamuni who was born at Lumbini is generally believed to be His Nivanakaya. That is how we look at its statues. The living Buddhism that we know in the world is the religion he founded. Now, it is very ironical that the real teachings of Buddhism that take the practitioners to very high levels of spiritual power represented by Yam-Yum (a deity with his consort) has become something that unknowledgeable people look down upon. This is the path leading to the realisation of great compassion, and Shunyata (Emptiness) and Bodhiccit. Most important of all, this teaching was also given by the Buddha himself in the form of Sambhogakaya. The Kalachakra Deity is, in fact, Buddha's Sambhogakya. So are Heruka, Chakar Samavara, Guyasamaja etc. Their real nature is the light of consciousness with no physical barrier. I always pray that I might become the Kalachakra deity, which some of you find not so attractive.

In almost all the places of Ladakh you will find representations of Avalokitesvara, Manjusri and Vajrapani. These three representations do not mean three different individuals. They are meant to represent the complete and perfect quality of one individual. If there is any one among us who wants to do a perfect service to mankind, he must possess Avaloketesvara's compassion, Manjusri's wisdom and Vajrapani's power. For example, if a person has succeeded in generating perfect compassion to a suffering sentient being without wisdom, he is handicapped. In the same manner, a person with perfect wisdom will not equally serve all because he does not have compassion to generate equanimity. When compassion and wisdom come together, power is born. All of these representations have an explanation like this.

In short, as His Holiness the Dalai Lama tells, Buddhism means helping others to attain happiness and never doing anything to bring suffering to them. The Nirmankaya Buddha tells us to not to harm others and His Sambhogakaya tells us to help others. The Buddhist philosophical tradition found in Ladakh is putting into practice the teaching of Sambhogakaya Buddha.

I hope my talk has proved useful.

REPORT

The Sixth Colloquium of the International Association for Ladakh Studies was held in Leh, from 16th to 20th August 1993. There were eight sessions on the following topics in which 43 papers were presented:

History, Culture, Religion and Philosophy, Health and Education, Anthropology, Environment, Development and Society.

Despite some problems with transport to and from Ladakh, partly due to heavy rain and landslides cutting the Manali road, this meeting proved most sucessful and enjoyable, being attended by 30 overseas members and a similar number from Ladakh and elsewhere in India; besides these were some official participants such as the Development Commissioner (Mr.Angurana) and the Secretary for Ladakh in the Kashmir Government (Mr.Arun Kumar). Strong support was provided by all three religious communities, Buddhist, Muslim and Moravian Christian, in the persons of H.H.Stakna Rinpoche, the President of the Ladakh Muslim Association (Mr.Akbar Ladakhi) and the Pastor of the Moravian Church (The Rev^{d}. E.S.Gergan), as well as by other official and unofficial organisations. Great satisfaction was expressed afterwards at our success in bringing together for friendly discussion such a wide range of local interests.

The main activities took place in a cool and capacious tent erected near the 'Ecology', but on two evenings we were hospitably entertained by the Development Commissioner at the Circuit House and by Rigzin Namgyal Kalon (Chairman of the Leh Citizens' Council) at his home. One day there was a tour of local gonpas, including Hemis, Thikse, Phyang, Likir, Spituk and Sabu, where we were welcomed hospitably. On the final evening the local committee invited all the participants to an evening of Ladakhi entertainments including *momos*, *chang*, music, dancing and singing, notably by Puntsok Ladakhi. Inspired by this and also perhaps by a few unlabelled bottles which were quietly circulating, there followed several more hours of rock-&-roll by almost all present, the like of which has never I am sure been seen in Leh before, and an example which many rather staid academic meetings might do well to follow. We particularly thank for financial and other support the Development Commissioner, Ladakh Ecological Development Group, Ladakh Nutrition project, Togdan Rinpoche, Helena Norberg-Hodge, Lions Club, Mahabodhi Society and the Students Educational and Cultural Organisation of Ladakh. All the participants thank Dr.Nawang Tsering, Mr.Sonam Dawa and other menbers of the committee for an enjoyable and interesting meeting.

During the colloquium many of the participants expressed deep concern on the following matters, both in presented papers and in subsequent discussions. at the final session the following summary was formally approved.

1. Serious concern was expressed regarding the deteriorating condition of many sacred works of art, historical places and monuments of great antiquity in Ladakh particularly the temples of the Rinchen Zangpo era and the wooden statue at Sumda Chenmo. The **Association recommends** that attention be given to the problems of their appropriate conservation, in relation to their ownership, ritual use and local sensitivity. Members with special interest in this field were urged to work with and through the existing Ladakhi cultural organisations such the Gonpa Association and Buddhist Association.

2. Concern was also expressed about current risks to the rich tradition of artistic activity in Ladakh and the **Association recommends** that concerted efforts should be made to encourage traditional arts, crafts and architecture. They also have important economic implications for the tourist industry.

3. The increasing problems of water and air pollution in certain parts of Ladakh, especially Leh, are matters of wide concern, and numerous **participants recommended** that all development in the fragile ecosystem of Ladakh should be carefully planned to meet the special environmental problems of this region. It was particularly emphasised that there should be local participation at all levels in the planning process. The opening of new areas for trekking would be a possible source of environmental degradation there; appropriate controls should be exercised from the start, and the effects carefully monitored.

4. Serious concern was expressed by **participants** about the marginalisation of the productive traditional agricultural system. They therefore requested that measures should be taken to increase the profitability of local agriculture.

5. Very serious anxieties about the current educational system were expressed by large number of **participants,** who felt that appropriate policies relevant to the social and economic needs of Ladakh were required and that special efforts should be made to encourage the use of local language in education.

6. Numerous papers were presented at the Colloquium on various aspects of social life in Ladakh, which it is hoped will be of use to the Administration and the people.

INTERNATIONAL ASSOCIATION FOR LADAKH STUDIES

6th. COLLOQUIUM, LEH, 16-20 AUGUST 1993.

The Development Commissioner,
Leh.
21 August 1993

Sir,

On behalf of the main and local committees of the Association I wish to express our appreciation and thanks for your help, encouragement and participation in our colloquium, which have made major contributions to its success.

We also thank you for your invitation to inform you of any recommendations which we might wish to express, arising from the papers and discussions. We have considered this very carefully, but feel that it would be inappropriate, except in two cases, for our Association to make formal recommendations on sometimes contentious matters, for the following reasons:

1) Ours is an International Association, and in most cases it would be wrong for us to try to influence the purely internal affairs of Ladakh.

2) We are proud that our membership comprises a wide range of backgrounds in Ladakh and we are determined to maintain this by remaining aloof, as a formal body, from sectarian interest. Any formal recommendations, even if apparently supported by a large majority of members, might well compromise the positions of a minority of members. This is especially so for some of our members, who hold official positions and for whom it would present problems if they were associated with recommendations which were not directly in line with current official policy.

3) Naturally, we do not restrict the personal and varied views of participants in our colloquia. However these should in no way be taken to represent the formal views of the Association.

We therefore respond to your invitation by making, in the accompanying report, two formal recommendations on the subject of the conservation and future of the artistic heritage of Ladakh, topics which we feel to be non-controversial, yet of considerable urgency and of legitimate international concern.

Other matters clearly aroused deep concerns and strong

feelings among many of the participants. We report the principal ones for your information, but without committing the Association itself to any formal position on them. We shall also be making these recommendations and report available to other relevant institutions, organisations and persons in Ladakh.

I am, Sir,
Your obedient servant

Henry Osmaston
Hon. Secretary, I.A.L.S.

****

INTERNATIONAL ASSOCIATION FOR LADAKH STUDIES

6th. COLLOQUIUM, LEH, 16-20 AUGUST 1993.

To:
The All Ladakh Gonpa Association
The Ladakh Buddhist Association
The Central Institute of Buddhist Studies.
20 Aug. 1993

1. At the Colloquium, concern was expressed at the deteriorating condition of some important sacred works of art in Ladakh. The Venerable Togdan Rinpochey advised all who were interested in remedying this situation to ensure that they worked closely with the Gonpa Association, Ladakh Buddhist Association and any local groups or villages concerned. We have emphasised this to our members, and look forward to the development of appropriate cooperative projects.

2. Several members also recommended that the Gonpa Association, the Ladakh Buddhist Association and C.I.B.S. consider the situation of nuns in Ladakh and discuss, in consultation with certain nuns, what measures might be appropriate for their support. Specific attention should be given to the educational and living situations in the nunneries.

Henry Osmaston
Hon. Secretary I.A.L.S.

THE INTERNATIONAL ASSOCIATION FOR LADAKH STUDIES

PATRON
H.E.The Ven.Kushok Bakula Rinpoche

PERMANENT COMMITTEE
Ravina Aggarwal (USA)
John Bray (U.K.)
Thierry Dodin (Germany)
John Crook (U.K.)
Philip Denwood (U.K.)
Pascale Dollfus (France)
Uwe Gielen (U.S.A.)
Kim Gutschow (U.S.A.)
Patrick Kaplanian (France)
Peter Marczell (Switzerland)
Gudrun Meier (Germany)
Maria Phylactou (U.K.)
Tashi Rabgias (India)
Harjit Singh (India)
Smriti Srinivas (India)
Nawang Tsering Shakspo (India)
Martijn van Beek (Denmark)

LEH COMMITTEE
Dr.Nawang Tsering Chairman,
Central Institute for Buddhist Studies
Abdul Ghani Sheik Treas.& Memb.Sec.
Yasmin Guesthouse, Leh, Ladakh 194101
Sonam Dawa
Dr.Mohamed Din
Rev. E.S.Gergan
Jamyang Gyaltsen
Thubstan Palden
Nawang Tsering Shakspo
Sonam Wangchuk

Hon. Sec.& Editor: Dr.Henry Osmaston, Thwaite End, Finsthwaite, Ulverston, Cumbria LA12 8BN U.K. Tel. & Fax (-44)-15395-31070

Only in the last two decades has Ladakh (northwest India, once known as Little Tibet) been readily accessible for study, but in that short time it has been the focus of much attention by students in many disciplines. These have been attracted by the interest of its physical situation at high altitude in the rain-shadow of the geologically active Himalaya; by the natural ecology of this rugged desert and the skilful adaptations of pastoralism and agriculture; by the sociology, history and cultural tradition, especially as a surviving example of Tibetan Buddhism; and by the problems presented by modern development and conservation. Informal study groups organised international colloquia on Ladakh in 1981 at Konstanz (Federal Republic of Germany), in 1985 at Pau (France) and in 1987 at Herrnhut near Dresden (German Democratic Republic). The 4th IALS Colloquium was at Bristol (UK) in 1989; the 5th at SOAS in London in 1992; the 6th in Ladakh in 1993; the 7th at Bonn in 1995. The proceedings of these have been published*. The 8th will be at Aarhus, Denmark, in 1997.

The I.A.L.S.

At Herrnhut the International Association for Ladakh Studies (IALS) was formed with an international committee of distinguished scholars. The functions of the IALS are to provide contacts between all who are interested in the study of Ladakh, and to disseminate information about proposed and completed research and publications. To do this the IALS organises colloquia, arranges publication of the proceedings, and publishes an occasional newsletter, "Ladakh Studies". This includes information about conferences, planned and current studies, requests for specific information and help, short reports, publications and general information about Ladakh. The close integration of resources, culture and religion in Ladakh demands a holistic approach, and members of the IALS are concerned with a wide variety of topics. Membership is open to all who are interested in Ladakh; for further information apply to the Hon.Sec.

*D.KANTOWSKI & R.SANDER (eds.) 1983 *Recent Research on Ladakh: history, culture, sociology, ecology.* Weltforum Verlag, Munich.

C.DENDALETCHE (ed.) 1985 *Ladakh, Himalaya Occidental: ethnologie, ecologie. Recent Research No.2.* Acta Biologica Montana 5, Pau.

L.ICKE-SCHWALBE & G.MEIER (eds.) 1990 *Wissenschaftsgesichte und gegenwärtige Forschungen in Nordwest-indien.* Dresden Museum of Ethnology.

H.A.OSMASTON & P.DENWOOD (eds.) 1995 *Recent research in Ladakh 4 & 5.* School of Oriental & African Studies, London; Motilal Banarsidass, Delhi.

H.A.OSMASTON & NAWANG TSERING (eds.) 1996 *Recent Research in Ladakh 6.* University of Bristol, UK; Motilal Banarsidass, Delhi.

T.DODIN & H.RATHER (eds.) (in press) *Recent Research in Ladakh* 7. Seminar für Sprach- und Kulturwissen-schaft Zentralasiens der Univ. Bonn.

N.B. The first two are out of print and the third is nearly so (apply Hon.Sec., price £11).

INFORMATION ABOUT CONTRIBUTORS

LADAKHIS

His Excellency The Venerable Kushok Bakula is Senior Lama of Ladakh and Rinpoche of Sankar and Spituk Gonpas, which are the main Gelugpa monasteries in Ladakh. The first Bakula is said to have been a disciple of the Buddha. He was a close associate of Pandit Nehru, which led to the establishment of the Central Institute of Buddhist Studies, Ladakh. From 1970-77 he was Minister of State of Kashmir and Ladakh, as member of Lok Sabha for Ladakh; then member of the Minorities Commission and is now Indian Ambassador to Mongolia. He is Patron of the IALS.

Dr.Mohamed Deen was a member of the Veterinary Department in Ladakh with a special interest in sheep and goat farming, and has managed the government farm at Upshi. He is now Director of the Desert Development Agency in Ladakh and has recently founded LEHO, the Ladakh Environment and Health Organisation, combating various local problems, particularly silicosis of the lungs. He owns the Himalaya Hotel in Leh.

Tsultim Gyatso comes from Nubra, and did his post-graduate studies at Varanasi Sanskrit University. He is Reader in Buddhist Philosophy at the Central Institute of Buddhist Studies, Ladakh.

Jamyang Gyaltsan comes from Matho village, and did his post-graduate studies at Varanasi Sanskrit University. He is a Tantra master who was formerly a monk at Mangtro gonpa but is now married with children and teaching at the Central Institute of Buddhist Studies, Ladakh.

Dr.Lozang Jamspal studied in Likir and Tashilunpo monasteries, starting from the mid-40's to the late-50's, then studied Sanskrit and earned the Acharya degree from Sanskrit University, Varanasi, in 1968. He came to the U.S.A. in 1974 to teach Tibetan at the Tibetan Buddhist Learning Center. In 1984 he went to Colombia University, earning his Ph.D. in 1991. His main interests are in Tibetan and Sanskrit literature and Buddhist philosophy.

Dr.Prem Singh Jina gained his Ph.D. at the Postgraduate Dept. of Economics, Kumaun University, Nainital. Since 1981 he has been Lecturer in Economics at the Central Institute of Buddhist Studies, Ladakh. Indus Publ.Co. has recently published his *Tourism in the Ladakh Himalaya*, and he has two other books on *Pasture lands in Ladakh* and *Phyang Monastery* in press with the same publisher. He has written over 30 papers on different aspects of the Ladakh and Kumaun Himalaya, presented at various national and international conferences. He is also a regular broadcaster on Radio Leh, his programme *Hemis Gonpa* being chosen for a national hook-up.

Dr.Tsering Morup was born at Likir and completed his medical (MBBS) training at the Govt. Medical College, Kashmir University, Srinagar in 1889. He has worked as Asst. Surgeon in Nubra, Chang Thang, Khalsi and Leh. He is convinced of the importance to the Ladakhi people of social and preventative medicine rather than curative treatment. This includes such positive measures as immunization and better maternity and health care, as well as negative ones such as discouraging smoking and excessive alcohol. He now works at the Sonam Norboo Memorial Hospital, Leh.

Sonam Morup comes from Hemis Shupkachan and is an engineering graduate from the Regional Engineering College, Srinagar. He is Assistant Executive Engineer with the Electric Power Division, involved particularly with the Stakna hydroelectric scheme. He is an active member of the Ladakh Ecological Development Group, interested in appropriate technology.

Contributors

Chhimet Namgyal is from Tingmosgang and is an officer in the District Cottage Industry in Leh. This year he received an award from the Cultural Academy for his Ladakhi writings. He is also an active member of the board of the Ladakh Ecological Development Group, particularly interested in handicrafts.

Jigmet Namgyal is an engineering graduate from the Regional Engineering College, Srinagar. He is Executive Engineer with the Electric Power Division, particularly concerned with power supplies to Ladakh.

Geshe Konchok Namgyal is from Phiyang village. As a youth he travelled to Sikkim and then walked for 25 days to Lhasa, where he studied for seven years at Drepung monastery and then for three years at at Varanasi University. For seven years he was *'chamdpon* (dance-master) and is now *cho stempo* (Commander of the Festival) at Phyang Gonpa. He is lecturer in Bhodi at the Central Institute of Buddhist Studies, Ladakh, and has given papers at many conferences. He is also a member of the Education Department in the Ladakh Ecological Development Group.

Fateh Chand Negi is a Research Fellow at the Central Institute of Buddhist Studies, Ladakh.

Dr.Tsering Norboo trained at the Srinagar Medical School and is now the senior consultant physician at the Sonam Norboo Memorial Hospital in Leh. He has researched various medical problems prevalent in Ladakh, including high altitude pulmonary oedema (mountain sickness), high blood pressure and chronic chest disease. An important cause of the latter is silicosis caused by breathing fine loess silt dust, aggravated by severe wind storms. The new rise in smoking among young men has prompted him to start LASH, the 'Ladakh Action on Smoking and Health' movement, which has had considerable effect.

Sonam Phuntsog is a headmaster in the village of Achinatang in Purig, west Ladakh. From his earliest childhood he has taken a keen interest in the history, culture and language of Ladakh and researched into these subjects. He is now a poet, scholar and historian, particularly interested in old traditions, especially among the Dards. Several of his writings on these Drogpa people and history have been published in the journals of the J & K Cultural Academy, Leh and he has written *Ladakhi Annals* in Tibetan.

Abdul Ghani Sheik has been a correspondent and news editor for All India Radio, and is a historian and dramatist, being the author of numerous books and papers in Urdu. He was a senior officer of the Indian Information Service and Principal of the Islamia School in Leh but is now retired and owns Yasmin Guest House in Leh.

Dr.Nawang Tsering obtained his doctorate at the Punjabi University of Patiala for a thesis on *The Yogins of Dzonkhul* (a gonpa in Zangskar). He has written a book *Buddhism in Ladakh: a study of the life and works of the 18th century saint and scholar Nawang Tsering* (Sterling 1979). He is now lecturer in English at the Central Institute of Buddhist Studies, Ladakh, and is chairman of the Local Committee of the IALS.

Dr.Stanzin Tondup is Chief Medical Officer, Leh District, and Medical Superintendent of the Sonam Norboo Memorial Hospital in Leh. He is the tuberculosis specialist for Ladakh and has especially studied the high incidence of chest disease there. He is a strong supporter of the Lions Club, which has raised considerable funds for the relief of Ladakhis with social and medical problems.

Lobzang Tsewang is from Taru village, and did his post-graduate studies at Varanasi Sanskrit University. He is now Lecturer in Comparative Philosophy at the Central Institute of Buddhist Studies, Ladakh, being especially interested in the common ground and contrasts between Buddhism and Christianity. At the IATS meeting in Oslo he presented a critical study of *rtsa.ba.shes.rab* (the Perfection of Wisdom).

OTHERS

Dr.Ravina Aggarwal is interested in Ladakhi poetry, politics and gender relations. Her doctoral dissertation was *From mixed strains of Barley Grain: person and place in Ladakh* at Indiana University. Subsequently she was a faculty member in the Department of Social and Cultural Sciences at Marquette University, and is now Asst. Prof. in the Anthropology Department, Smith College, Massachusetts, USA.

John Bray's reaearch interests include Christian missions in Ladakh and Tibet and the contemporary politics of the Himalayan region. After reading history at Cambridge University, he taught at the Moravian Institute at Rajpur, near Dehra Dun, then moved to Leh where he was the first superintendent of the new Moravian Mission School. Since returning to Britain he has worked as a country risk analyst based in London, specialising in South and South-east Asia. His publications include *Culture and Society in Ladakh* (an English translation of S.H.Ribbach's *Drogpa Namgyal* in German), *A Bibliography of Ladakh,* and articles in the *Tibet Journal* etc.

Dr.John Crook is reader in Ethology at the Dept. of Psychology , Bristol University. His scientific studies have progressed from the social systems of birds and baboons to those of humans. In 1977 he led an expedition to Zangskar, a pilot study for successive visits there, providing the material for *Himalayan Buddhist Villages* (Crook & Osmaston, 1994) and other papers. He is a teacher of Tibetan and Zen Buddhism, and recently received the Osman Hill Medal of the Primate Society of Great Britain.

James Crowden took a degree in civil engineering at Bristol University in 1976. While still an undergraduate he visited Zangskar in 1975, soon after it was reopened to foreigners, and was so impressed that he spent the 1976-77 winter there, being the first non-Ladakhi to go on the *chadur,* the winter passage of the frozen Zangskar Gorge. Since then he has travelled to Eastern Turkey, Iran, Afghan Hindu-Kush,, Yukon, Japan, New Zealand and Sikkim, besides revisiting Ladakh four times. His past and present occupations are Army officer, mountaineer, boatman, shepherd, sheep-shearer, woodman, poet, explorer and anthropologist.

Thierry Dodin studied Tibetology, Anthropology and Comparative religion at Göttingen and Bonn universities, his M.A. thesis being a study of the Losar (New Year) festival in old Tibet, followed by a research project on Buddhism and Society in the Himalaya. He is now a research student at the Seminar für Sprach- und Kulturwissenschaft Zentralasiens der Universität Bonn, working on processes of transformation initiated by Christian missionary schools in Ladakh and Darjeeling, supported by field studies in Ladakh, Himachal, Nepal, Sikkim and Darjeeling. He is organising the 7th International Colloquium on Ladakh at Bonn in June 1995.

Dr.Paula Green was until 1993 on the faculty of Antioch New England Graduate School, USA. She is now Director of the Karuna Center, exploring issues of Buddhism and social change. She spent 1993-94 teaching and learning in India, Nepal & Thailand. She is co-editor of *Psychology & Social Responsibility: Facing Global Challenges,* NYU Press, 1991.

Kim Gutschow is a Ph.D. Candidate in the Department of Anthropology at Harvard University. She has been doing fieldwork in Zangskar since 1991 on "Nuns, oracles, and madwomen: the marginal women in Zangskari society". This has involved spending three winters at Karsha nunnery and walking the *chadur*, the traditional winter traverse of the frozen Zangskar Gorge. She also has an M.A. in Anthropology and a B.A. in Social Studies (South Asia focus) from Harvard University.

Neil Howard took a degree in Geography at Liverpool and then, after teaching in Nigeria, pursued a business career. For the last decade however he has carried out research on the history and archaeology of the Himalaya and adjoining regions. He is now a research assistant at the University of Warwick, working on a *Dictionary of Manichaean Terms and Concepts* (a religious sect originally Persian). His interests in Ladakh and Himachal have been especially in the remains of old fortifications.

Contributors

Peter Marczell is a product and market development adviser and his consultancy firm in Geneva, Switzerland, also specialises in high net value asset management. His interest in the Himalayas and Tibet results from his researches on the life and work of Alexander Csoma de Körös (1784?-1842), the Siculo- Hungarian philologist, whose Tibetan dictionary and grammar were commissioned by Moorcroft in Ladakh.

Gudrun Meier obtained her diploma in ethnology from Leipzig University. Subsequently she worked in the Museum at Herrenhut, the headquarters of the Moravian Church, which stimulated her interest in their mission field in Ladakh. For the last twenty years she has worked in Dresden Museum of Anthropology, and was the main organiser of the Third International Colloquium on Ladakh. She has published papers on Sven Hedin, Jäschke and Hunza.

Helena Norberg-Hodge is a linguist by training who originally went to Ladakh to study the language. In the course of lengthy annual visits for the last sixteen years, she has mastered this and published an English - Ladakhi - English dictionary However her main interests are now directed to countering the cultural and economic problems arising from modern development. With John Page she founded the Ladakh Project which sponsored the indigenous Ladakh Ecological Development Group, with which she shared the 1986 'Alternative Nobel Prize'. Recently they have established the International Society for Ecology & Culture with worldwide targets, and she has written *Ancient Futures*, which relates Ladakh's problems to global ones.

Dr.Henry Osmaston was born in the Himalayan foothills and has been a forester in Uganda, a geographer at Bristol University and a pedigree dairy farmer. His thesis on the Quaternary glaciations of the East African mountains has been followed by similar studies in Ladakh and Tibet. These, with detailed studies of agriculture and pastoralism in Zangskar, provided material for *Himalayan Buddhist Villages* (Crook & Osmaston, 1994). He proposed the formation of the IALS at Herrenhut in 1987 and has been secretary and editor ever since.

Ali Mohmad Rather is a Research Scholar in the Centre of Central Asian Studies, University of Kashmir, in the field of sociology. He also teaches sociology at the Higher Secondary level Co-education Department of J. & K. State. He has completed his M.Phil. research project entitled *'Mons of Ladakh: An Ethnographic Study.'*

Dr.Peter Schweiger took his M.A. in Comparative Religious Science at the University of Bonn, followed by a Ph.D. in Tibetan Studies. He has published several books on Tibetan history, religion and language. He is now employed at the Academy of Science at Göttingen University, describing Tibetan manuscripts. At present he is working on the *Rin-chen-gter-mdzod*, a collection of *rÑing-ma-pa* texts.

Prof. Harjit Singh took his M.Phil. (*Ladakh - Analysis of its Regional Structure*) and his Ph.D. (*Ladakh - Problems of Regional Development in the context of Growth point Strategy*) at the Centre for the Study of Regional Development at Jawaharlal Nehru University, where he now on the staff, and has revisited Ladakh frequently with his students. His extensive travels in Ladakh made his theses the first detailed overview of the region since Cunningham's *Ladak*. His wife, Dr.Prem Lata, has worked similarly in Tadjikistan.

Dr.Smriti Srinivas studied sociology at the Delhi School of Economics, leading first to an M.Phil. thesis *Heteroglossia, structure and antistructure*, which combined theoretically a Bhaktinian perspective on language and society with anthropological studies of cultural variety. Her doctorate thesis, *Culture & Community on the Frontier: a study of Ladakh*, uses Bhaktin's social theory of language variety to relate the speech of oracles to shifts of religion and political economy. She is now Asst.Prof. at the Institute for Social and Economic Change, Bangalore, working on a project of the new liberalisation policy of the Indian government.

FROM UTOPIA TO HETEROTOPIA
Toward an Anthropology of Ladakh

Ravina Aggarwal
Dept. of Anthropology, Smith College,
Northampton, Massachussets, MA 01063, USA

Abstract

This paper investigates and critiques the atemporal anthropology of Ladakhi space by questioning the spaces of anthropology. A review of the academic literature on Ladakh reveals that it has often been claimed as "Little Tibet" or "Western Tibet" by Western scholars and "Eastern Kashmir" by Indian scholars. This academic and nationalist territorialism is explored within the paradigmatic framework of a reflexive and praxis-centered anthropology. In order to construct a more complete picture, it must be recognized that histories are contested, identities are fluid, meanings are conflicting and social practices are negotiated.

The terms "utopia" and "heterotopia" are borrowed from Michel Foucault (1986:24) who defines utopias as "sites with no real place" and heterotopias as counter-sites where "all the real sites that can be found within the culture, are simultaneously represented, contested, and inverted". The concept of heterotopia is well illustrated in the words of Apo Roziali, now deceased, one of my most knowledgeable informants from the region of Lower Sham which was the site for the major part of my field research. One summer morning, as we sat outside the little variety shop that was his window to the world outside, he said to me "We are mi-srar, made from mixed strains of barley grain. Some from here, some from there. A little bit of this, a little bit of that."

The relation between space and place is a problem in anthropological theory. Our discipline is grounded in the history of other places. Anthropologists are travellers in space, dislodged from familiar habitats. Anthropological writing derives its legitimacy and persuasive efficacy from "Being There", to use Clifford Geertz' (1988) phrase. Anthropologists have often forwarded their own locales, attributing totalizing essences to places which become reified demonstrations of the entire place itself (Appadurai 1988). Writing that validates its authority by producing environments that are inert, synchronic and timeless and histories that are universalizing, abstract and placeless, widens the distance between ethnographers and interlocutors. Inhabitants or "natives" living in these areas are then "incarcerated" and quarantined into the exotic confines of prison-like spaces and prison-like modes of thought which academic territorialism and imagination have defined and concretized (Appadurai 1991).

Although the technological shifts in communication have accelerated the pace of diaspora, the transnational movement of peoples and goods across locales is not just a special feature of modern and post-modern living, but rather, a given condition of our ever transient humanity. People from different nations have been invading, travelling and migrating to Ladakh for centuries, bringing with them cultural imports of commodities and ideologies which have shaped the topography of this region. Therefore, a rehabilitative anthropology must recognize that place is not vestigial or passive but that it is historically crafted and sensually experienced (Agnew 1989, Rodman 1991). "It is time to recognize that places, like voices, are local and multiple," writes Margaret Rodman (1991:643). In order to do so, it becomes necessary to undercover territorialism by placing under scrutiny not only the appropriations of nations but also those of academics.

In his book, *The Myth of Shangrila*, Peter Bishop (1989) provides a comprehensive view of Western travel writing on Tibet through the ages. Tibet, he alleges, was invented as a sacred landscape sculpted from the mythic fantasies of Victorian Romanticism. Through the topophilic visions of Western missionaries, traders and explorers in the eighteenth century, Tibet became an archetypical utopia in Western literature, with no geographical roots, an enterprise furthered by the imperial expansionism and trade interests of Britain.

Most visitors to Ladakh carry with them this romantic notion of an idyllic land, eclipsed from time and space. In the Himalayas, it is easy to let the magic of timelessness enfold you. But the mountains are not infinite texts of wisdom, frozen in eternity. There are roads linking Ladakh to Srinagar and Himachal Pradesh, the daily flights bring in tourists from all over the world, the same bureaucratic afflictions ail Ladakh as other parts of India, and so do similar religious tensions.

Bishop is influenced by Said's model of Orientalism, which presupposes that Western textual representations of the Orient can be traced to the dual propensity to radically dramatize the opposition between East and West and to deprive the Orient of its historical, diachronic being. However, there are other essentialisms that the theory of Orientalism ignores which must be considered to understand the process and not just the product of this objectification (Carrier 1992). Lying between these categories of Orient and Occident are other selves, other places - dialectical, shifting, slippery. When

Ladakhis present themselves to others, their depictions oscillate between categories of hospitality and privacy, simplicity and ignorance, patriotism and self-determination, business acumen and spirituality, harsh landscape and celestial abode, depending on the context, the situation and the position of their audience, whether Kashmiri, Indian, Tibetan, whether a wealthy tourist or a "hippy" (chad-po), army official or civillian. Within Ladakh itself, people of diverse regions, religions and classes claim to represent the authentic Ladakh. According to Michael Herzfeld (1990:305), "people themselves ignore human agency when it suits them to do so".

Ladakh has been represented in dual terms, as a surviving remnant of the glories and mystic secrets of an unsalvageable Tibet and as a primitive wilderness at the fringes of the Indian sub-continent. To quote one eminent writer, "Ladakh comprises the last remaining area of the world in which the original Tibetan religious culture remains untouched either by communism as in Tibet proper or by the modernization to which refugees in India and Nepal are generally exposed" (Crook 1980:140). Crook's article goes on to prophesy that "the tourist, however poorly informed, visits Ladakh for its authenticity. If that is lost the nature of tourism itself will change" (1980:160).

In academic literature, Ladakh has often been encapsulated under the domain of Tibet ("Indian Tibet", "Western Tibet", "Little Tibet") even though no Ladakhi that I have ever met classifies himself or herself as Tibetan, politically nor ideclogically. The rationalization forwarded is that Ladakh may be formally situated in India but that its culture is basically Tibetan. Thus, Barbara Aziz (1987) proposes to launch a Tibetan sociology of women, liberally disintegrating national and ethnic boundaries of diverse groups like the Ladakhis and the Lepcha, Sherpa, Tamang and Limbu people of Nepal, who she classifies as "fundamentally Tibetan, so strong has the influence from the northern civilization been" (1987:79) and then, later in the article, as "not pure Tibetan cultures" (1987:94). In investigating the position of women in Tibetan society, she infuses a diffusionist perspective where individual societies become mere proto-Tibetan emanations.

Patrick Kaplanian (1985) attempts to redress this problem with a quest to find a valid niche for Ladakhology. He welcomes a co-existence with Tibetan linguistics but decries the encroachment of phonological Tibetologists who demand an authentic, absolute and literary interpretation of texts and devalue the specificities of locale, dialect and experience with which their informants give new meanings to orthodox idioms. Kaplanian's plea to accord the Ladakhi language its due status is a welcome corrective but the debate is beyond a duel between just Ladakhi and Tibetan. In Ladakh, several languages are inter- woven by speakers including the official languages of Urdu and English. Unfortunately, as John Bray (1991:119) writes "Ladakh's religious links with Tibet tend to obscure the significance of its relationship with other neighboring countries". To understand comprehensively how people experience the world, it is necessary to situate the study of Ladakh in a larger universe, as I discovered when I asked for directives to visit Achinathang the first time.

You have to get an 'Inner line' [permit] to go to Achinathang, I was informed. Inner lines could be obtained from the D.C.'s office. If he wasn't in, I was to submit my petition to the A.C. Once he had sanctioned the Inner line, a copy would have to be submitted to the G.O.C. and the S.P. I was never to take a Shaktiman or a one-tonne going that way. If I was fortunate, then it might be time for a scheduled tour in a Gypsy by Block or Agriculture, the C.M.O. or B.E.O., or even Ecology which was building a hydroelectric project there. If none of these options were available, I could take the Service which ran on alternate days as a last resort choice which meant that I would have to identify myself at the three T.C.P.s en route. After I had reached my destination, it was unlikely that I would be bothered for there were only B.S.F. in the area. The I.T.B.F., I.T.B.P. and the S.B. (or R.A.W. as it was commonly called), might conduct routine inquiries but they were generally polite. It should be relatively uncomplicated. And if at all I had any complaints, I could address them to the A.C. in Khalatse.

Most of those who offered me this counsel spoke Ladakhi and Urdu with almost no English except for the acronyms which seemed almost impossible to decipher. One year of intensive training in Tibetan had not equipped me to decode this bureaucratese.

The inter-religious riots in Ladakh have exploded any fantasy of a timeless and homogenous Ladakh. Gerard Rovillé (1991:113) cautions scientific researchers in Ladakh to refrain from succumbing to partisan politics and parochialism, from sketching a lop-sided view of Ladakhi society, "bloquées dans leurs horizons par la ligne de cessez-faire". Seldom do texts on Ladakh make mention of the fact that almost half of its population practices Islam. Thus, Crook (1980:140) writes about Ladakh's "remoteness from Islamic and Hindu centers". In travel writings on Ladakh (Harvey 1983, Rizvi 1983), Islam emerges as a dark blemish on the otherwise pure and pristine society of Ladakh, with allusions to the hostile and sinister one-night stop-over in Kargil with its veiled women or in the form of avaricious, scheming peddlers of Kashmiri origin. Even distinguished authors like Pascale Dollfus (1987) assume that it was the Balti Muslims in conjunction with Kashmiri fleece traders and British trophy-collectors that endangered the ibex because Buddhism preaches non-violence toward living creatures, thereby prohibiting Buddhists from partaking in hunting. She falls prey to the official discourse, using stated ideals in place of experiential details. Rovillé (1991) further points to the total neglect of the study of Islam in Ladakh since Francke's article in 1929, which is fraught with references to the religious bigotry and conversion practices of the Muslims. Recently, there have been works which attempt to rectify this lacuna by voicing the political position of the Muslim organizations in Leh together with the demands of the Buddhist activists (Bray 1991, Crook 1990) and by researching the history of Islam in Ladakh (Dollfus 1992). There is, however, a greater need for anthropological revisionism and participation in this enterprise.

If Western academia has glossed over contemporary political realities, tending to dwell in wistful moments of paradise lost, Indian academics have also contributed to the process of partial representation. To most Indians the Himalayas are seen as sacred space, the abode of hermits for spiritual enhancement or as a protective frontier against invaders, sturdy, upright, impenetrable. There are songs that bear testimony to the heroic patriotism of those who shed their blood for the liberty of their motherland, defending the "wounded" Himalayas in the wars with Pakistan and China. From "Kashmir to Kanyakumari", we are taught, does the territorial sovereignty of India reign. The mention of Ladakh, however, does not evoke any sentiment of national pride or history despite its strategic importance and participation in the major wars since independence; in fact, very few Indians that I know have any idea where this place is situated. As Agehananda Bharathi (1978) maintains, "the Himalayas tend to be ascriptive rather than actual mountains" to most Indians except those who live there.

Bharathi (1978) adds that people in the Himalayas are considered to be mountain folk with strange body habits and stranger marriage relations. For example, B.L. Kak (1978:7) states that "judged from the outbreak of smallpox in Ladakh in 1834 with such fatal virulence that about 14,000 people were carried off, the mortal effect of such a contagious disease cannot be wondered at amongst filthy people, most of them living in the elevated tablelands, who never wash and only change their garments when the cloth has finished piecemeal off their persons". Kak (1978:23) takes an androcentric and derogatory stance in which polyandry ("the ugly system of plurality of husbands") is viewed as an abnormal aberration while "marital infidelity is nothing new in man's history, it has followed monogamy like a shadow" (Kak:24).

Bharathi further posits that Tibetan Buddhism is deemed a corrupt and distorted form of Buddhism, pejoratively labeled "Lamaism", and therefore scholars of Buddhism from the plains of India refuse to learn Tibetan. The problem of translation is highlighted in the anthropological works of Indian academics like R. S. Mann (1978) who indiscriminately intersperses Urdu terms, presumably translated for him by his interpreters, together with Ladakhi ones and attests that these are the words of usage in Ladakh. Thus Mann (1978:90) asserts that the Ladakhis refer to their fathers as Bada Baap and Chota Baap, both of which are Urdu terms. In the forword to his book *The Religion of the Dards in Ladakh* (1989), Rohit Vohra, in several instances, recounts the hardships he had to overcome in gathering data because of the inability of his informants to speak Urdu accurately, rather than self-consciously apologizing for his own failure to speak their language.

The process of fieldwork enhances the paradoxes of identities that are refracted and conflicting. My own position as an Indian educated in the United States unsettles the distinction between home and abroad, selves and others. Of course, I do not mean to imply that no Indian scholars learn Ladakhi or that all Westerners are accomplished Tibetologists. I have merely selected some broad problematic aspects of Ladakh studies with the hope that we can initiate a fruitful dialogue which scrutinizes not only the politics and practices of Ladakhis but also the politics and practices of the researchers who study Ladakh so that we may represent our experience as honestly and wholly as possible in order to bridge artificial chasms between East and West.

Acknowledgements

I should like to thank the Sigma Xi Foundation, the Skomp Foundation and the Institute for Global Change and World Peace at Indiana University for supporting my doctoral research. In addition I wish to express my gratitude to Michael Herzfeld and Michael Jackson for their comments on my dissertation writing, of which this paper is a part. To the people of Achinathang, particularly Sonam Phuntsog, and to all my friends in Leh and Kargil, I am especially grateful.

Notes

1. Although Bishop's approach is important because it probes the influences underlying textuality, there are some noticeable shortcomings. Bishop has been criticised for conflating the individual experiences of authors to collective imaginings, of succumbing tosubjectivism by skewing and selecting his sources to promote his theory (Sperling 1992). Moreover,

Bishop seems to be unaware of the genre in tibetan religion and literature which is itself concerned with hidden valleys and eternal places (*sbas.yul*).

2. In the light of some of the comments made when I delivered this paper, I think it necessary to clarify that I did not intend to suggest that there is no connection or identification of Ladakhis with Tibet but that this should not overshadow the multiple and multi-layered nature of Ladakhi identity. If Ladakh was called "Little Tibet" or "Western Tibet" in historical literature, these were points of reference used by outsiders in general, and not ethnonyms used by the people themselves. An old folk song, sung during the cultural programme on one of the evenings of the conference, underscores this distinction. With the assistance of Sonam Phuntsog, I have provided a somewhat rudimentary translation. The Ladakhi version can be found on page 66 in *Folk Songs of Ladakh* (1970) published by the J. & K. Academy of Art, Culture & Languages.

The Road around Lhasa

The road around Lhasa is narrow,
There are many travellers on it.
People from our birthland are even scarcer than gold.
People from our glorious capital of Leh are even scarcer than gold.

The water of Lhasa is of all kinds,
But nectar like chang and arak abound only in our birthland.
The water of Lhasa is of all kinds,
But nectar like chang and arak abound only in our glorious capital.

The grass in Lhasa is of all kinds,
But the grass of peacocks and turkey-hens abounds only in our birthland.
The grass in Lhasa is of all kinds,
But the grass of peacocks and turkey-hens abounds only in our glorious capital.

The trees in Lhasa are of all kinds,
But the best tree of all, the pencil cedar, abounds only in our birthland.
The trees in Lhasa are of all kinds,
But the best tree of all, the pencil cedar, abounds only in our glorious capital.

References

AGNEW, J. 1989 The Devaluation of Place in Social Science. In *The Power of Place* ed. John Agnew and James Duncan. Unwin Hyman, Boston, pages 9-29.

APPADURAI, A. 1988 Putting Hierarchy in its Place. *Cultural Anthropology* 3, 36-49.

APPADURAI A. 1991 Global Ethnoscapes: Notes and Queries for a Transnational Anthropology. In *Recapturing Anthropology: Working in the Present* ed. Richard Fox. School of American Research, Santa Fe, pages 119-210.

AZIZ, B. 1987 Moving Towards a Sociology of Tibet. In *Feminine Ground: Essays on Women and Tibet* ed. Janice Willis. Snow Lion Publications, Ithaca, p.76-95.

BHARATHI, A. 1978 Actual and Ideal Himalayas: Hindu Views of the Mountains. In

Himalayan Anthropology: The Indo-Tibetan Interface ed. James Fisher. Mouton, The Hague, pages 77-82.

BISHOP, P. 1989 *The Myth of Shangri-La: Tibet, Travel Writing and the Western Creation of Sacred Landscape*. University of California Press, Berkeley.

BRAY, J. 1991 Ladakhi History and Indian Nationhood. *South Asia Research* 11, 117-133.

CARRIER, J. 1992 Occidentalism: The World Turned Upside Down. *American Ethnologist* 19, 195-212.

CROOK, J. 1980 Social Change In Indian Tibet. *Social Science Information* 19, 139-166.

CROOK, J. 1990 Buddhist Ethics and the Problem of Ethnic Minorities: The Case of Ladakh. In *Radical Conservatism: Buddhism in the Contemporary World* ed. S. Sivaraksa. International Network of Engaged Buddhists, Bangkok, pages 376-391.

DOLLFUS, P. 1987 La representation du bouquetin au Ladakh, region de culture tibetaine de l'Inde du nord. In *Proceedings of the Fourth Seminar of the International Association for Tibetan Studies* ed. Helga Uebach and Jampa Panglung. Bayerische Akademie der Wissenschaften, Munich, pages 125-138.

FRANCKE, A. 1929 Islam Among the Tibetans. *The Moslem World XIX*, 134-140.

FOUCAULT, M. 1986 Of Other Spaces. *Diacritics* 16, 22-27.

GEERTZ, C. 1988 *Works and Lives: The Anthropologist as Author*. Stanford University Press, Stanford.

HARVEY, A. 1983 *A Journey in Ladakh*. Cape, London.

HERZFELD, M. 1991 *A Place in History: Social and Monumental Time in a Cretan Town*. Princeton University Press, Princeton.

KAK, B. L. 1978 *Chasing Shadows in Ladakh*. Light and Life Publishers, New Delhi.

KAPLANIAN, P. 1985 Ladakhologie - est elle une science? In *Ladakh Himalaya Occidental: Ethnologie, Ecologie* ed. Claude Dendaletsche and Patrick Kaplanian. Centre Pyreneen de Biologie et Anthropologie des Montagnes, Second Edition, Pau.

MANN, R.S. 1972 Intra and Inter Family Relations Among the Ladakhis of Ladakh. *Bulletin of the Anthropological Survey of India* 21, 88-101.

RIZVI, J. 1983 *Ladakh: Crossroads of High Asia*. Oxford University Press, Delhi.

RODMAN, M. 1992 Empowering Place: Multilocality and Multivocality. *American Anthropologist* 94, 640-656.

ROVILLÉ, G. 1991 Contribution a l'Étude de l'Islam au Baltistan et au Ladakh. In *Wissenschaftsgeschichte und gegenwärtige Forschungen in Ladakh* ed. Lydia Icke-Schwalbe and Gudrun Meier. Museum für Volkerunde, Dresden, 113-123.

SPERLING, E. 1992 Review of The Myth of Shangrila by Peter Bishop. *Journal of the American Oriental Society* 112, 349-350.

VOHRA, R. 1989 *The Religion of the Dards in Ladakh: Investigations into Their Pre-Buddhist 'Brogpa Traditions*. Skydie Brown International, Ettelbruck.

THE ROMAN CATHOLIC MISSION IN LADAKH, 1888-1898

John Bray
8 Glendall Street, Brixton,
London SW9 8AJ, U.K.

English and Dutch priests from the Mill Hill Mission lived and worked in Ladakh from 1888 until 1895. They founded a mission station known as 'St Peter's', studied the local languages, travelled widely, and engaged in medical and educational work. The missionaries wrote detailed accounts of their travels, their encounters with local Buddhists and their observations on Ladakhi life and culture. However, most of their writings are hidden either in unpublished archives or in specialist missionary periodicals. Thus, unlike the Moravian Church which maintains a congregation in Leh, the Roman Catholic mission is now largely forgotten in Ladakh. This paper, which is based on the Mill Hill Mission archives in London[1], aims to restore the mission's work to the historical record.

The founding of the mission

In 1866 Fr Herbert Vaughan founded St Joseph's Society of Foreign Missions, the first and only English Roman Catholic missionary society. Its initial centre was in a villa in Mill Hill, north London, and it later moved a short distance to its present, specially-built premises at St Jospeh's College. The society subsequently founded training centres in the Netherlands and in Austria, but it is generally known as the Mill Hill Mission because of the site of its English headquarters. Its founder went on to become one of the most prominent figures of nineteenth century English Catholicism: he was consecrated Bishop of Salford in 1872, became Archbishop of Westminster in 1892, and Cardinal in 1893.

In 1887 the Mill Hill Mission assumed responsibility for the Prefecture Apostolic of Kashmir and Kafirstan, which had been carved out of the Diocese of Lahore and had its headquarters in Rawalpindi[2]. The Prefecture's name reflected the missionary aspirations of its

1. I gratefully acknowledge the assistance of Fr W.J. Mol, the St Joseph's College archivist.

2. Rooney, John, *On Rocky Ground. The Catholic Church in the North-West Territories* (Rawalpindi: Christian Study Centre, 1987), p. 34.

founders who hoped to extend their work to the furthest frontiers of British India. However, the missionaries were never able to establish a foothold in Kafirstan, and therefore concentrated their attention on northern Punjab, Kashmir and, at first, Ladakh.

Ladakh had been an independent Himalayan kingdom until 1842, and was now part of the 'native state' of Jammu and Kashmir. The Maharaja of Kashmir owed allegiance to the British empire, and the British controlled most matters of foreign policy. However, the Maharaja exercised a considerable degree of independence over the state's internal affairs, and Europeans were not normally allowed to own land or buildings anywhere in Jammu and Kashmir.

The majority of Ladakhis were, and are, followers of Tibetan Buddhism, although there was also a large Muslim minority. Leh, the capital of Ladakh, was some two weeks' march from the Kashmir valley, and the road there was closed completely during the winter months because of snow on the mountain passes. However, it had obvious strategic advantages because it lay on one of the main Central Asian trade routes to Tibet and Chinese Turkestan (Xinjiang), and this meant that the mission would have access to travellers from far beyond the immediate locality.

Jesuit priests had travelled through Ladakh in 1631 and 1715[3], but the first missionaries to found a permanent station there belonged to the Moravian church (Herrnhuter Brüdergemeine) which is Protestant. The two Moravian pioneers, August Wilhelm Heyde and Eduard Pagell, passed through Leh in 1855 hoping to travel on to Mongolia. However, they were forbidden to cross the Tibetan frontier and therefore founded a mission station in Kyelang (now more commonly known as 'Keylong') in Lahul, a fortnight's journey to the south. Heyde visited Ladakh almost every year. In 1885, his colleague Friedrich Adolf Redslob opened a permanent mission station in Leh. He and his colleagues soon established the nucleus of an indigenous Christian community and set up a church, a school and a dispensary which was sponsored by the British government[4].

The first Mill Hill missionary to travel to Ladakh was Fr Daniel Kilty, who had been born in Liverpool in 1855 and had

---

3. These were Frs Francisco de Azevedo and John de Oliveira in 1615 and Ippolito Desideri and Manuel Freyre in 1715. See: Wessels, C., *Early Jesuit Travellers in Central Asia* (The Hague: Martins Nijhoff, 1924); Desideri, Ippolito, *The Travels of Ippolito of Pistoia S.J.* 1712-1727, Edited by Filippo de Filippi (London: Routledge, 1937).

4. For the beginnings of the Moravian mission see: Bray, John. 'The Moravian Church in Ladakh: the First Forty Years 1885-1925'. *Recent Research on Ladakh,* Edited by Detlef Kantowsky and Reinhard Sander (Munich: Weltforum Verlag, 1983), pp. 81-91.

previously served in north Borneo and Madras. Access to Ladakh was restricted, and Kilty first applied to the British Indian Foreign Department in Simla and then to the British Resident in Kashmir. In August 1888, the Resident issued Kilty with a permit to stay in Ladakh until 31 August 1890 'in order to learn the language'[5]. He arrived in Leh later that month.

At first Kilty stayed in the dak bungalow (resthouse) while waiting for a permanent residence to become available. Since the mission was not allowed to own land in Ladakh, he arranged for a building to be erected at government expense. The building cost Rs 800, and the mission was to pay the government an annual rent equivalent to 12% of its value[6].

Kilty was clearly a man of considerable zeal, and quickly embarked on a period of intensive language study with the help of a local assistant: he remarked that his work amounted to 'making a new dictionary'[7]. While studying, he shut himself away for days and weeks in the cold resthouse and paid little attention to material comfort, arguing that he needed to try to 'harden himself a little'[8].

However, Kilty's austerity contributed to a collapse of his health. In late April 1889 his superior, Fr Ignatius Brouwer in Rawalpindi, wrote back to London that he was concerned at the lack of news from Leh[9]. Four days later he received a letter from Captain H. Ramsay, the British Joint Commissioner in Ladakh, saying that Kilty was sick. Brouwer decided to set out for Ladakh, but on 6 May received a telegram stating that Kilty had already died. He apparently had suffered from a liver abcess which he had at first neglected. He had eventually reported to Dr Karl Marx at the Moravian mission hospital - but by this time it was already too late. He was buried in a small cemetery for Europeans in Leh[10].

The next Mill Hill missionaries to travel to Ladakh were Frs Ignatius Brouwer, Joseph Cunningham, Henry Hanlon and Michel Donsen. They set out from Srinagar in August 1890, and their first act

---

5. Letter from C.Plowden (Resident in Kashmir) 1 August 1888. British Library Oriental and India Office Collection (OIOC): R/2/1061.
6. H. Ramsay to C. Plowden. 24 September 1888. OIOC R/2/1061.
7. Letter from Kilty. *St Joseph's Foreign Missionary Advocate* (hereafter cited as SJFMA) 2 (1888-89), no. 1, p. 13.
8. SJFMA 2 (1890), p. 141.
9. Brouwer to Benoit. 29 April 1889. Mill Hill Mission archives.
10. The cemetery is in the Karzu district of Leh behind the army's 'Alpha mess', which used to be the British Joint Commissioner's residence. Kilty's grave is close to an obelisk commemorating Ferdinand Stoliczka, the Czech explorer who died in 1874.

on arriving in Leh early the following month was to kneel at Kilty's grave and recite the *De profundis*. They then proceeded to occupy the property which the mission was to rent from the Jammu and Kashmir government. The future 'St Peters' consisted of a three-room 'barn-like shanty' and some land in a plantation below the main bazaar[11]. Brouwer and Cunningham soon returned to Kashmir, but Hanlon and Donsen stayed on.

Hanlon and Donsen were the two missionaries who lived longest in Ladakh and who left the most dètailed accounts of their work. Hanlon was born in Manchester in 1862 and ordained priest in 1889. He stayed in Ladakh from 1890 until 1893. Donsen was four years younger than his colleague, and came from Vlissingen in the Netherlands. He worked in Ladakh, with intervals in Kashmir, from 1890 until 1895.

Research on Ladakhi language and culture

The two missionaries' immediate priority was to learn the language. Kilty's notes proved insufficiently organised to be of much value and they therefore had to start afresh. They started with colloquial Ladakhi - which they called 'Butti' - but found it necessary to combine this with the study of classical Tibetan as well. Kilty had acquired Tibetan catechisms prepared by the Société des Missions Étrangères de Paris, which had a mission near the Bhutanese border, but Hanlon and Donsen had to have these translated 'into proper Ladakh patois because...they were written in a language which is a mixture of Buthan patois, Lhassa patois, and book language'[12]. Their decision to translate the catechism into Ladakhi colloquial contrasted with the then Moravian policy which was to use a simplified form of classical Tibetan.

Language study led naturally to research on Ladakhi customs and religious beliefs, an area of knowledge which was of obvious importance for mission work. Thus, in the course of his language studies, Hanlon asked his *munshi* (clerk) to write out examples of conversations among the people. The *munshi* then brought a manuscript history of Leh[13]. Having digested this, Hanlon asked about folksongs, and requested the *munshi* to write them down:

> The collecting of these Ladakhi ballads was curious; they had never been written before; in many cases the writer

11. The building can be seen in the foreground of the picture of Leh in: E.F. Knight, *Where Three Empires Meet* (London: Longman, 1893), p. 168.
12. SJFMA 2 (1891), No. 12, p. 191.
13. Hanlon to Vaughan, 20 June 1892, MHM archives.

> had to hire the native musicians to play the tunes as the only means of recalling the words. These ballads number 130; and with the help of a native I have translated half of them. Religion in some degree enters into most I have read. They are in praise of the king, the queen and their court, of the head men of their villages; of the villages themselves; songs of their affections for weddings etc.[14].

Hanlon sent a paper on these songs to a Dr Casartelli in England; he in turn edited and presented the paper to the Ninth International Congress of Orientalists. A summary of Hanlon's contribution was published in the Congress proceedings[15], but it does not include any of the Ladakhi texts of the songs, and it is as yet uncertain whether the originals survive in any archive.

Hanlon wrote a substantial description of 'Ladak, the Ladakis and their popular Buddhism'. This was published in monthly excerpts by the *Illustrated Catholic Missions* magazine between October 1893 and April 1895[16]. Hanlon intended his work to:

> stand as an account of the Ladakis as they are in 1893, useful, when hereafter education, civilisation, and as we hope, conversions to our holy Faith will have obliterated many of their present customs and beliefs.

Hanlon drew on previous publications by Alexander Cunningham, Frederic Drew and H. Ramsay[17], but most of his work was original and, if brought together into a single publication, would have made a respectable book in its own right. His account has four parts: Land and People; Buddhist Public Festivals; Domestic Festivities; and Religion and Sacred Objects of Buddhism. Each part has up to nine chapters. Among other subjects, Hanlon gives a detailed description of Ladakhi wedding ceremonies and the negotiations which precede them. He was the first European to do so, and in this respect

---

14. *Illustrated Catholic Missions* (hereafter cited as ICM), 7, No. 75 (July 1892), p. 33.

15. 'The Folksongs of Ladakh and Baltistan', *Transactions of the Ninth International Congress of Orientalists*, pp. 613-615. 1895. 'The Wedding Customs and Songs of Ladakh'. *Actes du dixième congrès international des orientalistes, session de Genève,* 1894. pp. 183-184. Leiden: E.J. Brill, 1897.

16. ICM 8 (1893-94), pp. 81-83, 97-98, 113-116, 129-131, 113-116, 129-131, 145-147, 161-162; ICM 9 (1894-95), pp. 7-8, 21-24, 38-39, 54-56, 68-70, 86-88, 102-104, 119-120, 132-134, 146-148, 150-152, 167-168, 179-182.

17. Cunningham, Alexander, *Ladak*. (London: W.H. Allen, 1854); Drew, Frederic, *The Jummoo and Kashmir Territories, a Geographical Account* (London: Edward Stanford, 1875); Ramsay, H., *Western Tibet* (Lahore: W. Ball, 1890).

his work anticipates later research by the Moravian missionary A.H. Francke and more recent scholars.

Hanlon also wrote a shorter note for the *Journal of the Manchester Geographical Society*[18]. In the note he comments that the work of English officials in the Kashmir government had ensured that his countrymen were seen as 'men of fairness, uprightness, tolerance and good will' and gives hints on how to avoid mountain sickness when crossing high passes.

In addition to his more scholarly publications, Hanlon wrote regular letters and reports on his mission activities, and many of these were published in *Illustrated Catholic Missions* and the Mill Hill magazine, *St. Joseph's Foreign Missionary Advocate*. Hanlon's description of his adventures in travelling in the Nubra valey in northern Ladakh proved particularly popular. This was first published in the *Advocate* and then translated into Dutch for *De Annalen van het Missiehuis te Rozendaal*[19] .

Donsen's most important publication on Ladakh was a 46-page article published in the *Tijdschrift van het koninklijk Nederlandsch Aardrijkskundig Genootschap* in 1901[20]. This describes the geography of Ladakh; its political status; the characteristics of the local population; and Buddhist beliefs and rituals including birth festivals, marriage ceremonies and funeral rites. In addition to this article, Donsen wrote a series of letters on Ladakh which were published in *De Annalen van het Missiehuis te Rozendaal* between 1891 and 1896. Many of these contain ethnographic information as well as mission news. For example, in a letter dated 6th March 1892 Donsen gives a description of the King of Ladakh's participation in New Year ceremonies in Leh[21].

Mission work

Language study might have been a full-time occupation in itself but, as the two priests became more confident, they began to engage in various kinds of humanitarian work. For example in 1892, Hanlon wrote that six boys were coming to the mission school to study

---

18. 'Two Notes on Ladakh', JMGS 11 (1895), p. 183.

19. SJFMA 2(1892-93), No. 17, pp. 312-319; 334-346, 347-350, 390-397, 415-416, 430-431. AMR 4 (1893-94), No. 9, pp. 264-265; No. 10, pp. 270-272; No. 11, pp. 277-280; No. 12, pp. 283-286. The editor of AMR evidently had little idea of what Ladakh looked like: on page 271 he illustrates Hanlon's account with a picture of the pyramids.

20. TKNAG 18 (1901), pp. 416-462. I am grateful to Dr Wim van Spengen for bringing this article to my attention.

21. AMR 3 (1892-93), No. 2, pp. 110-112.

English, Tibetan and Hindustani. The missionaries did not teach Christianity at the school, which appears to have been short-lived, but regarded it as a form of service which was also a valuable point of contact with the local population. Similarly, the missionaries distributed sheep-skins to the poor during the winter, and did small-scale medical work such as smallpox vaccinations.

However, they would always have considered such activities to be a sideline to their main activity which was to preach the Christian message both in Leh and further afield: Hanlon made three evangelistic journeys to the Nubra valley. In order to get there he had to cross either the Khardong pass (c.18,500 ft) or the Sabu pass (18,200 ft) and, in addition to the problems caused by lack of oxygen at high altitude, he had to cope with snow and ice. On one occasion he was forced to turn back just after crossing the Kardong pass because he was suffering from frostbite.

On these journeys Hanlon would preach to local villagers using visual aids to help explain his message. He travelled with '40 large coloured prints of religious studies, covering the history of the world to the descent of the Holy Ghost upon the apostles'[22]. He began his sermon by showing a map of Ladakh, and then other maps to show his listeners their place in the world. In the course of his travels to Nubra, Hanlon also visited the Deskit and Tangyar monasteries but, not understanding the symbolism of Buddhist art, was repelled by the horrific pictures of deities which he found there.

Donsen wrote of his own travels in a series of letters published in the *Annalen van het Missiehuis te Rozendaal* between 1891 and 1896. For example, in August and September 1893, he marched via Lamayuru to the Zanskar valley, where he managed to preach to audiences of some 20 to 30 people in several villages. Donsen commented on the special difficulties of camping in a hostile environment some 4000 metres higher than his native Netherlands[23].

Buddhist reactions to Christianity

Hanlon wrote several accounts of his discussions with local Buddhists both in his letters and, in particular, in a series of articles entitled 'Buddhist dialogues' in *Illustrated Catholic Missions*[24]. In their first year in Ladakh, Hanlon and Donsen were pleased to find that people listened to their preaching with apparent appreciation, and

22. SJFMA 2(1892-93), No. 17, p. 318.
23. AMR 5 (1894-95), No.2, pp. 303-304; No. 3, pp. 307-312; No.4, pp. 314-319.
24. ICM 7 (1892-93), pp. 151-152; p. 165; pp. 179-180; Vol. 8 (1893-94), pp. 34-35; p 67.

they hoped that they might soon be able to establish an indigenous congregation. However, after two years it became obvious that the obstacles were much greater than they had originally supposed.

In Hanlon's view, there were major intellectual obstacles to conversion. The fundamental problem was that Buddhists had no concept of God the creator, and it was difficult to find an appropriate Tibetan word which matched the Christian understanding of the Deity. In the eighteenth century the Jesuit missionary Ippolitio Desideri, who had lived in Lhasa between 1715 and 1722, had coined the term *rang.drub.dkon.mchog*, which means the 'self-existent precious one'[25]. The Moravian Bible translator Heinrich August Jäschke also had used the word *dkon.mchog* for God. However, as Jäschke acknowledged, *dkon.mchog* had powerful Buddhist nuances because the term *dkon.mchog.gsum* is used to stand for the 'three precious gems' - the Buddha, the Dharma and the Sangha (monastic community)[26]. For this reason, French Roman Catholic missionaries working on the eastern and southern Tibetan borders favoured the term *gnam.gyi.bdag.po*, the 'Lord of Heaven'[27], and the Mill Hill fathers in Ladakh followed their example.

In expressing Christian ideas about God, Hanlon tried to draw on what Ladakhis already knew:

> In speaking of God to the people about Leh we had often found it difficult to give them the right conception. They would insist on their notion of Konchok [*dkon.mchog*]. Their idea of Konchok as the Supreme Being always seemed too vague to build upon. While in Nubra I overheard a Bot saying to his companion "nye mi shes; Konchok shes [*ngas.mi.shes, Dkon.mchog.shes*] - I don't know. Konchok knows (God knows)". In my next instruction, I made use of this telling them they already know who Namkai dakpo [*gnam.gyi. bdag.po*] (our word for God) was. I told them that if they were asked anything they didn't know they'd answer, "I don't know. God knows". If asked who has made anything very wonderful beyond the power of man, they'd answer, "God

---

25. Sherburne, Richard, 'A Christian-Buddhist Dialogue? Some Notes on Desideri's Tibetan Manuscripts'. *Reflections on Tibetan Culture*, pp. 295-306, Edited by Lawrence Epstein and Richard Sherburne (New York: Edwin Meller Press).

26. See: Bray, John, 'Language, Tradition and the Tibetan Bible'. *The Tibet Journal* 16 (1991), No.4, pp. 22-28.

27. *Dictionnaire thibétain-latin-français par les missionaires Catholiques du Thibet* (Hong Kong: Imprimerie de la Société des Missions Étrangères, 1899. For the history of French Catholic mission see: Launay, Adrien, *Histoire de la Mission du Thibet*, (Lille/Paris: Desclée, De Brouwer, c. 1901).

must have made it". No matter where they were if in great trouble they would pray, thereby showing that they believed God was everywhere. To the truth of this they assented, and I had the base to work upon of the omniscience, omnipotence and omnipresence of God[28].

Hanlon's listeners often responded sympathetically to some aspects of his teaching. For example, when Hanlon spoke of the example of martyrs who had followed the example of patience and goodness which Jesus Christ had given, the response might be:

> Ah yes; patience and gentleness! I don't wonder at the spread of the Christian religion; our holy books say that wherever these two virtues are, they will always do good[29].

However, Hanlon also found that other aspects of Christian teaching seemed quite alien to the Ladakhis:

> I shall always remember the expressions of horror with which they received the picture of the 'crucifixion'. Their horror was all for the atrocity of the act, and not at all for its origin - our sins. I made every effort to explain and repeat why Christ, God and man, suffered these things for our salvation. They appeared to comprehend what I would say, but hardly to apprehend it as applying to themselves.[30]

On occasion Hanlon drew on Western science to challenge the traditional Buddhist conception of the universe. Ladakhis would tell him that rain came from 'the Lhu yul, or lower regions of the earth and that the Lhu spirits live under the sea, and under the earth which floats on the sea'. The missionary responded by explaining:

> the true formation of the earth and its rotation; the known substance of sun, moon and planets; the causes of lightning and thunder; the formation of clouds and rising of winds, showing illustrations from Geikie's and Lockyer's large elementary books on these issues[31].

According to Hanlon the typical hearer's response was:

> Perhaps there is no Lhu country. But no - I must not say that; our holy books say there is a Lhu country.

---

28. Hanlon, Henry. Diary of Nubra trip (Mss). MHM archives.
29. ICM 7 (1892-93), p. 165.
30. SJFMA 1892-93, p. 348.
31. ICM 7 (1892-93), p. 180.

More educated listeners challenged Hanlon's exposition by comparing his ideas with Buddhist beliefs:

> I remember once, in the course of a quiet instruction which I was giving to a Buddhist at Leh, when speaking of the joys of Heaven, being interrupted by him. He calmly told me that our Heaven was but the inferior heaven of the Buddhist, whose supreme happiness is nirvana or extinction of all desires. When this stage is reached, there is no more joy or sorrow, heat or cold, hunger or thirst, or any other sensible feeling[32].

Even where Ladakhis proved sympathetic to Christian ideas, they showed no desire to foresake their own tradition. Hanlon writes of one listener:

> He had admitted the beauty of Christ's teaching; had expressed his delight with the prayers and doctrines of Christianity; and had frequently praised it; but generally concluded by repeating the Buddhist formularies '*rang rang gi chos*' - 'each one to the religion of his birth' and 'your religion is good enough for you, but Buddhism is the best religion'[33].

Hanlon tried to challenge this attachment to tradition by pointing out that the Ladakhis had accepted certain European ways of farming which were alien to their grandfathers: why should they not also accept new religious teachings? Similarly, he tried to challenge the pre-eminent position of the Buddhist monkhood by questioning the lamas' expertise as teachers and their faithfulness to their own moral precepts. He implies that this approach may have sown some doubt among his listeners, but adds that the response was generally to the effect that lamas 'could not sin'.

Hanlon believed that indigenous catechists would be better placed than Europeans to counter such arguments. With this in mind, the Mill Hill Mission opened negotiations with the French Roman Catholic mission on the borders of Bhutan to recruit 'native catechists' from there[34]. However, the negotiations appear to have foundered.

Hanlon's attempts to secure additional help from Catholic nuns also proved unsuccessful. In October 1890, soon after his arrival, he applied to the Kashmir state for permission to erect a house for 'a

32. SJFMA 1892-93, pp. 430-431..
33. ICM 6 (1891-92), pp. 86-87.
34. Rooney, p. xii.

teaching and nursing body of nuns'[35]. He believed that low moral standards - as exemplified by the practice of polyandry - were among the main obstacles to Christianity, and he thought that nuns would be best able to address this problem because they would have more contact with women and children.

However, the Kashmir government twice rejected his application: the first time it stated that it had no funds. On the second occasion the mission offered to pay for the building directly, but was again turned down. In November 1893 the goverment at last agreed to allocate funds for the building the following summer[36], but by this time Hanlon had already left Ladakh, and it seems that the mission never took up the offer.

Mill Hill missionaries and Moravians

As noted above, Kilty turned to the Moravian mission doctor during his final illness but, apart from this episode, the relationship between the two missions was one of competition rather than co-operation. For example, in March 1894 Hanlon wrote:

> An English-German Moravian was sent off in hot haste at our very heels when we went to Ladakh. He was to be a set-off and counteracting influence on our work. When they heard we were applying for nuns, they were in a great state of excitement and wrote to their board in Germany to have 'nursing sisters' forthwith[37].....

The 'English-German Moravian' was Becker Shawe, who came from Ockbrook in Derbyshire but had been educated in Germany. He served in Ladakh from 1890 until 1895. Shawe's assessment of Hanlon and Donsen was more generous: 'Personally, they are both well-educated and pleasant men'[38]. However, he added that their pleasantness 'only makes their presence here more galling': the sense of rivalry between the missions was obviously mutual.

Hanlon was keen to ensure that the Ladakhis understood the difference between the two churches. While travelling in Nubra he met many villagers who remembered the 'Kelang Sahib' (a reference to the Moravians' station in Kyelang), and wondered whether he belonged to

---

35. Hanlon to Mr Kaye, Assistant Resident in Kashmir, 17 October 1893. OIOC. R/2 1063.
36. Raja Sir Amar Singh to S.H. Godfrey, 23 November 1893. Ibid
37. Hanlon to Casartelli, 5 March 1894. MHM archives.
38. Becker Shawe to Br Connor, 6 March 1891. Archiv der Brüder-Unität, Herrnhut, Germany.

the same religion:

> I quickly brought forward the most striking of our differences, of which the youthfulness of Protestantism struck them most forcibly. A religion which counts itself by mere centuries seemed to them unworthy of serious consideration[39].

The Moravians themselves recorded that Ladakhis were more sympathetic to the Catholics in at least one respect:

> A Buddhist told one of our Christians a few days ago that he thought the Catholic religion better than ours because they have 'Skundra' [*sku 'dra*] i.e. idols. The images in a Buddhist temple are called Skundra[40].

The Mill Hill missionaries differed to some extent in method from the Moravians. For example, Hanlon believed that the Moravians were mistaken to distribute Tibetan translations of the Gospels because Ladakhis were likely to misinterpret the scriptures unless they had proper guidance[41].

However, in other respects the two missions had much in common. For example, both sets of missionaries believed in combining preaching with medical and educational work, and both undertook long evangelistic journeys outside Leh. Moreover, the Ladakhis' response was broadly similar. While often expressing polite interest, they tended to argue that all religions were the same, that the truths of Christianity were already expressed in Buddhism, or that Christianity was a religion for foreigners[42]. The social obstacles to conversion - especially pressure from the monastic community - applied equally to both churches.

The two missions' mutual suspicions were of course typical of their time. Like their counterparts in Europe, each regarded the other as representing a distortion of the Christian tradition. Nevertheless, from a historical perspective, one is struck more by the similarities than by the differences between the two groups.

The closure of the Mill Hill mission in Ladakh

In 1893 Brouwer pulled Hanlon out of Ladakh to support him in Rawalpindi. Hanlon's posting to Rawalpindi was supposed to be temporary, but in August 1894 he received a letter calling him to the

39. SJFMA 1892-93, pp. 347-350.
40. *Periodical Accounts Relating to Moravian Missions* 1891, p. 340.
41. ICM 7 (1892-93), p. 165.
42. See Bray 1983 cited in Note 4 above.

African mission field: he was to be ordained titular Bishop of Teso and first Roman Catholic Bishop of Uganda. He worked in Uganda until his retirement in 1911, and died in 1937.

Donsen continued working in Ladakh after Hanlon's departure. However, Brouwer did not wish to risk leaving him alone in Leh during the winter in case he suffered the same fate as Kilty, and therefore withdrew him to Baramulla (Kashmir) until the spring of 1894. Donsen returned to Ladakh in the summers of 1894 and 1895, and evidently felt optimistic about the future of the mission for he wrote in August 1895:

> I cannot mention as yet any conversions, but unless I read the signs wrong, I believe we are making a very good, favourable impression on the people to whom I have spoken. To bring things soon to a good issue, I have prepared an introduction to Catholicity for the Buddhists, and intend preparing one also for the Mahommedans....[43].

He concluded his letter by welcoming the news that new recruits were on their way to India - but regretting that they would not arrive before the snows closed the passes so that he would have to return to Kashmir for the winter. Evidently he had reason to hope that the newcomers would be sent to Ladakh.

It was not to be. In September 1895 Donsen was recalled to Rawalpindi, and he stayed in northern Punjab for the next four years. By this time Fr D.J. Reijnders had taken over from Brouwer as head of the mission, and he writes of Donsen with a mixture of admiration and exasperation: he was a man who worked with immense enthusiasm - but at the risk of damaging his health[44]. Reijnder's fears may have been justified because Donsen had to return to Europe in 1899 for health reasons. In 1905 he was sent to the Belgian Congo (Zaire), and he died there two years later.

In May 1898 Reijnders wrote a detailed report summing up the problems and prospects of the whole Prefecture of Kashmir and Kafiristan[45]. He believed that the main reasons why there were few converts included: a shortage of priests exacerbated by sickness and death; the fact that the mission's energies were diverted by chaplaincy work for the British army in Punjab and the North-West Frontier; difficulties of access; political instability on the frontier; and the poor moral example given by European Christians.

---

43. Donsen to Fr Henry. 8 August 1895. MHM archives.
44. Report by Reijnders, May 1898. MHM archives.
45. Ibid.

In reviewing the mission's activities Reijnders concentrated on northern Punjab, the mission's headquarters, and Kashmir. The Baramulla mission in Kashmir had been founded after Leh, but was now more firmly established. Reijnder's comments on Ladakh were pessimistic:

> Ladakh is for the present given up, not only on account of the fruitlessness of the labours spent there for more than four years, and of the unfavourable circumstances continuing, but also in consideration of the Bishop of Lahore's advice, supported by the Delegate Apostolic.
>
> Till the laws of the country permit foreigners to hold large tracts of land there, it seems useless to attempt christianising Ladakh; but even when the present prohibitive laws should be changed for the better, it will be a tremendous task to christianise Ladakhis, viz. on account of their practice of polyandria, their devil worship, and other difficulties which will have to be encountered.

Reijnder's report makes it clear that by 1898 the Prefecture had made a formal decision to close the Ladakh mission. Shortage of manpower was one of the main reasons for this decision, but it would not have been decisive if the mission had thought that the social, religious and legal environment had been more favourable.

Thus, the grave of Fr. Kilty, the first Mill Hill priest to operate in Ladakh, is now the only physical memorial of the mission's work there. However, both Hanlon and Donsen left valuable accounts of the Ladakh of the 1890's, and their role in the region's history - short though it was - deserves to be better remembered.

THE MEDITATION NOTEBOOK OF TIPUN PADMA CHOGYAL

John Crook
Psychology Department,
University of Bristol, U.K.

SUMMARY

In 1980 the author in company with Tashi Rabgyas and Tsering Shakya was asked by the late Khamtag Rimpoche to translate the text of the meditation notebook of his lama for use by serious Western practitioners of the Dharma.

The work is a notebook from which Tipun Padma Chogyal of Chimre in Ladakh taught his yogin disciples of the Drugpa Kargyu school in Tibet. It is a basic text describing the Mahamudra mental yoga still fundamental to yogin training in the Indian Himalayas.

This article describes the life of Tipun and his own lama, Shakrashri, a great exponent of the Ri-me tradition developed in eastern Tibet in the last century, and their importance in the training of yogins today. It also summarises the contents of the notebook which deals in depth with aspects of the Mahamudra system of meditation, its challenges and results.

Introduction

In the summer of 1980 during a research visit to the Mahe family in Leh I became acquainted with the late Khamtag Rimpoche a Tibetan refugee tulku revered and sponsored by this family. Although he was given to a dangerous liking for alcohol, which however never seemed to affect his behaviour, I soon realised that Khamtag Rimpoche was an exceptionally accomplished yogin. When he invited me to visit him at his little mountain temple at Urgyen Dzong near Shergola I could not refuse[1].

Travelling with my colleague Tsering Shakya then of the School of Oriental and African Studies, University of London, and with the good fortune of having Tashi Rabgyas in our company, I visited Urgyen Dzong. After some valuable interactions with the rimpoche we discussed the need for accurate translations of yogic documents in English. He then showed us a small notebook written in neat Tibetan which he told us was one of three copies of the meditation instructions of his own teacher, the well known Tipun Padma Chogyal originally of Chemre, Ladakh. To my considerable surprise he asked

1 See further in chap.22 of J.H.Crook and H.A.Osmaston (eds) 1994: *Himalayan Buddhist Villages*. Banarsidass, Delhi, and Bristol University.

me to photograph the entire text and prepare a translation useful for Westerners seriously wishing to practice the Dharma.

The text received a preliminary translation by Tashi Rabgyas and then James Low, himself a trained Nyingma yogin and a translator of texts, undertook the final work. The text in fact contains numerous difficult technical terms specific to the practice of Mahamudra and James consulted the Venerable Gegen Khyentse, the prime meditation teacher of the Dukpa Kargyupa yogin at Manali and the mentor of the present incarnation of Tipun, Sey Rimpoche, and his own teacher the Venerable Jigmet Rigdzin Rimpoche, formerly professor of Tibetan at Visvabharati University, Varanasi, as to their precise usage.

The Venerable Gegen Khyentse asked James Low and myself to be especially careful in presenting our translation and commentary lest it be a cause for confusion rather than clarification for Westerners. He also wished to preserve the secrecy regarding meditation methods which are characteristic of the Drugpa Kargyu and which we respect. After full translation and consultation we find however that the text does not contain either Tantric liturgical sadhana nor information on the psychophysical yogas of Naropa which might indeed confuse unprepared minds working without a qualified teacher, but is rather a straightforward account of the Mahamudra meditation system (Chagya chenpo). Indeed the basic text upon which the notebook is largely based has already been translated into English by Evans-Wentz and Lama Kazi Samdup in the 1930s[2]. We feel therefore that no harm will arise from its publication and commentarial examination[3].

Tipun Padma Chogyal, although a Ladakhi, spent most of his career in Tibet, becoming perhaps the most important teacher of the Mahamudra and related mental yogic systems from the turn of the century. We turn therefore first of all to an account of his life and that of his main teacher Shakyashri, a prime exponent of the Ri-me tradition.

Shakyashri and his lineage in Western Tibet

Towards the end of the 19th century a renewel of religious fervour developed in eastern Tibet (Kham) as a result of a syncretic movement led by remarkable scholars including Jigme Lingpa (1730-1798) and Patrul (1808-?). In particular a renaissance of Kargyu and

---

2 Evans-Wentz, W. Y. 1969 (Original 1935) *Tibetan Yoga and Secret Doctrines*. Oxford University Press.

3 The translation and commentary forms a major contribution to our forthcoming book, *The Yogins of Ladakh* (Crook & Low), in which we also discuss the necessary reticence needed in translating yogic texts to Westerners working without a guru.

Nyingmapa scholarship produced a merging of themes into a non-sectarian viewpoint known as Ri-me (*Ris.Med*) meaning impartial. The force behind these developments was the need both to collect and preserve numerous disparate teachings and practices and to synthesise a system of doctrine to compete with the powerful and highly formalised viewpoint of the Gelugpa. Drawing particularly on the rich spirituality of the yogins, Ri-me became an influential force in the development of Tibetan Buddhism. Indeed, I feel it is likely that rumours of these great masters reached India to stimulate Madame Blavatski ' s visions of imaginary meetings with teachers from beyond the Himalayas, thus indirectly stimulating the birth of theosophy and eventually the emergence of Krishnamurti as an independent thinker whose viewpoint is in many ways a radical Buddhism.

The great collection of material was brought together by Jamyang Khentse Wangpo (1820-1892) who inspired another great scholar Jamgon Kongtrul (1813-1899) whose philosophical writings have become the basis for modern Kagyu scholarship. Another great contributer to the *Ris.Med* movement was Mipham Gyatso (1846-1917, see S. Hookham 1991)[4]. An important disciple of these teachers was Shakyashri from Kham who was to take a great interest in the revival of Buddhism in the Himalayas.

The *Ris.Med* movement developed primarily among eastern Tibetan scholars but it was to be a Ladakhi monk who became the main transmitter of this viewpoint from Shakyashri to the contemporary generation of practitioners. Ngawang Padma Chogyal was born in 1877 at Chemre in the Sakti valley near the home of my friend Tashi Rabgyas. At an early age he entered Tragthog Gompa[5] where he completed his preliminary studies by the age of fifteen and began training in monastic affairs. Bored by administration, Padma Chogyal returned to his home and announced that he and a friend were intending to go travelling in Tibet.

The two of them journeyed to U (*dBus*) and thence to the holy place of Tsari (*gSang.sNgags.Chos.gLing*) where there was a Ladakhi lama for whom Padma Chogyal worked for some time as a servant. In Tsari lived a high authority of the Drugpa Kargyu (the Drugpa Kyabgon, *'Brug.Pa.sKyabs.mGon*) but, as he was not qualified to be a teacher, he wanted to invite to Tsari one of the great masters of the

4 Hookham, S.K. 1991 *The Buddha within*. State University of New York.

5 Barbara Aziz's notes show Tegchog Gonpa (*Theg.mChog*) as Padma Chosgyal's first monastery. However there is no such named Gompa in Sakti. Trak-thog (*Bra.thog*), the Nyingma gompa close to his home is the most likely place. The only other gompa nearby is Chendey (*lCe.bDe*) with which name confusion seems unlikely to have arisen.

period , Shakyashri, then living in Kham and well trained in the new movement.

When Padma Chogyal's own lama died, he too was in need of a teacher so he was receptive to the idea of travelling to Kham with a request to Shakyashri to come and work at Tsari. The journey was hazardous, for there were minor wars in the area at the time. None the less the determined traveller succeeded in locating the lama and persuaded him to return to Tsari as his personal teacher.

Back in Tsari, Padma and Shakyashri established themselves at both *rTsa.ri.gChig.Char* and the *sKyid.Phug* cave where not only did Padma Chogyal receive teachings based on Shakyashri' s account of his life (*rNam.thar*) but many other students came to join them. Shakyashri soon had so many disciples that he could no longer effectively teach them all and he appointed assistants to help him. Among these Padma Chogyal soon became pre-eminent as a teacher and was given the title of Tipun (*Khrid.Pon*) which means "Chief of Questions ". The title remained with him for the rest of his life and he was soon the supreme authority on the teachings of his master.

When Shakyashri died the demands on Tipun, as he was now known, gradually became excessive and he decided to go into retreat. He moved to Tsibri in Dingri in eastern Tibet where he lived alone in a cave called *dGon.gSang* for three years surviving on meager rations and without an attendant. On completing the retreat he moved to a location associated with Milarepa called *La.Phyi* where he again practiced meditation for several years. His fame was now such that many pressed him to teach them yet once again he sought solitude in mountain caves.

Dingri was already associated with the ascetic practices of outstanding yogins. In particular the Indian known as *Pha.Dam.Pa Sangs.rGyas* lived here in the eleventh century contemporaneously with the great Milarepa. Phadampa had brought to Tibet the *Zhi.Byed* system of meditation which he taught to a woman follower who became the great Yogini *Ma.Chig.Lab.Kyi.sGron.ma.* Phadampa and Machig jointly created the famous Chod practice wherein the yogin dances in a cemetary or wild place and donates his body to the spirits and other denizens of place to learn the nature of mental emptyness. Not surprisingly Tipun made use of their methods in his own meditations and also those of *Yang.dGongs.Pa*, a great Kargyu ascetic who had lived in Dingri in the eleventh - twelfth century[6]. Certain relics of Phadampa were rescued from Ding ri after the Chinese

---

6 Aziz, B. 1978 *Tibetan Frontier Families.* Vikas. Delhi.

invasion and are now kept secretly presumably in India or Nepal[7].

Eventually Tipun agreed to give teachings but only to those resolute and determined enough to pursue a steadfast life. He built a number of small communites each composed of huts for solitary meditation. These communities were each occupied by eight to ten monks. He also responded to the needs of his women students. One community for nuns held twenty one nuns while two others held eight and thirteen respectively. In all over 100 men and women trained in higher yogas with Tipun. In addition he had a great many lay disciples. Soon even reincarnating lamas found their way to him and even the new incarnation of his original sponsor, the Drugpa Kyabgon, studied with him. His influence gradually became widespread.

Tipun Padma Chogyal assembled a great library comprising more than ten thousand carved blocks for printing. The library, mainly concerned with the practice of meditation, was housed in a building called *Nye.Ring.Bar.Khang* on Tsibri mountain. The manuscripts for carving onto printing blocks came from Ladakh, Sikkim and Bhutan as well as from Tibet[8]. In addition he constructed and developed a number of small monasteries and meditation places around the Tsibri mountain. Tipun died[9] at the age of 81 in Tsibri. On the day of his death the sky was said to be absolutely clear until there was a great shower of flowers none of which reached the ground. A few days later there was an earthquake and many people felt great faith.

Shakyashri had been no celibate lama and had several children. His youngest son was Apho Ngawang who died as a monk at the age of twenty five to reincarnate as the son of one of his brothers known as *Kun.Lha*[10]. This boy was to grow into a yogin disciple of Tipun and eventually became an important yogic transmitter himself. As

---

7 Aziz, B. 1980 The work of Pha.dam.pa sangs.rgyas as revealed in Ding.ri folklore. In : M.Aris. and Aung San Suu Kyi (eds.) *Tibetan studies in honour of Hugh Richardson*. Aris and Philips. Warminster.

8 According to Aziz (1978), Gene Smith is undertaking a study of known sources concerning this library.

9 This account of the life of Tipun Padma Chogyal I owe to Barbara Aziz who found the details for me among field notes made for her book *Tibetan Frontier Families* (1978). She had collected this information in interviews with the former Kogno Shega Lingba of Dingri, Japyang Tempa. He had spent his early life in Lhasa returning home to Dingri when he was 27. His parents were lay devotees of Tipun and he received teachings from him working as his secretary while remaining married and living with his family. He was 37 when his teacher died. Three years later he had to flee with other refugees from Dingri because of Chinese invasions and came to Nepal. He became a monk in a meditation centre (Churung Kharka) in Solu founded by one of Tipuns disciples and later moved to Kathmandu to serve another teacher in the same tradition.

10 A contraction ; full name not known to us.

Awo Rimpoche (*A.Pho*) he was the prime teacher of nearly all the leading yogins James Low and I met during our study visit to Ladakh and Zanskar. Tipun asked Awo Rimpoche to marry but he was at first reluctant to do so. However, after he had had a number of auspicious dreams, he changed his mind and did as his guru wished. Then, when Tipun passed away, his incarnation was born as Awo Rimpoche's firstborn son. This young man, Sey Rimpoche, now lives at Manali with the Venerable Gegen Khyentse as his teacher and is training as a yogin[11]. Now assuming his duties, in 1993 he visited the yogin gompas of Gotsang and Khespang in Ladakh and inaugurated a new chorten at the latter

The structure and contents of the text.

The text we have is a notebook. It is not therefore a carefully worked over text book of instructions, rather it is a relatively systematic survey of the subjects taught by Tipun to his student yogins. Because Tipun was so influential in his time and because his work laid the foundation of the prime yogic training system still actively taught in the Indian Himalayas today the text is of interest not only to practitioners but also to scholars of this subject.

Although the text is uninterupted by headings or divisions, the work falls naturally into three parts.

1. A pithy account of Mahamudra practice clearly based on the original summary of Padmakarpo.

2. A more elaborated discussion of the nature of the obstacles to be faced in practising Mahamudra and the factors contributing positively to its main aspects, calming the mind (*Zhi.gNas*) and insight into its nature (*Lha.Tong*).

3. Tipun's recollection of his guru Shakyashri's oral instructions given as commentary to basic texts.

---

11 At Manali we were given the names of several noted teachers who received instruction from Tipun. Thuksey Rimpoche became the acting abbot of Hemis, sTagna Rimpoche governs the Lo-Drug monasteries of Ladakh and Lahoul, Gegen Khyentse is the foremost teacher of Mahamudra and the Yogas of Naropa and the teacher of Sey Rimpoche the present incarnation of Tipun. Awo Rimpoche was a fellow student with Gegen Khentse who established the monastery at Manali as a training centre and also taught for a time at Hemis after leaving Tibet. Khamthag Rimpoche, the wanderer, was based at Hemis, re-established the little gompa at Urgyen Dzong and asked Tashi Rabgyas and I to copy the meditation notebook of Tipun. Sentra Rimpoche teaches at the Parkhang Gompa near the Nepalese border with Tibet south of Ding-ri. There was also Nedun Puntsog who taught Tagtsang Rimpoche and Kenpo Nornang of Darjeeling on whom we have no information but whose photograph is extant in the Lhakhang of Khespang Gompa. Finally there is Drubten who lives with Gegen Khentse at Manali. Only Gegen Khentse, Drubten, sTagna Rimpoche and Sentra remain alive today.

4. Finally a discusion of the four main component yogas in Mahamudra, the practices of One Pointedness, Freedom from Limitation, One Taste and Non Meditation.

The first part of the text shows great similarities with the sixteenth century work of Padmakarpo one of the great scholars and systematisers of the Kargyupa tradition. Padmakarpo wrote his own work down at the request of a Zanskari king (*Zhan.phan. bZang.po* 1525-1561) who paid him in saffron for the work. This king [12]died apparently of dropsy while on pilgrimage in Tibet and his Queen established the Kargyupa in Zanskar at Bardan [13]. The Lama Kazi Samdup remarked to Evans Wentz that more information on these texts might be found at Hemis. Hemis was founded later than the yogin's monastery at Gotsang so we may presume that Gotsang was the location meant. Indeed, when visiting Gotsang we found that the Padmakarpo texts were the ones used in meditation training. Tipun may thus have known of these texts from his time in Ladakh but may just as well have come accross them in Tibet or from his teacher. At a subsequent date the Kargyupa split into two factions but this would not have effected the distribution or use of Padmakarpo's writings from an earlier period.

The main argument of the notebook, which is richly embroidered with alternative or parallel views and the awkward numerical listings traditional in Tibetan scholarship may be summarised briefly as follows:

By "mahamudra" is meant the arising together in a co-emergence of both the discriminatory function of cognition and the pure apperceptive clarity of its basis in non-duality.

Normally these two aspects of mind are split so that the subject is caught in a devisive intellectuality, however refined or coarse, that does not know its own basis.

The prime practice therefore is to calm the mind to create a basis within which the innate clarity can become apparent. To see into the depths the waves of the ocean have to have become calm.

Calming the mind may use many devices, such as looking at a pebble, watching the breath, visualising a Buddha image or gazing at nothing to cool down the fires of wandering thought.

When the mind is sufficiently calm the practitioner proceeds to question its basis endeavouring to perceive in actual experience the

---

12 See our further discussion in Chapter 16 of *The Yogins of Ladakh* (forthcoming).

13 See further Schuh, D. 1983. Zu den Hintergrund der Parteinahme Ladakhs fur Bhutan im Kreig gengen Lhasa. In : D.Kantowsky and R.Sander, eds. *Recent research on Ladakh*. Schriftenreihe Internationales Asienband. 1 Weltforum Verlag. Munchen

difference between a mind that is still and one that is active in thoughts.

Once the mind sees that both its movement in conceptuality and its stillness arise from the same basis - the practitioner abides in this meditative state practising Non Elaboration - i.e. no further investigative enquiry but a close focus on the basis itself.

Persistence in Non Elaboration leads to a state of One Pointedness where the mind is held steady in a stable focussed condition without any particular object of regard.

This practice develops into a sustained yoga of One Taste wherein everything simply appears in its own nature without cognitive descriminations deviding the mind.

Repititive training in these yogas leads to a condition in which practice arises simply and without intentionality. There is no goal in view. The ego is then no longer the root of intention to practice with an end in view because there is no deliberative activity. This practice is then termed Not Meditation or Non Meditation. The meditator cruises like an eagle in the sky free of care and of reference to self.

We may comment here that Kargyupa practitioners argue that once this stage is reached the practitioner does not differ in his method from a Dzogchen practitioner of the Nyingma school. The difference between Mahamudra and Dzogchen lies precisely in the presence or absence of intentionality. The Mahamudra practitioner initially intends to get somewhere by his practice and his method is thus called a "way of the path ". By contrast because the Dzogchen practitioner (when fully trained) activates a direct seeing identical to what is known in Non Meditation, the Dzogchen method is known as a "way of the fruit "- that is to say the apple has been found and one need only taste it. No more searching for the apple tree, no more path to the apple tree. When Mahamudra enters Non Meditation the practitioner has moved into a sphere not different from the way of the fruit[14].

Tipun closes his notebook with the following words: "To express it briefly, when the practitioner confirms clearly and without doubt his unmistaken recognition of the natural condition of mind just as it is, the ground Mahamudra itself, he gains a definite confidence. All the adventitious obscurations of the interactions between subject and object are purified on the path of Mahamudra. By thoroughly understanding the nature of view, meditation and conduct and practicing them one pointedly day and night without a break the mind itself manifests in the mode of its own nature. For as long as Samsara

14 These ideas arose from discussions with Khamtag Rimpoche, Staglung Rimpoche of Trag.thog Gompa at Sakti and the Gotsang yogins which are presented in *The Yogins of Ladakh (loc cit)*.

remains, the two modes of form, display and activity, effortlessly and spontaneously benefit beings. This understanding is called the resultant Mahamudra."[15]

Acknowledgements

This paper would have been impossible without the assistance of James Low who used his formidable skills in Tibetan to complete the translation of Tipun's Notebook begun by my colleague Tashi Rabgyas. James accompanied me in further researches among yogins in the field in 1986 and we have recently completed a joint book project (*The Yogins of Ladakh*) in which the full translation and commentary is presented.

In the initial fieldwork the assistance of Tsering Shakya and Tashi Rabgyas was invaluable. Our time together was a delight. Finally without the trust shown in us by the late Khamtag Rimpoche, I would never have received the text for translation in the first place. Conversations with the Venerable Gegen Khentse in Manali gave us much food for thought and helped to orient the writing of our book. We are also grateful for the comments of Professor Jigmat Rigdzin, Rimpoche of Visvabharati University, Bengal. Barbara Aziz has been most kind in checking through her notes on Tipun for me arising from her fieldwork for her book Tibetan Frontier Families.

I am grateful for the support of my work in the field by the Harry Frank Guggenheim Foundation and the Nuffield foundation.

15 Translation by James Low.

THE ROAD TO PADUM: ITS EFFECT ON ZANGSKAR

James Crowden
Forge House, Fore Street,
Winsham, Chard, Somerset TA20 4DY U.K.

Summary

For centuries Padum has been seven day's journey from Kargil on foot or horseback; since 1980 it is little more than as many hours. This change has been more significant than any other since the Dogra invasion. Zangskaris had mixed feelings about it: welcomed by the young but viewed with reservations by the old and those who had travelled in the outside world. Construction brought work and outside labourers to the valley. Completion has brought administrators, Kashmiri shopkeepers and goods, window-glass, new buildings, government rations and new foods, tourists and road accidents. More roads are planned and under construction; Zangskaris need to consider carefully if these will be beneficial.

First of all I would like to say how much I appreciate the relaxed and informal atmosphere of this conference, it is quite unlike any other academic conference that I have ever attended, and yet the transfer and flow of information is not only smoother but I think of sufficient breadth and depth that makes it a land mark, not only between east and west, but perhaps more importantly, between the Indian sub-continent and the traditions of Central Asia, whose future is very much on the point of change. Leh has always been a trading town and although the trade which made it important may have appeared to have died off, it has become a market place for ideas, and its location tucked in between the folds of the main Himalayan range and that of the Karakoram, make it central to the understanding of modern development. It is this change which is the focus of this paper.

Before the advent of the internal combustion engine, all travel and trade was made either on foot or with the help of horses, mules, yak, dzo, donkeys, and even sheep. It is the nature of their requirements which has led to the positioning and size of certain Ladakhi villages, i.e. as stages along the route. Kargil was, until recently, known as the town of 'seven days'. Seven days to Srinagar, seven to Leh, seven to Skardu and seven to Padum. True these distances could be shortened on a good horse and in times of emergency messages were carried by relays of riders and horses, but essentially seven days was the norm. Now it is one day in a truck or a bus. At once this measures distance in time rather than actual miles or kilometres as we have become accustomed. It is the way in which we render that distance down by our transport which matters. i.e. it is the time it takes which is fundamentally important, not the distance, and it is this which is far more important when assessing change to culture. As another small example it is only an hour or so from Leh airport to Delhi, and yet to walk that distance would take you at least a month and for nearly half of year be entirely impossible.

What is important when assessing change is not just the change itself, but more importantly the rate of change. It is in fact akin to differential and integral calculus, where the rate of change is more important than the actual speed. i.e. time is involved as well, not in some peripheral way but as a fundamental part of the equation. And here time is not in seconds, i.e. feet per second or miles per hour, but the unit of time is years or even decades. Like a tree growing imperceptibly, it is only when you return after a dozen years or so, that you notice the change most markedly. The change is so slow that the local people do not either notice it or attach little importance to it, and yet if it had happened overnight it would be obvious for all to see. It is the perception of change which is as important as the change itself. The real change may be more or even less, depending on who is doing the perceiving.

My main concern, however, is not just to itemise the major changes, although these are interesting and crucial, it is perhaps more important first to explore a psychological framework which can then be used in other situations not just in Ladakh or India.

Development is such a key issue and yet it is rarely looked at because it is itself changing so fast. You cannot stop countries developing and yet it is useful to have a point of reference with which to make comparisons.

Unlike the road to Leh, the road to Zangskar has little strategic importance, and so its construction has taken many years. Its actual volume of traffic is very limited in comparison to the great convoys that come over the Zoji La, and yet its effect in proportion to its size has been enormous. Very often what we might see as a small change is enormous for the people concerned. For instance the building of a single bridge over a fast flowing and dangerous river can bring vast changes in its wake not only to the day to day lives of villagers but to kinship patterns, demography and even grazing patterns. It is the knock-on effects of engineering projects which are so difficult to predict, not only on the human population but to the environment. Engineers rarely stay long enough to see the effect of their work, and to the more traditional anthropologists the sight of an engineer sends them running even further into the mountains. Consequently this is an area of great interest and I might say uncertainty.

During the last thirty years the coming of the roads to Ladakh has been as significant a cultural change as the invasion of the Dogras in 1834, which in itself tied Ladakh's fate to that of the subcontinent rather than to Tibet, China or Central Asia. Indeed the war with "Our Moslem brothers" in 1965 was centred on the road and their attempts to cut the road were numerous. These culminated in a desperate attempt to capture the road bridge just outside Kargil, and it was that war which more than anything else spurred the road building on to new heights. Significantly perhaps it is precisely at this bridge that the road to Zangskar starts.

Perhaps at this point it is worth just looking more carefully at what a road is, for in one sense there is nothing there at all. True there are natural paths that men and animals have taken, but these skirt round natural obstacles. Modern roads however are by their very nature less able to blend into the landscape, they dominate it, at least just long enough for a vehicle to pass over it. And when the vehicle has passed its usefulness is over, until the next vehicle comes along. Although a road may be several hundred miles long its usefulness is at least in one sense transitory. It lies there throughout the winter unused and its potency for change is still there, an invisible chord lurking deep beneath the snow. For many years the road to Zangskar was un-metalled and except for lengths of the Suru valley is still un-tarred. It is not so much a road, but a long thin strip without rocks snaking its way through the mountains, and yet its effects were felt long before it was ever completed.

All engineering projects have three phases. Planning and Anticipation, Actual Construction and then the Active Life of whatever it is that is being built.

1. The Planning Phase

This lasted many years having been started in 1962 and only finished in 1980. This has in a sense been the longest phase the further one goes down the road. The engineering planning was hampered by four things. The terrain, the weather, the lack of finance, and perhaps most importantly the lack of suitable machinery. That the road was built at all is extraordinary and I have the deepest respect for the road builders of Ladakh, who are in some ways the modern equivalents of Abdul Ghani Sheikh's 'Adventurers'. The roads are after all, only trade routes, and the truck drivers caravan leaders. The only difference is that all the horses are under the bonnet. A truck carries 60 quintals (1 quintal is 100 kg in the metric system) i.e. 6,000 kgs. or approximately 6 tons. A horse on the old trade route from Panikar to Padum would carry 80 kgs. or the weight of an average person, therefore on one truck is carried the equivalent of 75 fully laden horses, and it can do the journey in one day not seven. The advantages are clear. The only problem, as with so much in Ladakh, the trucks go back virtually empty apart from the human cargo.

In places such as Padum the coming of the road was greeted with mixed feelings. The younger people saw it as modern progress and welcomed it, particularly if it meant they could in some way benefit from it. I remember in a house in Karsha where I lived in the winter of 1976-77 I saw a picture painted by a young artistic monk and it showed very clearly a road leading up to his monastery and a bus driving up to it. The anticipation was positively joyful. The village headmen who acted as sub contractors did quite well out of the construction phase but even they found it difficult to encourage the villagers to work for a day rate as it then was of 15 Rs. for men and 12 Rs. for women. Masons got 30 Rs., How much the *gobas* made on this I am not sure for I have heard several quotes, some as high as 40Rs. Maybe this in some ways explains the villager's intransigence rather than any ill-feeling or lack of comprehension about the road. Certainly many of the fit young men were either off trading or looking after their animals on the *dok-sa*. The annual butter production was more important than working on the roads, and so it was left to the older men and the gangs of women, some of whom were feeding babies in between shifts. The women often sang as they worked.

Only the older men and some of the more intelligent lamas foresaw problems. One man in particular summed it up very neatly. "Today we are happy, we have enough food. When the road comes young people will want money, and we will lose our peace of mind" Not a few Zangskaris had travelled widely in India and some had even walked to Lhasa and back several times. They were aware of how the road had changed Ladakh and how influence crept up from Kashmir, an influence that they were not always entirely in favour of. Even before the road to Padum was completed they said that Leh was like Srinagar. Zangskar was very proud of its independence and also of its separateness from the rest of Ladakh. Indeed at one time it had even been part of Kishtwar, and in the upper reaches of the Lungnak is closer to Lahoul and Kulu, than the central Indus valley.

Be that as it may, the anticipation of the road caused political problems between the Buddhists and Moslems of Padum, and this led amongst other things to the riot and disturbances of 6th November 1976. Or as they referred to it, a 'small local problem'. It was as if the coming of the road had, like a bullet or jet aircraft. sent a shock wave before it. And this shock wave was felt quite a few years before the road actually arrived. To examine the causes of the riot is not the purpose of this paper but I think that the anticipation of the road, the uncertainty and economic forces that were associated with it cannot be ignored. It is not to say that the road caused the riot but I believe that it provided a feeling of uncertainty that allowed old feelings to come to the surface, which might have been resolved amicably in other circumstances. Some of the problems dated back to 1947/8 when Zangskar was for a short period, along with Kargil held by Pakistani forces. If nothing else this illustrates that the road is more than just a trade route, it is a vehicle for ideas and politics. A way of life, a new path. Zangskar is remote, but only to those that do not live there.

2. **The Construction Phase**

This of course was preceded by surveyors, and I well remember seeing their trail of yellow paint daubed on the rocks, not only blazing the trail but at every kilometre proudly announcing the distance from Kargil. It was, and still is 235 kms. to Padum, although the real distance should have been measured in centuries. Yellow is also the colour of Ratnasambhava and is associated with the south i.e. Delhi and central Government and has as its vehicle, appropriately enough, the horse. The story of the workmen has largely gone unrecorded and yet it is they that built the road single handed with picks and shovels and limited explosive. Compressors and drills were in short supply. The altitude and cold told heavily on the workmen who had come up from the plains. Biharis in particular suffered, and it is not known how many died in the snowstorm of September 1987. Some say 30, others far more. Some of the best outside workmen came from Nepal, and their women work alongside them, as do the Bakerwal women. The specialist bridge builders came from Punjab. The engineers were mostly from the Jammu and Kashmir Public Works Dept. and some of the most well known were Ladakhis themselves. The terrain is not at all easy and crossing the Pensi La required many years of explosive work. At this time the road-head was at Panikar. The onset of winter always stops work by the end of October, and sometimes earlier. The first few weeks of the next year from May onwards are spent repairing the damage caused by avalanches and rockslides. The stretch of road beneath Nun Kun before Parkachik, where the two ranges meet is particularly unstable. The mountains are young and still on their way up so to speak. Also the increased precipitation in the monsoon period has a detrimental effect, causing severe rutting and the collapse of retaining walls. Such is the maintenance work, that the road can hardly ever be called finished, that is the nature of the mountain environment. The road is an ideal example of the Noble Truth 2A namely that of Impermanence. Indeed it is interesting that in many cultures, the road or the way is used as a religious analogy for the spiritual path.

Ironically the first vehicles to reach Padum did so in mid November 1976 and these were two J&K police jeeps who were sent to investigate the riot and took away several prominent Moslems for questioning in Kargil. They spent the winter out of the valley, much to the consternation of their wives and families, although it may have been for their own safety. They themselves preferred to say that they had simply been transferred. To see the first vehicles coming over the fields was an awesome sight, and the noise of the first internal combustion engine had arrived. It was, I thought, not altogether boding well for the future that it should be the police inspectors who arrived first. They had crossed the river at Tungri over the ice. The first oil leak occurred and the local people viewed the jeeps with a mixture of admiration and awe, though they knew full well their purpose. Few of the women had ever travelled out of the valley, though some were accustomed to go down to Manali for work in the winter. For many it was their first glimpse of the road and of what the outside world had to offer.

As the road approached, the villagers from higher up the Lungnak and those like the Changpa and the villagers of Shun and Sha-de expressed concern because they feared that the excess grain would go out on a lorry and not be traded with them for salt or wool. Already the road was making its effect felt much further away, and the delicate balance of trade routes that had evolved over hundreds of years were being slowly eroded. Some people clearly remember Tibetans coming down to Sonnamarg with salt right up till the sixties. The road has pushed the old trade routes further and further back, and with it many of the subtleties and local variations. In its wake follows everything else. The road is in a sense a mirror through which one walks. It is also a rite of passage to a previously 'under-developed' community, though I use the words developed and under-developed carefully. The spiritual development of the monks and indeed lay people in Ladakh and Zangskar is of a very high order, and this development has been a by-product not of its apparent 'backwardness' but of its natural seclusion, a seclusion which it still retains more or less in winter. Indeed Leh was probably more cosmopolitan in the 1850's than it is today. The re-opening of certain trade routes may in the future make Leh once more the centre of an Asian trade network.

3. **Post Construction Phase**

The third and most extensive phase in term of change is the aftermath of the road arriving. I will try here to elucidate the nature and size of those changes, and for the most part I will be using Padum as the source for much of my information. Obvious visible changes include the following.

New Buildings. These have been built primarily along the route of the new road and comprise many Government Buildings, though the new offices of the Sub-Divisional Magistrate are situated near the Buddhist cremation ground, just above the old carvings. Previously the Tehsildar had lived in two rooms rented from the old Gyalpo Teshi Namgyal for the princely sum of 40 Rs a month. The whole infrastructure of government has arrived, and with it, its own architecture, which relies heavily on cement, concrete and reinforcing bars. The two styles of architecture in some ways highlight the differing attitudes to the environment. One natural, the other imported. Indeed one wonders if the people themselves actually need the government or whether it is not the other way round. To quote Ved. Prakash Gupta who was Tehsildar in 1976, who said in a moment of confidence over dal and rice: "These people are perfectly civilised. They have no need of government. It is we who should be learning from them". Since then of course the road has arrived and with it all manner of projects and schemes. Some of which work, some of which have yet to be finished. Others like the new bridge between Padum and Karsha have already fallen victim to the environment. Concrete does not respond well to the extremes of temperature and the ravages of the melt water put a severe strain on footings, particularly if the cement ratios and cover to reinforcing are not of sufficient standard. This is perhaps a minor detail but much the same thing which happened in Ladakh is happening on a smaller scale in Zangskar and it would be sad to see a plethora of half-completed projects.

With new buildings comes new architecture and glass has, I think, been the main difference, or rather large sheets of glass, which give big windows totally changing the style and living conditions of many new buildings. Insulation is as ever a major problem but a large glass room is very useful in winter during the day. Many of the modern 'Hotels' are simply left empty over the winter. Padum suffers from two types of development. The ribbon development already mentioned which also gives access to traders from Kashmir, and the more environmentally insensitive development in individual fields, which would have been unthinkable a few years ago.

In at least one instance I know that the *khang-chung* was larger and more modern than the *khang chen*. The father who was a teacher and village elder in Padum, instead of going to a smaller house, had in fact built himself a large new house in one of his fields, much to the consternation of his son who had 'inherited' the old but still substantial town house. His father would not let him alter or extend the old house because he said it would upset the *lha*. Also interestingly his 'uncle' who was in a polyandrous marriage with his mother, now lived with him, and not in the new *khang chung*. New architecture and settlement patterns may also in some ways reflect changing attitudes to the family structure. The main feature of new houses is that they are not suitable for the wintering of animals, a primary function of the older buildings, and this in itself highlights the first step away from the land. Increased wealth has undoubtedly changed Padum and will continue to do so for many years to come.

What one is witnessing is the transformation of a village into a town, and perhaps more importantly, the transfer of a predominantly non-cash flow society into a cash-flow one, and as in all cases there are winners and losers. What was stable almost to the point of ritual ten years ago is now no longer existent. The *changpa* with their caravans of a thousand sheep and goats no longer come. Salt comes in by truck. Bridges no longer have to be built by weeks of patient preparation twisting rope out of birch twigs. People can come and go with far greater mobility. There are cash jobs in the valley and here the tourists have played their part. Far from destroying the culture they have I think given a greater awareness to the local people of the worth of their culture and in particular the worth of their monasteries and the paintings and artefacts associated with them. However recruitment of monks is becoming a problem, although it is interesting to note that the nunnery in Karsha has actually increased its numbers. This maybe reflected in the fact that there is greater wealth around to support nuns whereas before unmarried women were kept at home to help with the agriculture. One very positive thing is that horses are still kept, particularly in Lungnak where the road has not reached and these are still used for government caravans of and for treking parties. The tourist industry has kept a significant number of young men in the valley who would otherwise have left for other jobs in Ladakh or elsewhere. Always it is a question of scale and in many ways the winter helps to preserve the Zangskari's individuality and thus the culture is not swamped. The tourists come and then they go. The trade comes to them as it does in Leh, and this means that there is a considerable income to be made from hotels and the sale of land near Padum has raised prices. Indeed before the road, land was rarely, if ever, bought and sold. The price of land has increased dramatically and in certain areas is worth as much as 30,000 Rs per kanal (1/8 acre; 506 sq.m.); the government rate however is only 13,000 Rs. and this is combined with compulsory purchase. A lot of the middle ground in the plain of Padum is being claimed by the government and may or may not be irrigated in the future.

One person who shall remain nameless, received a substantial grant for building a hotel, and in the meantime instead of building the hotel immediately used the money to purchase a tipper truck which is rented out to the PWD. The hotel was eventually built and is similar to several other hotels run, during the summer, by men from Manali. This same person admitted that although he still grew barley, he sold it off to the Buddhists for making *chang* and arak, whilst he and his family lived off the government rice ration, supplemented of course by government *atta* (wheat flour).

Supplies. Even before the road came, the government ration station was in full swing and accounted for many of the horse and mule caravans coming in from Suru, though issues were almost exclusively for government officials and some privileged families in the Padum plain. In the next decade there was a great increase, making rations available to most inhabitants of central Zangskar. The 1989 figures below are for supplies to the Padum area only; Karsha and more outlying villages were supplied from other depots, and it is impossible to say what population was served.[1]

	1977	**1989**	**1989 price**
Kerosene*	30,000 litres	120,000 litres	12 Rs/5 litre
Rice	1,000 kg.	23,000 kg	2.63 Rs/kg
Atta (flour)	1,000 kg	25,000 kg	2.36 Rs/kg
Sugar	1,000 kg	50,000 kg	5 Rs/kg
Salt	3,000 kg	50,000 kg	3 Rs/kg

*mainly for cooking stoves and lamps.

The necessity of getting supplies in before the middle of September was highlighted by the early and severe snowfall of 1987

1. The 1989 *atta* supply would only suffice for about 350 full rations; the population of Zangskar was about 7,000 in 1981. Only those with cash incomes, such as government officials, would be able to buy substantial amounts of *atta* and rice, but the uptake of sugar, salt and kerosene is much wider. (Ed.)

when not only were the road workers cut off and forced to cross the passes ill-clad, but government rations were so low that government officials had to subsist on the local diet, a state of affairs that they have no wish to repeat. The rations are carefully monitored. In 1989 the standard ration was 8kgs. of rice per head per month and for *atta* 6kgs. per head per month. Sugar was 400gms./head/month.

One of the main problems up Lungnak side was that the people in the villages there could not reach the government's ration station in Padum during the main winter months because of snow and the danger of avalanches. This I think has been alleviated and in 1993 I saw many caravans carrying government supplies to the upper reaches of that valley, to be stockpiled at Testa.

The availability of other foodstuffs in Padum has increased dramatically. In 1976 there were only three shops selling a very limited variety of goods, such as ink, cigarettes, biscuits, batteries, dried apricots, *dal*, matches, *naswar* (oral snuff), brown sugar, mirrors, tea and milk powder. Now in the height of summer you can get cabbages, carrots, bananas, coconuts, tomatoes, onions, eggs, Nescafé, butter, honey, lemon squash, etc. etc.

The sale of butter and salt is interesting as this made up the backbone of the long distance trade prior to the coming of the road. Butter produced on the *dok-sa* (summer grazing ground) would be traded down the gorge in winter for about 45-50 Rs/kg, when the government's Amul butter would sell for half that amount, 30 Rs/kg. The same with salt. 1kg of the *changpa* salt which was highly prized for tea was worth at least 2kg of government ration salt. The rate of exchange for grain being that a saddle bag of salt 3/4 full was worth the same as the same saddle bag filled up with grain, mostly barley, although peas were sometimes mixed in as well. Both trades survived the initial impact from the road but the *changpa* trade from Karnak has since stopped. They can take their salt into Leh direct by truck, thus saving a months grazing journey into Padum. They used to come twice a year, once in July and again in September. The wool from their larger sheep was much prized for making *nimbu* (woven woollen strips) out of which their *gonche* (cloaks) were made. It is this erosion of the apparently simple crafts which will in the end have the largest impact, making the differences in wealth between higher and lower villages even more marked. One thing which I noticed was that cattle were being brought over from Pangi and from Lungnak side and then shipped out by lorry to Kargil for slaughtering there. Prices for cattle and *dzo* were good. A good *dzo* being worth anything up to 5,000 Rs. and a good horse 4-12,000 Rs.

Electricity has arrived with generators at Padum, Sani and Karsha. These are worked intermittently and are in the main providing light. The charges are I think 9 Rs per month per light bulb. The diesel fuel to run them has of course to be brought in by oil tanker. There are moves afoot to construct the Haftal Hydro-electric project, but it is doubtful if this would function well in winter. Solar heating in the form of trombe walls would be good, as in the rest of Ladakh but so far there is no great evidence of them, though the villagers would undoubtedly benefit from them, the winter being more severe here than in Leh,

Labour: Patterns of labour have also changed and workers come over to help either at harvest, or on the various projects that are going on. Rates of pay vary but 45 Rs a day is fairly standard, though equivalent labourers in the central Indus valley get approximately 60 Rs. Most of the people that employ help at harvest have comfortable jobs which means that they can afford to pay for help. However it is a sign of the times that the agriculture is not standing on its own two feet, and this is because of the large government ration imports which are sold at reduced rates. The solution is not easy but farmers should be encouraged not to ignore their land, they do so at their own peril, both agriculturally and ecologically; fields that stand idle are liable to be blown away by the harsh winds in the autumn.

Diet has also changed, although not as much as in Leh. As an example I include the diet of a family[2] equivalent to six adults in Padum based on figures for the annual consumption of certain foodstuffs. The data has been obtained by oral cross referencing. People in Zangskar who rely heavily on their food reserves are usually very accurate on this point, though less accurate when it comes to estimating crop yields; this may be due to an underlying fear of government officials and taxation which prior to the relaxation in 1947 was burdensome.

The main swings are obvious: a great increase in the use of Government *atta* which releases land for more barley. Peas are down and rice is up. Indeed this prosperous family was unusual for Zangskar in general to be eating so much rice in 1977, but not so unusual for Padum. Reckoning two children as equivalent to an adult, these figures give an adult daily ration of about 800 gm of grain and

2. This family should not be regarded as typical of the valley. Besides having a farm, the man is both a salaried government employee and a local dignitary who has to provide food at traditional meetings. (Ed.)

ANNUAL FOOD CONSUMPTION OF A FAMILY IN PADUM

	1977		1989		% Change
	4 adults 4 children		2 adults 8 children		
Staple foods					
Barley for food	500 kg	(hg)	450 kg	(hg)	-10%
,, for *chang*	150 kg	(hg)	150 kg	(hg)	} +100%
			(150 kg)	(hg)*	}
Peas	300 kg	(hg)	180 kg	(hg)	-40%
Wheat	500 kg	(hg)	150 kg	(hg)	} +14%
,, flour (*atta*)	—		420 kg	(Govt.)	}
Rice	300 kg	(bt)	700 kg	(bt)	+130%
Total domestic use	1,750 kg		2,050 kg		

* 150 kg homegrown barley for brewing *chang* for harvest labourers, excluded from domestic total. hg = homegrown bt = bought

Remainder of diet:		
Ghee	5 kg	5 kg
Mustard Oil	10 kg	15 kg
*Dalda**	-	23 kg
Rape seed Oil	-	4 lt
Dal	30 kg	30 kg
Butter	36 kg	33 kg
Churpe (cheese)	25 kg	15 kg
Potatoes	35 kg	80 kg
Cabbage	-	10 kg
Local Vegetables	6 kg	6 kg
Yak Meat	70 kg	120 kg
Sheep/Goat meat	20 kg	20 kg
Onions	5 kg	21 kg
Salt	20 kg	20 kg
Sugar	12 kg	60 kg
Red Tea	20 kg	15 kg
Lipton Tea	1.5 kg	5 kg
Milk/Yogurt	1500 litres	1000 litres
Chang (beer)	500 litres	500 litres

* A cheap margarine, mainly used in Ladakh for 'butter' lamps.

peas per day in 1977, rising to 940 gm in 1989.[3]

The other significant changes are an increase in vegetables, notably cabbage, onions and potatoes. Twice the amount of meat is eaten. Sugar is up considerately but I think this is not just an increase in the amount of Lipton tea that is drunk, but an increase in the amount of sugar taken to sweeten the *tsampa* in the making of *kolak*.

---

3. But WHO recommendations indicate that food requirements of children aged 0-18yr average about 2/3 of adults. Use of this factor and exclusion of grain used for *chang* would remove the change and reduce the amount to about 650g/adult/day (c.2200 Kcal). However this is still nearly double the consumption found in a survey at sTongde, so entertainment may account for some. (Ed.)

Change of diet is undoubtedly important particularly for the children.

Dress: This has changed considerably, particularly in the summer. Traditional dress is however worn on festive occasions. The Buddhist women prefer to wear a colourful scarf which is much more comfortable than the old *perag*. Men love to sport their down jackets, jeans, cotton shirts etc. but still have deep respect for the traditional dress. In winter all revert to the old style *gonche* and many prefer to wear two.

Language: The use of English has increased and a new school at Pipiting has started. Also some Buddhists are sending their children to be educated at the monasteries. The best education is still outside the valley. Pay for teachers is low and often delayed. The importance of children learning Ladakhi and Bhoti is essential, even though their teachers may prefer Urdu.

Politics: In the wake of the 1976 disturbances in Padum, a new system of deciding contentious affairs has been in force for a number years. So ingenious is the system that it could well have applications in other small scale areas of conflict, and even larger ones. The notion is simple. It consists of a village committee which is made up of five members. The *goba* or headman and four others, two Buddhists and two Moslems. The difference is that the Buddhists are elected by the Moslems and vice versa which tends to lead to moderates, rather than extremists, on either side, and hence the greater chance for compromise in difficult situations.

Road Accidents: These have been severe, though not as severe as the avalanches. The most common accident is that of a tipper truck going over the edge if a retaining wall collapses, and with many people on the back fatalities are common. About twenty people have died from road accidents since the road was opened. In 1987 avalanches killed 45 people in the village of Skagam and another 9 in Uberag. Although in no way linked to the road, they maybe linked to a change in overall world weather patterns. Particularly heavy and sudden snow falls are rare, and village sites usually very safe.

Conclusion

The changes in Padum have been very significant, but not as bad as they could be. The most important changes are probably to do with the economics and in turn the politics of decision making. The view of the outside world has no doubt shifted. The tourist season is short but welcome. It is perhaps significant that both the Buddhist and the Moslems have both built new religious buildings, namely the new monastery at Photang and the new mosque at Padum. The most significant changes however may occur if the road to Lahoul over the Shingo La is completed or the road down the gorge linking Zangskar to central Ladakh. The changes would then be far greater.

It is interesting to note that in 1993 when the road was progressing slowly up the Lungnak valley, there were heated discussions in Padum about the rate of progress, which seems to have slowed in the last two or three years. The villagers would like it speeded so that they are not left behind the development in the rest of central Zangskar. On the other hand I believe that the important leaders in Lungnak and Testa, who have a significant income form organising government caravans and supplying horses and mules, are keen that certain bridges are NOT improved. They realise that when trucks come this livelihood will be taken out of their hands. In the early 1970's in Afghanistan I heard of various villages in the Hindu Kush in Nuristan which elected not to have a road, foreseeing the problems of a loss of independence — a view which was justified after the Russian invasion a few years later. That aside, this choice highlights the problems of the shift in local economy which are often not considered as part of the overall equation.

How the problem will be resolved is up to the Zangskaris and the engineers. A road through to Darcha in Lahoul would change the whole balance and nature of Zangskar. Instead of being a remote valley, it would simply become another corridor. Time, terrain and weather will however keep Zangskar cut off for half the year. They may lose their peace of mind but there will still be many thousands of square miles of nearly inaccessible mountains.

HANDICRAFT DEVELOPMENT IN LADAKH
An Approach Paper

Mohammed Deen Darokhan
Director, Desert Development Agency, Leh, Ladakh.

Summary
Traditional local handicrafts could make a great contribution to the prosperity of individuals and Ladakh as a whole. There is now a good potential market among tourists, but better quality is essential, especially in luxury goods such as pashmina shawls. Improvements in training, technical equipment, cooperatives and marketing are proposed.

This paper is published with the aim of explaining the great potential for income generation provided by local resources and personnel in Ladakh through the production of handicrafts. The raw materials and skills are rapidly available, and scope for marketing, both locally and for the export trade is considerable. Opportunities are available to people in urban and rural areas alike.

The department of handicrafts and industries and indeed other organisations have been trying to develop these skills for many years, but because of some inherent problems, little has been achieved.

One of the reasons for the lack of such development may well have been due, in the past, to the isolation of Ladakh from the outside world because of its topography. Such an excuse so longer exists since the opening of road and air communications to Ladakh, bringing in tourists and allowing the Army to establish a permanent and plentiful presence there. The main — perhaps the only — constant export from Ladakh over the last five or more troubled years has been its valuable animal fibre from the pashmina goat and the antelope.

Even these, though have been exported in the raw states, no attempt being made to send finished products, or to try and enhance the quality of fibre before despatch.

The situation has now changed, as a greater awareness of the needs of development has become apparent. It is time to examine the weakness of the existing training, production and marketing systems, and to establish the proper links between local industries, integrating them into developmental planning processes. It is also time to upgrade skills, perhaps introduce new ones, and make use of technology available to improve production. Finally, it is important to try and understand how the climate, topography, lack of power and illiteracy bear upon the problems that Ladakh faces, and find measures to minimise their disadvantageous effects.

TOPOGRAPHY

Ladakh is situated in the Northern part of India, and is spread over an area of 45,110 sq. km but with a population density of only two persons per sq. km. Inhabited areas range from 8,000 to 15,000 feet above sea level. Winter temperature can fall to -30 degrees during the months of December to February and in the months other than June to September, sub - zero temperature are frequently recorded. During summer the temperature can rise to 20 degrees Celsius. Rainfall is less than 100mm annually, making the climate generally dry and cold. There are 112 inhabited villages, scattered over a vast area, with sometimes 20-50kms separating them.

THE PEOPLE AND THEIR OCCUPATIONS

There are 68,380 people in Ladakh, of whom 59,662 live in rural areas, and only 8,718 live in urban areas (Census 1981). Of these, 17,415 are cultivators, 2,191 agricultural labourers, 1,443 forestry and livestock breeders, 546 constructors, 735 in commerce, 306 in transport business, 760 in the manufacturing services and 6,439 in other services. Those in work form 43.55% of the total population, while those without work amount to 29,586 in rural areas, and 4,339 in urban areas. (Census 1981)

The dependence of a large portion of the population upon agriculture, forestry and animal husbandry, as a means of livelihood, will be noted. This is not suprising in view of the vast areas of land available for cultivation and grazing. Utilisation of this land is limited, however, by the lack of rainfall and insufficient irrigation, and the harsh topography in many areas will not allow any of these activities to take place.

PRODUCTION OF HANDICRAFT RAW MATERIAL IN LADAKH

The main raw material produced in Leh District, for handicraft purposes, is wool/fibre. The average quantity produced in one year is as follows:

Pashmina	30,000 kg
Wool	1,42,000 kg
Mohair	5,000 kg
Goat hair	20,000 kg

Pashmina. This is one of the softest of animal fibres. It is produced by the Changra goats, in Ladakh, during winter. A comparative study of its quality in relation to the fibre of other pashmina goats is as follows:

Country	Breed	Fibre Diam.	Staple Length	Colour
Russia	Predonskays	18-19μ	8-12 cm	grey
China	Xinjiang	15μ	4-5cm	white
Mongolia	Koigurvansakhan	16-17μ	7-10cm	grey
Ladakh	Changra	10-15μ	3-7cm	white

Ladakh produces one of the best pashmina fibres in the world. There is further scope for a production of 10,000 to 15,000 kg. of pashmina from goats in the areas other than Changthang. At the moment, because of the short staple of this fibre, its production is not seen as commercially sound.

More than 95% of the 30,000 kg of pashmina presently produced every year, leaves the District. Traditionally, the pashmina trade has been controlled by Kashmiri traders, known as Tibet Baqals, who generally purchase the fibre at exploitative rates. Recently traders from Himachal Pradesh have been going to Changthang direct, advancing money to the breeders before harvesting takes place, and taking away the raw fibre when produced. Alternatively, these traders offer domestic goods as barter for pashmina. However, the majority of pashmina goes to Kashmir from Leh, or from Himachal Pradesh.

Wool. The wool produced is medium grade, suitable mainly for carpets. The Changlok breed of sheep has very long fibre-up to one foot-which makes for better and easier spinning. Wool from Leh District has a low grease content in comparison to other breeds in the world. Most of the wool is white, but black, grey and brown colours are also produced.

More than 15,000 to 20,000 kg of wool leave the District for Himachal Pradesh each year. More of this is used to make pattu, a negligible amount of sweaters, socks, gloves, caps etc.

Mohair. Mohair is produced from a breed of goat known as Angora and its crossbreeds. 5,000 kg of mohair are produced in Leh each year. This is a little known fibre to the local people, though they are now acquiring a taste for it. Its most common use is for decorative fabrics, and for blending with ordinary wool.

Goat Hair. This hair is known as "*Rawl*" in Ladakhi. Traditionally people use this hair for making challies (a rough blanket), barley bags, ropes and papu shoes.

THE PRESENT POSITION & STATUS OF HANDICRAFTS AND SCOPE FOR DEVELOPMENT

In this paper only a few of the main handicrafts will be considered. These are:

Wool based handicrafts: pashmina shawls, woollen pattu, sweaters, socks, gloves, caps and carpets.

Thangka making.

Wood carving.

Metal working.

Pashmina The value of the fibre is determined by its staple length, colour and diameter. Currently, the best prices are paid for white fibre, with a staple length of more than 5cm. However, even the best prices offered in Ladakh fall far short of the real value, and the small farmer remains hostage to the whims of the middlemen. Until such time as some form of competitive purchasing is established, the situation is unlikely to change for the better. Cooperatives could provide such competition and if effective would encourage the small farmers to produce more pashmina.

In addition to staple length, colour and diameter, other factors will obviously affect the decision of any purchasers to invest their money in sources of Pashmina. These are:

The yield, and the ratio of fine fibre to coarse hair and waste material.

The cleanliness of the fibre.

The quantity of pashmina available and nearby alternative sources, if any.

Wool garments and carpets. 80-90% of the 142,000 kg of wool produced in the district is utilised locally to make the items already listed above.

If any new progrmmes were to be introduced e.g. knitting of sweaters, making carpets etc. there would be a real likelihood of depriving the existing wool-users of their raw materials, as there would not be enough wool for all purposes. Any such new programme would therefore require that more sheep be produced. Pastures are available for an increase of livestock, though not in Changthang. There are, however, many areas where the numbers of flocks have been significantly reduced during the last three decades, which could again provide effective grazing. If necessary, wool could be imported for the pattu, leaving the local product to be used for making marketable items attractive to foreigners and visiting Indians alike. While visitors might wish to buy the relatively expensive

Pashmina shawls, they are more likely to purchase less costly items especially if these are well made. Whatever changes are made to the existing local wool industries, however, it would be necessary to ensure the survival of the art of pattu making in the villages.

Like pashmina fibre, wool is sold on a whole-sale basis or is used, occasionally, as a barter for other goods or services. There is a need to organise a retail wool counter, on the lines suggested for pashmina, in Leh town. At the moment there are very few shops selling wool at retail prices.

Rawl goat hair. There is a huge production of goat hair, both from the Changra and other goats. The 30,000 kg of raw pashmina contains 18,000 kg of pure pashmina, and 12,000kg of goat hair. At present this hair is used for making ropes, barley bags, shoes and challies. Much is wasted in the process of de-hairing pashmina. A closer look needs to be taken at the uses to which this wool is put.

Thangka making and wood carving. The raw material required for making thangkas is readily available and is cheap. The base is made of tricot, and normally a stone colour is used, as it does not fade. In the expensive thangkas, pure gold powder is used for painting.

Wood carving is done in the traditional way, and wood is reasonably plentiful. *Choktse* (tables) are a speciality.

Metalworking. There is little to be said about this except that the art is dying and needs to be revived.

PRODUCTION

Pashmina shawls. The shawls produced in Ladakh are not standardised in weight, dimension, colour, or quality. The present estimated production from all sources, is about 500 a year, and these are produced in an unorganised way. Despite this, the best of the shawls are in high demand.

There are seven main processes involved in making pashmina shawls:

1. Grading of pashmina by colour and quality, if this has not already been done by the breeders. 2. Dehairing. 3. Combing/Spinning. 4. Weaving. 5. Clipping. 6. Finishing. 7. Dyeing.

Wool grading. Fibre colour is an important factor when assessing the value of pashmina. This point is not sufficiently recognised locally, to the extent that fibres of mixed colours are used when making shawls; to the obvious detriment of their finished value. Grading, both for quality and colour of pashmina should either be done at source or the raw material should be pooled and graded centrally. The result would be a far greater uniformity in the production of shawls and consequently a better price for the finished product. It would be a mistake to allow colour grading to take place at small manufacturing units, as this would lead to wastage and a lack of standardisation. For example, at present, because of poor grading, grey and brown fibres are not accorded the higher value that their rarity should confer on them. It would not be difficulty to train producers to recognise the standard required, until such time as the premium prices paid for properly graded fibre, dictated their own requirements.

One of the problems has been the lack of a retail counter for the sale of raw pashmina in Leh. Traditionally pashmina fibre has always been sold wholesale, in quantities far beyond the demands and the pocket of individuals to purchase small quantities of fibre, which they could then, according to their abilities, spin and de-hair. This, of course, they would only do if they were ensured of a market, or wished to use the fibre for their own weaving purposes. If, then, the same retail counter was obliged to buy back the finished fibre at a realistic price, the market would be assured, with the result that a large number of people would be encouraged to take up the work.

Another problem that has seriously hindered the production of shawls by individuals or small units, has been the cost of the raw material. Few have the funds to purchase enough pashmina to make more than two or three shawls at any one time.

It is appreciated that any change in the present system and processes of the pashmina fibre trade, will take time to implement. By no means all the fibre can be diverted from the middleman to individuals and units in Ladakh, even when the new system is working at full capacity. The transition must be slow, both to allow for an essential consultation, education and training of the people, as much as to permit the middlemen to adjust to the decline of their business.

De-hairing. This is the most difficult task in the process of making shawls. Separating the fine fibre from the coarse guard hair takes much time, and can only be done by those who have good eye-sight. This, by and large, confines the task to those aged between 18 and 45. However, sometimes whole families can assist in de-hairing, which does not require much training, although it does require considerable practice to acquire any dexterity in the skill. Some figures below may illustrate the tedium involved in de-hairing 30,000kg of Pashmina annually.

One skilled man/woman can de-hair 150-180 gm in 6 hours.
1kg of raw pashmina will take about 6 days to de-hair.
30,000 kg of pashmina will take 180,000 man/days to de-hair.

After de-hairing the pashmina is soaked overnight in a rice-flour solution. Next day the pashmina is dried when it is much easier to identify the true colour of the fibre. It should be noted, however, that this process is much more time consuming than the less professional methods applied in Ladakh.

The efficacy of de-hairing depends on the quality of the Pashmina and the effectiveness of the worker. It takes from one to two months for a worker to become really familiar with the work.

At present, the District Industries Centre, Leh, pays only Rs.25 for de-hairing 1kg of pashmina, which, on a full time basis takes about 5 days. Some agencies pay Rs.50 - 60 per kg. The low de-hairing rates are the main cause for poor work, which results in the finished shawls having an unacceptably high content of coarse fibre in it.

There is much scope in this process for improvement, laborious and tedious as it is. One of its unattractive aspects, which ought to be faced, is the hazard to health caused by the dust given off while de-hairing. Other health problems arise as a result of the hours given to the work: among these are back pains and eye-strain. It is not a job for elderly people. The first task must be to raise the rates. These should be based, not on the number of kg. de-haired, but on the amount of coarse hair left in the fibre after de-hairing, as judged by samples already graded for their hair content.

Spinning. In Ladakh nearly all the women know how to spin, but with different degrees of skill. It is quite a simple art, conducted on a drop spindle. On the whole, spinning is done for domestic needs only, using the wool that the household produces. Those living in urban areas would have to purchase their wool.

The quality of spinning is the crucial factor in the production of shawls, and this is variable, depending on the experience and application of the spinner. Fibre length plays an important part in spinning, the longer staple being easier to spin, and producing a finer thread. The average required length is 7cm, but anything less than 5cm produces a rougher and thicker yarn. Most shawls are made of a blend of the long and short staple, and this detracts from their quality, to allow the spinners to produce a finer thread.

To spin well, training, experience, dedication and good quality pashmina are required. The spindle could be improved in size and shape, and so could the pot (bagur). These items are hand made, often by the spinners themselves, and traditional models. Often the same spindle used for wool is use for pashmina. Of course this so-called drop spindle is not nearly as effective as the spinning wheel (charkha) which produces a finer thread,(and - importantly - can thus produce more shawls from the same quantity of fibre) but there are solid reasons why this may be difficult to introduce into Ladakh. These are:

It does not fit into the culture and traditions.

It is expensive.

It occupies space.

It is not readily portable. Ladakhi women are used to meeting at selected gathering spots to talk and spin. When they go to the fields they sometimes take their drop spindles with them, which they employ while resting from their agricultural labours.

The preparation of the cone is much easier on a drop spindle than a charkha. No-one, at the moment, possesses a charkha, whereas in Himachal Pradesh they are fairly common, while differing from the standard one by having a small disc near the base of the spindle. Until recently the spinning of pashmina has never, in Ladakh, been viewed as a source of income. Women in Leh have seldom spun and recently, some spinners in the rural areas have abandoned their skill.

Fixed rates for spun pashmina, given by the District Industries Centre, leave little incentive to produce high quality spun thread. Fine spinning takes time and care, and should be rewarded accordingly. Too many spinners work as fast as they can, in pursuit of as much of the flat rate as possible.

The time factor involved using the drop spindle

1kg of de-haired pashmina takes one woman (usually) 15-20days to spin.

18,000kg (60% of the total) requires from 270,000 to 360,000 (wo)man days to spin.

18,000 kg will require the services of 900 to 1200 permanently employed spinners working 300 days in the year.

Weaving

The fly shuttle is used for shawl-weaving in Ladakh. Before the yarn is placed on the loom, it has to go through a twisting process in order to reduce the weak strands in the thread.

Preparation of the warp has been poor in the past, which led to tension related weaving faults. Except at Government Centres, no warping rams are available. These are very efficient and can prepare ten shawl warps to one prepared by the local system. Using the latter, there is a wastage of about 50gms thread on each shawl, as opposed to a loss of 50 gms on ten shawls when using the warping ram; this saves a significant amount of thread, and becomes thoroughly economical when one considers the cost of a warping ram is only about Rs.1500

The following points need immediate consideration:

One warping ram is required in each village at the local

community centre.

Proper training must be given in the preparation of warps.

Looms. Fly shuttle looms are used both in Kashmir and in Ladakh. There is scope for improvement in the looms, and this can be done locally. Such improvements will be required to meet the demand for finer spinning, by which the best shawls are produced. Michael Henderson, a consultant to J & K Handloom, Cooperation, in the report under the title "Pashmina Shawl Weaving in Ladakh" has recommended discontinuation of the steel heddles in the shaft as soon as possible, because in his view, it is totally unsuitable for this type of yarn. The present loom needs a slight improvement to reduce the weight on the thread-especially the finer thread - in order to avoid cuts when weaving. This problem might be solved by dipping the thread in rice gruel, as is presently done in Kashmir.

Kani shawl looms are reported to be different from those in Ladakh in that they make use of bamboo seeds.

At present, in Ladakh, there are only about ten looms owned by local people, and these are in use part time only. There is, however, a good demand for the purchase of looms which cost about Rs.3,000.

One local shawl requires 500-550 gms of pashmina yarn for its production. It would weigh up to 450 gms on completion. In Kashmir, 1kg of yarn will produce three shawls, each weighing 300-325 gms.

One person can weave one or two shawls in a day, so an annual production of 30,000 shawls would require 15,000 to 30,000 man days, i.e. a workforce of 50 to 100 permanent weavers (working 300 days a year).

Clipping. Clipping is not done properly. It is carried out, on the upper side, while still on the loom and on the other side after the shawl is removed from the loom. There is proper frame for clipping, which can be made for the purpose, without this shawls can be badly damaged.

Finishing. This is rarely done in Leh, as there are no facilities available in the private sector.

Woollen pattu There is a high demand in Ladakh for this fabric (strips several metres long and about 25 cm wide) which is used for making the Ladakhi *gonche* (overcoat). At present almost 90% of pattu is made by the people themselves. They normally buy Changlok sheep wool for preparing the warp, and the wool from their own sheep, which is slightly finer, is used for the weft. Nearly all the ladies of the household, except girls going to school, do the spinning. There are many weavers in each village, using local looms, who will do this work at cheap rates. The only problem connected with the pattu industry is that of dyeing. The colours tends to fade. Sales, however, are good.

Knitting This is not an organised industry, but most of the ladies in urban areas know how to knit and make socks, caps, gloves and sweaters, mainly for their own consumption. These items are rarely for sale in the markets.

Carpets Ladakhis do not produce a significant number of carpets, as the market is dominated by the Tibetans, who have better quality carpets, at cheaper prices for sale in Leh.

Thangkas. These are traditional paintings, on fabric, that hang from the wall. Thangkas are virtually obligatory components of the *chotkhang* the private place for worship for Buddhist families. Materials for making thangkas are scarce, and they take a long time to complete. Each village will have the skill to make the hangings of the few that are required, but there is no large scale production. There is a demand for more Thangkas locally, as those with the artistic ability to paint the religious depictions are few and far between, and require many years of training to reach any sort of perfection.

Choktse, the small table, is traditional to Ladakhi culture, and is required by nearly all families within the district. There are different qualities of this product, which depends for its value on the amount of carving along the three sides open to view, and the skill with which the carving is done. The fourth side of the table is open to accommodate the feet of whoever sits, cross-legged, in front of it.

Other handicrafts There are a few other items produced locally, but these are now rare. The only one of any note is the wooden phekor (satto pot) cups, which used to be made in the past, but are now seldom seen.

TRAINING AND FOLLOW-UP ACTION

Proper training and follow-up action are essential aspects of any improvements in the development of the handicraft industries. While training has been in progress for three decades or more, there is little visible evidence of it. Any follow-up action there might have been, has been out of step with the training itself and it a sad reflection on the whole process, that many people who have been trained in different crafts, may now be seen doing other work, and commenting unfavorably on the industries as a whole.

There are several reasons why this situation has come about, and a few of them are listed:-

Lack of proper leadership

This applies particularly to trainers/instructors. Much of the problem may be due to lack of supervision on the part of management, and lack of motivation on the part of trainees who are selected simply to fill gaps in the vacancy lists. Even enthusiastic trainers can lose interest under these conditions. By and large, the standards of training are low and this reflects adversely on management, and trainers alike. The same can be said for any follow-up action, which is either mostly irrelevant or non-existent.

Lack of qualifying standards

No particular experience, background or qualification were required by trainees to take part in training. At the same time, because of high employment, there were few applicants, and courses were packed with any that could be found. Now the situation has changed, there is higher unemployment, and the committees that control courses can be more selective.

Lack of proper facilities in the training centres.

Very rarely are the training centres properly equipped, and the replacement of existing equipment is virtually non-existent.

Frequently training centres are located in very old buildings, dry, uncleaned and dusty. There is very little, if any, furniture and the trainees have to sit all day on the floor. The weaving centre in Leh, which might have been a model for other training centres, functions in relative darkness, whereas it is particularly important that good light is available to see defects in the cloth being woven. Besides there being little light, there is no heating system at all, which makes training in winter, with any sense of enjoyment or satisfaction, a virtual impossibility.

Low pay

Trainees are paid Rs. 100 a month, some deductions being made from this at the end of the training. With costs at they are, this is a very poor incentive to aspiring trainees.

Lack of advanced training/refresher courses for instructors.

It is important to provide these.

How matters may be improved.

The first step would be to draw up, for each craft a brochure, fully illustrated, describing the type of craft in simple terms, the benefits from being trained, the length of any course and the incentives offered to attend it, and the qualifications required (if any) from an applicant. This would need to be carefully explained to each applicant, especially, of course, the illiterate. Where possible, the candidate should be allowed to make a conducted tour of any courses in progress.

Selection for training must be based on the aptitude and qualifications of the applicant.

Selected candidates must be made to sign an agreement to complete the course, and continue working in the same craft thereafter for a specified period.

The pay must be increased. Part of the extra cost could be defrayed by the sale of the goods made by the trainee during training. Some of the pay could be deducted during training, in order to build up a lump sum, that could be used to set-up the trainee on his own after the course.

Incentives to attend a course might include the provision of food and accommodation for those who live far from the training centre. This is a system presently employed by the Tibetans at Choglamsar for their trainees.

A commitment must be made to obtain constant supplies of raw material, and find markets for the sale for finished goods. This means that co-operatives, or associations will have to be established or, where they already exist, revived, to organise and control these vital aspects, and to administer the training establishment.

Advanced training and refresher courses must be organised for the trainers/instructors. Similar facilities must be made available to those exceptional craftsmen who show interest and aptitude.

Good instructors must be encouraged and given status, salaries and promotion prospects. It is essential that they be supported administratively, and that there is an official, clearly appointed by name, whose task is to meet their administrative needs.

Training in handicrafts skill should not be seen only as preparation for full time employment in the chosen crafts. Many people can profit from the training to do part time work only, on completion. Advantage should be taken of trained workers in their own villages. An honorarium could profitable be paid to such individuals as an incentive.

Training centres must be properly equipped to a minimum standard. An inventory for a fully functioning training centre should be drawn up by Government, and this must be the authority for equipping and re-equipping training centres to the standard laid down. Instructors should understand that they are responsible for the training centre and its equipment, as much as for training trainees. Particular attention must be given to the provision of proper heating and lighting arrangements.

Supervision and Co-ordination. The need for good supervision cannot be over stressed. This applies to all levels of direction, from head of Government Department to the individual trainee. Almost equally important is the co-ordination of all departments and institutions involved, such as the District Industries Centre, Handicraft

Department and the financial department involved.

Improving the present standards of training. If the measures recommended above are fully implemented, the standards will automatically improve. There will be no room for poor or lazy instructors if proper supervision is carried out, and given material and moral support, the students themselves will probably demand higher standards. Instructors can be brought to Leh from Kashmir for shawl making, and from Dharamsals for carpet making to train instructors and to raise the standards generally. An element of competition between training centres will add an edge to the work, and this might be done by organising displays of work centrally, prizes being given for the best artifacts.

Duration of training.

Carpet making. At present only one year's training is given, whereas four years are required for a trainee to reach an acceptable standard.

Thangka painting. This requires four to five years training.

Shawl weaving. A trainee can make fairly good shawls with only six months training. The ideal is one year.

De-hairing can be learnt within one month, but the official requirement for training is one year.

Spinning. A trainee can spin fairly good yarn after five to six months training . Required training, at the present is for one year.

MARKETING

On present assessment, the crafts of making pashmina shawls, knitting sweaters, pattu weaving, thangka painting and wood carving could contribute greatly toward raising the income of the people of Ladakh, provided, of course, that the markets are assured and constant. It will not be sufficient to assume that the present market will absorb the greater number of goods produced by the renewed interest in making these crafts. Outlets will have to be sought both locally and outside.

Fortunately there is a growing interest by the outside world in the crafts of the Himalaya region and the unique art, culture and tradition of Ladakh expressed in its handicrafts will have great appeal. The Ladakhi shawl, for example is a lovely product, and is in high demand from Indians and foreign tourists alike. The attraction of a shawl made of pashmina is its lightness for those travelling by air. These and the other products will sell well, provided the quality of work is of a high standard.

Suggestion for improving marketing.

1. Standardisation in the production of all similar goods.

1. Standardisation in the production of all similar goods.

2. All finished goods should bear a label to show their authenticity, by whom made and the material used, e.g. "Shawl made in Ladakh from pure pashmina fibre". This should be certified by the Government or non-government body responsible for the production, and will act as an endorsement that the product has attained the required standard of quality.

3. Until production units are established, the Government should assist by securing markets for the items produced. This can be done by fixing a support price. When the production units are established and operating, the Government can withdraw.

4. Those items which are not easily sold, should be pooled at Leh, where they will be more open to public view. Advertisements in the local press and leaflets left in places frequented by tourists will help promote sales. There will be a need for a show room, with capable staff to explain details of production, prices etc. This could perhaps be combined with a museum exhibiting local handicrafts, used through the centuries for domestic and agricultural work. It would be essential, once created, that any such show room would be assured of a regular supply of finished goods.

5. Costs of products from Government training centres should be fixed at moderate levels, to make sure that products from the private sectors are not undermined. At the same time, inferior products should not be allowed to be sold, as these are a waste of raw material, and a poor reflection on the crafts that are being promoted.

Co-operatives, Associations and Agencies

Such organisations will be needed primarily to deal with the two essential aspects of providing raw materials, and of marketing the finished goods. A revolving fund will be required. It is appreciated that good co-operatives are not easy to run, but they are an important link in the chain of events between the provision of raw material and the finished product, and they do represent the participation of the people involved, providing a focal point for help, discussion, and for legitimate dissension. They also, of course, ensure a fair distribution of profits and stablise prices. While direction from an agency may be necessary in the initial stages of any new re-vitalizing of the handicraft industry, it will be the co-operative that sustain it.

Most Ladakhis are extremely busy in the summer months with their chosen ocupations, but have time on their hands in the winter. If co-operatives are well organised, they will be able to offer additional opportunities for income generation to those that would otherwise have little to do, by providing raw materials and market outlets. The Government can help this process by providing centrally located markets.

Appendix A

Recommended Co-operative system

Advisory Board
Agency for Handicraft Development
Independent Co-operative Societies
Main society in Leh
Supply of raw material, and finished and semi-processed items.
Sale of finished semi-finished items.
Associated members from all villages producing handicrafts.

The raw material can be supplied against the cost of the finished article, and the price of the finished article fixed by the producer and co-operative together. The latter will add its own commission, and ensure a uniformity of price of similar articles that will satisfy both the producer and the consumer. Naturally, whoever manages the society will have to have the necessary commitment to the ideals of the cooperative, as well as a basic knowledge of all the crafts represented by it.

Costing 1 Pashmina shawl 3ft by 6ft

	Rs.		Rs
Pashmina fibre 1kg	400	to	600
De-hairing 1kg	25	to	50
Spinning 600gms	126	to	144
Twisting 600gms	10	to	10
Weaving	100	to	100
Finishing/Washing	20	to	20
Total	Rs.681.00	to	924.00

Sale price Rs. 1100 to Rs. 1500 for one pashmina shawl

Costing: 1 Carpet 3ft by 6ft

Wool yarn 7kg @ Rs.130/140	910	to	980
Cotton 1.5 kg @ Rs. 45/50	68	to	75
Labour 1 month	1000	to	1200
Total	Rs.1978	to	2255

Sale price less than Rs. 2000. It is not in demand because the quality is much lower than the Tibetan carpets which may be bought for the same price.

Knitting

Local wool for one kg	75	to	80
Spinning	50	to	50
Dyeing	50	to	50
Total	175	to	180

Sale price Rs. 400/600 per kg. Local wool is preferred in Leh, especially when it is dyed. This will sell very fast for making sweaters etc.

Thangka painting
Cost depends on the size, and of course the amount of detail in the painting. Prices reach about Rs. 3000, and it takes 3 months to complete a thangka.

Appendix B

Those consulted in the preparation of this report.

1. Sh. Sonam Dawa	Director, LEDeG Leh
2. Sh. Abdul Majid	Deputy Register, Cooperative
3. Sh. Ali Raza	Manager, Industries Dept. Leh.
4. Sh. Sonam Wancghuk	Secretary SECMOL, Leh
5. Sh. Tserig Stobdan	Supt. Industries Dept. Leh
6. Sh. Tsetan Spalbar	Supt. I.T.I. Leh
7. Sh. Rinchen Tundup	Manager, Tibetan SOS Handicrafts Training Centre Leh.
8. Smt. Rigzin R/O Mulbek	Pashmina de-hairer
9. Smt. Lal Dedi R/O Leh	Spinner
10.Smt. Yangchan R/O Leh	Spinner
11. Smt. Tashi Dolma	Weaver
12. Smt. Zenab	Instructor, Carpet Centre Chushot
13. Dr. Phuntsog	Laboratory Officer, Upshi
14. Sh. Abdul Qadir	Butcher

List of weavers of pashmina shawls - Leh

1. Disket	Tshangspa yurthung Leh
2. Zara Watul	Leh
3. Tsering Choskit	Changthang
4. Yangchan	Nochung Leh
5. Phuntsog	Lamagon Chanspa Leh
6. Laskit	Khema
7. Chewang	Ragsha Choglamsar
8. Tundup Yangskit	Housing Colony Leh
9. Tashi Dolma	,, ,,
10 Tsering Dloma	,, ,,
11. Sonam Deskit	,, ,,
12. Tseing Wakhama	Skalzangling.

List of spinners and de-hairers.

1. Ashey	Stagophelok Leh
2. Samstan Paldam	Stalam, Leh
3. Zila Juma Bhat	Zangsti Leh
4. Hajira	Tagophelok Leh
5. Rabi Juma Bhat	Zangsti, Leh
6. Maryam	Zangsti, Leh
7. Halima	Near C.M.O. office Leh
8. Zila Matto	Stagophelok
9. Aziz Saraban	Stagophelok

NEGI LAMA TENZIN GYALTSEN
A preliminary account of the life of a modern Buddhist saint.[1]

Thierry Dodin
Zentralasiens Seminar, University of Bonn,
Regina-Pacis Weg 7, 53113 Bonn, GERMANY

Summary

Negi Lama (1894-1977) of Kinnaur. though never a monk, was one of the foremost Buddhist scholars of his time. After mastering classical Tibetan so as to understand fully the classical philosophic texts, he went to Tashilhunpo and Lhasa, receiving teaching there and himself teaching Tibetan grammar. Professional jealousy drove him to Khams where he spent 19 years, partly at the royal court, mostly at successive monasteries and yogins' retreats, studying in libraries and gathering tantric initiations. He then returned to Varanasi in India to learn Sanskrit, the original language of Buddhist philosophy. While living there in very poor circumstances, the Dalai Lama heard of his reputation and made a special visit to meet him, subsequently arranging for him to move to Bodhgaya and instruct H.H. and others. By his collection and critical study of many little known teachings, otherwise lost in the Chinese occupation of Tibet, he gave a new impetus to Buddhist study. Tashi Rabgyas of Leh was one of his disciples.

The man who is the subject of this presentation will probably be unknown to most of the readers. His name was Tenzin Gyaltsen (*bstan 'dzin rgyal mtshan*), but among the different ethnic groups of Tibetan culture in the Himalaya he was also known under various other names like Kunu (*khu nu*) Rinpoche, Kunu Lama and Negi Lama (*ne gi bla ma*)[2]. While working on a research project on modern Buddhism in the Himalaya[3] I often had come across his name and became aware that he must have been an important personality of contemporary Tibetan Buddhism. However, apart from some fragmentary information I was able to get from some of my informants - who all spoke about him with deep respect - I could not find any complete account of his life, so that I was in the situation of having some pieces but being unable to complete the jigsaw.

By chance, while spending some time at the Ladakh Bauddha Vihara (Ladakh Buddh Vihar) in Delhi at the very beginning of 1993, I met Mr. Roshan Lal Negi, a scholar of Buddhism from Kinnaur, who introduced me to his father, Sangnak Tenzin (*gsang* sngags bstan 'dzin*)[4], who had himself been a disciple of Negi Lama for many years of his life. From Sangnak Tenzin's narration I could record quite a complete account of Negi Lama's life which is the main source of information I used for this paper.

Although it was an unexpected opportunity to get a first-hand account of his master's life from Sangnak Tenzin, I stay aware of the fact that relying upon one single testimony as the source of information implies a certain lack of reliability for a scholarly contribution of this kind. Nevertheless Sangnak Tenzin, by the beginning of 1993 an old blind man of 82 years who since the death of his wife had lived a life consecrated to religion, had received his knowledge about the early life of Negi Lama from his master's own narrations. The later parts of his account were Sangnak Tenzin's own reminiscences.

Although Sangnak Tenzin's account was quite different from the type of biographical accounts that can be found in traditional Tibetan hagiographies (*rnam thar*)[5] it was not a purely historical account either.

Sangnak Tenzin's obvious intention was to relate what he considered the most important episodes in the life of his *guru*, and not to give a historical account of his life in the scholarly sense of the word. His discourse was very enthusiastic and he conspiciously emphasized certain episodes which seemed to be of great importance to him while just passing over several years of time which he considered to be of lesser significance. Moreover, precise dates as well as topographical and personal names were rare and quite inaccurate in his account. I tried to cope with that problem by noting down problematic points during the interview and trying to clarify them afterwards. After each single part of the interview, which more or less coincided with the different phases of Negi Lama's life, I inquired about some of the passages which I thought had not been treated intensively enough. However, although he doubtlessly tried his best, Sangnak Tenzin was not always able to give an accurate answer, obviously because I asked questions which seemed to be of secondary importance to him, and about which he therefore had never really thought or enquired. The antinomy between critical-scholarly and devotional-religious discourse in the interview situation is a well-known methodological problem of fieldwork research on which I do not intend to elaborate further here. Pointing out the existence of this problem is, however, important in the present context since it may explain some of the shortcomings of this contribution. Nevertheless, in spite of those limitations Sangnak Tenzin's account also included many anecdotal items, which I think cast an interesting light on the personality of his master by making him appear in a very human perspective.

I completed the basic material from Sangnak Tenzin's

testimony with some pieces of information I had been able to collect in the course of my research work before and after my encounter with Sangnak Tenzin. Thus, in spite of some contradictions, I could in parts amend for the almost total lack of dates in the interview. Where sources apart from the interview have been used, the name of the informants or the references of the sources used are given in the footnotes[6].

Although I still am aware of the fact that some points need further investigation, I have come to the conclusion that enough material is available for giving a preliminary but valuable account of Negi Lama's life, as well as for an appreciation of the influence he exerted on Tibetan Buddhism as a whole.

The early years

Negi Lama was born in 1894 in the village Sunam which lies in the forest-clad province of Kinnaur in the western Himalaya[7]. In contrast to most well-known lamas he was neither an incarnation or tulku (*sprul sku*) nor even a monk (*dge slong*, Skt.*bhikçu*) but chose to live the life of a layman for his lifetime. The only vows he took were those of a lay practitioner or genyen (*dge bsnyen*, Skt.*upâsaka*). We must presume that he never felt the need to take more than layman vows, for he would obviously have had enough opportunities to do so in later years while staying in several monasteries for long periods of time.

He was still a teenager when for the first time he considered becoming a student of religion. His parents, who were very wealthy, were strongly opposed to these plans, but he was sternly determinated and at the age of 18 or 19 he decided to ignore their objections and secretly go to Sikkim, where he hoped to meet a proper teacher. The final decision to leave home must have come very suddenly, for, according to the narration of Sangnak Tenzin, he did not even take the time to put shoes on, so that it was bare-footed that he set out for a journey which was to last for almost his entire life time[8].

From his native country of Kinnaur he first headed for Spiti, then to Lahaul and from there to the town of Manali in Kulu valley, the first destination he had set for himself on his journey to Sikkim. Because of his hasty departure from home, he had not been able to bring any money with him and soon had to look for some financial resources. As he knew some people in Lahaul and Kulu to be debtors to his family, he claimed to have been sent in order to collect partial refunds. After he had gathered enough money he left Kulu for Sikkim.

In Sikkim he stayed with his brother-in-law, Sonam Zi Negi

(*bsod nams gzigs*(?)*ne gi*), and began to study Tibetan grammar with Urgyen Tenzin (*(db)u rgyan bstan 'dzin*), a famous Sikkimese scholar of that time[9]. The fact that Negi Lama put so much emphasis on beginning his studies of religion by intensively learning grammar with a renowned scholar is quite remarkable. It clearly shows that, even though a young and unexperienced student, he was already convinced of the futility of learning by heart religious texts as the monks generally do, without previously acquiring a proper knowledge of classical grammar which first makes them understandable. He studied with Urgyen Tenzin for about 3 months in order to reach the grade of "Master of Tibetan language"[10]. Then he decided to go to Tibet.

His plan was to study Buddhist philosophy and since Tashi Lhunpo (*bkra shis lhun po*), the seat of the Panchen Lama, was the first monastery of importance on his way from Sikkim to Lhasa, he stayed for about eight to nine months and acquired the grade of gyugchung (*rgyugs chung*) there.[11] After that he continued his journey to Lhasa[12].

About seven kilometres from Lhasa there was a small monastery of the Drukpa Kagyu (*'brug pa bka' brgyud*) tradition, known as "Kamda Tulku Monastery"[13]. In this monastery Negi Lama received teachings on *phyag rgya chen po (mo)/Mahâmudrâ* from Kamda Tulku[14] and he himself taught Tibetan grammar to his teacher, a subject in which he, although still being very young, had by now become an expert. For about 6 years he met Kamda Norbu every day, teaching him and getting teachings from him[15].

His exceptionally good understanding of Tibetan grammar quickly made him famous in the Tibetan capital. He taught at many places, and many people came to listen to his lectures. Most of the time he used to stay at the medical college of Mentsi khang (*sman rtsis khang*). The fame Negi Lama had won with time, however, was not to everyone's taste. A great scholar of Tibetan language, whose name we unfortunately do not know, became jealous of Negi Lama and started spreading rumours against him, pretending that his teaching was not proper and that, as a non-Tibetan, he could not have a correct understanding of Tibetan language[16]. Confronted with this situation Negi Lama decided that he should better leave Lhasa, for he had no powerful protector. He left the Tibetan capital for the eastern province of Khams where he hoped to escape this kind of intrigue[17].

The years in Khams

Negi Lama was to remain in Khams for 19 years. He first lived in Derge (*sde dge*) where he stayed at the king's palace teaching Tibetan language and grammar to members of the royal family. He is said to have had a very good relationship with his pupils, the son and daughter of the King. After his death some rumours occured among the Tibetans pretending that the king's daughter's child was in fact Negi Lama's illegitimate offspring.

During the years following his stay in Derge, Negi Lama went from monastery to monastery and from master to master in order to gather as many tantric initiations (*dbang*) as he could get. In all those years Negi Lama had about 100 teachers, some of them famous scholars but many unknown ascetics, a large number of them being lay practitioners, living a life of retreat in caves hidden in the mountains. One of those lay practitioners, whose name we unfortunately do not know, seems to have been one of Negi Lama's most important masters. He is said to have been living for years alone in a cave wearing nothing but a goat skin. From him Negi Lama received extensive teachings connected with the Dükhor (*dus kyi 'khor lo*)/*Kâlachakra*-Tantra, which took about nine months.

Out of all these teachers from Khams only one, Jamyang Khyentse Rinpoche (*'jam dbyans mkhyen brtse*), managed to escape the Chinese invasion and later lived in Indian exile. The destiny of most of the others remains unknown but, given the well-known political troubles which were to occur some years later in Tibet, we can reasonably assess that the very most of them died or had to give up their contemplative life without being able to transmit their teachings to another generation of Buddhist ascetics. We can therefore presume that history left Negi Lama the only holder of many teachings which have now vanished in Tibet itself.

Negi Lama also visited every monastery on his way in order to explore their libraries. He also attempted to visit the library of the "Kaya" Bonpo Monastery[18], but the head-lama of the monastery did not give him the permission to do so, because he did not belong to the Bon tradition.

Through the years Negi Lama became famous in Khams under the name of Gya-Lama, Gyagar-lama (*rgya (gar) bla ma*) or Indian Lama and his fame as a great scholar of Buddhism spread all over the province. However, he still felt unsatisfied with himself. Having become a master in all branches of the traditional Tibetan curriculum and having collected many tantric initiations, among which many were known in Central Tibet only by name, he felt the need to learn Sanskrit, the original language of Buddhist *Mahâyâna* philosophy and tantrism. As he was not able to find a Sanskrit teacher in Tibet, he decided to return to India[19]. At that time - it must have been in the first half of the 1940's, some years before India's independence[20] - Negi Lama was about fifty years old already.

Back to India

On his way to India Negi Rinpoche passed through Kinnaur, his country of birth where he had not set foot since he had left home secretly as a young man[21]. The news of his coming raised a wave of enthusiasm among the Kinnauris who had come to know about his high level of Buddhist scholarship through some of their compatriots who had been among his disciples about twenty years before in Lhasa. He stayed in Kinnaur for some years and went from village to village giving basic teachings appropriate to the simple people who came to welcome him. While in Kinnaur, besides giving teachings, Negi Lama took the opportunity to correct the draft of an extensive grammatical treatise - a commentary on *ngag sgron* - which was a written version of the lectures he had given years ago in Lhasa. This was to be Negi Lama's first book and shows once more the importance he laid upon the right understanding of classical language as the basic step on the Buddhist path. After having received the final touch, the manuscript was sent to Lhasa where it was printed on woodblocks at the Mentsi khang. Negi Lama was still in Kinnaur when he heard of Mahatma Gandhi's death under the bullets of a Hindu fanatic in 1948. On that day he refused to take food as a sign of mourning.

After his stay in Kinnaur Negi Lama left for Calcutta where he stayed for one year. A rich Khampa family living there was sponsoring him. He first tried to learn Sanskrit in the Bengali metropole but as he couldn't get a good teacher he decided to move on to Varanasi. In Varanasi Negi Lama stayed at the Hindu temple of Lakshmi Kund Tekramat. Since he had no sponsors there and very few money to live on, he used to take only one meal a day. He is said to have been living like a *sâdhû* at that time. In Tekramat Negi Lama could realise his dream of learning Sanskrit. He had found a proper teacher, an Indian pandit, who taught him Sanskrit-grammar for about 5 to 6 years.

Meanwhile, although Negi Lama was still living the life of a recluse, his fame had began to spread among the Indian Buddhists of the western Himalaya. In 1956 Kushok Bakula Rinpoche, the head-lama of the Spituk Monastery (*spe thub*), came to know about him and invited him to Srinagar in order to receive teachings from him. Negi Lama stayed in a government bungalow in Srinagar where Kushok Bakula was supposed to come and meet him. But as Kushok Bakula was too busy with his duties for the Government of Jammu & Kashmir, Negi Lama after some time returned to Varanasi in order to continue his own studies[22].

In the same year Negi Lama first met the Dalai Lama,

although this was to be a very short meeting. The Dalai Lama and the Panchen Lama had come to India for an official visit on the occasion of the festivities for the 2500th Buddhajayanti. The well known Ladakhi writer Tashi Rabgyas was accompanying them as a translator, for he knew Lhasa Tibetan as well as Hindi/Urdu and English. Tashi Rabgyas had got to know Negi Lama during the latter's stay in Srinagar short before, he had been his disciple and therefore knew what a great master he was in spite of being still unknown outside the western Himalaya. Once, while standing in the middle of a crowd of people who had come to welcome the two high lamas and get their blessing, Tashi Rabgyas recognised Negi Lama in the crowd. He grasped his arm, pulled him in front of the Lamas and introduced him to them[23]. After a short while, however, Negi Lama disappeared again, pushed away by the unruly crowd. It was only many years later in Tekramat that Negi Lama was to have his first true meeting with the Dalai Lama[24].

Teacher of the teachers

After many Tibetans had come to India as refugees, the Dalai Lama organized an inter-school meeting in Mussoorie in order to take proper measures to assure the survival of the Tibetan Buddhist tradition in exile, while it was obviously being destroyed in Tibet itself. All important khempos, gehes and rinpoches from all schools were invited. It was probably the first time in the history of Tibetan Buddhism that so many prestigious lamas participated in one meeting. Although he was not among the official guests and therefore most probably did not take part in the plenary sessions[25], Negi Lama was also present on that occasion. He left a lasting impression on many participants because he was obviously the most learned among them. It is told that, though many Khenpos were particular experts in a certain branch of knowledge, no one knew a tradition or a specific teaching which Negi Lama was not acquainted with. On the contrary he knew many teachings which they were not familiar with.

After the meeting, the Dalai Lama was told about this scholar, who - apart from the short encounter they had in 1956 - up to then had been unknown to him, and since at that time he was collecting all initiations (*dbang*) and teachings of Tibetan Buddhism, he decided to meet him as soon as possible and to become his student. He therefore rushed to Varanasi and came to meet Negi Lama accompanied by his personal secretary only.

At that time Negi Lama was just recovering from a serious illness and was still feeling very weak. As the disease had affected his eyes he couldn't see properly. He was also very poor and his only property was the old torn-up blanket he was wrapped in in his empty cell. Negi Lama noticed two monks entering his room and asked who they were. When he was informed by the private secretary who the visitor was, he objected that he wore no appropriate clothing and had no chair for His Holiness to sit on. He claimed not to be able to receive him under such conditions. As the Dalai Lama insisted on speaking with him they both remained standing and had a talk.

The encounter was quite short, although more fruitful than the previous one: the Dalai Lama and Negi Lama only fixed a place and a schedule for further meetings. The Dalai Lama made up his mind for Bodhgaya as the proper place. From then on Negi Lama mostly stayed in Bodhgaya in order to give teachings to the Dalai Lama as well65 as to other high lamas among which Ling (*glin*) Rinpoche, the senior-preceptor (*yongs 'dzin*) of the Dalai Lama, was one of the most well known. He settled in Bodhgaya with two nuns from his native province of Kinnaur, who are said to have been his closest disciples and stayed with him for the remaining years of his life[26].

Although it is not exactly known which teachings the Dalai Lama received from Negi Lama, the central matters obviously were the concept of Bodhicitta - a concept which plays a major role in the teachings nowadays given by the Dalai Lama[27] - and other aspects of Buddhist philosophy, like epistemology. The Dalai Lama naturally had other highly qualified teachers and counsellers for religious matters (a.o. the so-called "*mtshan zabs*"), but the philosophical concepts which seemed still not clear enough to him he used to discuss with Negi Lama. Those meetings with Negi Lama left a deep impression on the Dalai Lama: when he gave his *Kalachakra* initiation in Bodhgaya 1985, he qualified Negi Lama as the "*Shantideva* of our time", referring to the great Buddhist philosopher. Ling Rinpoche, himself one of the greatest gelugpa lamas[28] received from Negi Lama teachings based on several Sanskrit texts which he himself handed down to his own disciples[29].

After having given most of his knowledge and experience to so many illustrious students Negi Lama, now an old man in his seventies, came to consider his life-work as accomplished and decided to look for a proper place to spend the last years of his life in a peaceful atmosphere. He first settled in Nalanda, the most well-known place of Buddhist erudition, where a new Pali-Institute had just been opened. He enjoyed the place and decided to stay there. Soon after his coming, however, the then Prime Minister of India Smt. Indira Gandhi came to the institute on an official visit. For matters of security all persons living in and around the institute were made to leave their place and had to stay in some surrounding villages.

༄། ཁུ་ནུར་འཁྲུངས་ཞེས་བསྟན་འཛིན་རྒྱལ་མཚན་ཞབས། །

Tenzin Gyaltsen from Kinnaur
***khu nur 'khrungs zhes bstan 'dzin rgyal mtshan zhabs*[33]**

Negi Lama had to stay for a while in a small village house where he didn't feel comfortable. He therefore left Nalanda and went back to Bodhgaya, where he spent the last 8-9 years of his life together with his two nun-disciples in the Tibetan monastery which at that time was headed by his former disciple, Ling Rinpoche[30]. Two months before his death he left Bodhgaya for a visit to Kinnaur and Lahaul, where he went from village to village teaching mostly from Gampopa's (*sgam po pa*) "Jewel Ornament of Liberation" (*dvags po thar rgyan*)[31]. He died at the age of 82 on February 23rd, 1977 at Shashul monastery while on his way through Lahaul[32].

The legacy of Negi Lama

Giving an appreciation of Negi Lama's life and work first means pointing out the fact that he was in many ways an unusual lama. While in the past as well as today the leading figures of Tibetan Buddhism exclusively consist of *Tibetan monks*, he was neither a Tibetan nor even a clerical in the true sense of the word, The traditional academic "career" of Tibetan Buddhism, an almost life-long programme of studies following a curriculum fixed centuries ago at one of the well-established monastic institutions, progressing slowly but steadily from lower to higher academic titles was not the path he chose to go. Rejecting that kind of strictly institutionalised form of religious life, he instead actively searched for the best sources of erudition and spiritual experience of his time by which his personal quest might be satisfied. Accepting two young nuns as his disciples and spending the last 15 years of his life in their company was in open contradiction to the generally accepted view of nuns as passive participants of religious life, and, by the way, exposing himself to accusations of promiscuity. Instead of following one single line of transmission which he would have recognised as "the right one", he collected and followed the teachings of different scholars, irrespective of the tradition (*chos lugs*) they belonged to. He rejected dogmatism and all the more the widely spread sectarian thinking.

To be sure, Negi Lama was a man of faith; faith alone, however, was insufficient for him. In true Buddhist spirit he had to check out the basis of things and to test affirmations before accepting them. For all these reasons, and because of his extraordinary capacities rousing jealousy among established authorities of his time, he was repeatedly the object of enmities. Because he was such a non-conformist he became the object of intrigues and injurious rumours several times, even after his death as has been noted above. Gifted as he was, he could have led a secure life and have become a geshe or Khempo covered with honours, but this would not have been in accordance with his understanding of the path of religion. He preferred to live the life of a wandering ascetic searching for spiritual perfection, like the Buddha himself did.

Considering the impact Negi Lama left on Tibetan Buddhism, two aspects should be distinguished: his innovative role and his role in the preservation of the Tibetan spiritual heritage.

Although Negi Lama has truely been an innovative personality in the modern history of Tibetan Buddhism, he was no reformer in the true sense of the word, for he never held any official position. However, through his writings and much more still through personal charisma, his own example, and the influence he exerted on his disciples - in particular the Dalai Lama - he gave new impulses to Tibetan Buddhism. The emphasis he put on proper understanding of the scriptures instead of mechanical learning left traces on the type of education given nowadays by some Buddhist institutions. Besides that, this attitude inspired some of the "progressive" Tibetan intellectuals in-exile, despite the scepticism they otherwise generally show towards everything traditional, including the institution of the Dalai Lama[33]. The central position he gave to the concept of bodhicitta as the basic step on the Mahayana path seems to have particularly influenced the Dalai Lama. The study of Sanskrit which Negi Lama initiated in the late fourties today forms part of the curriculum of several modern Buddhist institutions like the Central Institute of Higher Tibetan Studies in Sarnath or the Central Institute of Buddhist Studies in Choglamsar[34].

To state that Negi Lama alone was the initiator of these modern developments would surely be an exaggeration, but he was one of those who definitely inspired them, for - beside his lasting influence on the Dalai Lama - we should not forget that many of his other disciples today hold leading positions in contemporary Buddhist institutions.

The role Negi Lama played in the preservation and spreading of the Tibetan Buddhist heritage seems even more obvious. By collecting many little known teachings and traditions, particularly from eastern Tibet, he saved them from vanishing for ever in the course of the Chinese crack-down on Buddhist culture in Tibet. By handing down those teachings to a new generation of practitioners in India, he did not only carry on the line of transmission but even made them accessible to many more Buddhists throughout the Himalayan range and beyond, more accessible than they had ever been in Tibet itself.

As for a conclusion we should therefore point out that Negi Lama has been one of the most influential figures of Tibetan Buddhism in our century. I could only give a short account of his life and an appreciation of his work here. Further studies, providing more evidence about his life, will be necessary to appreciate the role of this outstanding lama in full[35].

NOTES

*For technical reasons it was unfortunately impossible to print the author's standard diacritics. In Tibetan the Wylie transliteration has been used; in Sanskrit the following convention has been used: â for a, û for u, ç for s, Sh for S.

1. As a testimony of gratitude, I would like to dedicate this contribution to the memory of my main informant, the late Sangnak Tenzin from the Jangi village, Kinnaur (Himachal Pradesh), who passed away on January 15th, 1994. I also want to thank my friend Roshan Lal Negi, son of Sangnak Tenzin for arranging for me a meeting with his father and translating the interview from Kinnaurese language. The material presented here has been mainly collected during fieldwork for the research project "Buddhismus und Gesellschaft im Himalaya" ("Buddhism and Society in the Himalaya") which was sponsored by the Volkswagen Stiftung, Hannover, between January 1991 and August 1994. It was the Volkswagen Stiftung too, which enabled me to participate at the 6th Colloquium of the IALS, and thus made this presentation possible. I am also very indebted to Susanne Kamüller, Bonn, who proofread the draft of this paper.
2. Kunu (*khu nu*, sometimes also "*ku nu*") is the traditional Tibetan name for the province of Kinnaur while Negi (*ne gi*, sometimes "*ni gi*") is a very common clan and family name among Kinnaurese Buddhists.
3. See note 1.
4. Full name: *grub bla gnyis pa mdo gsang sngags bstan 'dzin*. This name, respectively title, was given to him by the late XVIth Karmapa.
5. It particularly lacked any feature of the customary teleological patterns and the stereotypal mentioning of wonders which are usual for this kind of literature.
6. I tried to make this contribution as accurate as possible; however, I naturally take the full responsibility for any mistakes, misunderstanding or omissions that the reader may find in it. Moreover all views and appreciations expressed here are mine and do not commit any of my sources and informants.
7. Sources: Negi Lama's place of birth was taken from *The Mahabodhi*, June- July 1977, p. 371. His date of birth was given to me by Mr. Fateh Chand Negi, teacher at the Central Institute of Buddhist Studies, Choglamsar, Ladakh. The village Sunam (called "Summam" in the *Mahabodhi*) is situated in Upper Kinnaur, in the vicinity of Poo (*spu*), close to the junction of the Spiti (*spi ti/dpe ti/spyi ti*) and Sutlej (*glang chen kha bab*) rivers (Manis Kumar Raha & Satya Narayan Mahato, The Kinnaurese of the Himalayas, Anthropological Survey of India, Calcutta 1985, p. 357; Peter, Friedrich, A Glossary of Place names in Western Tibet, in: *Ethnologische Zeitschrift Zürich* II, 1975).
8. Since Negi Lama was born in 1894 and left home while being about 19 years old, his departure must have been around 1913.
9. There were obviously more Kinnauri students of religion at that time in Sikkim. In the preface of his *English-Tibetan Dictionary* the well-known Sikkimese scholar Kazi Dawa Samdup or Dousamdup (*zla ba bsam 'grub*), who was to become famous in the West as teacher of W.Y. Evans-Wentz and translator of the "*Tibetan book of the dead*" (*bar do thos grol*), mentions a certain "*Negi-Amar Chand Babu, a bright Tibetan scholar from Bashahr State=*" (i.e. Kinnaur), who had studied Tibetan in Sikkim since 1915 (Kazi Dousamdup, *An English-Tibetan Dictionary*, Calcutta 1919). Whether this Kinnaurese scholar had any connection with Negi Lama or his relative is unknown. The date of arrival of Negi Lama in Sikkim is uncertain since we do not know how long his journey

from Kinnaur to Gangtok took. The fact that a close relative of Negi Lama was residing in Sikkim may be interpreted as an indication that his family was involved in the trans-Himalayan, respectively Central Asian trade. There are two reasons for this supposition: A. The family has been described as being very wealthy although living in an otherwise quite deprived region. Their village was situated on the "Tibet-Hindoostan Road" which was one of the two main traditional trade routes to Tibet and Central Asia on the Western sector (the other one being the Ruthok (*ru thok*) route, which led to Ladakh and Yarkand). B. Because of the decline of the Tibet-India trade through Western Tibet, many families who had been involved in it for generations moved their main activities to Sikkim and North Bengal and sent relatives to Gangtok and Kalimpong in order to continue the family's business in the southern sector, on the Lhasa-Kalimpong-Calcutta route, which in this century had emerged as the most prolific trade link between India and Tibet. (On this topic see a.o.: Abdul Wahid Radhu, Caravane tib3taine, Paris 1981; Hisao Kimura, Japanese Agent in Tibet, London 1990 and Wim van Spengen, Tibetan Border Worlds. A geo-historical analysis of trade and traders, Universiteit van Amsterdam 1992 (unpublished Ph.D. diss.))

10. I couldn't find out what the title "Master of Tibetan language" exactly means. As far as I know there is no appropriate equivalent for it in Tibetan, so that one may consider it an indication that Negi Lama visited a western-type school, conferring grades related to the British educational system. If this was the case he should probably have visited the "Bhutia College", headed by Kazi Dawa Samdup (see previous note) which at that time was the only western-type school teaching Tibetan language in Gangtok. This, however, is only a supposition.

11. "Gyugchung" (*rgyugs chung*) was an academic title peculiar to Tashi Lhunpo, the passing of which was the minimum requirement for beginning studies at this monastic university. In the course of an exam which took place every year in January, the candidates had to recite by heart a very extensive ritual text known under the short title "*bkris lhun chos spyod*" (full title: "*chos grwa chen po bkra sis lhun po'i phags tshogs dus sde rin po che zhal don chos spyod rab gsal*"). In order for the candidates to fullfil this requirement intensive one-year preparatory classes were held at the monastery. However, those who - like Negi Lama - did not wish to or could not attend these classes were welcomed to participate in the exam as free candidates. To acquire the grade of a gyugchung it was sufficient to recite one of the two volumes (about 14 cm thick each!) of the text. Those who knew both volumes by heart were rewarded with the title of "gyugchen" (*rgyugs chen*). I am indebted to Geshe J. Zongtse, Göttingen for this information as well as to Dr. Siglinde Dietz who put the question to Mr. Zongtse and diligently communicated the information to me.

12. The reason why Negi Lama left Tashi Lhunpo just after passing his gyugchung examination is unclear, for as the title was nothing but a test of aptitude for beginning scholarly studies in Tashi Lhunpo and as study was Negi Lama's aim, he should rather have been expected to stay there at least for some time. Since passing the gyugchung exams only made sense in the case the candidate stayed at Tashi Lhunpo for study afterwards, we must presume that either Negi Lama first planned to study there but for some unknown reasons changed his mind, or that he had subjected himself to this exam as a test of proficiency but never had planned to stay at Tashi Lhunpo. As Sangnak Tenzin's account seems to imply that Lhasa was Negi Lama's destination when leaving Sikkim, the second supposition seems to be more probable.

13. I was unfortunately unable to find out which monastery is exactly meant and who the lama called here "Kamda Norbu Tulku" (phonetic rendering) may be. After consulting several persons well acquainted with the Lhasa region - both Tibetans and Westerners - I could, however, gather some information out of which the following hypothesis can be proposed: The monastery was probably one of the several small monasteries belonging to the Drukpa tradition and situated above

the right bank of the Kyichu river (*skyid chu*), approximately between Nyethang (*snye thang*) and Chaksam (*lcags zam*), where the Kyichu runs into the Brahmaputra (*gtsang po*). The fact that this region is about twice to thrice further from Lhasa than the quoted 7 kilometres should not automatically be seen as a contradiction to Sangnak Tenzin's account since the distance was obviously guessed in the course of the interview. According to the reminiscences of Mr. Gonpo N. Ronge, Königswinter, there was in this region a "holy place" situated some kilometres above the well-known monastery of Dolma Lhakang (*sgrol ma lha khang*). Because sage (*Salvia officinalis*) used to grow there in abundance, the place was called "*kan mda'*", which means "terrace of sage" (correct spelling of *kan* (sage) is uncertain; *mda'* given here as "terrace" may also connotate the lower part of a plain or plateau). Although there was no consecrated monastery there, many meditation practitioners from the Drukpa as well as other traditions used to reside at this place. They lived in caves and in different buildings. The chapel (*lha kang*) was one of those connected with Ling Repa (*gling ras pa*). Since many incarnate lamas are popularly known after the name of their main seat, we may assume that the "Kamda Norbu Tulku" in Sangnak Tenzin's account was the lama heading this institution. This, however, is to be seen as an hypothesis which would need futher investigation.

14. Since *Mahâmudrâ* is mostly practised in hermitages, this information would fit with the hypothesis proposed in note 13.

15. It is not clear whether Negi Lama's stay in Lhasa lasted only 6 years or longer. Since no expressed affirmation about this topic was given in the interview, we could argue that he might have met Khamda Norbu long after his arrival in Lhasa, or that he stopped seeing him regularly long before he left the Tibetan capital, or both. Those 6 years have to be admitted as being the shortest possible duration of Negi Lama's stay in Lhasa.

16. This is in accordance with the, particularly in Central Tibet, commonly accepted view on people coming from the border areas as being uncultivated. Kinnauris, like other members of ethnic groups from the southern slopes of the Himalayas related to the Tibetans, like the Tamang and Lepcha, would have been widely considered as "*mon (pa)*", a term which could be freely translated as "southern barbarians". The *mon (pa)* are the southern counterparts of the *Hor (pa)*, the "northern barbarians", by which name turco-mongolic nomads have been known in Tibet in ancient times.

17. The use of gossip and rumours was a common device for carrying out political and personal quarrels in old Lhasa. On this topic see M. Goldstein, "Lhasa Street Songs: Political and Social Satire in traditional Tibet" in *Tibet Journal*, vol. 7, Nr. 1&2, 1982; also Lobsang T. Lhodrakpa, "Voice of the People in Old Tibet" in *Tibetan Review*, Vol. XII No. 7, July 1977.

18. I could neither find out the location nor the proper spelling of the name of this Bonpo monastery.

19. We do not know whether Negi Lama came by himself to the idea of learning Sanskrit or whether he had been influenced by some other persons. He may have come under the influence of the non-sectarian movement (*ris med*) while travelling through Khams and staying for a longer period of time in Derge, which had been one of the centres of that movement. It is known that although Sanskrit has generally not been taught in the monastic centres of Tibet, the *ris med* movement under Kongtrul Rinpoche (*kong sprul blo gros mtha' yas*, 1813-1899) had reinitiated the learning of this language in Eastern Tibet in the first half of the last century. (On this topic see: Dieter Schuh, Tibetische Handschriften und Blockdrucke Teil 6 (Gesammelte Werke des Kon-sprul Blo-gros mtha'-yas), Wiesbaden 1976) In this case, however, since Negi Lama was not able to find a proper Sanskrit teacher in Tibet, although having been travelling through the province for 19 years, we must suppose that this tradition

had been lost or at least was on the decline at Negi Lama's time.

20. According to *The Mahabodhi*, June-July 1977, p. 371, it was at the beginning of the 1940's.
21. We don't know for which reasons Negi Lama went to Kinnaur on his way to India and at which time he decided to do so. We must however presume that he was strongly motivated to do so since, as he came from Khams and headed to the gangetic plains, going through Kinnaur did not make any sense and - by the length of his stay - considerably delayed his aim of learning Sanskrit.
22. These informations about Negi Lama being invited by Kushok Bakula to Srinagar were provided to me by Mr. Tashi Rabgyas.
23. We should remember that Negi Lama had stayed in Tashi Lhunpo while on his way from Sikkim to Lhasa
24. This anecdote was related to me by Mr. Tashi Rabgyas.
25. Dagyab (*brag g.yab*) Rinpoche who was in charge of the organisation of that meeting could not remember that Negi Lama's name was on the list of the official participants, which he himself compiled.
26. According to the information given to me by Acarya Sherab Gyaltsen Negi from the Lava Monastery, Kalimpong one of the nun was called Bogti Negi, while the other one could have been Hirmal Negi, who also spent some years with Negi Lama. The identity of the second nun is not clear since there is a discrepancy between on one side the interview in which - in accordance with what I heard from other sources (for instance from Dagyab Rinpoche a.o.) - it was clearly stated that both nuns have accompanied Negi Lama until his death and on the other side the information given to me by Sherab Gyaltsen after which Hirmal Negi only stayed about 3 years with Negi Lama. However, the reliability of this last information seems more probable to me, since Hirmal Negi is an aunt of Sherab Gyaltsen. Possibly the nun who stayed with Negi Lama and Bogti Negi was a third one. As the nuns were about 50 years old in 1993, they must have been about 20 at that time, since the Mussoorie-meeting mentioned above took place in 1963.
27. The concept of "universal responsibility" propagated today by the Dalai Lama is clearly a modern interpretation of the classical buddhist concept of *Bodhicitta*.
28. Ling Rinpoche (1903-1983) has been *shar pa chos rje* since 1949 and *dga' ldan khri pa* since 1965, i.e. second-highest lama respectivly head of the Gelug (*dge lugs*) school of Tibetan Buddhism. Beyond that, according to the second autobiography of the Dalai Lama "Freedom in Exile", he appears to have been the most important preceptor of the XIVth Dalai Lama. Ling Rinpoche is told to have been very impressed by Negi Lama, whom he seems to have met before, while both of them were still staying in Tibet.
29. I am endebted to Mr.Tashi Rabgyas for this information.
30. It is unlikely that Negi Lama stayed in the monastery itself, since no nun would be allowed to spend the night in a Gelug monastery. All three of them most probably stayed in the guesthouse situated next to the monastery and belonging to it.
31. Source: Bhikkhu Pasadika & Rev. Nawang Tsering, Some excerpts from the "Spiritual Diary" of Grub-Chen Ngag-Dbang Tse-Ring in memoriam Negi Rinpoche, alias Kunu Lama or Ven. Bstan-'Dzin Rgyal-Mtsan, in: *The Mahabodhi*, 85/4-5, April-May 1977, p. 145.
32. The information about date and place of Negi Lama's death was provided to me by Mr. Fateh Chand Negi, CIBS Choglamsar. However *The Mahabodhi*, June-July 1977, p. 371 and *The Mahabodhi*, 85/4-5, April-May 1977, p. 145 (see note 31) state: February 20th, 1977. The Shashul or Shashur monastery (*sha shur dgon pa* or more rightly *bkra shis shugs gling*), which belongs to the Drukpa (*'brug pa bka' brgyud*) tradition is situated above Kyelong (*kye glang*), the capital of Lahaul.

33. It seems that particularly his book "*byang chub sems kyi bstod pa rin chen sgron ma* ...", a collection of 356 stanzas on bodhicitta composed in Varanasi, which was widely distributed, left a lasting impression on them. (I have to thank my friend Dr. Dawa Norbu for this information and for making that book available to me.) The portrait on p.91 is from this book.
34. The principal of that school, Mr. Tashi Paljor, has been a student of Negi Lama.
35. It seems to me that the most important tasks would be to find out what Negi Lama did after his departure from Kinnaur and before entering Tibet as well as who his many teachers - particularly those in Khams - have been. This may cast a light on the influences he has been the object of. After I had had finished this article, I heard that a biography of Negi Lama in ṭraditional style (*rnam thar*) has been published in *dpe cha*-form in 1989. The author is a Lahauli, Mr. K. Angrup, retired professor of Tibetan Language at the University of Chandigarh and former student of Negi Lama. The study of this work as well as of Negi Lama's own writing would surely contribute to elucidate those questions.

BUDDHIST NUNS IN LADAKH

Paula Green
Karuna Center, 49 Richardson Road,
Leverett MA 01054, USA

Summary

The nuns of Ladakh, most of whom traditionally lived with their families, are facing big social changes. As the extended family crumbles, the nuns are no longer assured of a place at home. Visits to 3 villages (comprising 100 nuns), showed that each is in a different stage of achieving their aims of communal living and full education, that of Wakkha being the most successful.

Since the time of the Buddha, the question of ordination of religious women has been a challenge. Out of his Great Compassion, the Buddha agreed to ordain women, despite the cultural norms of patriarchy and caste prevalent in his day. He encouraged the spiritual pursuits of his female initiates and did not distinguish between monks and nuns regarding the attainment of enlightenment. Among the first female disciples were members of the Buddha's own family.

In the 2500 years that have elapsed since the life of the Buddha, the opportunities and responsibilities of nuns have been subject to interpretation by the male dominated Sangha. Since the days of the Buddha, women throughout the Asian Buddhist world have been given a lesser ordination and fewer precepts than their male counterparts. Southeast Asia nuns of the Theravadan tradition currently have a greatly reduced position. In Thailand, with a Buddhist population of more than 90%, the lineage of ordained women has been broken and is thus completely extinguished.

In the Mahayana traditions of Ladakh and Tibet, the nuns have never enjoyed the high status, reverence or support given to monks and their monasteries. In Ladakh, the nuns lived with their families throughout their lives, participating in the seasonal routines of agriculture and handicrafts, involved in the life cycles of the newborn, the old and those in need. The nuns were given neither a Buddhist education nor the opportunity for a life of spiritual devotion and meditation.

What the nuns did receive, however, was a life embraced by family connections and a sense of belonging to the land and village community. Throughout the centuries, this tradition must have had its own rewards, both for the religious woman and for her extended family.

The process of modernization and the influence of western-based development now facing Ladakh is having a profound effect on the nuns, as it is on all sectors of society. As the extended family system crumbles in the face of contemporary pressures and the new demands of a money economy, the place of nuns is less secure. Many Ladakhis feel that unless some positive response is made to this changing situation that few women will choose ordination or remain within the order. The nuns themselves are articulating a need for change.

In the summer of 1993, at the request of a Ladakhi monk and a community of nuns, I visited groups of nuns in three villages. All of the villages, Shargol, Mulbek and Wakkha, are connected to the road between Kargil and the high mountain passes, a full day's drive from Leh. A Ladakhi laywoman who lives in Leh is closely associated with these nuns; she served as guide and liaison on during our exploratory visit. Translation was supplied by a monk from Shargol with fluent English and by a Shargol government employee who is secretary of the Shargol Nun's Welfare and Cultural Program. In the three villages we spoke with approximately one hundred nuns, ranging in age from six to seventy-three years old. Perhaps 20% of them were children or young adolescents; the majority were women in their twenties and thirties. We spoke also to several lamas responsible for teaching the nuns.

Almost all of the ordained women we interviewed had been given to the order of nuns by their parents when they were children, generally between the ages of six and ten. Although the decision to ordain was not an adult choice made by the religious calling of a developed mind, the women are quite committed to the life chosen for them and have no inclination to leave for the lay responsibilities of marriage and family. What they clearly articulate, however, is a need for change in their living arrangements.

The nuns in these three villages all have the same wish: to live as a monastic community, to study broadly, and to practice Dharma together on a daily basis. Historically nuns have not attended the government schools. Thus, when there is no lama available for instruction, the nuns remain illiterate in both the vernacular and in sacred texts and practices. The nuns we spoke to are requesting education and no longer find their exclusion from the educational system acceptable.

Furthermore, these ordained women spoke of exhaustion from the pressures of agricultural and domestic demands. They have a strong wish to live together in order to focus their energies on a full spiritual life. They want the experience of a religious community that supports their meditation practice, and the opportunity for solitude that is available to their Dharma brothers.

Their vision is that each of the three villages would have a small assembly hall (*dukhang*) for *puja* and meditation, a kitchen, gardens, a classroom, and small connected cells where the nuns would live individually. Ideally, each village would have a resident lama as teacher, as there are currently no nuns trained and available to teach the Dharma.

The actual situation for the nuns is different in Shargol, Mulbek and Wakkha. The Shargol nuns have a Tibetan *geshe* as teacher and have built with their own hands a small classroom and adjacent kitchen. Those who are free from domestic duty attend class each day, but some of the women reported with tears in their eyes that they were not able to study because of family work demands. The Shargol nuns have land for their residence and assembly hall, but no funds with which to build. They raised the money for their classroom by begging funds from many villagers, but feel that the costs of building, even with their own labour wherever possible, makes fund raising from villagers beyond their capacity.

In Mulbek there is no resident teacher for the nuns, and one part-time teacher who is just beginning to work with them. These women are illiterate, and although they have applied to the Central Institute of Buddhist Studies for a teacher for the past four years, they have not yet had a favourable response. They also begged for money with which they hand-built a modest assembly hall, but are eager both for a full-time teacher and for funds to create residential spaces.

The nuns of Wakkha have accomplished something unheard of in Ladakh. They, under the guidance of a strong minded and forward thinking Tibetan *geshe*, have built a beautiful *dukhang* and nine residential cells. A solar room was donated by the Ladakh Ecological Society and the Ladakh Project, and the nuns have planted trees and lovely gardens in front of their rooms. The complex has an air of peace and harmony; one can feel the love that was put into this twenty year building project. The residential quarters are very crowded: three to a room meant for one. The sisters are eager for cells to have individual practice and living space. They showed us scars on hands and backs from so many years of clearing land and making mud-bricks, and dread the idea that they might have to face construction work again to obtain more living space. They credit their teacher for the vision of the nunnery, as well as for the loans he secured for them to accomplish their building project.

As of the present not many groups of nuns have come to visit the Wakkha nunnery, but it is a shining example of a model community that it may well become an ideal to which others can aspire. We attended the evening *puja* with the thirty nuns of Wakkha, and found great pleasure in joining a hall full of Buddhist women chanting the ancient Buddhist scriptures with confidence and robust voices.

The reality for the nuns is that they will likely remain tied to their agricultural tasks of their families and villages in order to secure their own food. Indeed the nuns at Wakkha, who no longer live with their families, were all participating in the barley harvest the day we visited. Because of the deeply entrenched traditions, in the immediate future it will not be possible for the nuns to receive the gifts of food and supplies offered to the monks. However, once they are living the community, they will no longer be accessible to their families as a constant source of labour, and their days will be more largely focused on spiritual practice and education. In the future, the time may come when villagers perceive the value of the nuns as full daughters of the Buddha, and offer them necessary support.

At a conference of Dharma teachers in the spring of 1993, His Holiness, the Dalai Lama affirmed the importance of educating nuns as a chief goal for the coming years. In India there are already five Tibetan nunneries offering full training and education for women in both secular and religious subjects. there are long waiting lists for entrance into these new institutions.

Perhaps the encouragement of His Holiness and the models being established in India will inspire the movement of Ladakhi nuns. One project in the planning stages in Choglamsar, near Leh, is an educational centre for current and future nuns that would offer a seven year in-depth training programme in both Buddha Dharma and general curriculum. It is hoped that eventually these women would become teachers for Ladakhi nuns throughout the region.

There are other small models of Ladakhi nuns living and studying together, in Zanskar, Temisgam and elsewhere. Clearly, change is in the air for the nuns of Ladakh, in this case a shift which they welcome and consciously seek for their own growth and spiritual progress.

Let us hope that these changes will increase the strength and depth of the Ladakhi nuns and enable them to contribute their own love and understanding of Dharma to their fellow villagers and to future generations. A renewed order of nuns, supported and educated by the Ladakhi people and Ladakhi institutions, would be of enormous benefit in this era of rapid development. Spiritual guidance will be greatly needed as the pressures of modernization intensify in the villages, and an order of educated, confident and spiritually developed nuns might be an important resource in difficult times. Let us hope this change brings great benefit to all.

'LORDS OF THE FORT', ' LORDS OF THE WATER', AND 'NO LORDS AT ALL': The Politics of Irrigation in Three Tibetan Societies.

Kim Gutschow

Dept. of Anthropology, Harvard University,
Cambridge, MA 02138, USA.

Summary

Water is life in the high altitude desert of the west-Tibetan region. The traditional political and social systems which regulate the distribution of water through the irrigation systems of the villages provide a carefully balanced method of ensuring equity in this. They also provide an insight into the sources of, and checks on, power in the community.

"Power must be analyzed as something which circulates, or rather as something which only functions in the form of a chain....not only to individuals who circulate between its threads; they are always in a position of simultaneously undergoing and exercising this power." (Foucault, 1980: 98).

Irrigation schemes present microcosms which offer a glimpse of the mechanics of power and politics in village societies. I do not wish to analyze power in the sites where it has been spoken of more conventionally — the realms of kings, presidents, the military, or other agents of the state repression. Instead, I intend to examine the webs of water, or irrigation systems, which bind Ladakhi and Zangskari villagers to each other. These webs reflect a shared source of life; for water is life in the high altitude desert of the west-Tibetan region. However, these webs of solidarity are also webs of restraint that bind villagers to an all-seeing village order they cannot easily escape. The tightness of the web reflects the dark and the light aspects of village politics. The easy intimacy and consensus-based decisions which flow from webs of village solidarity might suggest an ideal form of Greek democracy. However, the same webs create claustrophobic techniques of surveillance by which villagers keep each other in check.

The irrigation systems of central Ladakh and Zangskar are fine-tuned mechanisms for distributing water equitably and efficiently.

I mention systems in the plural, for each and every village has its own rotational scheme by which certain channels or houses are allotted water throughout the growing season. The rotational scheme is largely determined by village topography, total village acreage, relative exposure to sun, average temperature, size of the glaciers or snowfields from which most villages draw their water, soil type, and seepage in the irrigation channels, among other factors. Most central Ladakhi and Zangskari villages (with the exception of those directly on the Indus plain such as Chushot, Spitug, Thikse, etc. and those on the Stod River plain in Zangskar such as Reru and Yulang) do not take their water from the major rivers along which they are situated. Instead, villages obtain their irrigation water from tributary streams that flow down from the glaciers high above.

The amount of water that a village receives varies by year, season, day, and even hour. Variations in daily temperature and sunshine are enough to turn a calm morning rivulet into a raging afternoon torrent. In order to accomodate these variations somewhat systematically, Ladakhi and Zangskari irrigation systems are both fixed and flexible. They take an extremely variable water supply and distribute it equitably and efficiently in a series of waterings throughout the summer. The main grain crops in Ladakh and Zangskar are barley, wheat and buckwheat, with peas in Zangskar and mustard seed in Ladakh. These crops ideally require eight to ten waterings in a single growing season. Using figures from Crook and Osmaston (1994: 152), barley takes 85 days to mature along the Indus and between 105 and 120 days to mature in Zangskar. In comparison, wheat matures in 95 days along the Indus and in 120 days in Zangskar, while peas mature in 90 days and buckwheat in 75 days in Zangskar. In sum, the fields require a watering every seven to ten days, which is no easy task in larger Ladakhi villages. Leh has a cultivated area of over 5000 hectares (ha.) and 80% of Ladakhi villages have between 100 and 1000 ha. (Census of India, 1971).

Irrigation water is a critical source of food and wealth in Ladakh and Zangskar (99% of the rural population were farmers as late as the 1961 census). One might expect to find a complex politics of distribution and exploitation in these circumstances. Distribution is certainly complicated, but exploitation is rare. Of course there are inevitable abuses and conflicts in the distribution of water, but they are managed through a variety of political mechanisms which I shall investigate.

Ladakhi and Zangskari villagers are implicated in an intricate web of power. Villagers are continually being watched at the same time that they are watching out for their neighbors. It is difficult to disguise the telltale signs of cheating: a moist field when all the surrounding fields are dry. In short, the distribution of water is managed by an ingenious network which provides fairness but exacts scrupulousness. The formalization of the village bureaucracies which manage water distibution depend primarily on the size of the village concerned. I shall look at several cases of irrigation which range from the more formalized (Tibet) to the more *ad hoc* (Zangskar).

I'll begin with an unknown district in Tibet, as described by Charles Bell (1928), the British representative under the thirteenth Dalai Lama. Tibetan irrigation suggests a highly centralized polity, in which village level water disputes could ultimately land in the Lhasa courts. Bell notes that irrigation in Tibetan villages was managed according to written schemes stored in the archives of local dzongs or district forts. These forts were the administrative centers of the Lhasa government in its outlying districts. Because the schemes by which each house or estate received water were stored at the dzong, the *dzong dpon* or "**Lord of the Fort**" had first rights of adjudication in case of a dispute. However, since he was often an absentee landlord who lived the 'good life' in Lhasa, disputes would be referred to him there. Ultimately, disputes could end up in the Lhasa court system if the underlying politics got too messy. Although Bell (1928) does not say so, I would surmise that it was necessary to appeal to higher authorities of the Lhasa judiciary when the players involved in the dispute were themselves aristocrats or monastic estate owners with more power than the dzong dpon himself. Unfortunately, there are no descriptions of disputes or specific village rotational schemes in the English language sources which mention Tibetan irrigation (Aziz, 1978; Bell, 1928; Carrasco, 1959; Dargyay, 1982). A similar lack of detail is apparent in the sources which mention Ladakhi and Zangskari irrigation (Asboe, 1937; Friedl, 1983; Heber, 1903; Moorcroft, 1837; Norberg-Hodge, 1992; Ribbach, 1906; Rizvi, 1989). Only Crook and Osmaston (1994: 81-90) provide a detailed account of the irrigation schemes in Stongde, Zangskar.

While Tibetan irrigation was managed at several levels of government including the highest authorities in Lhasa, Ladakhi and Zangskari irrigation schemes are managed at the village level, although the officials involved and the degree of power they wield varies with the size of the village. Basically, there are no categorical differences between Ladakhi and Zangskari modes of irrigation, for a small village in Ladakh uses a system very similar to that used by a small village in Zangskar. However, because most villages in Zangskar are much smaller than those of central Ladakh, one finds more complex distribution schemes and a more formalized bureaucracy in the

Ladakhi villages along the Indus valley. For instance, villages in the lung nag region of Zangskar have between 3 and 90 houses; central Zangskari villages have between 150 and 200 houses; and central Ladakhi villages between 100 and 400 houses (excluding Leh).

Because Leh is the largest town in Ladakh (with a population of nearly 11,000 as estimated in the 1991 census), its water distribution system is fairly complex. Most of the fields of Leh below Sankar monastery obtain their water from (and are said to "belong to") one of three major watersheds (*'drog po*): Drugchu, Sheldan, and Shenam. The areas above Sankar, known as *sNgan pa* (literally, "those before") and *Yur thung*, have separate water schemes which are interwoven with the main cycle of the three major watersheds. This occurs as follows: the official daytime and nighttime periods when the three watersheds are given water are 10 a.m. to 4 p.m. and 10 p.m to 4 a.m. respectively. In the intervening blocks of time, water is routed to the upper parts of Leh watershed such as *sNgan pa*, *sGang las*, and *Yur thung*, which have their own water distribution schemes.

The three major watersheds alternate water as follows. For the initial watering (tha chu) which takes place from March to mid May (i.e. before the fields are even ploughed), each watershed consecutively receives water for a period between 20 and 29 days and nights. The exact number of days is not fixed for it is measured by however long it takes to water all of the fields along the watershed. After this initial watering, the watersheds take turns receiving water according to the following schedule: while watershed 'A' receives water during the official daytime period, watershed 'B' receives water at night. This lasts as long as it takes to water the fields along the full length of the watersheds. Thereafter, watershed 'B' receives water in the daytime and watershed 'C' at night; then 'C' in the daytime and 'A' at night, and so on all summer long.... Villagers whose fields lie along the watershed that receive water at night divert the water into storage tanks (*zing*) and let it out the following day to make watering more convenient. Because the flow of water is heavier after mid May, it usually only takes 10-15 days to water all of the fields along a watershed; thus, fields are ideally watered every 7-10 days. In practice, because the upper areas of the Leh watershed receive a stronger flow of water (as natural topography would suggest), fields in these areas receive more frequent waterings than fields in the lower—and thus poorer and drier—sections of Leh township such as Skalzangling and Skara. This system of distribution (with many more nuances I have to space to go into) functions for most of the summer. In periods of excessive water or aridity, extraordinary measures are called for by the Leh *chu dpon* or "**Lords of the Water**".

The "**Lords of the Water**" in Leh manage and monitor this complicated water distribution scheme. Each year, ten *chu dpon* are chosen on a rotational basis from the following subsections of Leh: four from *Skya ngos*; four from *sGo gsum*; one each from *Chans pa* and *dGon pa*. Sankar and *Yur thung* have their own *chu dpon*, as they are on a separate distribution system. The *chu dpon* duty is rotated between all the main houses (*khang pa*) in a given subsection. This duty is a difficult summer job with rather low pay (*chu dpon* are paid 1000 Rs. per summer by the Indian government as of 1982; previously payment was in kind, i.e. one *khal* of grain per family in Leh). Each day, in principle, all of the *chu dpon* must serve duty. In practice, all ten *chu dpon* rarely show up, especially if they have more pressing things to do that day. They are required to pay someone to come as their substitute, but often fail to do so. Each day, the *chu dpon* go up to the head of the Leh valley: eight men go to *Ta zas*, the principal junction where the Drugchü and Sheldan watersheds split off from one another, and two men go to Sgang las, where they check that by 10 a.m. all of the channels (*yur ra*) are closed off and no water is being diverted to fields in this area. During the day, the *chu dpon* are supposed to watch the channels along the watershed in order to insure that water is not diverted higher up and is being sent down to the appropriate channels which are to receive water that day. As there are more than 100 channels along any given watershed, each *chu dpon* is assigned to monitor a certain number of channels. At night, one or two *chu dpon* sleep by the storage tanks along the watershed which is receiving water (*tsan chu* or "night water") and in the morning this water is released to the appropriate fields.

Ideally, the *chu dpon*s insure that all of the fields along a watershed receive an equitable share of water throughout most of the summer. At the end of each day, two of the most senior *chu dpon* (the oldest or most experienced) go down both of the watersheds which received water that day and previous night to check how many fields were irrigated that day. This monitoring is necessary, I was told, for otherwise people would simply divert the water to their willow groves and demand more water for their fields on the next day. The population increase in Leh has put a premium on wood as a lucrative construction material. Informants noted that disputes, cheating, and bribery are more prevalent in recent decades due to the changes in the Leh economy and demography. The *chu dpon*s are responsible for reporting any abuses to the head man of Leh, who mediates the dispute and arranges the fine to be paid (as high as 500 Rs. in some cases).

While the present *chu dpon* is a part of the Indian bureaucracy, the system of selecting *chu dpon*s was different before 1947, when

Ladakh first became a part of the Indian nation. According to an informant who served as a *chu dpon* some sixty years ago, selection used to be on the basis of merit, in a proccess that included both royal and ecclesiastic authorities. Every year the headman (goba) of Leh, in consultation with his deputies (khotwal), would select a group of candidates from five subsections of Leh (*sGo gsum*, *sKya ngos*, *Chans pa*, *dGon pa*, and *bSangs dkar* (Sankar)). The candidates chosen were men known to be virtuous and upright (mi rgyal ba) who came from large and wealthy households. On an auspicious day in the third Tibetan month, all of the candidates, as well as one Sankar monk, the Prime Minister (*bKa' blon*), the headman, and the Wazir of Leh would gather at the *Byams pa Lha khang* below the palace. A lottery (*tag ril*) was conducted to determine who would be chosen as *chu dpon* from each of the subsections that year. The names of all of the candidates from a given subsection were written on slips of paper which were rolled into little tsampa balls (*ril bu*). The Sankar monk, who was the key-keeper (*sGo gnyer*) of the *Byams pa Lha khang*, then placed all of the the balls into a wooden tsampa bowl and invoked *Byams pa* (Maitreya) and various other deities for their blessings upon the following procedure. He swirled the balls around until one dropped, or jumped, out. The name on the paper indicated the *chu dpon* chosen for that subsection. the process was repeated until all seven *chu dpon* were chosen (two from *sGo gsum*, two from *sKya ngos*, one each from *Chans pa*, *dGon pa*, and Sankar).

Shortly thereafter, on an auspicious day chosen by a local astrologer (*rtsis pa* or *dbon po*), the *chu dpon* would proceed to the head of the Leh valley, to ceremonially inaugurate the watering season. The *chu dpon* climbed to a small temple at sGang las, which lies at the top of the valley, above the first irrigation channel. At the temple, the *chu dpon* prayed to Tsongkhapa for plentiful water and a bountiful harvest. They offered beer (*chang*), butter, tsampa, butter lamps, and blessing scarves (*kha tag*) to the deity. My informant recalled one year when his fellow *chu dpon* prayed so fervently that tears came to his eyes. Sure enough, there was more water than ever that year! The ceremony concluded with the official "opening" of the uppermost irrigation channel. A child is specifically chosen for this task. The child must be born in an auspicious year chosen by an astrologer and must be the legitimate offspring of parents who are still alive. When the child diverts water into the uppermost channel, the irrigation season is begun. This ceremony recalls the use of a child to "open" the earth when building a house in Tibetan societies as desribed by Wongmo (1985), Dollfus (1989), and Brauen (1980).

In contrast to the *chu dpon* bureaucracy of Leh, smaller

Ladakhi villages such as Sakti and Chemre have a different but equally complex system of water distribution. Because Sakti lies above Chemre along the same tributary stream, one might expect a fundamentally assymetrical or exploitative relationship of power to exist between these two villages. In fact, an interesting relationship of reciprocity exists between them. For most of the summer (from the tenth day of the fifth Tibetan month—*Hemis Tse bCu*—until the tenth day of the seventh month), Chemre is allotted water every seven days in what is known as a *'bab phyi*. This *'bab phyi* (literally, a "general descent" or perhaps *'bab chu*, "falling water") is a period of 36 hours (two nights and the intervening day) when Sakti villagers must desist from taking water and all the water in the stream is fed down to Chemre. In return for this service, the Chemre villagers bring a ceremonial gift to Sakti village. On the third day of the third month, the treasurer (*phyag mdzod*) of Chemre *dGon pa*, two Chemre *chu dpon*, and three or four assistants (*zhab zhi*) proceed to Sakti bearing 16 jerry cans of chang and 500 Rs. It used to be a sheep instead of the Rupees, until *'Drug chen* Rimpoche of Hemis changed the practice a few years ago. This gift, which is provided by Chemre dGon pa, is taken to a house in Sakti known as the *gzim khang*, where the *chang* is immediately consumed in a large feast. The rupees are given each year to one of the four subsections (bcu tshogs) of Sakti village, turn by turn. The traditional reciprocity between Sakti and Chemre is expressed symbolically by the gifts of food and chang in exchange for the gift of water. Sakti villagers speak of an obligation to provide Chemre with water, as if there were no choice but that of Buddhist compassion. The religious power of the Chemre monastery and Chemre's strategic location at the bottom of the valley, near the Leh-Manali trade route may provide Chemre some leverage to "demand" water from Sakti. Nonetheless, the villagers I spoke to denied this.

The arangement between Sakti and Chemre suggests an unusual degree of cooperation between two villages. Nonetheless, this trust does not preclude a certain pragmatism in the sharing of water. Whenever there is a *'bab phyi*, the Chemre villagers send four *chu dpon* and several other villagers up to Sakti to ensure that no water is 'accidentally' diverted to Sakti fields during this period. An informant told me that this was not because the Sakti villagers are known to cheat, but that they do sometimes "fall asleep at the channels" and forget to block them off for the *'bab phyi*. I could imagine a very different scenario with a lot less compassion and more capitalism in the United States.

In addition to intra-village distribution between Sakti and Chemre, each village has its own rotational scheme as well. Roughly speaking, one could divide Sakti and Chemre each into two portions: (a) channels and fields below and (b) channels and fields above the reservoirs. In the daytime, water is diverted to fields above the reservoirs and at nightime, water is channelled into the reservoirs and let out the following morning. If the reservoir is not particularly big, then it may fill up in the middle of the night. At this point, the water will be released by a villager sleeping next to the reservoir. When water is scarce, the Sakti villagers whose fields lie below the reservoirs go up the watershed in the evening to check that all of the upper channels are indeed blocked off for the night and all water is routed into the reservoirs. In brief, while there are no *chu dpon* in Sakti, the system depends on a balance of surveillance and trust, in which each member of the system abides by an implicit honor code. When disputes arise, they are mediated by the village headman and his deputies, who call upon both parties of the dispute for an explanation and set a fine to be paid by the abusing party. In Chemre, where there is less water and thus more cause for disputes, *chu dpon* exist who monitor and mediate the distribution of water.

In the smaller villages of Zangskar, irrigation is managed in a more ad-hoc and less formalized style. The amount of acreage and the number of irrigation channels in any given village seem to determine which kind of rotational scheme is used. If the village is small enough and the irrigation channels are few enough, rotational schemes of water distribution are pegged to the household, rather than the irrigation channels. In Leh, where a single watershed has more than 100 channels, and in Sakti, where the two watersheds (*'brag nag* and *'brag dkar*) have 17 and 26 channels respectively, the water distribution is arranged by channels. Karsha, Zangskar—which is one of the largest villages in Zangskar with 308 ha. of cultivated land—has only nine major irrigation channels and yet it also distributes water by channel rather than by household. In Karsha, the four channels which are located above its four reservoirs receive water during the daytime, while the five channels which feed into the reservoirs let out water into the fields which has been stored the previous night.

Three smaller villages of the *Yul gsum* region in central Zangskar —Rizhing, Hongshet, and Testa — are situated along the same watershed. Each of these three villages have a unique mode of distributing water internally among their attendant households, in addition to being part of an overarching system which divides water between them. During much of the summer, when water is plentiful, there is no rotational scheme at all. However, by mid August water is usually scarce and the following rotational schemes are called into effect. For an 18 day cycle, Hongshet and Rizhing both receive water during the day, while Testa is allotted water at night. Hongshet and Rizhing each have their own distinct schemes of distribution. The ninemain houses (*khang pa*, or *khang chen* in Zangskar) of Hongshet village are divided into two groups of four and the ninth house is put into a separate group. The small houses (*khang chung*) which consists of extended kin from the larger houses receive water along with their brethren houses. For four days the first group (of four houses) jointly waters its fields, and for the next four days the second group waters its fields. Finally, on the ninth day the ninth house waters its fields. Two such cycles are repeated to form an 18 day cycle. Meantime, Rizhing village is undergoing its own version of the 18 day cycle. In Rizhing there are 10 main houses (*khang chen*): the four largest are given four days, three mid-sized houses are given three days, and finally the three smallest houses are given two days to water their fields jointly. This forms a nine day cycle which is repeated to make up the 18 days. After 18 days and nights in which Hongshet, Rizhing, and Testa share water, for one day and night water is diverted along a channel to the grasslands (*'ol thang*) owned by Karsha monastery. Karsha monastery is the largest landowner in the Yul gsum region and is the only landowner granted this special privilege of having its grasslands watered. The monastery, whose fields are leased and cultivated by lay villagers, does not receive any other benefits in terms of water rights.

Tentatively, the smaller the village and the more plentiful the water, the less likely one is to find a *chu dpon* system. Only one village in Zangskar with an extremely limited supply of water—Zangla—has a *chu dpon* office. Most Zangskari systems of irrigation are more flexible and *ad hoc* than the Ladakhi systems because they are managed by household rather than by channel. When only several houses obtain water on a given day, it is fairly easy to arrange whose fields will get water. In larger village systems, where distribution is arranged by channel, the fields lying along any given channel may belong to a large variety of households. Thus, larger villages often have a pre-arranged system by which houses share water from the channels receiving water on a given day. These pre-determined rotational schemes between households are recorded in the land records stored at the Patwari's (Tax and Revenue) office in Leh or on silk documents in the village itself (as in Sakti, Tashi Rabgyas has noted). The documentation of these rotational schemes suggests that disputes could be taken to the courts in Leh, for example. While this is beginning to be the case in Leh, villagers in Sakti and Chemre still prefer to negotiate their disputes at the village level.

Water distribution offers a means to analyze the mechanics of power in different village societies of Ladakh and Zangskar. While this paper is an introduction to the subject and far more research is called for, one can make some preliminary conclusions about the nature of power in Ladakhi and Zangskari society. Irrigation systems involve village players as both subjects and objects of power. The modes of distributing water suggest systems in which power is not concentrated in any one individual's hands, and thus the more conventional notions of domination do not fully apply.

Power in these systems circulates among each of the member households, who are both the targets and the agents of its articulation. Surveillance appears to be the most significant coercive element in the system. Because village affiliation is often a lifetime sentence, the ignominy of being caught cheating may provide a sufficient deterrent to abuses within the system. However, as the villages become larger, more anonymous, and more influenced by a cash economy, the increasing anomie may result in a more contractual mode of managing power.

Acknowledgements: I would like to thank Meme Tsewang Norbu, Dorje Rinchen, Tashi Rabgyas, Sonam Gyatso, and Gonbo Anchug from Ladakh; Lonpo Sonam Angchug, Ani Yeshe Kundzom, Ani Thuje Drolma, and Sonam Tsomo from Zangskar for their assistance.

References

Asboe, W. 1937. Agricultural Methods in Lahoul Western Tibet. *Man* 37(90): 74-77.

AZIZ, B. 1978. *Tibetan Frontier Families*. New Delhi: Vikas Publishing.

BELL, Sir C. 1928. *The People of Tibet*. Oxford: The Clarendon Press.

BRAUEN, M. 1980. *Feste in Ladakh*. Graz: Akademische Druck und Verlags Anstalt.

CARRASCO, P. 1959. *Land and Polity in Tibet*. Seattle; University of Washington Press.

CENSUS OF INDIA. 1971. *District Census Handbook*. Ladakh District: Village and Town Directory. Srinigar: Census Publications.

CROOK, J. and OSMASTON, H. 1994 *Himalayan Buddhist Villages*. Bristol, Bristol University Press; Delhi, Motilal Banarsidass.

DARGYAY, E. 1982. *Tibetan Village Communities*. Warminster: Aris and Phillips, Ltd.

DOLLFUS, P. 1989. *Lieu de neige et de genevriers: Organisation sociale et religieuse des communautes bouddhistes du Ladakh*. Paris: C.N.R.S..

FOUCAULT, M. 1980. *Two Lectures, in Power/Knowledge: Selected Interviews and Other Writings*. ed. by C. Gordon. New York: Pantheon.

FRIEDL, W. 1983. *Gesellschaft, Wirtschaft und Materielle Kultur in Zanskar (Ladakh).* Sankt Augustin: VGH Wissenschaftsverlag.

HEBER, R. and K. 1903 (1978). *Himalayan Tibet and Ladakh.* New Delhi: Ess Ess.

MOORCROFT, W. and G. TREBECK. 1837. *Travels in the Himalayan Provinces of Hindustan and the Punjab, in Ladakh and Kashmir, etc.*. London: John Murray.

NORBERG-HODGE, H. 1992. *Ancient Futures.* New York: Random House.

RIBBACH, S.H. 1906 (1986). *Culture and Society in Ladakh.* tr. by J. Bray. New Delhi: Ess Ess.

RIZVI, J. 1989. *Ladakh: Crossroads of High Asia.* New Delhi: Oxford University Press.

WONGMO, C. 1985. Rituals of Bhutanese House Construction. in Aziz and Kapstein, eds. *Soundings in Tibetan Civilization.* New Delhi: Manohar.

THE INTRODUCTION OF BUDDHISM INTO LADAKH

Jamyang Gyaltsen
Central Institute of Buddhist Studies,
Choglamsar, Leh.

Ananda, one of the important disciples of the Buddha, had five hundred students named Nima Gungpa. Chief among them were Nima Gungpa Chen & Chu Thuba Chenpa. They lived in the period 550 BC.

Nima Gungpa Chenpo visited Kashmir with the help of his power of performing miracles. Kashmir was then an important Buddhist country with nine big cities, many rural towns, one fort and twelve monastic Institutions. It was during his stay in Kashmir that Nima Gungpa also visited Ladakh. He blessed the land where Lamayuru Gonpa now stands.

King Kanishkas began his reign in the year 125 A.D. Under his rule Buddhism became a popular religion in Kashmir. It is quite clear from the scholar Kalhon's book that King Kanishka built a large number of Stupas and Viharas all over Kashmir. From this fact, we can also conclude that the might have built Stupas and Viharas in Ladakh too. In the Kani Fort at Sani in Zanskar, we can still find a Stupa known by the name of Kani Stupa. Thus it is evident that Buddhism came into Ladakh around 130 A.D. At Teri there is still a Stupa called Ashoka Stupa. We can, therefore, come to the conclusion that if Buddhism was not introduced in Ladakh before the time of Christ, it was brought to Ladakh in the 1st and 2nd century A.D.

Kanishka had conquered Yarken and Khotan. Therefore, it is very probable that he had come to Ladakh also. If Buddhism had shone like the sun in Skardo and Gilgit in those days, there was no reason why it should not have spread to Ladakh.

In the year 975 Skide Nyima Gon reigned in Nyari (western Tibet). His three sons viz. Lhachen Palgyi Gon, Tashi Gon and Getsul Gon ruled over Ladakh, Purang and Zanskar respectively. Lha-Chen Palgyi Gon built the first Fort in Ladakh at Likir to carry on the tradition of the Kadampa sect founded by Dipamkara Atisha.

The Nyingmapa sect and its introduction into Ladakh

Secret Tantric teachings are divided into the Old Tradition and the New Tradition. Those who follow and practice the Old Tradition are called Nyingmapa.

During the reign of King Trisong Detsen in the 8th century, Guru Padma Sambhava and Khanchen Bodhisattva propagated the highest yoga Tantric teachings by way of giving empowerment, and teaching of the Tantric texts etc. The Guyasamaya Tantra and the other eighteen Tantric teachings were of that time. The main practice resolved round the eight great oral traditions.

In the 8th century Padma Sambhava visited the Zanskar, Sakti and Phokar regions of Ladakh. That was also the beginning of the introduction of the Nyingmapa sect in Ladakh. In the year, 1430, the saint-ascetic Padma Thinley sat in retreat in the famous Cave-Hermitage of Padma Sambhava. An unending line of his lineage continues to this day. He built Dak-thok monastery at Sakti. Many people still practice the great compassionate teachings of this sect.

The Kagyud Sect and its introduction into Ladakh

The Kagyud sect was started by Marpa Cheikyi Lodoe. He was born in 1012 and his teacher was the famous Naropa. Marpa visited India three times to receive teachings. He later became very famous as a translator. His four chief disciples were:

1. Tsurton Wangpo
2. Nyontan Choedor
3. Menton Chenpo
4. Milarepa.

The Kagyud sect is further divided into eight sub-sects;-four big and four small.

In the year 1010 Naropa came to Lamayuru and the Zanskar regions of Ladakh. Then Marpa, Naropa's most important disciple built Marpaling in Zanskar. Gotsang Gonbo Dorje came to visit Ladakh during the reign of King Tashi Namgyal from 1225 to 1250. He spent a lot of time in meditation at Hemis Gotsang, Igu, Matho etc. It seems that even before Lama Stak-tsang Raspa, the Kagyud sect had already been followed in most regions in Ladakh. The most glorious period in the life of the Kagyud sect in Ladakh was when King Singey Namgyal (1590-1620) patronised Lama Stak-tsang Raspa leading to the establishment of Hemis Gonpa and many other Gonpas professing the Druk-pa Kagyud sect. The other important contribution to the spread of the Kagyud sect was made by King Tashi Namgyal (1500-1530) when he invited Choeje Denma who then founded the Dri-khung

Kagyud sect in Ladakh.

The Sakya sect and its Introduction into Ladakh

Khon Konchok Gyalpo, the holder of the New Tradition of Tantra was born in the year 1634. He later built the Sakya monastery in 1091. The famous Sakya Lama, Kunga Nyingpo was born to him in 1092. Kunga Nyingpo propounded the Sakya doctrine of the Path and the Truth. Sakya Pandit Kunga Gyaltsan and Dro-gon Choegyal Phagspa established the political rule of Tibet by the Sakya sect. Ngorchen Kunga Zangpo built the monastery of Ngo in 1435.

The Sakya sect started spreading in Ladakh from the year 1300. Then in the year 1430, the scholar-hermit Drungpa Dorje arrived at Matho. King Drakpa Bumde patronised him and built the Matho Gonpa. Two other monasteries were built at Skidmang and Chite. However, in the war between Baltistan and Ladakh during the reign of King Jamyang Namgyal, Matho Gonpa was pillaged. The monks and the villagers were forced to carry the loot all the way to Baltistan. Matho Gonpa then passed through a period of decline, but with time it has regained a semblance of its past glory.

The Gelug sect and its introduction into Ladakh

Tsong-Khapa, the founder of the Gelug sect was born in the year 1357. In the year 1413, he started the great prayer festival of Lhasa. He built the monastery of Ganden in the same year. His Chief disciples later built the famous monasteries of Sera, Drepung and Tashi Lhonpo. Thus began the great tradition of the Gelug sect.

During the reign of King Drag-pa Bumde (1400-1440), two ascetics arrived from Tibet carrying with them a statue of Amidayus sent by Tsong-Khapa to be given to the King. The King took the Statue to indicate the importance of propagating the Gelug sect traditions in Ladakh. He therefore patronised Lama Lhawang Lodoe who built the monastery of Spituk. Many monasteries in Nubra, Zanskar and other places were built to preserve and promote the Gelug sect teachings.

WHAT HAPPENED BETWEEN 1450 AND 1550 AD ?
and other questions from the history of Ladakh.

Neil Howard
27, Clarendon Road,
Birmingham B16 9SD, U.K.

Summary

A number of important developments in the history of Ladakh took place during the years between approximately 1450 and 1550 AD, and yet we know almost nothing about the dynastic history of Ladakh during that time. This survey of the readily available historical material suggests that the period of 100 years under discussion was one of widespread political instability in the western Himalaya, that it has a number of causes which have not been thoroughly explored and that it may be possible to reconstruct some, at least, of the missing dynastic history of Ladakh.

****

The years between approximately 1450 and 1550 AD seem to have been of the greatest importance in the history of Ladakh, yet we know almost nothing about them. At the beginning of this period Ladakh was apparently still ruled by the "Lha Chen" Dynasty, as it had been for the previous 500 years, according to the rGyal-rabs; but when it ended the second or "rNam-rgyal" Dynasty was coming to the throne, or had recently done so. No reliable details of the dynastic change are available to us today.

Approximately half of all the great monasteries of Ladakh (except Lamayuru) was founded, or refounded, by the Gelugpa before this 100-year period was fully under way: Spitok, Likir, Tikse, Karsha and Phugtal; and Matho was founded by the Sakyapa before 1450 too[1] (Shakspo 1988 p.8). Soon after the end of the period, the Drikungpa monastery of sGan-sngon-bKra-shis-chos-rdzong was founded at Phyiang and the Dukpa influence began to be felt in Zanskar (Schuh 1983b). The great Dukpa monasteries all belong to the 17th century: Stakna, Bardan, Hanle, Himis, Chimre. The same pàttern seems to be revealed in the history of the building of the great fortresses: their defences and their principal temples and palaces seem to have been

1. I am grateful to Mr Jamyang Gyaltsan for the information that the foundation of Matho monastery during the reign of Grags-'bum-lde is recorded in an incomplete document in Matho monastery.

built either in the early 1400s or (with considerable rebuilding and new work) in the later 1500s (Howard 1989). If we consider the spread of Islam in Ladakh, we find that between the 1380s and the early 1500s three great teachers are believed by Ladakhi Moslems to have made converts in greater Ladakh, particularly in Purig and Baltistan: Sayyid Ali Hamadani, Sayyid Muhammad Nur Bakhsh and Shams ud Din, and there must have been other missionaries. Mosques in Mulbhe, Padum and Shay are believed to have been founded at this time. Whether or not Islam received a set-back later, we cannot say; but it is noticeable that Mirza Haidar does not record the presence of Islam in Ladakh during his campaigns there from 1532 to 1535. The advance of Islam seems to have been resumed during the reign of 'Jam-dbyangs-rnam-rgyal.

In which ever field we look, we seem to find at this time a break in the historical development of Ladakh. In this paper I shall suggest that the years between 1450 and 1550 were a time of great political instability in Ladakh and that the instability was not confined to Ladakh alone but also affected a number of her neighbours. Some of the possible causes of that instability will be identified as having their origins outside Ladakh; and further questions - historical problems awaiting solutions - will be elaborated. Finally, the paper proposes a speculative outline reconstruction of the dynastic history of Ladakh during the second half of these 100 years.

THE DYNASTIC CHRONICLES

The dynastic chronicles of Ladakh and its neighbours contain some interesting similarities and will be briefly examined first.

LADAKH

From the La-dvags Rgyal-rabs we learn of the following kings spanning the 15th and 16th centuries (Francke 1926 pp 99-108). Francke's estimated dates of their reigns will not suffice in the light of more recent research and Prof. L Petech's are preferred here (Petech 1977); also his suggestion of 25 years for the average length of a reign has been used where no other information is available (Petech 1977, p 20). All dates are in the Christian Era, AD.

Grags-'bum-lde - ruled c.1410-1435 (Petech) He appears to have relocated the capital of the kingdom to Leh and he was the builder of several religious monuments and monasteries. He received an emissary from Tsong-kha-pa, the founder of the Gelugpa sect, who died in 1419, and he was a patron of Bṿang-sems Shes-rab-bzang-po. He may be the mNa'-bdag-pa, king of Mar-yul stod, who donated revenues from land in Rupsho to Phugtal monastery (Schuh 1983a PH

I 75,76; PH II 16,17; PH III 3,4,5).

Grags-pa-'bum - ruled c.1410-1435? He was the brother of Grags-'bum-lde and the ruler of Lower Ladakh who built a new capital at Temisgam. The Rgyal-rabs, if it should be so interpreted, tells us that he rejected the emissaries of Tsong-kha-pa who therefore went to his brother.

Blo-gros-mchog-ldan - ruled c.1435-1460 (Petech) He was the son of Grags-'bum-lde. The only information about him in the Rgyal-rabs is that he conquered Ngaris and received enormous tribute. Petech tells us that he was a patron of gSan-phu-ba Lha-dbang-blo-gros who was a pupil of, and therefore younger than, mKhas-grub-rje (1385-1438) and that he sent presents to the First Dalai Lama (1391-1475).

Bhagan - ruled c.1460-1485? or earlier. Bhagan was, according to the Rgyal-rabs, "very fond of fighting" and combined with the people of Shay to depose "the sons of the king of Leh", Grags-'bum-lde, *viz*: Blo-gros-mchog-ldan, Drung-pa A-li and Slab-bstan-dar-rgyas.

He was the grandson of Grags-pa-'bum, the ruler of Lower Ladakh, and the son of his son Bara about whom we are told nothing. The Zanskar Chronicles might lead us to place Bhagan earlier than 1460 (see below) in which case it is possible that Bara is fictitious. Bhagan's reign could possibly, therefore, be set earlier than 1460-1485 but not later.

bKra-shis-rnam-rgyal - ruled c.1555-1575 (Petech). According to Inscription 10 in the Sum-tsek temple at Alchi, bKra-shis-rnam-rgyal was born in Alchi, defeated Mon and Hor and ruled a territory extending from Dras and Suru to Ngaris, including Nubra, Zanskar and Spiti (Snellgrove and Skorupski 1980 p 149). This is confirmed by the Rgyal-rabs which lists other meritorious works, and states that he drove out the Hor (Turks or Mongols from Central Asia) - perhaps finally?

The Rgyal-rabs tells us he was the younger son of Bhagan; that he blinded his older brother and usurped the throne; and that he then set his brother to breed an heir in Lingshet - we are not told why he did not have heirs of his own to follow him on the throne. He invited the *rdor-'dzin-pa* lDan-ma Kun-dga'-grags-pa to be his *mulaguru*, who founded the sGang-sngon-bKra-shis-chos-rdzong monastery at Phyiang; Francke's Inscription no. 179 records offerings made by bKra-shis-rnam-rgyal, in Temisgam, Basgo and Leh, on lDan-ma's death (date not known). We can accept that lDan-ma was in Ladakh in late 1550s (Petech 1977 pp 29-30). The reign of bKra-shis-rnam-rgyal cannot be moved far from the dates suggested by Petech, on the basis of the available evidence, but it is not impossible for it to have begun a little earlier.

Tshe-dbang-rnam-rgyal, rNam·rgyal-mgon-po and 'Jam-dbyangs-rnam-rgyal - ruled c.1575-1616 (Petech). 41 years may be the maximum total one could expect for the successive reigns of these three brothers, one generation. We know from Diogo d'Almeida that 'Jam-dbyangs-rnam-rgyal was king in 1603; we know he corresponded with sTag-tshang-ras-pa in 1613. It is therefore difficult to place the accession of Tshe-dbang-rnam-rgyal earlier than 1575.

ZANSKAR

Fragmentary chronicles of the rulers of Padum and Zangla in Zanskar have been published by Francke, Schuh and Dargyay (Francke 1926 pp 151-162; Schuh 1983a; Dargyay 1987). From them we learn of the following rulers:

Seng-ge-ldor/lde - ruled c.late 14th century? He had three sons: one (un-named) received Kishtawar; Blo-bzangs-lde received Padum and the south; and Khri-nam-(dpal-)lde received Zangla and the north.

Zangla

Khri-nam-(dpal-)lde c.1400+?

Rin-chen-dpal-lde (or Rin-po-che dpal-lde) - ruled c.1425-1450? Son of the above. He was a patron of Byang-sems- Shes-rab-bzang-po (a pupil of Tsong-khapa) who was still active in Ladakh in the 1450s (Petech 1977 p 168).

Khri-dpal-lde - ruled c.1450-1475? (Dargyay: c.1450-1460). Son of the above.

Nam-kha-dpal-lde - ruled c.1475-1500? (according to Dargay, ruled in the early second half of the 15th century). Son of the above. His religious works involved people in sTong-sde and Sa-ni (which were in the southern kingdom - does this indicate a decline in the power of Padum?).

It must be noted that Francke also provides a "Register" of the Zangla rulers which bears little resemblance to the above (Francke 1926 pp 163-166). Much work is needed before a proper understanding of the history of the early rulers of Zangla can be arrived at.

Padum

Blo-bzangs-lde - ruled c.1400+? He had three sons:

Tshang-rgyal-po (or Tshe-dbang-rgyal-po). Schuh suggests 1430-1460 for his reign (Schuh 1983a p 34); but as he was a cousin and therefore a contemporary of Rin-chen-dpal-lde of Zangla, perhaps he ruled slightly earlier, c.1425-1450? He ruled Padum and was also a patron of Byang-sems Shes-rab-bzang-po.

Ra-dug-rgyal-po - ruled c.1425-1450? He ruled sTong-sde. He was also a cousin of Rin-cen-dpal-lde. The only known event of his reign is his war with Bhagan of Basgo (Schuh 1983a PH I 64, PH II 12-16).

Bde-mchog-skyabs-pa. He ruled Ste-sta.

Tshang-rgyal-po II - ruled c.1530-1550? During his reign Mirza Haidar raided Zanskar c.1532-35[2].

Seng-ge-lde - lived 1525-1561? His name, only, is given in a biography of Ngag-dbang-tshe-ring of Dzongkhul (Snellgrove and Skorupski 1980 p 11). He may have been the unnamed king of southern Zanskar (lived c.1525-1561) who became a Dukpa monk under the religious name of gZhan-phan-bzang-po and a follower of Padma-Dkar-po (who lived 1527-1592); possibly also his nickname was 'Bo-go-so-to, because of his dropsy, and therefore he was the Zanskar king who became first a Gelugpa monk before converting to the Dukpa[3] (Schuh 1983a pp 14-15; Schuh 1983b pp 7-8; Evans-Wentz 1935 pp 153-154, 251).

Tshe-ring-dpal-lde - reigned some time between 1575 and 1610? He was the son of Seng-ge-lde (Schuh 1983a pp 14-15).

SURU-KARTSE

From Hashmatullah Khan (Khan 1939), and Kaju Sikander Khan (Khan 1987) who copies him here, we learn of the following kings of Suru-Kartse, descended from the line of "Nyati Astani" who came from Tibet. These kings seem to have ruled Suru and Purig as one kingdom, and are presented to us as ruling in the following dated sequence (in Hashmatullah Khan's spellings[4]).

Rgyal Bum-lde - 1345-1400. His wife was Muslim Begum, *née* Ganga Rani, daughter of a ruler of Kashmir. He ruled all the land from Suru to Mulbhe, in which latter place he built the original Kachay Masjid (Kashmiris' Mosque).(Khan 1939 p 694) He and his brother (see below) are said to have converted to Islam in Kashmir. Unfortunately Hashmatullah Khan does not give his sources. Could Rgyal Bum-lde be the same as Grags-pa-'bum? - in fact ruling a kingdom which stretched from Basgo to Suru with capitals at Temisgam and at Mulbhe where a *chos rgyal* 'Bum-lde (but which

2. or late 1540s, see Schuh 1983a p.34.
3. I am grateful to John Crook for putting me on to this interesting ruler's history.
4. I am most grateful to Dr Rohit Vohra for the opportunity to study the Suru section of an English translation of Hashmatullah Khan's book upon which he is working.

one?) has left a Buddhist inscription? (Francke 1906 p 75)

Chos Bum-lde - 1400-1430 The brother of the above, married to a Buddhist. No further information.

Yng-lde - 1420-1470. Son of Chos Bum-lde

Thong-lde - 1470-1530. Son of Yng-lde.

Tonba Gyalpo (Ao Tonba) - 1520-1530. Son of Thong-lde. Very pious, he gave up his throne to become a lama in Tibet.

Lobzang Gyalpo - 1530-1560. The younger brother of the above and a lama before becoming king. During this reign, according to Hashmatullah Khan, occurred the attack on Purig by 'Jam-dbyangs-rnam-rgyal (c.1575-1616); but Lobzang Gyalpo's name receives no confirmation from the Rgyal-rabs and Lobzang Gyalpo's dates are inconsistent with those of 'Jam-dbyangs-rnam-rgyal as calculated by Petech. Lobzang Gyalpo left the throne to his nephew and became a lama again.

Konchok Sherab Stan - 1560-1600. The nephew of Tonba Gyalpo. He divided his kingdom amongst his five sons; one Kungda Namgyal received Suru-Kartse.

KULU

The *vansavalis* provide a long list of rulers in the time before 15th century, whose regnal dates are almost universally unknowable (Hutchison and Vogel 1933 pp 413-473). Then we learn of:

Raja Urdhan Pal c. early 15th century (Hutchison and Vogel). This king's name is found in two inscriptions in Jagatsukh, dated 1418 and 1428.

Raja Kelas Pal. His dates are unknown but he was the successor of the above.

Raja Sidh Singh c.1500 (Hutchison and Vogel). This date is derived from the authors' study of the *vansavali*. After a period of exile of the ruling family, Sidh Pal, a descendant of the last king, reclaimed the throne and changed his dynastic name suffix to Singh.

Raja Bahadur Singh c. mid 1500s. This ruler's name occurs in two documents, dated 1533 (perhaps doubtful) and 1559, the year of his death (Hutchison and Vogel 1933 pp 454-457). There is also an inscription of his, dated 1553, on the Hidimba Temple in Manali.

Raja Partap Singh 1559-1575 (Hutchison and Vogel). He is followed by an apparently complete succession down to the 19th century.

WHAT CAUSED THE POLITICAL DISRUPTIONS OF THE PERIOD c.1450-c.1550?

The lists of kings summarised above for Ladakh, Zanskar and

Kulu have one striking characteristic in common: a gap covering the period of the second half of the 15th century, which in the case of Ladakh and Zanskar runs on into the 16th century. We know nothing of any independent rulers who might have existed contemporaneously in Spiti and Lahul; and the currently incomplete lists for Guge (Petech 1980) cannot at present be interpreted as being especially incomplete in this period. But Hashmatullah Khan's sequence of rulers for Suru-Kartse (including Pashkyum and Mulbhe) arouses suspicion because he provides only 7 rulers covering a period of 250 years, which suggests that some names have been lost here too. Since the records of royal dynasties are likely to be lost only when those dynasties themselves suffer severe disruption, taken all together even the information we have can be interpreted as pointing towards the period c.1450 to 1550 as being one of unusual instability in the western Himalaya.

We cannot guess at any single cause of that instability but we can discern a number of historical developments which may have taken advantage of the weakness of these states and have contributed to its continuance. Something of the range of threats to the stability of Ladakh and its neighbours may be illustrated from the following.

Firstly, there are the expeditions of the Muslim rulers of Kashmir, beginning back in the 14th century with attacks on Little Tibet (Baltistan), probably, during the reigns of Shihab ud Din and Sikander. Better known is the great raid or conquest by Zain ul Abidin which included Sheya-desa (Shay[5]), Goggadesa (Guge) and Kuluta (Kulu, but the exact parts not known) (Sahni and Francke 1908 pp 188-189). He may himself have led another raid against Ladakh towards the end of his reign (Hasan 1959 p 72); meanwhile in 1451 his son Adham Khan raided Little Tibet. During his reign he received tribute from Manasorawar (Briggs' *Firishta* 1910 p 470) which coincides interestingly with the list of tribute received from Guge by Blos-gro-mchog-ldan - perhaps the Ladakhi ruler accompanied him on his campaign against Goggadesa? In 1483 Jahangir Magre and Sayyid Hasan raided Ladakh. But thereafter a succession of feeble rulers and violent internal struggles kept Kashmir weak until Mirza Haidar conquered it for Humayun Padshah in 1540. In (possibly) 1544 he raided Ladakh, taking several unnamed places including "Looshoo" (Suru?) (Elias and Ross 1895 Introduction p 20) and in 1548 he reimposed his rule on Baltistan and Ladakh and appointed governors. In 1551, after his death, a party of his followers under Sabr Ali were killed endeavouring to cross Ladakh to the safety of Yarkand and

5. Perhaps destroying the monastery of Nyar-ma? see Snellgrove and Skorupski 1977 *The Cultural Heritage of Ladakh* Vol. 1. p 106.

Kashgar (Hasan 1959 p 142) (is this one of bKra-shis-rnam-rgyal's victories over the Hor?).

Secondly, there was recurrent danger from the Hor (Mongols, Turks) from Central Asia, Turkistan, to the north. Again their incursions begin before our period, for example Shihab ud Din is said to have defeated a Kashgari leader in Little Tibet. But in 1447-1448 there was an invasion, by Hor from Yarkand or Khotan, of Western Tibet, Guge and "Man-yul", which was repelled by the *lama* Thang-stong-rgyal-po; later, in 1459, he is said to have visited some 60 villages in Ladakh which had been settled by Hor (Petech 1980 p 102). Mirza Aba Bakr of Kashgar raided or conquered "Tibet" sometime after 1499 (Elias and Ross 1895 pp 253-4) (for the Mongols, Tibet included all the lands between the borders of Kashmir and the eastern Tibetan border with China, but here greater Ladakh is probably intended). In the years before his defeat and death in 1514 Aba Bakr's minister Mir Vali raided "Bolor and Tibet as far as Kashmir", presumably the Hunza, Nagar, Gilgit district and Baltistan (Elias and Ross 1895 p 320). When Mirza Aba Bakr was defeated by Sultan Said he fled to "Tibet" where "he found that all the forts which he had garrisoned had been abandoned by his men" but he was still able to leave his wife and family there in safety. Since he fled via Khotan, "Tibet" in this case must mean Ladakh (Elias and Ross 1895 p 324). In 1517 a follower of Sultan Said, called Mir Mazid, was killed in "Tibet" during another raid. Mirza Haidar's activities in Ladakh will be discussed in more detail below, but he states that before his entry into Ladakh in 1532 there had been a number of earlier raids under the orders of Sultan Said (Elias and Ross 1895 p 403). All these pieces of information may be a clue to the statement Lata Jughdan and Tashikun, rulers of "Maryul", made to Mirza Haidar that they had always been, or should have been, loyal subjects of the Hor (Mongols) (Elias and Ross 1895 p 460). The last notice of a Hor raid into Ladakh tells us of the death there of its leader, the third son of Sultan Rashid (Rashid was the son of Sultan Said) sometime before 1565-1566 (Elias and Ross 1895 Introduction p 121). Inscription 10 at Alchi may be celebrating the fact that bKra-shis-rnam-rgyal had finally rid the country of a long-standing Mongol nuisance.

Thirdly, while these events were happening in Ladakh, the kingdom of Lo (Mustang) under its rulers A-mgon-bzang-po (Petech 1978 p 320) and bKra-shis-mgon (Jackson 1984 p 148) exerted some sort of suzerainty, however temporary, over Purang and Guge - roughly second and third quarters of the 15th century.

Finally, in Kulu, following the end of the reign of Kelas Pal, the state of Suket extended its power over all the Beas valley south of approximately the present town of Kulu. Meanwhile the eastern side of the valley north of that, up to the Rotang Pass, may have been held by people of Tibetan or Ladakhi origin known to history as the Piti Thakurs. They may have been in uninterrupted occupation of their district since the time of Utpala of Ladakh or they may have recently expanded from a base to the east, to occupy this part of Kulu; they are presumed to be the Tibetans whom Zain ul Abidin found occupying Kulu during his raid (Sahni and Francke 1908 pp 188-189). What is certain is that the central power of Kulu, after centuries of uninterrupted rule, had collapsed.[6]

WHAT HAPPENED BETWEEN C.1450 AND C.1550 IN LADAKH?

The 100-year gap in the history of the kings of Ladakh was first revealed in 1895 by N Elias and E Denison Ross in their edition of *The Tarikh-i-Rashidi* of Mirza Mohammed Haidar Dughlat (p 418). A H Francke managed to hide it again by calculating regnal dates on the basis of impossibly long reigns for those kings whose dates were not given in the Rgyal-rabs. Prof. Petech brought the gap to notice once more in 1977 and Dieter Schuh discovered a similar gap in the available chronicles of Zanskar (Schuh 1983a p 34). Of the few sources available to help us fill in part of the 100-year gap in the dynastic history of Ladakh, the most intriguing is *The Tarikh-i-Rashidi* and Petech has considered this evidence; but there seems to be room for a different interpretation.

The relevant parts of Mirza Haidar's career in and around Ladakh can be summarised as follows (Elias and Ross 1895 pp 417-423, 442-464). He was a Mongol, born in Tashkent in 1499/1500; at approximately the age of 15 he entered the service of Sultan Said Khan and quickly rose to a position of prominence; in 1514 Sultan Said defeated his relative Mirza Aba Bakr and became the ruler of Kashgaria and thus the northern neighbour of Ladakh. In July 1532 Mirza Haidar led 2000 of the Sultan's men into Nubra where he defeated the Ladakhi leader who opposed him and then advanced to "Maryul", ie. presumably the district of Leh and Shay. Here he found that "there were two rulers, one called Lata Jughdan and the other Tashikun. They both hastened to wait on me". He then joined forces

6. Since writing this I have considered the chronology of the Piti Thakurs further and come to the new conclusion that their period of power in upper Kulu may have lain in the late first and early second millenium AD, that they were of no political significance (perhaps no longer there at all) in the late 15th century, and that there must be doubt whether Zain ul Abadin ever campaigned in Kulu — see N.F.Howard 1995 "The Fortified Places of Upper Kulu, India" in South Asian Studies 11 (J. Soc. for South Asian Studies, London).

with Sultan Said and his 3000 men, the Sultan already suffering from the altitude sickness which was eventually to lead to his death. During the winter the Sultan and 1000 of his men wintered in Baltistan while Mirza Haidar took the remaining 4000 plus a number of "Tibetans" (Ladakhis) via the Zoji La to Kashmir, which they plundered.

In the spring of 1533 the Mongols occupying Nubra were faced with a rebellion and were forced to take refuge in Maryul where Mirza Haidar found them on his return from Kashmir. He put to death one Tashikun for aiding this revolt whom we may presume from the context was a Nubra chief and not the Tashikun of Maryul who appears again later[7].

In May of the same year Mirza Haidar left Kashmir by way of Lar, "as we had come" (and by the Zoji La, presumably). He was generally welcomed "on the frontiers of Tibet" except in the case of "Karsa, a district of Tibet", which refused to pay tribute, thinking itself safe at the end of a deep, narrow - and therefore easily defended - ravine. Karsa must be Kartse, the seat of the principality of Suru and apparently at the time the dominant power in Little Tibet. But the resistance was overcome and then tribute was collected from "Purik" (Purig). And so they arrived at Leh where Sultan Said deputed Mirza Haidar to sack "the idol temple of Ursang" (Lhasa) with 2000 troops. Meanwhile the Sultan set off for Yarkand but died on the journey.

In the autumn of 1533 Mirza Haidar gave up his attempt on Lhasa and turned back, reaching Guge in January 1534. While he was collecting tribute there most of his army deserted him on instructions from Sultan Said's successor, Rashid. With 50 men who were still loyal, of whom 40 or so suffered frostbite, he struggled back during 25 days to Maryul where "the chui (*jo*, plural) of Maryul, named Tashikun and Lata Jughden .... hastened out to wait upon us. Since we had [on a former occasion] treated them with violence, both plundering and killing [their people], I was inwardly in great fear of them". But they professed loyalty to the Yarkandis saying they had always been, or should have been, their loyal subjects. "They gave us the castle of Sheya (ie Shay), which is the capital of Maryul".

There some of his deserters returned to him and Rashid, seeking to mend his broken relationship with Mirza Haider, sent 200 men under Maulana Kudash, so that by the end of winter in 1534 he had 700 under his command "and most of Tibet submitted". So they raided Baltistan to collect tribute.

But Suru, "a department of Balti' refused to accept occupation

7. *pace* Petech 1977 p 26; and not 1535, presumably a misprint for 1533.

although its people offered to send whatever tribute was demanded to Mirza Haidar's camp. This is the second year's levy and is not to be confused with the first. Maulana Kudash, however, insisted on collecting the levy personally and was killed along with 24 of his men by the people of Suru; and Mirza Haidar was too poor and too short of arms to avenge them.

In summer he moved with his army to Zanskar in order to collect tribute when the harvest ripened. Here he received a proposal from "Tangi Sakob" the chief of Sod, whom he describes as "one of the chui of Balti", that they should jointly raid Suru in revenge. However negotiations with this chief of Sod and the death of his cousin Mahmud Mirza caused Mirza Haidar two months' delay and in the end only a party of 70 men was sent to raid Suru under the leadership of Maulana Darvish Muhammad Kara Tagh. This expedition too was a failure and its leader was killed by one Baghan "a chui of the provinces of Tibet". Baghan seems also to have been killed, but the translator acknowledges that this passage is unclear.

Mirza Haidar and his remaining men retreated again to Maryul "at the commencement of the cold season" and suffered greatly during the winter of 1534-1535. The following summer he gave Ladakh up and went first to Badakhshan, then via Kabul into the service of the sons of his late cousin, the Padshah Baber, in Lahore.

Although the geographical context of these events is generally recognisable and may be presumed to be accurate, there are imprecisions which prevent firm identifications being made. However, two conclusions seem at least worth suggesting. The first is that Tashikun and Lata Jughdan were the rulers of upper Ladakh - at least - and in possession of Shay fortress, the twin capital with Leh. The fact that their title is given as "chui", ie *jo*, chief, rather than a version of rgyal-po, king, need not worry us too much if Mirza Haidar found greater Ladakh, indeed all of the "Tibet" in which he campaigned, in a generally weak state with local rulers holding the only effective power. Chui is the title he gives to all rulers whom he mentions.

The second is that although Baghan might at first sight appear to have been a chief of Suru, Mirza Haidar does not say that, nor does he say where Maulana Darvish Muhammad Kara Tagh was killed; and he might be understood to be saying that his men had attacked Baghan instead of attacking Suru as was intended. The passage reads: "Meanwhile a messenger arrived from the party which I had dispatched against Suru, saying that .....[they]..... had gone to attack Baghan, who was a chui of the provinces of Tibet". Note that he does not call him, either, a chui of Maryul, of Balti, or of any other named province. If Baghan's province were lower Ladakh (Basgo to

Temisgam) he would not have found it either difficult or improper to conduct warfare over the mountains into Zanskar or Purig or Suru in summer and autumn.

In order to fill in the names of the missing kings from c.1500 to c.1555 Petech first accepted that Tashikun is a clear transcription of the Ladakhi name bKra-shis-mgon and he recalled two inscriptions containing a king of that name, at Nyar-ma (next to Shay) and at Matho. He concluded that bKra-shis-mgon was only a local ruler although perhaps in some way independent. But he was reluctant to accept that Lata Jughdan is a transcription of Blo-gros-mchog-ldan and proposed that an unknown Lata Jughdan was king "of the main portion of Ladakh" and suggested the dates c.1510-1535 for his reign, although neither Mirza Haidar nor any other source indicates why such a reign should end in 1535. Finally he introduced a *lha-chen* Kun-gda'-rnam-rgyal of the Taru inscription (Francke's no. 102) as the ruler of Ladakh from c.1535-1555, on the basis that he is mentioned in the company of his minister Phyag-rdor-jo who also served under bKra-shis-rnam-rgyal (Petech 1977 pp 26-27).

Stepping further along the path of speculation, we may propose the following alternative - and emphasise that it is pure speculation - that Lata Jughdan *is* a transcription of Blo-gros-mchog-ldan and that Tashikun was known, perhaps at different stages in his life, as both bKra-shis-mgon and as Kun-gda'-rnam-rgyal, his full name being bKra-shis-kun-gda'-rnam-rgyal. In this case, at the time of Mirza Haidar's invasion Lata Jughdan/Blo-gros-mchog-ldan was the Father King and Tashikun the Young King. A similar relationship existed between the old king bDe-ldan-rnam-rgyal and his son bDe-legs-rnam-rgyal in the later 17th century (Petech 1977 p 69), and between Tshe-dpal-rnam-rgyal and the mChog-sprul in the 1830s (Petech 1977 p 137 quoting Gergan). Perhaps when he became sole king, Tashikun took, or was known by, the formal name of Kun-gda'-rnam-rgyal?

Over what territory did Lata Jughdan and Tashikun/Kun-gda'-rnam-rgyal rule? In theory they may well have claimed suzerainty over upper and lower Ladakh, all Purig and even Baltistan, as their predecessors had done; but by Mirza Haidar's time they may in practice have ruled upper Ladakh only. It should be noted that Taru is the most westerly village of upper Ladakh. The ease with which Mirza Haidar conducted his operations in most of greater Ladakh suggests that it was under no firm rule. He commented himself that the fortresses of Guge would have been very difficult to capture and the fortresses of Ladakh are no less strong (Howard 1989). Except briefly, he never had more that 2000 men under his command in Ladakh and for most of the time far fewer.

At the farthest limits of speculation, we may suggest that lower Ladakh (Mar-yul-smad-pa, Petech 1977 p 28) was at that time as independent in practice as Baltistan, and Purig and Suru, and that its ruler - its chui - was Baghan with twin capitals at Basgo and Temisgam. Two items of information point to this suggestion. The first is the welcome which Mirza Haidar received from Lata Jughdan and Tashikun when, much to his surprise and despite his obvious weakness, he was given the castle of Shay. Although he tells us nothing about it, Lata Jughdan's and Tashikun's most likely reason for befriending this outstanding Mughal soldier was that they hoped for his help against their enemies. The second is the Rgyal-rab's short entry for Lha-chen Bhagan, that he was "very fond of fighting, he and the people of Shay, having formed an alliance, deposed and subjected the sons of the King of Leh.......Blo-gros-mchog-ldan, etc". In other words Bhagan and Baghan are variant spellings of the same name and the rulers of Leh (and Shay) feared for their throne and were prepared to accept any help they could get, at whatever cost. We can now accept that bKra-shis-rnam-rgyal was Bhagan's (Baghan's) son, as the Rgyal-rabs says.

The foregoing solution to the second half of the problem of the missing 100 years (that is the years from c.1500 to c.1555) has the demerit of being more complicated than Petech's and much more complicated than Francke's. Francke's must be abandoned since it is based on impossibly long reigns and conflicts with the findings of later research but Prof. Petech's solution, the fruit of deep and lifelong scholarship, may yet stand the test of time. The solution being proposed here has at least the merit of answering more questions than did the previous attempts but it must be recognised that it raises just as many new questions.

The first question must consider the possibility: could Tashikun be King bKra-shis-rnam-rgyal? I believe this is impossible because the pusillanimous behaviour of Tashikun (and Lata Jughdan) towards Mirza Haidar is quite uncharacteristic of the vigorous, military king bKra-shis-rnam-rgyal described in the Rgyal-rabs and the Alchi inscription. Furthermore he cannot be both the son of Bhagan or Baghan and the joint ruler with Lata Jughdan/Blo-gros-mchog-ldan who was deposed by Bhagan; nor can he have been on the throne from 1533 to 1575 without having a reign of unlikely length, since his nephews and successors cannot be estimated to have come to the throne before 1575.

The second question is: can we accept two kings called Blo-gros-mchog-ldan in the lists? This is acceptable. There were two kings called Tshe-dbang-rnam-rgyal, two kings called bKra-shis-mgon (including Tashikun) and three kings called Grags(-pa)-lde; further part-repetitions may be found among the combinations of name elements in the list. The list of Guge kings is even more repetitious.

The third question is: how can Bhagan and Baghan be the same person when as much as 100 years separates their lives? They are not; and there may even have been four rulers bearing these names. Some Ladakhi historians derive the name Bhagan from *bha-gan*, old bull (eg. Shakspo 1988 p 10). If they are correct then Bhagan, alone of the kings of Ladakh who are known to us, is remembered by a nick-name whereas all the others have good religious Tibetan manes, with the exception of Lha-chen rGal-po and Lha-rgyal, which are good Tibetan titles. Most western Tibetologists would prefer Francke's suggestion that Bhagan may be a corruption of the Sanskrit Bhagavan(t) (Francke 1926 p 102) and Petech's that he came from a Hindu state (Petech 1977 pp 25-26) although we have no suggestion of from where he might have come. One wonders if the first Bhagan might have married the female heir of lower Ladakh? This original Bhagan can be accepted as having ruled in the middle of the 15th century, or a little earlier, and as being the Bhagan who attacked sTong-sde in Zanskar. Reverting to speculation again: it is possible that Bhagan then became the dynastic name of the rulers of Lower Ladakh, much as bTsan-po was used to refer to the ancient kings of Tibet, Khri-sultan for various rulers in Purig and Suru and Akabat Mahmud Khan for the kings of Ladakh since the nominal conversion of bDe-ldan-rnam-rgyal to Islam - all being names used by outsiders. Thus Baghan is merely Mirza Haidar's spelling of what he thought was the name of the third or fourth ruler of lower Ladakh to bear Bhagan as a dynastic title-name.

This latter speculation is prompted by the appearance of the Rgyal-rabs as it has come down to us in Francke's *Antiquities of Indian Tibet* and Petech's further researches. The reader is struck by the fact that of all the kings in the first dynasty only Skyid-lde-ni-ma-mgon, Lha-chen Utpala, Lha-chen Dnos-grub, Lha-chen Grags-'bum-lde and Blo-gros-mchog-ldan are presented to us with any quantity of distinctive detail - 5 kings out of a total of 19, and more have been lost completely (eg. Petech 1977 p 20). But from bKra-shis-rnam-rgyal onwards each king is presented with a considerable quantity of information about his deeds. One must conclude that large amounts of detail from the earlier periods have been lost. Prof. Petech observes that the Rgyal-rabs was "compiled probably in the 17th. century, but continued later till the end of the kingdom and beyond". (Petech 1977 p 1). The first writer of the Rgyal-rabs as we have it must have known who bKra-shis-rnam-rgyal's father was since he knew about the blinding of his brother and he must have known something of his ancestry. His readers would have known too, it not being long before; which is why he was not able to hide this discreditable element of the story. Therefore we can believe his statement that bKra-shis-rnam-rgyal's father was called, or used the title, Bhagan. However, this first writer, or a successor, desired to extend the history of the kings back to the founding of the Ladakhi kingdom and to the ancient kings of Tibet but he did not have a complete set of records covering the 600 years preceding bKra-shis-rnam-rgyal's accession. He did the best he could; but he confused the two Bhagans and the two Blo-gros-mchog-ldans - and thus 100 years fell out of the history.

THE CHANGE OF DYNASTIC TITLE/NAME FROM LHA-CHEN TO RNAM-RGYAL

Since Francke's time it has been widely accepted that the name change took place when Bhagan deposed the last ruler of the first dynasty. He suggested that Bhagan named himself Lha-chen Kun-dga'-rnam-rgyal when he became king (Francke 1926 p 102). This is pure speculation on Francke's part for which there is no proof in the Rgyal-rabs, particularly now that we recognise that there is a 100-year gap in the records at the very time when this change took place. Furthermore, we may note that Blo-gros-mchog-ldan is not given the title Lha-chen but Lha-chen Kun-gda'-rnam-rgyal has both. Resolution of this matter of the dynastic name change must await the discovery of more source data.

CONCLUSION

The period of Ladakh's history which runs from the middle of the 15th to the middle of the 16th centuries is of the greatest interest. It not only contains - and currently hides - the events surrounding the change of dynasties but it is a period during which the fortunes of Ladakh may have been closely bound up with those of her neighbours. Yet we know almost nothing certain about the history of the period. We need new sources. They may lie forgotten in Ladakh still. In monasteries, in family boxes, in the minds and memories of the old people are great stores of history and tradition - in Ladakh, in Nubra, in Purig, in Suru and in Zanskar. Progress has been made; but there is much more to do and time is running out, as old people die, old records decay or are lost and as young people turn to the excitements of the cinema, the television and the transistor radio. The traditional culture of the region will, of course, live on but the facts of its history are slipping away. Facts are what we need. We must all make haste.

Acknowledgement: the author very gratefully acknowledges the generous financial support which he received from the Society for South Asian Studies in the preparation and presentation of this paper.

POST SCRIPT

After writing this, I have read Dr Jamspal's extremely interesting paper and had correspondence with him in which he has generously provided me with further information. It is my opinion now that the reign of King Grags-'bum-lde should, perhaps, be moved forward one generation or so. This may have implications for the dating of other dynasties; and it reduces the length of the break in Ladakhi history which I have been trying to fill - but it does not remove it.

REFERENCES

BRIGGS, J. (reprint) 1910 *History of the Rise of Mahomedan Power in India (Tarikh-i-Firishta)*. London.

DARGYAY, E. K. 1987 "The Dynasty of Bzang-La (Zangla, West Tibet) and its Chronology - A Reconsideration". In BECKWITH, C. I. (ed.) 1987 *Silver on Lapis*. Bloomington, U. S. A., pp. 13-32.

ELIAS, N. and ROSS, E. Denison 1895 *The Tarikh-i-Rashidi of Mirza Muhammad Haidar, Dughlat*. London.

EVANS-WENTZ, W. Y. *Tibetan Yoga and Secret Doctrines*. London.

FRANCKE, A. H. 1906 "The Rock Inscriptions at Mulbe". *Indian Antiquary* 35, 72-81. Bombay.

——— 1926 *Antiquities of Indian Tibet*. India (reprinted S. Chand and Co. New Delhi 1972, and others).

HASAN, M. 1959 *Kashmir under the Sultans*. Calcutta.

HOWARD, N. F. 1989 "The Development of the Fortresses of Ladakh c.950 to c.1650 AD". *East and West* 39, 217-288. Istituto per il Medio ed Estremo Oriente, Rome, Italy..

HUTCHISON, J. and VOGEL, J. Ph. 1933 *History of the Punjab Hill States*. Lahore.

JACKSON, D. P. 1984 *The Mollas of Mustang*. Dharamsala, India.

Khan, HASHMATULLAH 1939 *Tarikh Jammun, Kashmir, Laddakh aur Baltistan*. Luknow.

KHAN, KACHO SIKANDER. 1987 *Qadim Laddakh tarikh va tamaddun*. Published by the author, India.

PETECH, L. 1977 *The Kingdom of Ladakh c. 950-1842 AD*. Istituto per il Medio ed Estremo Oriente, Rome, Italy.

——— 1978: "The 'Bri-gun-pa Sect in Western Tibet and Ladakh". In LIGETI, L. (ed.). 1978 *Procedings of the Csoma de Kôrös Symposium September 1976*, pp.313-335. Budapest, Hungary.

——— 1980 "Ya-ts`e, Gu-ge, Pu-ran: a new study". *Central Asiatic Journal*, 24, 85-111.

SAHNI, D. R. and FRANCKE, A.H. 1908 "References to the Bhauttas in the Ragatarangini of Kashmir". *Indian Antiquity* 37, 181-192. Bombay.

SCHUH, D. 1983a "Historiographische Documente aus Zans-dkar". In SCHUH, D. and WEIERS, M. (eds.) 1983 *Archiv für Zentralasiatische Geschichtsforschung*, Heft 6. Sankt Augustin, Germany.

——— 1983b "Frühe Beziehungen zwischen dem ladakhischen Herrscherhaus und der südlichen 'Brug-pa-Schule". In *Archiv*...etc, Heft 2 (as above).

SHAKSPO, N. T. 1988 *A History of Buddhism in Ladakh*. Ladakh Buddhist Vihar, New Delhi.

SNELLGROVE D. L. and SKORUPSKI, T. 1980 *The Cultural Heritage of Ladakh* Vol. 2. Aris and Phillips, Warminster, England.

TABLE SUMMARISING THE DYNASTIC HISTORY OF LADAKH, ZANSKAR, SURU-KARTSE AND KULU BETWEEN 1400 AND 1600 AD

	LADAKH		**ZANSKAR**		**SURU-KARTSE**	**KULU**
			Sen-ge-ldor		Rgyal-Bum-lde	
	LOWER	**UPPER**	**PADUM**	**ZANGLA**		
1400			Blo-bzang-lde	Khri-nam-lde		
						Urdhan Pal
	Grags-pa-'bum	Grags-'bum-lde			Chos-Bum-lde	
1425						
			Tshang-rgyal-po (+ brother Radug)	Rin-chen-dpal-lde		
						Kelas Pal
1450	Bara?	Blo-gros-mchog-ldan			Yng-lde	
				Khri-dpal-lde		
1475	Bhagan					
				Nam-kha-dpal-lde		
1500	*Bhagan II?*	*Latajugdan/ Blo-gros-mchog-ldan II*			Thong-lde	Sidh Singh
	Bhagan III?					
1525					Tonba-gyalpo	
	Baghan?	*Tashikun/ Kun-dga'-rnam-gyal*	Tshang-rgyal-po II			Bahadur Singh
1550		(Lha-dbang-rnam-rgyal)	Seng-ge-lde (a monk)		Lobsang-Gyalpo	
		bKra-shis-rnam-rgyal				Partap Singh
1575						
		Tshe-dbang-rnam-rgyal			Konchok Sherab Stan	
1600		'Jam-dbyangs-rnam-rgyal	Tshe-ring-dpal-lde			

NB: names in oblique type are the author's speculative additions to the royal chronology of Ladakh.

N.Howard. The dynastic history of Ladakh etc. 1400-1600 AD.

THE FIVE ROYAL PATRONS AND THREE MAITREYA IMAGES IN BASGO

Lozang Jamspal
606 W. 116th Street,
New York, N.N.10027, U.S.A.

Summary

Three Maitreya images and their temples were constructed in the sacred Basgo valley of Ladakh by the Kings Takpa Bumde, Tshewang Namgyal, Jamyang Namgyal & his Queen Khatun - the Balti Princess, and King Sengge Namgyal in the period 1450-1650 C.E. Although in neglected condition, the extraordinarily beautiful images and mural paintings within the temples are still visible and are very important from cultural and artistic viewpoints. The temples and their contents are in immediate need of preservation to protect them from collapse due to erosion. The author earnestly asks for patrons to help in this restoration project.

The author clarifies and corrects the statements of previous Western and Ladakhi scholars on the chronology of the construction and patronage of these temples, and the reigns and lifetimes of the five main patrons. Two appendices are based on incidents in the life of one patron and a Basgo hero.

Introduction

Basgo valley, the ancient capital of Ladakh, is very important in the history of Ladakh. It is about four miles in length, varying in width from a mile to some few hundred yards, situated about 11,000 to 11,500 feet above sea level. The lower part is widest and it narrows to its upper part where many springs originate, all having the eight good qualities of coolness, delicious taste, etc.[1] Flowing through the valley, these springs provide water for both drinking and irrigation.

At the sides of the valley there are many hills, cliffs, and mountains, standing as though competing with each other, astonishing the eyes of the viewer. Especially impressive is the rocky mountain of Ngang pa looming over the east side of the valley, considered both gracious and holy as it is surrounded by many ancient hermitages.

At the bottom of the valley the mighty Indus flows from east to west and, in the summer, it roars loudly with spectacular waves. At this time the valley is full of terraced fields growing wheat, barley, beans, peas, mustard, as well as other crops. There also can be found many kinds of trees, such as willows and poplars, as well as fruit trees producing apricots and apples. Throughout, there are hundreds of

1. As it has been stated in the commentary of *Abhidharmakosha* by Yashomitra:— *The eight-fold good qualities of water are as follows: cool, good tasting, light, smooth, clear, pure, and neither harmful to the stomach nor to the throat.*

chortens (*mchod-rten*, Skt. *stupa*), strung like ornaments of the valley, standing on roadsides to bless passing travellers. In the ancient period before the Dogra invasion of the 1830s, family houses were built below the royal castle inside the fortified wall, but now they are scattered throughout the countryside. There are more than 150 families containing about 800 inhabitants.

The magnificent ruins of the ancient royal castles of Ladakh stand on the eastern cliffs, in the central portion of the valley[2]. Among these ruins one finds three temples to the bodhisattva Maitreya, the future Buddha. In these temples there are many priceless images, beautiful murals, and sacred manuscripts of the Kanjur[3] and Tanjur[4] produced by highly skilled artisans and craftsmen and consecrated by holy persons many centuries ago. The patrons of these images and paintings were the Kings Grags pa 'Bum lde, Tshe dbang rNam rgyal, 'Jam dbyangs rNam rgyal, the Balti Princess, and King Seng ge rNam rgyal. Scholars have proposed various chronologies for the royal patrons, but the following table is based on the best current evidence.

A TENTATIVE CHRONOLOGY

King	Reign	Accomplishment
Grags pa 'Bum lde	circa 1450-1490	Original builder of the big Maitreya at Basgo.
Tshe dbang rNam rgyal	circa 1580-1600	Brother of Jam dbyang rNam rgyal. Had Maitreya temple painted.
'Jam dbyang rNam rgyal	circa 1600-1615	Husband of Balti princess, Khatun. Started construction of the golden image.
Queen Khatun, Balti princess		The builder of the smallest Maitreya temple at Basgo.
Senge rNam rgyal	circa 1616-1642	Completed the gilded Maitreya image.

---

2. See Howard 1989 "The development of the fortresses of Ladakh c.950 to c.1650 A.D." *East & West* 39, 217-288. Inst. medio ed estremo Oriente, Rome.
3. There is still a Kanjur set among these, and the valley people bring them down to the villages and read them once a year in the spring.
4. The set of Tanjur, written in gold, is incomplete due to robbing by the attackers from Jammu in 1830s. See Yoseb, p. 594.

Grags pa 'bum lde

Cunningham and Yoseb do not include a date for Grags pa 'bum lde, while Francke and Tashi Rabgyas put his date at c. 1400-1440 C.E. and Petech gives c. 1410-1435 C.E.

An error which is made in *The Chronicles of Ladakh* continues up to the latest histories of Ladakh[5] by Luciano Petech and Tashi Rabgyas. This is in regard to the two ascetic messengers who are sent to king Grags pa 'bum lde or his younger brother Grags pa 'bum by Tsong khapa himself with a miniature of Amithayus made of Tsong khapa's nasal blood.

There are couple of reasons to doubt this statement:

Firstly Tsong khapa would not make such an image of Amitayus Buddha with his own nasal blood because traditionally no Tibetan Lama would openly represent himself as holy. Of course, having great faith in Tsong khapa and in the Buddha, his disciples could make such a holy object and send it to a pious Buddhist.

Secondly, about four decades after Tsongkhapa's death, the two ascetics were sent to Ladakh by dGe 'dun grub pa, the posthumous first Dalai Lama (1391-1474 C.E), in order to raise funds for the construction of a Maitreya image in Tashilhunpo monastery. One of the ascetics was really practicing the bodhisattva path, as Ye shes rTse mo tells us. [6]

According to *The Chronicles of Ladakh*, the ascetic messengers were not successful in meeting Grags pa 'bum, the younger king, in Nubra, but later on they were received by Grags pa 'bum lde, the elder king, with great honor in Leh.[7]

According to Ye she rtse mo, the ascetic messengers brought back a huge turquoise as an offering from Grags pa 'bum lde,[8] as well as other wonderful offerings made by the people of the region. The date given for the ascetics' return to Tashilunpo is the lCags mo sBrul [1461 C.E.][9].

Grags pa 'bum lde's dates are connected to the Te se ru (Te'u

---

5. Petech, pp 20-22
6. Ye shes rTse mo became the abbot of Tashi lhun po and composed dGa' 'dun grub biography in 1698.
7. Francke, vol. II, pp. 36, 99.
8. Ye shes rTse mo calls him the king of Western Tibet (mNga' ris), Lord (Jo bo) Grags 'bum lde.
9. Ye shes rTse mo, f. 37a

ser po) stupa temple, namely the Te'u bKra shis 'Od 'phro (Te'u Auspiciousness Radiating Light) at Leh. Neil Howard wrote me that this had a similar structure to the Great Stupa Temple at Gyangtse, which was built in 1427 C.E. according to the chronicles of Tibetan events in the *Tibetan Chinese Dictionary*.[10]

According to the regent, Sangs rgyas rGya mtsho, Gyangtse Monastery was founded by mKhas grub Chos rje dGe legs dPal bzang po (1385-1438) and Rab brtan Kun bzang 'phags, the local chieftain.[11] The regent also mentions that the renovation of the dPe thub (Spituk) monastery was done by gSang phu pa, Lha dbang bLo gros, a disciple of mKhas grub rje.[12]

Therefore, we can conclude that being a disciple of mKhas grub rje, Lha dbang bLo gros had been in rGyal rtse (Gyangtse) and had seen the great stupa. Then, he might have advised king Grags pa 'bum lde to build a similar stupa at Te 'u ser po at Leh. When Grags pa 'bum lde died, his son bLo gros mchog ldan became the patron of the Lama, Lha dbang Blo gros.[13] This would seem to establish the reign of King Grags pa 'Bum lde as having occurred between approximately c. 1450-1490 C.E.

Petech and Rabgyas tell us that Blo gros mChog ldan made great offerings to the first rGyal ba (Dalai Lama,) dGe 'dun grub and Tashi lhun po. It seems that their source was the defective passage of Vaidurya ser po of the regent regarding bLo gros mchog ldan. The Tibetan text is as follows: *Mang yul stong ba'i* (*sic*, it should be*: Mar yul stod pa'i) rgyal po blo gros mchog ldan pas mkhas pa lha dbang blo gros pa'i sbying bdag mdzad/ gTsang du rje bla ma'i yang srid gong ma pan chen dgd grub la 'bul chen phul //* [14] The translation of this passage should be as follows: "The king of upper Mar yul (Ladakh), bLo gros mchog ldan pa became a patron of the savant Lha

---

10. Krang dbyi sun, p. 3247.
11. Sde srid, p. 244.
12. Ibid. p. 280
13. "This king still continued to make offering to dGe 'dun grub, the incarnation (Tib. yang srid, sprul sku) of the Lord Lama," the regent Sangs rgya rGya mtsho says. However, in his statement there is a mistake when he mentions dGe 'dun grub pa is the incarnation of Lord Lama. dGe 'dun grub pa was not recognized as a reincarnation of any former lama in his lifetime. The regent himself could not make such a mistake, it had to be the informant about dPe thub monastery and not the regent.
14. sDe drid, 280.

dbang bLo gros. He, the king, made a great offering to the incarnation of the Lord Lama, the former Savant dGe 'dun grub pa in the gTsang province. Francke states that "Probably during the reign of this king (bLo gros mChog ldan) the expedition of the Kashmir king Adam Khan to Tibet took place. This king is also mentioned in the *Ta'rikh-i-Rashidi* as still living in 1532; probably his descendants are called by his name. There his name is spelt Lata jughdan" [Francke, p.101]. Petech's study refers to the same events, although Petech is probably more correct when he says the invader came from Central Asia, while Francke states that he came from Kashmir. According to Petech, when Mirza Haidar invaded Ladakh in 1532, Haidar mentioned the names of both Jo bo Bhagan and Lata Jughdan (bLo gros mChog ldan?). Neither Francke nor Petech accept that these were Bhagan and bLo gros mChog ldan of the chronology of Ladakh.[15]

I have tried to prove that King Grags pa 'bum lde's reign was as late as 1490, and that the two Jobos of Ladakh during Haidar's invasion of Ladakh must have been bLo gros mChog ldan and Bhagan who are written about in the Ladakhi Chronicle. Also it is possible that the author of the history of Mirza Haidar's invasion of Ladakh miscalculated the year of the invasion as 1532, some years too late.

To prove this point the following passage is very important. In the *Biography of the saint Thang stong rGyal po* who lived in the 15th century (written by 'Gyur med bDe chen in the beginning of the 17th century), there is a passage implying the possibility of the two kings being bLo gros mChog ldan and Bhagan who were mentioned by Mirza Haidar. The translation of the passage is as follows:

> "The great saint [Thang stong rGyal po] together with about twenty of his disciples, who had renounced attachment to their own lives, visited Maryul [Ladakh] in order to subdue the Mongols of the West. The saint pacified the dispute of the two kings of upper and lower Maryul through his clairvoyance and miracles. He bestowed the transmission of **Om mani padme hum** to the Western Mongol people, who settled in about sixty settlements in Maryul. Through using meditation to overcome the Western Mongol army, he caused rains of mice in the country of the Mongols and destroyed their grain, so famine and bubonic plague occurred. Thus he destroyed the opportunity of the Western Mongols to enter the Nation of the Snow Land [Tibet]."[16]

---

15. Petech, pp. 26-27.
16. 'Gyur med bDe Chen, Biography of Thang stong rGyal po gyi rnam thar, p.309.

Although this is legendary in part, the author does have the historical knowledge of the dispute of the two kings of Maryul and the invasion of Ladakh by Western Mongols (Central Asians). Thus the two kings **must** have been bLo gros mChog ldan and Bhagan. Only during these two kings did Upper and Lower Ladakh dispute, then finally Bhagan united the two kingdoms of Upper and Lower Ladakh.

In dGe 'dun grub pa's life time, there was no custom of choosing an incarnation (*yang srid* or *sprul sku*) by most of the monasteries, although some Kargyud pa Lamas did so. However, when dGe 'dun grub pa passed away in 1474 C.E., a boy born in 1475 in gZhis ka rtse district was chosen as incarnation of him. This is the first incarnation of the dGe lugs pa. He was named as dGe 'dun rGya mtsho, and from his age 11 up to 19 he studied at Tashilhunpo monastery.[17] At age 19 (1494) he left for 'Bras spung monastery and studied there. Around 1509 he was preaching all over central Tibetan and lived again in Tashilhunpo for several years.

Therefore, the defective passage can be edited as follows: *gTsang du rje bla ma sku gong ma pan chen dGe 'dun grub kyi yang srid dGe 'dun rGya mtsho la 'bul chen phul/* "In gTsang province, he (bLo gros mchog ldan) made a great offering to the incarnation, (dGe 'dun rGya mtsho,) of the former Savant dGe 'dun grub pa."

Tshe dbang rNam rgyal I

Several dates have been suggested for Tshe dbang rNam rgyal I. Cunningham dates his reign as c. 1580-1600, [18] while Francke gives c. 1532 -1560, [19] Petech c. 1575-1595, and Rabgyas c. 1530 to 1560.[20] Yoseb places his death in c. 1569.[21] Of all of these suggestions, Cunningham and Petech seem most likely. There is a solid evidence placing the death of his successor, 'Jam dbyang rNam rgyal, sometime within 1614 and 1615 C.E. met Lama Stag tshang ras pa in the Zanskar valley.[22]

---

17. Ya han krang, pp. 37, 38, 40, 42.
18. Cunningham, pp. 318-9.
19. Francke, Vol. II, p. 105.
20. Rabgyas, p. 155.
21. Yoseb, p. 355.
22. See below the second paragraph about 'Jam dbyangs rNam rgyal.

Jam dbyangs rNam rgyal

Cunningham puts his reign at c.1600-1620,[23] while Petech gives c. 1595-1616 and Francke c. 1560 to 1590,[24] which Tashi Rabgyas agrees with.[25] Corroborating Cunningham and Petech's view, it is recorded that when the Venerable Yogi sTag tshang Ras pa arrived in Ladakh, he did not find the king at all, but met only the queen, the Princess of Balti, and her two sons, Seng ge rNam rGyal and Nor bu rNam rgyal, at Basgo in circa 1616 or 1617 C.E..[26]

We know that Tshe dbang rNam rgyal was succeeded by his younger brother, 'Jam dbyang rNam rgyal, sometime in the late 16th or early 17th century. Moreover, a meeting of King 'Jam dbyang rNam rgyal and the Venerable Yogi sTag tshang Ras pa (1574—1651 C.E.) is documented sometime within the Water Bull year (1613 C.E.) and the Wood Rabbit year (1615 C.E.) in the Zangskar valley. In those years sTag tshang started his journey to Uddiyana from central Tibet and from Zangskar, respectively,[27] and, when he returned from Uddiyana to Zangskar and eventually arrived in Basgo, he did not see the King 'Jam dbyang rNam rgyal, who had presumably passed away. After his s death, Seng ge rNam rgyal probably became king, around 1616 C. E.. When the Venerable Yogi sTag tshang arrives in Basgo, he bestowed an empowerment of the integration of Hayagriva and Amitayuh to the Queen Khatun and the King, Seng ge rNam rgyal, and his brother, Nor bu rNam rgyal, at the Basgo Castle. Lord sTag tshang then stays on in Ladakh for four years before returning to central Tibet in 1620.[28]

Seng ge rNam rgyal

Various dates have also been put forth for Seng ge rNam rgyal. Cunningham places his reign c. 1620 -1670,[29] Francke c. 1590

---

23. Cunningham, p.322.
24. Francke, vol. II, p. 106.
25. Rabgyas, p. 162.
26. Kun dga' Lhun grub, f. 26b.
27. Kun dga' Lhun grub, ff. 24b and 25b..
28. Ibid. fb. 26.
29. Cunningham, p.324

-1635,[30] Yoseb from 1567 to 1596,[31] Snellgrove and Skorupski 1570 -1642,[32] Petech, c. 1616-1642, and Tashi Rabgyas[33] from 1590 to 1620. Although Cunningham is more accurate about the beginning of his reign, he is not correct about the end,[34] whereas Snellgrove and Skorupski give his date of death correctly. Although his date of birth remains hard to establish, evidence suggests Seng ge rNam rgyal might have died in his late 30s or early 40s. Seng ge rNam rgyal passed away in 1642, according to the *Life of Ngag dbang rGya mtsho.*[35] This occured during a campaign in which he led his army to the highlands of Western Tibet, a rugged journey no aged person would ever consider making.

Consistent with this view is the fact that there is no mention of his bride in the Life of Tag tshang. When he first time arrived in Basgo in 1616 or 1617 C.E., he just met the Queen Khatun along with her sons, the two prince- brothers. This would suggest that he may have been in his teens then, and thus too young to have yet married.

The First Maitreya Image

The main Maitreya temple is the most ancient of these buildings and is very important from the standpoint of its artistic beauty. Historians have different theories about the time and patron of its construction.

Francke credits the building of the temple itself to King Tshe dbang rNam rgyal I on the basis of his inscribed portrait and those of his two brothers on the wall murals of the temple.[36] If Francke is correct, then it would have been constructed sometime in the late 16th century. Snellgrove and Skorupski also agree with Francke about the date and patron of this temple's construction.[37]

---

30. Francke, p. 108
31. Yoseb, pp. 359, 386.
32. Snellgrove and Skorupski, p. 86.
33. Rabgyas, p. 178
34. Kun dga' Lhun grub, fa. 40.
35. Kun dga' Lhun grub, fb. 40.
36. Francke, Vol. I, pp 86-7.
37. Snellgrove and Skorupski, p. 93.

But in the *Chronicles* there is no mention of constructing any temple by Tshewang rNam rgyal. However, it does say that he objected to his ancestors having placed the Buddha-relics on a hilltop which did not have an easy access for people who wanted to worship and circumambulate the relics. Therefore, he said, "I will build a temple for the benefit of sentient beings and will make the Buddha's teachings known, as did my ancestor Ral pa can"[38]. Thus he had a good thought, but unfortunately he passed away without fulfilling his wish.[39] But the mural paintings of the Maitreya temple of Basgo were certainly painted in the time of his reign, and it shows his royal retinue at the bottom of both the right and left sides when one enters the temple.

Cunningham certainly misunderstood the passage of the *Chronologies* about King Tshe dbang rNam rgyal when he wrote that the king resolved to erect a temple of Buddha,[40] which contradicts the passageof the *Chronicles of Ladakh*. But Cunningham's dates regarding this king were more accurate than the dates suggested by later scholars.

Francke interprets this passage fairly well, except for the last phrase, which is in Tib. *sems can gyi las zad pas / rgya; po de sku bde bar gshegs so //* He translates this: "as his work on earth was finished, he went to heaven."[41] This should be corrected to: "due to exaustion of the good karma of people, the king died peacefully."

The learned Ladakhi historian Shri Tashi Rabgyas disagrees on both points of Francke. In his monumental work, the *History of Ladakh,* he states that when King Grags pa 'bum lde had the Maitreya of gTing mo sgang constructed, he simultaneously made the Maitreyas of Basgo and Leh, too.[42]

Yoseb and Rabgyas do not agree about the identity of the patron of the construction of Tingmosgang Maitreya. Yoseb says that it was constructed by Grags pa 'bum according to Tsongkhapa's advice, while Rabgyas claims that it was constructed by Grags pa 'bum

---

38. Ral pa can is known as Khri ral pa can (866-896? C.E) and he was one of the three best ancestor kings of Tibet.
39. Francke, pp. 38, 105
40. Cunningham, p. 319.
41. Francke, pp. 38, 105.
42. Rabgyas, p. 122.

lde according to Tsongkhapa's advice, (Yoseb, pp. 346-7 and Rabgyas, pp. 121-2.

The former statement is disproved and latter is proved by the *Chronicles of Ladakh* itself, which says that when the ascetic messengers from Tsongkhapa arrived in Nubra valley they asked for an audience with Grags pa 'bum. He did not see them, but in Leh, his elder brother, Grags pa 'bum lde, received them with great respect and honor. (see Francke, pp. 38, 99). However, the messengers were not from Tsongkhapa, but from dGe 'dun grub pa, as shown above.

If Tashi Rabgyas is correct, then this Maitreya temple was constructed over a century earlier than that proposed by other scholars.

Furthermore, Tashi Rabgyas tells us:

> "In the early part of life, Grags pa 'bum lde reigned in both upper and lower Ladakh, but in the later part of his life, his reign in lower Ladakh was usurped by his younger brother, Grags pa 'bum. Although some ministers of upper Ladakh objected to this usurpation, Grags pa 'bum lde was quite tolerant and both brothers successfully reigned in different parts of the country.[43] Then, Grags 'bum, with great faith and respect, served the Maitreya image, erected by Grags 'bum lde, as well as the image of Avalokiteshvara, which was received by Grags 'bum lde."

Tashi Rabgyas' statement is supported by the *Chronicles of Ladakh*, which states that when the two ascetic messengers arrived in Ladakh, Grags pa 'bum was in the Nubra valley,[44] instead of in lower Ladakh, c.1559 C.E.

The Chronicles of Ladakh particularly do not mention the Maitreya construction at Basgo and Tingmosgang by Grags pa 'bum lde. However, it does mention that he constructed many temples and Matreya? (Maitreyas):

> "Grags 'bum lde built many[45] temples (red temple, sic) and in them [put] Lord Maitreya? (Maitreyas)[46] the size of eight year olds [boys in the future eon],[47] and by his right and left

---

43. Ibid. p. 127.
44. Francke vol. II pp. 30, 99.
45. The London MS. of the reads *mang po* instead of *dmar po*. I take the meaning of the former one.
46. Here I use plural, because having constructed **many** temples, it is unreasonable to say constructing **one** Maitreya.
47. Tibetan Buddhists believe that in the future, when Maitreya will become Buddha, the people will have enormously huge body and will live for many thousands years. Thus the people say that the Maitreya at Basgo, Tingmosgang and Leh are eight years old boys, sized as in the good future aeon.

sides two bodhisattvas, Manjushri and Vajrapani, which are one storey high, on the mural the portraits of Sugatas (Buddhas), worldly displays (*'jig rten brtan bzhag*[48]) and complete tutelary deities. Thus, the three storey high temple? (temples)[49] were erected on the model of mTho gling." [50]

In the present reading of the *Chronicles*, the word **'red'** , (Tib *dmar po*) is certainly a corrupted form of **'many'**, (Tib. *mang po*) which is correctly read in the L. MS (London MS). [51]

This Basgo Maitreya temple exactly corresponds to the Maitreya temple, built by Grags pa 'Bum lde as described in the *Chronicles*, in the above passage. The Maitreya temple is three storeys high, on the right and left sides of the main Maitreya image are two one-storey high bodhisattvas. When one enters the temple on the left wall there are three portraits of Sugatas, representing the Buddhas of the past, present and future. The display of King Tshe dbang rNam rgyal's retinue corresponds to the worldly display as stated in the *Chronicles*. The portraits of Tsongkhapa, Vajrasattva,[52] the white and green Taras, as well as others, represent the tutelary deities. On the eastern side wall the painting of Padma dkar po and others are significantly different from the paintings on the other walls in their style and painting colors. Therefore, we can conclude that they are products of a later time.

This Basgo Maitreya temple has survived better than the temples at Tingmosgang and Leh, thanks to the additional buildings surrounding it, except for the southern front part. These additional buildings were constructed much later, as Neil Howard has suggested.

As a result, we can surmise that Grags pa 'Bum lde constructed this Maitreya temple too, but could not complete the mural paintings, or in time his paintings were damaged by dripping water

---

48. A.H.Francke has misinterpreted the phrase, *'jig rten brtan bzhag* as follows, **of the preserver of the universe,** Francke vol. II p. 99; he tried to make the phrase as adjective to the Sugatas, Buddhas. But this phrase is an independent one in the list of things.
49. Yoseb thinks that three storey high temple is separate from the Maitreya temple at Leh Chu fyi.
50. mTho gling in Zhang zhung, erected by Lha bla maYe shes 'od (*The Blue Annal,* p. 83.)
51. Francke, vol. II pp. 36 and 99.
52. Here Snellgrove and Skorupski mistakenly recognized Tsongkhapa as Atisha and Vajrasattva as Vajrapani. Snellgrove and Skorupski, pp. 95, 96.

from the roof, as was usual in mud building. Then, in Tshe dbang rNam rgyal's time, it was painted or repainted in the present form on the model of the paintings of the Maitreya temples at Tingmosgang and Leh, which no longer exist due to the deterioration of the walls.[53]

After the ancient Maitreya Temple at gTing mo sgang fell into decay a new one was reconstructed during the mid 1940s.[54] There is no ancient mural left to view, only the image of Maitreya and some pleasing floral and circular patterns on the ceiling of lower temple hall.[55] Nevertheless, the Maitreya image and the paintings on the ceiling of the lower shrine of the Maitreya Temple at gTing mo sgang are comparable in artistic style to the images and the designs on the ceiling of the Maitreya Temple at Basgo.

There is reasonable evidence to date the murals. Snellgrove and Skorupski describe the Maitreya and its temple at gTing mo sgang:

> "It is one of the most beautiful representations we have seen of this very popular divinity. The ceiling of the lower temple with its pleasing floral and circular patterns is reminiscent of the Maitreya Temple at Basgo."[56]

THE SECOND MAITREYA IMAGE

Above the main gate of the castle, a small old Maitreya Temple stands (very precariously and can fall at any moment!). The outer structure of this temple is in the shape of a Balti mosque.[57] According to Yoseb, in his *History of Ladakh*, the Balti Princess, Khatun, had three mosques built at some important sites in Ladakh: one below the gTing mo sgang Castle, one below the Leh Castle, and one in Hundar in the Nubra valley. He then asserts that she remained a life-long follower of Islam.[58] This last statement could not be true.

Several records indicate her acceptance of Buddhism. Had she not accepted Buddhism, sTag tshang, who was free from the eight

---

53. Snellgrove and Skorupski, p. 102.
54. As I was then a novice , I was fortunate to be able to join in the consecration ceremony.
55. There are still some people who can tell us about the ancient mural paintings of the Maitreya temple of Tingmosgang.
56. Snellgrove and Skorupski, p. 104.
57. Rabgyas, p. 167.
58. Yoseb, pp. 621-2.

worldly concepts,[59] would not have allowed her to sit in the tantrika secret mandala, for this would have transgressed the rules of esoteric Buddhism. At the time, he performed this kind of empowerment for very few people. Another point is that she also was a patron of the gilded Maitreya image at Basgo Castle.

Furthermore, it seems that not only was she a Buddhist, but she was a patroness of the dGe lugs pa sect. There are two reasons to state that she had faith in the dGe lugs pa sect. First, in the *Life of sTag tshang* there is no mention of the death of the royal mother, the Balti Princess, or of any posthumous offerings by King Seng ge rNam rgyal, despite mention of posthumous offerings for some royal relatives, including Senge Namgyal wife's brother. Second, Seng ge rNam rgyal, who did not have much faith in the dGe lugs pas in his later life,[60] made a large posthumous offering to the great dGe lugs pa Lama, Pan chen Chos kyi rGyal mtshan (1570-1662 C.E.).[61] Therefore, we can surmise Senge Namgyal made the offering according to his mother's own wish.

Although it is not mentioned anywhere that the Balti Princess built a mosque in Basgo, if she built three mosques at other places in Ladakh, she should surely have built one in Basgo where she spent nearly her entire life. So it is conceivable that the building of the small Maitreya temple was originally built as a mosque and then turned into the Maitreya temple when the Balti princess later embraced Buddhism.[62] Then it must been completed by the early beginning of the 17th century. The mural paintings in this small temple and those of the upper old Maitreya temple are stylishly quite similar, especially the portraits of Tsong kha pa, although the countenance and the hat of the Tsongkhapa portrait in the small Maitreya temple are much

---

59. Nagarjuna, Suhrllekha(verse. 29) states the eight worldly concepts:
O knower of the world, the eight worldly concepts — gain, loss; happiness, unhappiness; sweet words, harsh words; praise, and blame — should be regarded equally as not worthy of your mind.

60. Kun dga' Lhun grub, F 42b

61. Francke, pp. 30, 108, and Rabgyas, p. 182.

62. In 1974/75, Snellgrove and Skorupski found an inscription which informs that it was dedicated by bsKal bzang sGrol ma on the 25th day of the 2nd month of the Water Horse year (= C E. 1642). This summer, 1994, we looked for this inscription, but could not find it. Instead we found a new inscription about donations and voluntary works for a renovation done ten or fifteen years ago. Unfortunately, they probably destroyed the ancient inscription and wrote a new one over it.

distorted at a later time by an unskillful repairer. Thus, we can guess that both the mural paintings of the biggest and the smallest temples were done under the guidence of the same person or by different persons in the same tradition.

Snellgrove and Skorupski mistakenly mentioned that the Balti princess and bsKal bzang sGrol ma are same person. This is incorrect. The Balti princess was the mother of Senge Namgyal while bsKal bzang sGrol ma was his wife.

The Third Maitreya Image

In the year of Water Dog (1622 C.E.) Lama Stag tshang ras pa returned to Basgo from central Tibet. Senge rNam rgyal and his royal family consulted to restart the late King Jam dbYang rNam rgyal's project of constructing of Maitreya. The image is called either gSer zangs or gSer sbyangs, made of gold and copper or made of purifying gold, respectively. King 'Jam dbyang rNam rgyal probably had been able to finish the image only in copper, its gold work was interrupted by the war with the Balti Muslims. The gilding process and the work were recommenced in the Water Dog year, 1622 C.E. The Princess Khatun offered all the jewels that make up the ornaments on the crown, necklaces, and bracelets of the image.[63] This very radiant image of Maitreya, the deity of loving kindness, and its beautiful surroundings were completed in 1623, and the Venerable Yogi sTag tshang made the consecration of the image and its temple.[64]

At that time the two princes were competing for the royal throne. The Lama Stag tshang raspa made the two princes compromise: the younger prince, Nor bu rNam rgyal, would become the king of Ladakh, and the older prince, Seng ge rNam rgyal, would practice Dharma and live in the monastery of Wanle. Both princes agreed, but later, due to the advice of cunning ministers, prince Norbu rNam rgyal died[65] and prince Seng ge rNam rgyal began to reign in the year of the Wood Mouse (1624 C.E.).[66]

Snellgrove and Skorupski describe the ruined castle and the temples as follows:

---

63. Many of these jewels were taken to Jammu during the Dogra invasion of Ladakh,Yoseb, p. 594.
64. Kun dg' Lhun grub. f. 30b.
65. Ibid. f. 31a.
66. Ibid. f. 30a.

"This is certainly the most impressive of Ladakhi citadels despite its ruined state. In earlier times it must have been also well-nigh impregnable, as was illustrated by the three-year siege that it withstood in the late 17th century (see p.870). .. It is first mentioned in the Ladakhi Chronicles in the early 15th century as the capital of Grags pa 'bum, whose descendants were to become the Namgyal Dynasty of Ladakh (p. 82). Here it is known by its Tibetan name of *Rab brtan lha rtse, 'Divine Peak of Great Stability'*.

Amidst the ruins of the fort there are two large temples and adjoining one of them is a small shrine. They all contain images of Maitreya in due proportion to their size. The most beautiful one is the higher one, which is known as the Chamba Lhakhang (Maitreya Temple) and which was built by Tshe-wang Namgyal, son of [sic] Tashi Namgyal, about the middle of the 16th century ... This is probably the only temple in Ladakh to have survived with some of its murals intact from the 16th century. Thus after Alchi, which is exceptional ... the Basgo Maitreya Temple is likely to be the oldest available to us for comparative study."

In conclusion I would like to ask the people of Ladakh, and especially the authorities of Hemis monastery, who own these temples, to continue to strive to rescue these beautiful images and paintings from further deterioration by the strong wind, rain, and snow. These historic and irreplaceable monuments are national treasures not only of Ladakh, but also of India, as well as ancient art treasures of world class stature. They are now in a state of ruin and near-destruction. Although the people of Basgo have volunteered their labor and money, there is not much that such poor farmers can do without help.

In 1982 my friend, Maurice Lowe, Professor of Art at the University of Pennsylvania in Philadelphia, offered a generous contribution to save these ancient monuments. This enabled the building of a passage in the steep cliff, for otherwise it would remain difficult to reach even the main hall of the Maitreya Temple. Later I myself made a small contribution to secure the roof of the temple. Last year Professor Lowe again sent a contribution to the Basgo Welfare Committee to try to save the Bya rgya mchod rten erected by Seng ge rNam rgyal.[67] Also this year Mrs. Hideko Wayman, Miss Keiko Nakayama and Drs. Philip and Natalie Hauptman sent their help to the committee to preserve the Maitreya temples and other ancient monumental stupas in Basgo. It is difficult to imagine how, without outside help, the Basgo people can succeed in rescuing and preserving these exquisite ancient monuments.

---

67. Rabgyas. p. 181.

Appendix I

Some Events related to Seng ge rNam rgyal from the Life of Ngag.dbang rGya. mtsho

In the Iron Horse year of the 11th Rab 'byung Era (1630) Venerable Yogi sTag tshang founded He mi Monastery. In the same year, there was a revolution in Chu mu rti, which brought the nomadic state of Gu ge into Seng ge rNam rgyal's kingdom.[68]

In the Water Monkey year of the eleventh Rab 'byung Era (1632) the great Venerable Yogi sTag tshang, at the age of fifty-nine, wanted to return to Central Tibet; but Seng ge rNam rgyal insisted that he remain in Ladakh.

In the Water Horse year of the eleventh Rab 'byung Era (1642), Seng ge rNam rgyal led his troops to Western Tibet. Fulfilling his mission successfully, he returned to Ladakh and halted at Wan le, where Venerable Yogi sTag tshang was residing. Seng ge rNam rgyal received some Dharma teaching and blessings from his Lama. Then he passed away to the divine state; and his retinue secretly brought back his body to the great royal castle at Leh.[69]

In the Iron Tiger year of the eleventh Rab 'byung Era (1650), King bDe ldan rNam rgyal, his wife, and a small retinue visited the Venerable Yogi sTag tshang to ask him to name their infant. The Lama named their son Prince bDe legs rNam rgyal.[70] After a few days, Queen sKal bzang sGrol ma, wife of Seng ge rNam rGyal, visited the Venerable Yogi sTag tshang to pay homage to the Lama before leaving for the Mountain of Snow. "This year some obstacle to your life will arise, do not go to any distant place. It is better to stay at He mi or Ma gro," the Lama said to her. But the Queen did not obey his advice and went through dByi gu, Nyo ma, and Wan le to Zangskar. The Lama told his disciples, "I have had a bad dream. This year she will die." And indeed she did, passing away at Zangla. Her body was cremated at the royal palace of Shel dkar.[71]

Appendix II

An Event in the Life of Nono bSod nams, hero of Basgo

The Basgo Fort was surrounded in vain by the Mongols and the Tibetan troops of dGa' ldan Tshe dbang between 1680 and 1684.[72]

The Dogra invasion (1834) destroyed all the manuscripts and many other religious objects of Basgo's temples. The invaders gathered all the precious things, including the jewels on the gilded Maitreya image, loaded them onto many horses and

---

68. Kun dga' Lhun grub, F. 33a.
69. Ibid. F. 40a.
70. Ibid. F. 48a.
71. Ibid. F. 48b.
72. Krang dbyi sun, p. 3270 and Yoseb, p. 433.

sent them to Jammu. They also took books to cover the ceilings of the Kila fort at Leh.[73]

Nono bSod nams was a hero among the Basgo people. (A legend of the Tashilunpo monastery states that the Panchen Lama said to Nono bSod nam: "If you prevent the invasion, I will pray to ensure that you are reborn in Shambhala." This message was accompanied by a painting of Shambhala.)

Nono bSod nams, looking for a chance for revenge, obeyed the Dogra general, Zorawar Singh, but inwardly hated him. When Nono bSod nams got his chance, he did not waste time putting Zorawar Singh on the road to face the Five Elements. He was captured by later Tibetan armies and taken to Tibet. Of course, this story was kept secret from the Dogra invaders for many reasons, but the fact was known by the high Tibetan officials and was rumored among the monks of Tashilhunpo monastery.

I also heard other legends about Nono bSod nams and Zorawar from many elderly monks of Tashilhunpo during the 1950s. It is hard to believe them, but there is some evidence. Nono bSod nams became cherished (spyan gsal) in the eyes of the Pan chen bsTan pa'i nyi ma (1781—1888) who constructed the Shagaran polo ground for Nono bSod nams and planted apple trees at Kun skyob gling, the summer residence of the Panchen Lama, in order to dispel Nono's nostalgia for his homeland.

Furthermore, the Tibetans considered Nono bSod nams a hero and did not even confiscate his gun and sword. He kept them with him until his death. After he died his gun and sword went to his countrymen's college at Tashilunpo, dPe thub Khams tshan, as did his other wealth. The college kept the weapons in the temple of the Protector Deity (mGon khang) in memory of Nono bSod nams for more than 150 years, until 1960. I have seen the gun and the sword: the gun was called *topidar* in Ladakhi, *rang 'bar* (self-igniting) in Tibetan; in the sword's handle there was small gold ball which moved up and down when the sword moved.

Historians of Ladakh have introduced Nono bSod nams to the reader in different ways. Cunningham recognized him as the brother of Tshe dbang Rab brtan, the Kalon of Basgo. Francke identified him as "the Ladakhi (chieftain) Nono Bsod nams," not related to the Kalon of Basgo; bSod namsTshe brtan's *Account of the Dogra Wars*[74] does not mention Nono bSod nams, but does mention "the astrologer[75] Tshe dbang Rab brtan, the chief sGo lam khan of Chu shod, the minister of Basgo". bSod namsTshe brtan's text does not clearly recognize him as the minister of Leh or of Basgo due to lack of precise punctuation. Several pages below, he mentions "ga ga bSod nams from Basgo." In short, in his history book, it is not clear whether Nono bSod nams and the minister of Basgo were one and the same person or not. bKra shis Rab rgyas unequivocally recognizes Nono6 bSod nams as the minister of Basgo, but who then was Tshe dbang Rab brtan? There is no word about Tshe dbang Rab brtan in the history book of bKra shis Rab rgyas, but he was recognized as the minister of Basgo by Cunningham and Francke.

Selected Bibliography

BSOD NAMS TSHE BRTAN YOSEB DGE RGAN, *La dags rgyal rabs 'chi med gter*, New Delhi, Sterling, 1976.

CUNNINGHAM, ALEXANDER, *LADAK, Physical, Statistical & Historical,* 1853, reprint New Delhi, Sagar Publication, 1970.

DKON MCHOG BSOD NAMS, YONG 'DZIN, *La dags dgon pa rnams kyi lo rgyus padmo'i*

73. Yoseb, p. 594.
74. It is included in Francke, Vol. II, p 255.
75. I think that the spelling of *dpon po*, chief, was mistaken for *dbon po*, astrologer.

phreng ba, 1978.

FRANCKE, A. H. *Antiquities of Indian Tibet,* Volumes I and II, Calcutta Suprintendent Government Printing India. 1914 and 1926 respectively.

HOWARD, N.F., 1989 "The Development of the Fortresses of Ladakh *c.950 to 1650*", *East and West*, 39, 217-288. Inst. medio ed estremo oriente. Rome.

KRANG DBYI SUN, *Bod rgya tshig mdzod chen mo, Tibetan Chinese Dictionary*. Mi rigs dpe skrun khang, 1984.

KUN DGA' LHUN GRUB, *rNal 'byor gyi dbang chug odiyana pa ngag dbang rgya mtsho'i rnam thar legs bris vaidurya dkar po'i rgyud mang*. Hemis or lCe bde block printing.

PETECH, LUCIANO, *The Kingdom of Ladakh*, Rome, M.E.O., 1977.

RABGYAS, TASHI, *Mar yul la dags kyi sngon rabs kun gsal me long*, *History of Ladakh,* Leh, 1984.

SANGS RGYAS MTSHO, SDE SRID, (1652-1705) *The Yellow Vaidurya, the History of dGe lugs pa Monasteries* (*dGa' ldan chos 'byung vaidurya ser po,* composed in 1698), new editon, 1991 Ze ling.

SNELLGROVE, DAVID and SKORUPSKI, TADEUSZ, *The Cultural Heritage of Ladakh,* Boulder, Prajña Press, 1977.

THUB BSTAN DPAL LDAN SA PHUD PA. *Mang yul skyes chen kun gyi rnam thar*, Leh, 1988.

THUB BSTAN DPAL LDAN SA PHUD, *Chags rabs kun gsal me long*, Leh 1976.

YA HAN KRANG, *Dalai lama's rnam thar* (*The Biographies of the Dalai Lamas*), Zi ling, 1986

YE SHES RTE MO, *rJe thams cad mkhyen pa dGe 'dun grub pa dpal bzang po'i rnam thar ngo mtshar nor bui' 'phreng ba*, composed in 1486, Tashi lhunpo edition.

IMPACT OF TOURISM ON THE ECOLOGY OF THE LADAKH HIMALAYAS

Prem Singh Jina.
Lecturer in Economics,
Central Institute of Buddhist Studies,
Choglamsar, Leh.

Ladakh is exposed to accelerating environmental changes. Tourism which is a recent occurrence in Ladakh, has now recorded 3,000 per cent growth during the past eighteen years, with the result that the ecological set-up of Ladakh region is greatly affected. No doubt tourism has brought improvement of living standards of local inhabitants, provides jobs and employment of all kinds at all levels and for every conceivable form of regional development (Verma, 1989). Therefore, in this context the development of tourism has now become a need of the day.

The increase of the tourist industry, though it is supporting the economy of the Ladakh region, also results in indiscriminate converting of cultivated land of Leh and Kargil towns to Hotels, Guest Houses and Government buildings. Villages in the vicinity of these towns do not have enough land for grazing animals.

Farmers of these villagers are becoming more and more money minded, using chemical fertilizer in excessive quantity, causing the land to become dry and more hard.

The traditional practices which were once prevalent to protect their crops from insects or pests such as Sadak-don-dol, Sadak-tuk-chos etc., are now hardly seen in these villages. Instead villagers of these areas are now using pesticides like Dithen-Z, which is no doubt killing the harmful pests. But sometimes the excess use of such kinds of pesticides is harmful to the other animals and insects who are helpful for the crop production. Thus, decreasing the population of one harmful pest ultimately causes the increase of the population of new pests and diseases in crops as well as among other living beings.

Increasing water-borne disease among human beings and stomach disease among livestock are quite common in Leh, because the water used by them is no more free from pollution. Air pollution caused by motor vehicles, aircraft, road transportation, coal-fuel, oil, natural gas, wood-fuel etc. is now gradually emerging as a new problem before locals, resulting in eye and throat problems. To meet the tourists' demands, a large amount of food stuff is imported to Leh by Kashmiri merchants. These vegetables and semi-ripe fruits bring infections to Leh and its surroundings. During the tourists season diarrhoea is now becoming a common feature among the children in the Leh area, because of tourists and labourers, especially Nepalis and Biharis, brought in by tourism, who are mostly engaged in construction works in Ladakh.

In addition to the problems of air and water pollution, a new kind of disturbance, noise pollution, has come into prominence specially in Leh and other tourist centres due to frequent travel and population growth. Variety of sounds produced by vehicles, machines, radio and television at these centres intensify the noise pollution.

In the past couple of years, trekking and mountaineering has become popular among tourists. Every year trekkers and climbers climb on mountains (Jina 1986), thus, polluting the environment in the following ways:

1. Throwing all wastes such as plastic bags, tins, water bottles along tracks.
2. Polluting water near the camping sites.
3 Using shrubs for fuel.
4 Disturbing wild animals.
5. Catching butterflies and other helpful living beings.
6. Trampling the vegetation and soils.

Hence, many species like snow leopard, marmot and black necked crane are becoming rare; varieties of butterfly and plants along the treks are becoming extinct. This degradation of vegetation leads to an acceleration of erosion.

Other changes in the ecology are due to the increase of the human population in the recent decades, including the presence of the army. Population increase and increase in agriculture have modified the climate of Ladakh. Three days of unprecedently continuous rain fell in September 1988. Exceptionally heavy snow fell on 14th December, 1986, and around 450 vehicles were snowbound, with the result that around 50 dead bodies were recovered; not only this but a number of person suffered from snow or frost bite (Jina 1990). Recently the unexpected snow fall during 2nd week of May and heavy rain fall on 12th to 15th July 1993 resulted in around five rooms of Central Institute of Buddhist Studies collapsing. These are a few examples which show the reactions of the environment in Ladakh.

The need for the conservation of resources is in fact a problem of human ecology. In its present form, therefore, an understanding of the emergence of many ecological and environmental problems of the present day may be associated with such dynamic processes as population growth, changes in technology, or the changing social and political circumstances. In Ladakh, the increase in population from 85,551 in 1961 to 163,710 (Jina 1993) has largely been due to changing traditional system viz. the ban against polyandry, providing modern education for children instead of monastic education, and a decrease in donating one son or daughter to their respective monasteries.

Therefore, keeping to the above facts, if only a few groups of tourists are occasionally passing through so that the intervals betwen them are longer, their impact will be little and incidental on the ecological set-up of Ladakh Himalayas.

Careful studies are needed of the impact of tourism. If tourism greatly increases it will result in ecological disturbances in Ladakh. In this case local people will be more and more busy during tourists season. They will have much less time to stay with their families and parents in villages. Ultimately cultural erosion will be serious. Similarly road and transportation changes will change the infrastructure. New urban areas will come into existence. More and more hotels, guest houses, shops and restaurants will meet the tourists' demands. Migration of rural youths towards cities will take place. Thus population pressure in and around urban areas will increase. Such activities will generally upset the ecological balance.

References

JINA, PREM SINGH 1986 *Eco-Environment study of tourist industry of Ladakh*. Paper presented to All India Seminar, Centre for Central Asian Studies, Kashmir University, Srinagar.

——— 1990 "Pasture ecology of Leh, Ladakh", pp.171-180 in L.ICKE-SCHWALBE & G.MEIER (eds) 1990 *Wissenschaftsgesichte und gegenwärtige Forschungen in Nordwest-indien* (Proc. 3rd Coll. Ladakh). Dresden Museum of Ethnology.

——— 1990 *Environmental Stress of Tourism on Ladakh Himalayas*, unpublished report.

VERMA, S.S. 1989 "Tourism, Environment and Remote sensing". In: S.C. Singh (ed.), *Impact of tourism on Mountain environment*. Res. India Pub., Meerut, p.34.

WILLIAM MOORCROFT'S COMMERCIAL PILGRIMAGE TO MANASA SAROWARA IN 1812

P.J.Marczell
24/b rue Lamartine, CH-1203 Genève,
SWITZERLAND

Summary

Disguised as a *gosain* (pedlar), William Moorcroft (1767-1825) made an unauthorised pilgrimage to Mânasa Sarôwara in 1812 in order to explore its hydrography, appraise and start tapping the economic and commercial potentials of its region, reconnoitre the socio-economic and political conditions there and assess the military strength of its rulers. It was during this successful pioneering trip to the Undes (Nari) that he developed his style of travel and Proconsul-like approach to the Himalayas, Central Asia and their peoples and also affirmed the anti-Russian bias of his political outlook. The paper attempts to make up for the neglect of this journey in H.H. Wilson's account of the travels of Moorcroft and Trebeck published in 1841. It highlights the especial interest which the East India Company's Superintendent of the Bengal stud and veterinary surgeon took in *pashmina* and Russian commercial penetration.

I shall deal with Moorcroft's (1767-1825) secret trip to Tibet in 1812. I shall describe its setting, define its nature, follow its log-book, assess its results and point out its consequences. The subject is of interest for several reasons.

It was Moorcroft who commissioned Csoma de Körös to study Tibetan, when he met in Ladakh the Hungarian scholar who was pulling back from Leh to Srinagar after his failure to cross the Karakoram. Their contract of March 24th, 1823, provided for the extension of the Tibetan project to Tangut, [as Bethlenfalvy (1976) reported it] thus preparing a strike-out to Central Asia, the original destination of the Siculo-Hungarian hiker who stuck to it to the very end of his life. This was how his search for the supposedly Asiatic "cradle" of his people got diverted to the language and canonical texts of the Himalayan Buddhists.

The character and endeavour of the providential and fatal sponsor who induced this distraction are worth publicizing. They are revealed for the first time in the expedition and the ensuing official correspondence which I want to highlight. The enterprise let free Moorcroft's nomadic drive and for the leader and two of his most valuable companions (considered by Le Calloc'h, 1989, 1991) it became a general rehearsal for the long march to Bokhara of no return; in which the stay in and around Leh from September 24th, 1820, to the last day of the same month, 1822, was just a stage. It typified a remarkable figure of the expanding British colonialism in the Indian subcontinent. His venture reconfirmed his nation's peculiar sensitivity to international affairs which Ralph Fitch had already made manifest in Tudor England. Its commercial stake and hydrographic findings showed the true stature of the entrepreneur who behaved like a Proconsul in the guise of the versatile trading doctor and extremely well paid veterinary surgeon he was. Its pretext was inspired by Indian tradition. Its utilitarian bias contrasts with the remarkably idealistic motivations of Csoma, a pilgrim of another kind.

Moorcroft's position and problems

William Moorcroft had spent three and a half years in India when he set out for Tibet. He was then 45 and felt bored. The East-India Company had appointed him Superintendent of the stud and Veterinary Surgeon at Pusa in all its branches. Against the exceptionally high, tax-free salary of 30,000 Sicca rupees a year[1], he had to supply the local British forces through reproduction and breeding on the spot with cavalry remounts strong enough to carry the 252-lb load of the dragoon and his equipment at speed over great distances in rough country.

Moorcroft was quick to realise that he could not fulfil this task. The Pusa estate on the overpopulated plain of Tirhut comprised 5 000 acres of land, but neither its climate, nor its pasture on the bank of the Burhi Gandak suited the use to which it was put. Most of its stallions lacked the necessary size, form, bone structure and movement. Under the exisiting arrangement with neighbouring farmers, they were seldom put to standard-height mares. Only too often the colts left with the subcontracting breeders suffered from neglect or inferior ones took their place for admission to the stud. It would have been better to meet the annual demand of 800 horses (in

---

1 According to Yule & Burnell (1866) in *Hobson Jobson* a Sicca rupee was a coin containing 176.13 grs. of pure silver, replaced in 1835 by the 'company's Rupee', worth only 15/16ths as much. In 1779 about SRs 10 were equivalent in value to one pound sterling, making Moorcroft's salary about £3,000. The high level of this is shown by comparison with Csoma de Kôrös's monthly pay of SRs 100 + lodging as librarian to the ASB, and with his receipt of SRs 300 from Moorcroft for compiling a Tibetan Dictionary, Grammar and Anthology in about one year in Ladakh-Zangskar. The contemporary value of the Kacha [=inferior] rupee is not clear. In modern usage Sicca rupee refers to the coin, and Kacha rupee to paper notes.

peacetime) through purchases in the big traditional markets, but these lay outside the British confines.

Moorcroft started to approach them as early as 1811 when he went to Hajipur (near Patna), visiting Butwal on Gurkha terriroty, and pushing forward to Hardwar close to the mountains of Kumaon. In the first quarter of 1812, he returned to the annual fair of Hardwar better prepared with fresh commercial information. As his inquiries confirmed the decline of trade in big Turki and Turkoman remounts in Rajasthan, Jungle Lakhi and Punjab, he placed his hopes north of the Himalayas and also in supplies from Bokhara. He hired a young Muslim educated in Persian from Delhi, Saiyid (Mir) Izzat-Allah (1790-1826) to cross-check his optimistic assumptions in these directions, reconnoitre the going prices and commercial practices, explore the ways of access and prepare an expedition (if feasible and worth undertaking). This civil servant was a tested interpreter and spy. He set out on April 21st, 1812, and in approximately one and a half years covered Kashmir, Ladakh, the Karakoram, Chinese Turkestan, the Pamir highlands, Transoxiania and returned to report. (The publication of the information which he had gathered in those remote regions, hardly known in Europe, caused a sensation.)

The Tibetan escapade

Having several months at his disposal before the obligation to resume his duties at Pusa, the Superintendent decided to avoid the summer heat by an excursion to the North. The prompting came from his acquaintances in the region who explained to him all the interest of such a venture. The government agent in the area, Sir Edward Colebrook, approved the plan. Moorcroft did not wait for other permission. He requested authorisation from his superiors in a formal letter without caring for the reply (which could be only negative). He also dispensed with official Gurkha consent by crossing *incognito* their territory, choosing the shortest, least obvious and most loosely guarded path. In order to stave off Tibetan suspicion, he opted for the trading pilgrim's disguise and for taking the traditional itinerary of the Indian worshippers to Mount Kailas and to the lake which is associated with it. In case of need, the natives could be bribed to vouch for the good behaviour and *bona fides* of the devout travellers. Presents and lucrative business proposals might help obtain the goodwill of the security officials involved. The expenses were defrayed out of Moorcroft's personal income.

The company took shape near Chilkia and Ramnagar at a mart clearing the products of the plains for those of the hills. It comprised 45 participants (including the porters). Most of them were armed.

They drove a herd of goats along with them. The only white member, Moorcroft (alias Mayapoori), concealed his true identity by marking his eyes with lamp black, darkening his face and neck with the juice of walnuts and smearing them with the ashes of burnt cowdung. His Afghan retainer, Ghulam Hyder Khan and his two guides (the illegitimate half-caste son of a British infantry officer, Captain Hyder Hearsey [as Hargiri] and an old Kumaoni brahmin, Pandit Harbalam or Harbullubh) could pass unnoticed more easily. Yet the two officers were well known by the Gurkhas on the south-western border.

They loaded spices (nutmeg, cloves, cardamom, black pepper), European broadcloth, coloured glass beads, trinkets from Hardwar, cutlery and scissors and three telescopes. They also secured large provisions of brandy, peppermint essence and sugar. Their bargaining power was enhanced with 2,000 rupees in gold coins.

The caravan set off on the 9th of May, advanced North through Kumaon, passed by Karnprayag at the junction of the Pindar with the Alaknanda River, reached Josimath, then climbed to Tapoban. Edging its way further in the Dauli gorge between summits like Kamet and the two-peaked Nanda Devi, it attained Niti on the 4th of June. During its three-week halt there, it succeeded in negotiating its progress to the top of the pass and beyond and ensured its entry into Tibet at Daba. Moorcroft's healing performances and guns helped achieve this result. Gartok, the administrative centre of western Tibet, was caught sight of on the 17th of July, with its population swollen by the big summer fair. Thanks to the cooperation of the governor (*garpon*), Moorcroft could buy the animals and wool he wanted and left the bulk of them at Tirtapuri. He got to Lake Manasarowar (Mapama; Tso-ma-vang; Tso-rinpoche; etc.) by what came to be called the Ladakh-Lhassa Trade Route, but fever and bad weather prevented him from exploring the full circumference of its shoreline. From the 5th to the 8th of August he and Hearsey (after him) examined the western side and Pandit Harbalam's nephew, Harkh Dev walked round to the southern edge. Instead of extending their discoveries to Rakas Tal (Rawan Rudd; Lankan; Langak-tso; etc.), the twin expanse of water without the sacred connotation of its sister, they turned back to Tirtapuri as quickly as they could to collect the belongings they had left there. They made haste along the Sutlej to Daba, where they were welcomed by the natives like old friends but claimed publicly as impostors by the Tibetan officials in charge. They sold part of their freight, replenished their supply of food and purchased additional quantities of gold dust, turmeric and flocks of goats. They bid farewell to their hosts on the 26th, sticking to the road by which they had come in compliance to Tibetan order. In the vicinity of British territory, however, a Gurkha patrol stopped, disarmed and arrested them. After a custody of 16 days, the party was led to the border without any extortions whatever. Moorcroft could be satisfied: the aims of his expedition were accomplished.

Sven Hedin's view of the expedition

With Hearsey, Moorcroft made an impressive number of scientific and technical observations. He carried back with him a lot of dried plants and flowers, several of which bear his name. He also collected seeds and samples of a wide range of plants. [A 172[2]]. In his view, the Europeans had much to learn in and borrow from Asia, especially if they wanted to give new impetus to the activity of their economies in the wake of the devastating Napoleonic wars.

As we can see today, his expedition to Tibet had two objectives: one geographic, the other economic.

In the sphere of hydrography, it verified and completed the discoveries made by two of its members four years earlier. Encouraged by the Governor of Bengal, Hyder Hearsey and two other officers (Webb and Raper) followed the Ganges to its source at Gangoktri and thereby established that, in contradiction to prevailing belief, the river could not flow from Lake Manasarowar. Their guide, Pandit Harbalam had noticed in 1796 a river which discharged to the West from this body of water and which was considered as the holy spring of the Ganges, the Indus, the Sutlej and the Brahmaputra at the same time. In the third volume of his book *Trans-Himalaya*, Sven Hedin discussed this belief and explained how it was progressively refuted. Moorcroft is given pride of place in this historical overview which presents his account on the mystical lake in the *Asiatic Researches* of 1816 as one of the best pieces of information on the subject. [H 223[1]] The English doctor found the lake completely closed to the West under the effect of drought. In a rainier period, under more propitious circumstances, he would have witnessed a situation more in accordance with traditional Tibetan and Chinese representations. Thus, he would have perceived it with the Racas Tal as two pearls pierced and connected into a set of ornaments by the Sutlej welling forth from the Ganglung Glacier under the name of Tage-tsangpo and following its course as the recognized main tributary of the Indus. However, this relationship was proved only in 1907. [H 233 & 221-22[1]] Suffice it to say that Moorcroft got a good glimpse of the Indus at Gartok and trailed the Sutlej (Langchen-kamba) from

2 My paper relies heavily on three authors, *viz.*, Garry Alder, Sven Hedin and John Irwin — see references. They are acknowledged in the text respectively by A, H and I followed by the number of the page concerned.

Tirtapuri to Kyunglung.

In the same book, Hedin also glorified the place of Moorcroft's feat. He compared it to a fine ring, a turquoise set between two diamonds. Manasarowar or Mânasa Sarôwara, "the most beautiful of lakes created by the soul" (of Brahma / Buddha), 4,570 m above sea level, guarded by the north-westerly, 6,714 m high Kailash (Kang-rinpoche, Gangri) and to the South-South-west by Gurla Mandatta (Naimo, Memo-nami) rising to 7,728 m. Its fresh water is praised by the Skanda Purana for purifying those who drink from it, bathe in it or sprinkle their body with it. The mountains towering over its edge were hailed by Kalidasa in the poem *Maghaduta (The Cloud-Messenger)*. To many, Kailash is identical with the fabulous Mount Meru, the axis of the world. The Hinduists hold that Shiva elected it for his dwelling. The Buddhists regard it as the ideal support for meditation where hosts of Tibetans have achieved *nirvana*, like Yogi Milarepa [as summed up by Dak-Pa (1987)]. A few fancy that the abode of Samvara (*Bde-mchog*), the Tantric divinity is there. By their ritual circumambulation (*parikrama*) of these holy sites (*tirta*), the Hindu and Tibetan pilgrims believe that they have acquired extraordinary merits.

Moorcroft could not walk around the place like them. He did not believe in the role of *gosain* (*gossyne*) which he acted with Captain Hearsey out of sheer expediency (trying even to seduce - without success - the pretty women on their way).

Moorcroft's true design and merit

Accoring to the *Glossary of colloquial Anglo-Indian words and phrases, and of kindred terms, etymological, hystorical, geographical and discursive HOBSON-JOBSON* by Yule & Burnell (1866), the word was derived from the Sanskrit *Goswami* meaning *Lord of Passion* (literally Lord of Cows). It characterises "one who is supposed to have subdued his passions and renounced to the world". It is "applied in various parts of India to different kinds of persons not necessarily celibates, but professing a life of religious mendicity, and including some who dwell together in convents under a superior, and others who engage in trade and hardly pretend to lead a religious life". George Bogle's account of the trade of Tibet depicts them under the latter aspect emphasising that many of them are quite rich. As Markham (1875) pointed it out, they deal in articles of "great value and small bulk" which they sell "without noise or ostentation and often by paths unfrequented by other merchants". (Bogle had had plenty of opportunity to observe this practice during his mission to the Tashi Lama from 1774 to 1775 when he had availed of the services of *gosain*

Purungir who also accompanied the Panchen Lama to Peking in 1779-80 and reported his death there in 1780. He took part in the Embassy of Captain Samuel Turner to the new Rimpoche of Sigatse in 1783 and acted as the representative of the Bengal Presidency in Tibet until about 1785.)

Moorcroft's trip to Mânasa Sarôwara ended in implicit blasphemy, as it denied the existence of a complex of lion, elephant, peacock and horse-shaped rocks gushing into the human world the Indus, the Sutlej, the Karmali and the Brahmaputra. Its economic stake outclassed the usual calculations of a normal *gosain*. It boiled down to breaking to British benefit the monopoly of the so-called cashmere wool shared among Tibet, Ladakh and Kashmir. The annual turnover of this restricted trade was estimated at more than 2 million Sicca rupees[1]. The merchandise consisted of the fine hair of the breed named today the Central Asian Down. The fibres of the highest value were combed from the undercoat of ventral areas. This fine wool known as *pashmina* (average diameter not exceeding 15 microns) were processed into shawls by Kashmiri handicraft. They found lucrative outlets all over Asia. Their expensive, ostentatious vogue spread mainly among men and hit Europe around 1767. Society women were quick to favour the soft, light, sensuous touch of the new warm fabrics which enabled them to replace their former clumsy overcoats by elegant yarns revealing their shapes to best effect. The fad reached its climax in the wake of Napoleon Bonaparte's invasion of Egypt which gave rise to a wave of enthusiastic orientalism. The fashion lasted until 1870 when it fell victim of its own popularity and collapsed under the weight of cheap imitations.

The British would have liked to divert the flow of the valuable primary product to their Indian possessions. To channel it directly, for instance, through Garwhal and Kumaon, even at the price of liberating these economically promising provinces from Gurkha occupation - as they did over 1814-16, partly under the influence of Moorcroft. They would have preferred, however, to move the large scale breeding of the peculiar *Capra hircus* to Scotland with the help of males imported from Tibet and/or its adjacent regions. Moorcroft worked simultaneously on both solutions with no more luck than predecessors like George Bogle in 1774 and Captain Samuel Turner in 1783 (both trying to implement the instructions of Warren Hastings, Governor General of Bengal). In this attempt, he renewed previous efforts by Sir John Sinclair [I 21-22], the physician John Gilman and Lieutenant-Colonel Robert Colebrook [A 129-30] and eventually shipped to England 25 pairs of shawlwool-goats. However, half of this cargo perished on sea and the remainder died soon after landing. [I 22-23].

Those who strove later to succeed where he failed (like the French Amédée Joubert, professor of Turkish at the Royal Library) did not fare better. According to Mr. James Crowden (1992), an Anglo-Australian group is now tempted by the experience discontinued for one and a half centuries.[3]

Despite all his drive, Moorcroft was unable to add impetus to the agro-industry of his country by organizing the production of genuine *pashmina* on British soil, although he went as far as proposing to bring over from India and settle in Great Britain spinners, weavers and designers of kashmiri patterns. [I 37-39] Instead of relaxing his development effort, he channelled it into a global strategy. He referred to it as the 'Himalayan concern' which implied the expansion of Indian trade based on liberal principles to the remote corners of Central Asia. (Other expatriates also overestimated the potential of these little known areas.) For him it was a vital issue in checking the growing Russian encroachment attested by his partners and noticed by his party at Daba and Gartok. (In particular *ooroo* [Russian] dogs, red leather, blue linen, sword blades ... of Russian origin.) He attached crucial importance to it because he presumed that it was boosted by French cooperation and benefited from Chinese connivance. His suspicion was vindicated much later. In his time his compatriots were well advised to remain friendly with the Russians in Europe and prospects looked too poor for doing good business in Central Asia to fall in with his crusade.

Körösi's destiny

Csoma de Körös had to bear the consequences of this conflict. He was hired by Moorcroft to provide linguistic means for penetrating the states of Tibetan culture and comprehending the population around the Koko Nor. The Hungarian scholar narrowed the scope of this assignment to the elements and structure of a language preserved fossilized in canonical texts of no practical use for colonial purposes. His sponsor lost his credit because of his dare-devil lack of discipline, militant russophobia and commercial imperialism in countries put down for buffers (i.e., left practically to themselves). He disappeared in 1825 before Csoma could meet the requirements of his contract. (There is sufficient testimony witnessing that he died of fever on the 27th of August 1825 at Andkhoi, 160 kms off Balkh, in northern Afghanistan. [A 357, etc.])

The bureaucrats in the colonial administration felt little

3 Successful breeding trials are currently in progress in Scotland. Ed.

inclination to step into his place and made no hurry to do so. Without letting Körösi down altogether, they left him in a precarious situation which hardly improved to the very end. Its amelioration, with the tenure of librarian at the Asiatic Society of Bengal, did not last more than three years (from May 1838 to May 1841). Hiding his sense of exposure to ridicule for the poses of a Siculo-Hungarian obsessed by the rather absurd search for his ethnic forefathers, the Transylvanian apparently did nothing to make things easier for himself. It is singular that the Hungarians honour him as a prominent cultural hero.

Acknowledgements

Herewith I should like to express my sincere thanks to the authorities of the National Archives of India for their help in my work. I am also most grateful to Dr. Erzsébet Tóth, archivist in the Oriental Collection of the Hungarian Academy of Sciences, for having photocopied and brought to me in Rome Moorcroft's description of his "Journey to Lake Manasarowara in Undes" published in the *Asiatic Researches* in 1816. My colleague and friend, Mr. Jason Spencer-Cook was kind enough to read my draft and pointed out the grammatical and spelling errors in it. My sincere thanks are also extended to him.

References

ALDER, G. 1985 *Beyond Bokhara*. Century, London.

BETHLENFALVY, G. 1976 "Alexander Csoma de Körös in Ladakh". In LIGETI, L.(ed.). *Proceedings of the Csoma de Körös Memorial Symposium*. 1978 Akadémiai Kiadó, Budapest, 10-11 etc. (7 - 26).

LE CALLOC'H, B. Oct. 1989a & April 1991b "Mir Izzet Ullah, voyageur cachemirien; Ghulam Hyder Khan soldat-voyageur afghan." *Institut National des Langues et Civilisations Orientales - Bulletin de l'Association des Anciens Elèves*, 23-33 & 29-42.

CROWDEN, J. Personal communication, 5th Colloquium on Ladakh, SOAS, London. 1st and 2nd of June, 1992. It confirmed the information given A 171.

DAK-PA, N. 1987 "Les pèlerinages bouddhiques en Tibet". In CHÉLINI, J. & BRANTHOMME, H. (ed.) 1987 *Histoire des pèlerinages non chrétiens*. Hachette, Paris, 275 (etc.).

HEDIN, SVEN (reprint) 1991 *Trans-Himalaya*. SBW. Vols. II-III; New Delhi.

IRWIN, J 1973 *The Kashmir Shawl*. H.M.S.O., London.

MARKHAM, C. R. 1876 (signed 1875) *Narratives of the Mission of George Bogle to Tibet and of the Journey of Thomas Manning to Lhasa*. 1989 Cosmo Ed., New Delhi, etc., 125.

YULE, H. & BURNELL, A.C. 1866. *Hobson-Jobson*. 1990 Bengal Chamber of Commerce Ed., Calcutta, etc., 389.

APPENDIX

Moorcroft's Self-justification, Politico-economic Assessment and Military Outlook

As attested by the records kept in the National Archives of India in New Delhi for 1812-13, the Foreign Department, Political Branch, filed three documents pertaining to the escapade discussed. They were entered under the name of William Moorcroft in the class of "Persons not in the Service". The first (N. 29) was a 40-page memorandum addressed by the veterinary from "Neetee in Boothunt" to J. Adam, Secretary to Government in Political Department, on September 7th, 1812. The second (N. 53) and third (N. 63) consisted of an exchange of correspondence between John Monckton, Persian Secretary to Government, and William Moorcroft, bearing on charges by "The Rajah of Nipaul" of having maltreated local government officers while returning to British India through the raja's "dominions".

Monckton's letter signed on March 5th, 1813, was remarkably accomodating. It referred repeatedly to the direction of the Governor General in Council when asking for "an explanation of any transactions to which you may suppose the Rajah's letter to refer", "for the purpose of framing a reply", and stressed that his Lordship gave no credit to the accusation and had "little hesitation in ascribing it to the misrepresentations of the Rajah's officers who were anxious to justify their own proceedings".

The addressee did not fail to describe at length these "proceedings" to his advantage from "Hajeepoor" on March 15, 1813, only ten days after he had been summoned to do so from Fort William (Calcutta). To start with, he denied energetically the representation of the raja of Nepal "That on my return from the Oondes, and when in persuance of the orders of the Gorkeah Government certain Chokeedars required me to produce my Passport, I beat them in an unwarrantable manner, and prepared to give them Battle, in consequence of which they seized upon my person and confined me". Then he went on giving full details on two attempts to provoke him to an attack: two insults to which he reacted by displaying his readiness to defend himself and his party. He fired and recharged his gun as a matter of routine every morning. Nearly <u>two hundred soldiers</u> could not "be put into bodily fear by <u>two persons</u> very indifferently armed, attended by a few servants, of whom the greater part were not armed at all", and even less "feel alarmed at one person loading a Gun and this individual not of the Military profession". The servants were "expressly enjoined ... not to leave the line of road; not to take the most trifling article of any kind without paying it; not to give the slightest cause of offence; and for the better insuring this point they were forbidden to enter into conversation with any persons they might meet". The "Gorkeah" Government did not exercise effective control over the Oondes: in the hills under its nominal authority, especially towards the most Northern range, it stationed no regular guards and had "not the power of defending the weak farmers against the attacks of the strong ones". "Many people both of the borders and far in the Southern portion of the Mountains ... going into Bhote" carried no passports. It took two months to intercept Moorcroft and his men by "Sepahis drawn [from various sites] for the express purpose of interrupting our return to the Company's Provinces" after the intrusion had been reported by an authorised spy.

This protest against a "Slanderous Aspersion" demonstrates what in French may be called "la cocasserie de l'incident" (drollery of the affair). It was natural enough that the Gurkha overlords prove their sovereignty over Kumaon and Garhwal by subduing an arrogant, politically critical armed band traversing these provinces twice without their permission. The more so the more their authority was flouted there, as by Moorcroft.

In contrast to this rather extravagant, "hair-splitting" pleading not guilty, the report from Niti is a major piece of commercial, political and military intelligence. From the observations made during a trek, information through conversations and knowledge of the contemporary balance of power in Europe, it draws far-reaching conclusions and warns of the threat of war for which it spells out the causes and defines the logistic constraints. It is quite straightforward in its anti-Russian stand, as it opens by the statement: "a trade is at this moment carrying on by Russians in the neighbourhood of the Honble Company's possessions immediately and highly prejudicial to the Company's commercial interests, and which, if not timely counteracted, will probably lead to events that may disturb the tranquillity and endanger the safety of the Company's Provinces contiguous to the northwestern and northern frontier of British India, provided the war fare now existing in Europe be prolonged under the present alliances".

The trade in question covered "Chinese Tatary", "Latakh", "Cashmeer" and spread over to "Punjab" and "Hindoostan". It involved horses and a wide range of merchandise like textile materials and leather, swords and telescopes, beads, large mirrors and glasses paid in rupees or exchanged against fine muslins, woollen shawls, sugar, grain and other items. They included French cloth labelled

"Drap très fin", probably from Abbeville (of which Moorcroft dispatched a sample). They were brough to the "Himachul" massif of mountains by "Ooroos [Russians] under the garb and character of Moosulmans" and followed by persons who looked more like political emissaries and their Armenian associates than real merchants. Despite the disadvantage of long overland transportation across high mountains, the subsidized goods imported from the North were selling very well compared to superior, initially low-cost, moderately marked-up products of British make which were probably priced out of the local markets by greedy middlemen. The supply of shawls from Kashmir seemed to contain low-quality specialities intended expressly for the Russians - an indication of high volumes flowing through well-established channels - should we comment today.

The French woollens "Drap très fin" provided a clue. "In whatever manner the extension of the Russian trade in the Countries just mentioned may have been produced its continuance, whether stationary, or progressive, will interfere with the course of British Commerce, and by giving to the Russians and French an acquaintance with the state of the tract behind the Himachul afford them facilities for attempting the invasion of India which they have not enjoyed heretofore." In fact, it could be feared that Buonaparte lured Tsar Alexander (however reluctant) into an alliance, by promising him the "plunder of India and the addition of its immence territory to the Russian Empire". "Experience ... must have abundantly proved to the Statesmen of Russia that the strength of their Empire is not yet sufficiently consolidated to give it the preponderating influence in the politics of Europe they were formerly willing to impute to it, the reflection may lead to the idea of its aggrandizement as an Asiatic Power." Buonaparte, who sought "to improve the Commerce of France and to depress that of Britain" but was "baffled in his views of wresting the sovereignty of the Ocean from Great Britain or of distressing her Commerce upon that element by direct means", may have ordered the opening of a new, Indian "line of Commercial Speculation for enterprising adventurers in the continental part of Europe." Should he "once be acquainted with the fact of the Russian Merchants travelling amongst the Nations at the back of the Indian Caucasus, the resources of these countries appropriable to his use and the defenceless condition of these hills, he would instantly abandon all idea of crossing the Indus except by fording its stream in some part either of Independent or of Chinese Tatary, an operation of great facility, nor would the passage of the Sutleej be more difficult in the same Country."

British India prepared for attacks from the South or West, not from the North. She presumed "the Tatars" fit to act as a buffer and "the Gorkalees have been thought competent to repel any attempt at invasion they might make." However, the military force of the former appeared "truly despicable ". "And all resistance on the part of the Gorkalees to an European Army proceeding from this quarter would be as transient as unavailing." A company of one thousand French and Russian soldiers could subdue these peoples and encroach on the territories belonging to the East-India Co. They could easily outflank the British if thrusting forth through Yarkand if they secured the cooperation of "the Chief of Punjab" for traversing his country, marched East and attacked on that side. The sparse nomadic population scattering from Yarkand to Kashmir had "no communication except by mere chance with any of the inhabitants of Hindoostan". The Raja in Lahore debarred Englishmen from visiting his country and had lately enlisted one Russian and two Armenians for disciplining his infantry. So the British Resident on the Sutlej could not know what was happening in these inhospitable areas. "It is to be presumed that arrangements would be made previously to the actual invasion with the principal Chiefs of the Tatar Hordes but, if these should not have been effected, the imposing presence of an European Army and the promise of a Share in the spoil of Hindoostan would ensure their co-operation." Ranjit Singh might be tempted to take advantage of French and Russian forces dividing the attention of the British Army and attack on several fronts: beside entering Hindustan from Kashmir, send many columns to "defile by the foot of the Mountains towards the eastern part of the British possessions"... Given his vested interest in the trade in shawl-wool and in French and Russian commodities, the "Rajah of Latakh" was likely to be friendly to the cause of the invasion. The natives of Oondes, "the country of wool", were "not only a timid, unmilitary race, but from living in insulated spots by single families ... [were] ... incapable of acting in concert, and of making any combined and effectual opposition." "In fact from the general thinness of population in the vast tract of country between Latakh and Lassa no Enemy is to be apprehended sufficiently powerful to interrupt any operation the invader might think proper to carry on within." "The Grand Lama in the event of his territories being invaded ... [had] ... no military force capable of making face against a Column of five hundred Europeans". He depended on succour from Chinese and Tatar campments too far away to provide adequate protection. "The contact of the power of leathern Cannons, of Bows and Arrows, and of ill-served Matchlocks with European instruments of war would lead to the certain defeat of the Chinese, and afford an experience that might ultimately tend to the subversion of that weak and unwieldy

Empire". "Having reached the northern front of the Himachul an invading Army would find a Climate not unfriendly to the constituion of Europeans, and ... the Oondes would give a supply of animal food and of grain without delay, and of the former in quantity sufficient to suffice for a large consumption during a long time." However, it could not provide other fuel for cooking "than a species of low Tamarisk and two varieties of Furze". Abundant sheep could be used to carry loads "of twenty pounds and upwards walk as fast as a man in a hilly country, and perform daily journeys of six or eight miles without being distressed, requiring no other food than the grass he meets with at the end of his days work." Roughly the same held true of goats also in profusion. Nevertheless, the extremely rugged surface made progress difficult and precluded the transportation of artillery, with the exception of very light pieces. This difficulty might be partly overcome by cutting sloping roads in zig zags and building temporary causeways. The twelve major passes of the region had to be considered also.

The final point of the memorandum: "the paltry force of twelve thousand Gorkeeahs, ill-paid, ill-fed, ill-equipped and ill-disciplined, even if concentrated, would be capable of making little substantial resistance against the well appointed Soldiers of France and Russia, but divided as it now is between the extremities of the long line of subjugated Country running from Nepal to the Jumna, the moment of invasion would be the signal of destruction to the thinly scattered bands in the intermediate Provinces from the resentment of the wretched oppressed mountaineers, who would rise in mass against the instruments of oppression employed by their detested Masters. And the deposed Rajahs, who have now long struggled with poverty, would fly with alacrity to join the Standards of those, who would promise to re-instate them in their former possession the condition of their assisting the invaders in their designs upon Hindoostan".

The document made no allusion whatever to the feasibility of an invasion by British troops, nor did it advise any pre-emptive sweep through the Nepalese Empire to "Tatary". Yet Hearsey (and no doubt also Moorcroft) lent a lot of thought to such prospects and one can safely infer that their analyses helped two years later in triggering the war against Nepal, whose military capabilitry they had grossly underestimated. Moorcroft's assumption of a collusion between Napoleon Bonaparte and Tsar Alexander I was proven wrong in the same year by the former aggressing the latter. Russia's glorious come-back to the political scene in Western Europe in the wake of the defeat and annihilation of three fourths of the "Grande Armée" in local snow and mud further discounted Moorcroft's proposition about a sense of political inferiority and consequent subservience to France in the tsardom. These radical changes in circumstances did not prevent, however, the veterinary's stated apprehensions crystallizing into an *idée fixe*. His criticizers and contradictors in whose opinion he was chasing shadows and causing only constant embarrassment to Government, were vindicated until later in the century when the imperatives of the "great game" became manifest.

NOTES

(i) Besides echoing one of the commemorations of Csoma de Körös and of his initial sponsor in Ladakh, the purpose of the lecture is twofold. First, to provoke a debate on what a pilgrim is; second, to question trading potentials across the Himalayas.

(ii) Next year, in 1994, alpinists in the country where I live will remember the Swiss expedition to Garhwal 55 years earlier whose itinerary overlapped in part with that of Moorcroft's. It had attained its first two objectives: conquering the Dunagiri and exploring the amphitheatre of Kosa with ascension of the Ghori Parbat, but it was carried away by an avalanche before reaching the top of Badrinath (Chaukhamba). Two sherpas hired from Darjeeling lost their lives in that disaster. (ROCH, A. 1947 *Garhwal Himalaya*. Ed. Victor Attinger, Neuchâtel-Paris).

(iii) Much more significant then will be the 100th anniversary of the death of B. H. Hodgson, "the most brilliant young scholar whom the Indian Civil Service has produced..., the masterly diplomatist who held quiet the kingdom of Nepal and the warlike Himalayan races throughout the disasters of the Afghan war..., the munificient Englishman who enriched the museums of Europe with his collections, enlarged the old boundaries of more than one science, and opened up a new field of original research..., the founder of our Buddhist studies". His career started in 1818 in the position of Assistant to George William Traill, the Commissioner of Kumaun. It is striking how closely their reports on local conditions echoed those of Moorcroft. (HUNTER, W. W. *Life of Brian Houghton Hodgson British Resident at the Court of Nepal*. Asian Educational Services Reprint 1991, New Delhi - Madras).

(iv) "A Journey to Lake Manasarowara in Undes, a province of Little Tibet" published in the *Asiatic Researches* in 1816 (12; 375-534) by Henry Colebrook (President of the Asiatic Society of Bengal) is a "curtailed" account of Moorcroft's notes in which the "narrator's own words [were] scrupulously retained". Most probably its actual editor was H.H. Wilson who, in his own words, had "occasionally digested some of Mr. Moorcroft's rambling epistles for the public press of Calcutta, and the use of the Asiatic Society" - hopefully to a lesser extent than he did in *Travels in the Himalayan Provinces of Hindustan and the Panjab from 1819 to 1825 by William Moorcroft and George Trebeck*. John Murray, London, 1841 (lxx, vol. I of its 1979 Reprint. Oxford University Press, Karachi.) It reveals its author the promoter of economic growth through agricultural and industrial innovation and unfettered trade expansion. It deals with geology and topography, botany and zoology, economy and trade, without neglecting humans and their contact. This lively geographic approach occasionally encompasses shrewd ethnography. However, the chronological sequence of the reported data allows few syntheses. Perhaps the most valuable informant was Ahmed Khan Kazalbash, the Kashmirian Vakil (principal agent) of the Raja of

Ladakh. (443-44, etc.)

What is particularly striking is the desolation of Kumaon and Garwhal, as reflected by the Journal even in its 1816 published form. "The upper part of Butan is now suffering much from scarcity of grain, in consequence of the Juaris and Dharmis plundering the Gungaris, or people living on the banks of the Ganges within the hills, who were in the habits of bringing up grain they raised, and that which they procured from below." (496) Said a Malari man:"the tenants had been plundered of their goats by the Juaris; ... unable without these animals to carry on their usual traffic of grain and salt with the Unias, they were deprived of the means of paying their rent to the Gorkiahs, who took the remainder of their cattle, their cooking utensils, the rings out of the noses of their wives and daughters, and seized their children as slaves. Many persons were actually starved to death, and others fled.'" (499) "... if a man by his industry raises a small flock of goats, a Juari or a Darmi plunderer attacks him and carries them off, and we can get no redress from our present masters, nor are we strong enough to resist or make reprisals." Comes the scathing generalisation: "Independently of the direct plunder they obtain, without any other caution than putting a number of men under arms, the Juaris are interested in destroying the trade of the Niti Ghati, in order that they may have a larger proportion of the profitable traffic with the Undes." (500) There are other details of pillage and devastation resulting in quasi- genocide. "The inhabitants of the whole tract between Lata and Niti complain much of the extortions of the Gorkiahs. The poorest man is compelled to pay a poll tax of four kacha rupees[1]. This has caused many villages to be deserted; and the population is now much diminished." (499) Instead of keeping peace and maintaining security, the Gurkhas are depicted then as quickening the pace of regression to savagery and poverty. Later in Kashmir Moorcroft's judgment was not less lenient. This contrasts with his sympathy for the Ladakhi.

(v) Treating patients is mentioned only once in connection with a boy "relieved by tapping for dropsy". (530) Hearsey's manuscript notebook processed by G. Alder, however, provides ample evidence of Moorcroft putting his skill of a physician to good use all along his expedition, even among his Gurkha captors. (A 162, 164-66, 168). He never gave up his medical practice on humans. At Pusa he usually saw patients waiting in long queues on Fridays and did surgery on Saturdays. H.H. Wilson's quoted transcript gives more examples during the "Great Journey", especially with regard to removals of cataracts.

(vi) Ladakh is still involved in the production, processing and trade of Moorcroft's favourite commodity: *pashmina*. In the estimates of Miss Monisha Ahmed (Oxford University), approximately 80 families of nomads in Rupshu derive their livelihood from this sector, each selling annually 10-50 kg of the precious hair for Rs 500-700 per kg. There is additional production in Zanskar. Both sources meet fierce competition from Tibet under Chinese rule. According to Dr. Mohd Din (or Deen, veterinary project officer with the Desert Development Agency in Kargil), about 140 thousand changra goats in the Ladakh region provide 30 metric tons of raw pashmina a year to be processed domestically. (Contribution to 1992 Luxury Fibres. Special Report No.2633 by Philippa Watkins and Alexandra Buxton. The Economic Intelligence Unit, London) [see also Deen in this volume].

(vii) Many participants in the Workshop had hoped for the imminent reopening of the Kailash-Manasarowa route for pilgrims from the South, stressing the archeological, cultural and spiritual interest of the traditional tracks. Their optimism gained support from the advanced negotiations over Himalayan territorial disputes between India and China. A prominent member of the Colloquium Committee, Mr. Sonam Dawa looked forward to exploring in September with Chinese counterparts the advantages of the agreement.

THE CONTRIBUTION OF MORAVIAN MISSIONARIES TO THE SCIENTIFIC EXPLORATION OF LADAKH.

Gudrun Meier
Staatliches Museum für Volkerkunde,
8060 Dresden, Germany

English Summary

In 1722 Moravian emigrants came from Bohemia and Moravia to Herrnhut in Saxony in Germany, where they founded the new Moravian Brotherhood. Their members were farmers and weavers, used to working with their hands. Ten years later, in 1732, the first missionaries went to the Virgin Islands (Caribbean) and Greenland. Later they worked in Suriname, East and South Africa, Australia, also in Sarepta, South Russia, among the Calmuc people who follow the Tibetan religion.

In 1853 two missionaries, Wilhelm Heyde and Eduard Pagell were sent to Mongolia. They had to learn the Mongolian language and some medicine and they had to have a good training in the practical things of life. They wished to go to Mongolia across Russian territory but it was forbidden, so they went by ship around Africa to India, where at last their travels ended in the Himalaya. The first Moravian mission station was in Kyelang. Heyde and Pagell had only Buddhist neighbours, and they had to learn the Tibetan language and the local dialects.They had to work for their existence, to build a house for themselves and rooms for guests and a school; they had to cultivate soil, build canals for irrigation and so on. Exploration then was learning to live in their surroundings.

Looking back in the diaries, letters and reports we find that they also worked on dictionaries, collected words in the local dialects for word-lists and wrote schoolbooks and Christian literature in Tibetan language. Especially after Heinrich August Jaeschke arrived to Kyelang as Head of the station. He was a linguist able to read and write 20 languages, and his work is the basis for most other later Tibetologists. But he also worked in botany, zoology and meteorology, as we can find from papers in the archives; for example ten plants in the Himalaya were named after Heyde and Jaeschke.

The best known missionary as a scientist is August Hermann

Francke. In his time as a member of the Moravian mission in the Himalaya he collected Tibetan literature variants of the Gesar Epic, spring and winter songs, and he translated and published this literature in both English and German. He worked as an archaeologist, studying the history of Western Tibet. All this was his work besides working as a teacher, a priest, a translator for Christian literature and a poet for Christian hymns...

Other missionaries, such as Friedrich Redslob, a good translator of Bible texts, the medical doctor Carl Marx, and Samuel Ribbach, later a member of the Museum für Völkerkunde in Hamburg, brought information from Ladakh to the knowledge of scientists worldwide.

In these days of our conference we will hear many new findings in different disciplines, but the basis for many of them came from knowledge collected by the Moravian missionaries.

HERRNHUTER BEITRÄGE ZUR ERFORSCHUNG LADAKHS

Gudrun Meier
Staatliches Museum für Volkerkunde,
8060 Dresden, Germany

Die Herrnhuter Brüdergemeine - Moravian Church - hat seit ihrer Gründung 1722 Missionsarbeit in fast allen Erdteilen betrieben und daneben zur wissenschaftlichen Erforschung dieser Weltgegenden beigetragen, auch in Ladakh. Die Voraussetzung dafür war eine Gemeinde, deren Mitglieder über eine gute Ausbildung verfügten und der wissenschaftlichen Entwicklung aufgeschlossen gegenüber standen. So sammelte sich schon bald nach der Gründung Herrnhuts ein Kreis bedeutender Gelehrter um den Grafen Zinzendorf, die neben der Theologie auch Naturkunde, Medizin und Sprachwissenschaft betrieben. Waren es 1735 zwanzig Wissenschaftler, die sich unter dem Anspruch einer "herrnhutischen Universität" zusammenfanden, so konnte Zinzendorf 1739 in einem Brief schon von dreißig Gelehrten berichten, die zum "Seminarium" gehörten.

Das Ziel aller Bemühungen war eine gute, allseitige Ausbildung für Theologen. Enge Verbindungen bestanden zur Universität Jena. Von dort kamen Studenten und Professoren nach Herrnhut und in andere Zentren der Brüdergemeine. In Berichten über die ersten Jahrzehnte der Brüderkirche wird betont, daß aus Jena wichtige Mitarbeiter kamen.

In den folgenden Jahren wurde die Arbeit am Pädagogium - einer Schule, die zur Hochschulreife führte - zu einer der Säulen der wissenschaftlichen Arbeit. Außer Griechisch und Latein wurden Philosophie, Geschichte und Kirchengeschichte gelehrt, daneben Jura, Medizin mit den Fächern Anatomie und Gesundheitspflege, allgemeine Naturkunde, insbesondere Botanik betrieben.

In den Wetterauer Anstalten, die nach der Ausweisung Zinzendorfs aus Sachsen in Herrnhaag entstanden, gingen die Bestrebungen dahin, den Lehrstoff auf praktische Fragen in den Missionsgebieten auszurichten. Es gab die Fächer Geographie, Sprachkunde, "Apotheke", die der Gewinnung und Verarbeitung von Heilpflanzen aus der Umgebung diente, Medizin, Mathematik, Baukunst, Mechanik, Zeichnen, Geschichte, Handwerk, Künste. Am Pädagogium in Barby entstand ein" Naturalienkabinett" als Sammlung von Anschauungsmaterial für Schüler und Studenten. Zum Unterricht gehörten immer Exkursionen zur praktischen Übung des Lernstoffes.

Missionare, die seit 1732 in alle Welt gegangen waren, bereicherten das Naturalienkabinett mit Pflanzen, Tieren, Gesteinen, und ethnographischen Gegenständen aus den Missionsgebieten.

Diese Ausbildung war natürlich in erster Linie zur Anwendung in der Missionsarbeit gedacht und Berichte über einzelne Missionsgebiete, z.B. Crantz über Grönland, Oldendorp über die Westindischen Inseln und Zeisberger über die Indianer Nordamerikas enthalten immer auch ausführliche, z.T. erstmalig gesammelte, Angaben zur Geographie, Topographie, Anthropologie, Botanik, Zoologie etc.

Als Heyde (1825-1907) und Pagell (1820-1883) im Jahre 1856 nach Kyelang kamen, kam ihnen diese umfassende Ausbildung sehr zustatten. Die Auswahl des Ortes, der Bau des Missionshauses, die medizinische und pädagogische Arbeit waren die Grundlage für den Beginn der Missionsarbeit.

Für den Lebensunterhalt waren landwirtschaftliche Kenntnisse erforderlich, um unter den Hochgebirgsbedingungen ertragreiche Ernten durch Bewässerungsbodenbau zu erzielen, widerstandsfähige Obstbäume zu pflanzen und Vieh zu halten. Der heutige Kartoffelanbau in Ladakh und im Kulu-Tal beruht auf Versuchen und Erfahrungen von Wilhelm Heyde, der mit wenigen Knollen aus Europa begann die Pflanze hier heimisch zu machen.

Vor Beginn der Arbeit am Missionskrankenhaus in Leh war Heyde auch der "Mediziner", der in Kyelang und den umliegenden Siedlungen und in den Sprechstunden im Missionsgehöft den Patienten nach bestem Wissen half. Dabei spielten die Heilkräuter in seiner Apotheke eine entscheidende Rolle. Da für Zinzendorf der Satz "mens sana in corpore sano" nach den alten Griechen auch für die Christen Geltung haben sollte, wurde die ärztlichen Arbeit sehr geschätzt und in die Missionsarbeit integriert.

Der erste Senior der Missionsstation Kyelang, Heinrich August Jaeschke (1817-1883), und Wilhelm Heyde haben bei ihren botanischen Studien 6 neue Pflanzenarten in Ladakh entdeckt, die botanische Namen mit dem Zusatz Jaeschkeana oder Jaeschkei und Heyde erhielten.

Meteorologische Beobachtungen und Aufzeichnungen über lange Zeiträume gehörten zu den wissenschaftlichen Tätigkeiten, die neben dem unmittelbaren Nutzen für die eigene Arbeit - Planung der Missionsreisen, Termine für die Feldbestellung auch europäischen Forschungsreisenden sehr nützlich und wertvoll waren. Sven Hedin schreibt darüber in seinem Werk "Transhimalaya". Die Daten aus

Kyelang nutzte er zur Ergänzung seiner eigenen Meßreihen aus dem Inneren Tibets. Nach der Gründung der Missionsstation in Leh 1885 wurde auch dort eine meteorologische Station eingerichtet.

Detailierte Aufzeichnungen von den Reisen in Lahoul, nach Spiti, Ladakh und den Indus entlang, enthalten die Tagebücher der Missionare, die in dieser Hinsicht noch wenig ausgewertet sind.

Die wissenschaftliche Arbeit der "Moravians" als Sprachforscher fand schnell internationale Anerkennung und ihre Arbeiten wurden in England, Deutschland und Britisch-Indien veröffentlicht. Neben Wörterbüchern, Gramatiken und Wörtersammlungen der lokalen Dialekte, die die Grundlage für die Erforschung tibetischer Literatur und die erste Bibelübersetzung bildeten, schrieben die Missionare Schulbücher, Lieder und Gebete in Ladakhi und klassischem Tibetisch. Bedeutendster Forscher war neben Heinrich August Jaeschke, der das erste Wörterbuch und die erste Grammatik verfaßte und große Teile der Bibel übersetzte, August Hermann Francke (1870-1930).

Er sammelte verschiedene Formen des Gesar-Epos, die in der Folklore Ladakhs noch lebendig waren, veröffentlichte eine Übersetzung der Frühlings- und Winterlieder der Ladakhi. Angeregt durch zahlreiche Funde von Inschriften, Steinzeichnungen und Ruinen, die Francke auf seinen Missionsreisen antraf, schrieb er "History of Western Tibet". Dieses Werk dient noch heute vielen Forschern als Grundlage für ihre Projekte in Indien und Pakistan. Dabei wurden z.B. von Mitarbeitern eines Deutsch-Pakistanischen Forschungsprojekts entlang des Karakorum Highway mehrere Hunderte weiterer Steinzeichnungen, Reliefs und Inschriften gefunden, die aus verschiedenen historischen Straten stammen. Die ersten Inschriften veröffentlichte Francke 19o4, der sie am Indus bei Khalatse entdeckt hatte.

Moderne Reiseführer enthalten Hinweise auf "Dardengräber" oder Burganlagen. Der Begriff "Darden" wurde zuerst von Francke verwendet und ist seitdem in jeder Geschichte Ladakhs, NW- Indiens und NW-Pakistans zu finden.

Neben den archäologischen und historischen Forschungen finden sich in den Aufzeichnungen der Missionare Studien zu den verschiedenen Dialekten im Bereich der Mission. Die Kenntnis dieser Dialekte und ihre Verwendung in Schulbüchern und christlicher Literatur war ein Zugang, um die Bewohner benachbarter Täler für die Mission zu erreichen, denen die Verwendung des klassischen Tibetisch fremd war.

Heyde, Jaeschke und Francke, die selbst mehrere Instrumente spielten, bemühten sich auch um Kenntnisse der tibetischen Musik.

Von Francke sind einige Kompositionen erhalten, die aber keinen Eingang in das damalige Liederbuch fanden.

Nach Wilhelm Heyde war es besonders der Arzt Carl Rudolf Marx (1857-1891), der die medizinische Betreuung im Rahmen der Missionsarbeit am Krankenhaus in Leh vorantrieb. Seine großen Erfolge hatte er in der Behandlung der häufigen Augenerkrankungen. Neben der medizinischen Arbeit war er als Lehrer tätig und sammelte tibetische Schriften. Seiner früher Tod 1891 verhinderte, daß er die Übersetzung der westtibetischen Chronik, deren erster Teil bereits vorlag, beenden konnte.

Neben ihren Aufgaben als Mitarbeiter der Mission waren auch später die Missionare der Herrnhuter für die Wissenschaft tätig. Friedrich E.Peter, der einzige Bischof der Herrnhuter im Himalaya, und sein Sohn, Friedrich A.Peter (1904-1988), beschäftigten sich mit Sprachen und Geschichte des Missionsgebietes, befaßten sich mit der Architektur Ladakhs und der tibetischen Ikonographie.

Friedrich Adolf Redslob (1838-1891), Samuel Heinrich Ribbach (1863-1943), Theodor Daniel Lorenz Schreve (1860-1930) und Wilhelm Karl Julius Weber (1851-1934) arbeiteten als Übersetzer, Historiker und Geographen.

Dem Arzt Frederick Ernest Shawe (1871-1907) verdankt die Forschung Berichte zu den medizinischen Problemen des Hochgebirges und seiner Bewohner. Neben seiner medizinischen Tätigkeit war auch Shawe als Sprachwissenschaftler tätig.

Diese Übersicht ist keineswegs vollständig und läßt die Arbeit der einheimischen Helfer, die zuerst als Sprachlehrer und Gehilfen in Haus und Landwirtschaft am Leben der Europäer teilnahmen und später selbst Lehrer in der Missionsschule, Übersetzer und Drucker von Bibeltexten, Schulbüchern und der ersten ladakhischen Zeitung wurden, ganz aus. Das Kolloquium hier in Leh, ganz in der Nähe von Kirche und Schule der "Moravians", zeigt am besten, daß die wissenschaftliche Arbeit der Missionare in Ladakh nicht vergessen ist.

Literatur

BECHLER, THEODOR, Beiträge der Brüdergemeine zur Pflege der Wissenschaft und Kunst in zwei Jahrhunderten.Bilder und Gestalten. In: *Jahrbuch der Brüdergemeine*, S.4-48, 35.Jg., Herrnhut 1941/42.

MEIER, GUDRUN, Sven Hedin und die Herrnhuter Mission. In: *Kleine Beiträge aus dem Staatlichen Museum für Völkerkunde Dresden*, S. 37/38, Heft 5, 1982.

MEIER, GUDRUN, August Heinrich Jaeschke - Person und wissenschaftliche Wirksamkeit. In: *Wissenschaftsgeschichte und gegenwärtige Forschungen in Nordwest-Indien*, S. 15-27, Dresdner Tagungsberichte 2, Dresden 1990.

SCHULZE, ADOLF: *200 Jahre Brüdermission. Bd.II. Das zweite Missionsjahrhundert, Teil III: Asien*, S.530-557, Herrnhut 1832.

UTTENDÖRFER, OTTO, Die Entwicklung der Pflege der Naturwissenschaften in der Brüdergemeine. In: *Zeitschrift für Brüdergeschichte*, S. 89-127, X.Jg. Herrnhut 1916.

WALRAVENS, HARTMUT und MANFRED TAUBE: *August Hermann Francke und die Westhimalaya-Mission der Herrnhuter Brüdergemeine.* Eine Bibliographie mit Standortnachweisen der tibetischen Drucke. Mit einem Beitrag von M. Hahn. Stuttgart: Steiner 1992. 532 S.281 Abb. auf Tafeln gr. 8= Verzeichnis der orientalischen Zeitschriften in Deutschland. Im Einvernehmen mit der Deutschen Morgenländischen Gesellschaft begr.von W.Voigt, weitergef. von D.George. Im Auftrag der Akademie der Wissenschaften in Göttingen hrsg. von H.-O.Feistel, Supplementband 34.

HYDEL POWER POTENTIAL IN LEH DISTRICT

Sonam Morup
Civil Engineer, Leh

The programme and planning for the development of electric power.. forms one of the most integral parts of the overall economic strategy. Like in the irrigation and agriculture field, there is a basic production of energy in hydel schemes in the form of electric power from the available water resources. . Certain factors are very essential and to be kept in the mind at the stage of planning. These are the efficient use of resources, long term sustainability. freedom from the effects of environmental pollution and economic feasibility. Keeping in view these factors, the micro, mini and small hydel schemes meet these requirements and are the most suitable sources of energy or electric power in the Ladakh region. The sites identified for the construction of hydel schemes are as under:

Micro Hydel Schemes

1. **Sasoma Nallah Hydel Scheme (in Nubra Valley)**

Head available = 170 m
Minimum discharge = 1 cumec
Power Generation = 1 MW (Winter) 3 MW (Summer)
Estimated cost = Rs. 18 Crores[1]

2. **Hanu Hydel Scheme (Leh - Khalatse Block)**

Head available = 165 m
Minimum discharge = 1 cumec
Power Generation = 1 MW (Winter) 3 MW (Summer)
Estimated cost = Rs. 12 Crores[1]

3. **Upshi - Igo Hydel Scheme, Indus River**

Head available = 30m
Minimum discharge = 11.33 Cumec
Length of Power Canal = 7 Km
Power Generation = 2.5 MW (Winter) 7.5 MW (Summer)
Estimated cost. = Rs. 37.5. Crores[1]

4. **Micro Hydel Scheme, Tingmosgang.**

Head available = 65m
Minimum discharge = 0.4 cumec
Power Generation = 167 kw (Winter) 500 kw (Summer)

[1] 1 crore = Rs10 million.

5. Nimo Hydel Scheme, Zanskar River

Head available	= 40m
Minimum discharge	= 32 cumec
Length of tunnel	= 15 km
Power Generation	= 10 MW (Winter) 30 MW (Summer)
Estimated cost	= Rs. 120 Crores[1].

6. Domkhar Hydel Scheme (on River Indus)

Length of water conductor (tunnel + open channel)	= 7 km
Head available	= 25m
Power Generation	= 6.5 MW (Winter) 19.5 MW (Summer)
Estimated cost	= Rs. 78 Crores[1].

Sites for a Low Head Run-of-river schemes are easily available at more than six places with a total generating capacity of 12 MW (in winter) and 40 MW in Summer. The overall cumulative power potential in Leh district is not less than 30 MW in winter and 100 MW in summer. This power potential is more than enough to meet the requirements of lighting, cooking, irrigation and agricultural operations, industries and various other related activities of the whole Leh district for a period of about a half century.

Before the start of the eighth five year plan, the work of all the micro-hydel schemes up to 3 MW was transferred to the Department of Non-Conventional Energy Sources (DNCES). The Hydel schemes up to 3 MW are now treated as Micro-Hydel scheme under the head of Non-Conventional. Funds and & other incentives are available from the Ministry of Non-conventional Energy Sources.

Freezing and icing problems in the Hydel Structures.

Due to the severe climatic conditions prevailing in the Ladakh region, there are acute problems of freezing and ice-formation in the hydel structures. As observed in the Stakna Hydel Project for more than the last six years, the hydel project with a gravity canal system can be run only for a period of 9 to 10 months i.e. from March to December. The problems faced due to ice formation at the intake structures and power house are manageable with some difficulties, but the problem faced in the canal system is totally unmanageable.

The ice formation in the power canal or water conductor can be divided into two parts.

1. The freezing of water surface and ice formation on the wetted perimeter due to sub-zero temperature and low velocity.
2. The adhesion of suspended crystals of frazil ice to the inner surface along the entire length of the canal and pipes.

The second icing problem is the most acute and uncontrollable. Normally trash racks are installed at the intake structure to trap the debris and ice sheets but these trash racks cannot control or retain the flowing frazil ice. In the winter season, when the ambient temperature falls below -10°C, the formation and flow of frazil ice starts in the river and enters into the water conductor system. The accumulation of frazil ice reduces the sectional area of the channel and the discharge of the canal is progressively reduced. The power generation is similarly reduced and at a certain minimum limit closure of the project becomes unavoidable. Some suggestions and solutions to minimise the ice formation in the channel are:-

Water conductor and Hydel structure.

1. Materials with low heat-conductivity should be used for the water conductor system, with further insulation.
2. If possible the gravity type open conductor should be totally eliminated or the length should be minimised.
3. Preference should be given to a tunnel type water conductor or the cut-and covered type canal system.
4. A Low Head or Medium Head Run-of-River Scheme with standardised Tubular, Bulb and Package type Turbines is more suitable on the Indus River.

Low Head/Medium Head Run-of-River Scheme

Keeping in view the severe climatic conditions and water resource constraints especially during the winter months, the Low Head/Medium Head Run-off-River schemes are very suitable on the river Indus particularly down stream of the Zanskar-Indus confluence.

The Bharat Heavy Electrical Limited (BHEL) has now standardised Tubular type Horizontal Machines for a low head of 5m to 10m to generate power from 500 kW to 1000 kW with a river discharge of 6.8 cumec (250 cusec) to 13.6 cumec (500 cusec)

Bulb Turbines and package type turbines are also available for a low head of 5m to 20m with a discharge requirement of 10 to 50 cumec (i.e. 350 cusec to 1880 cusec) generation power in the range of 1500 to 7000 KW.

Energy Data[2]	**1990-91**	**1991-92**	**1992-93**	**1993-94**
All India				
Installed Capacity(MW)	68261	74619	83352	91593
Peak Availability (MW)	40430	43610	49045	52846
Peak Load(MW)	46509	50431	54634	59122
Energy Availability (MKWh/yr)	264125	283631	314471	348998
Energy Requirement (MKWh/yr)	262393	284501	308162	333407
All India per capita energy	411 KWh	or 63 watt		

[2] The derivation of some figures in this table is not clear. (Ed.)

Energy Data (cont.)[2]	**1990-91**	**1991-92**	**1992-93**	**1993-94**
J&K State				
Installed Capacity (MW)	457	463	472	507
Peak Availability (MW)	526	562	637	691
Peak load (MW)	654	727	808	896
Energy Availability(MK Wh/yr)	2888	3294	3716	4243
Energy Requirement (MKWh/yr)	3150	3503	3893	4318

J&K State per capita energy available = 653 KWh/yr or 106 watt

Leh District, Energy Generation				
Stakna Hydel project (MKWh/yr)	6.007	7.078	10.520	13.565
Diesel power station (MKWh/yr)	0.823	1.467	1.678	1.522

Leh District per capita energy = 135 KWh/yr

The per capita energy available of 135 units/yr is very low as compared to the State and All India level. To meet the normal requirement of energy consumption it should be increased by 4 to 5 times. Thus a minimum power generation of 15 to 20 MW is needed for the Leh District.

Solar and Wind Energy

Other renewable and sustainable sources of energy in the Leh District are Solar and Wind Energy. As compared to the Hydel Energy, the equipment and installation cost of energy from Solar and Wind is very high but from the ecological and environmental stand point the harnessing of energy from Solar & Wind is preferable to Diesel and other polluting sources.

Solar Photo Voltaic (SPV)

In a solar photo voltaic system, solar energy is converted directly into electricity. The existing technology is based on single and poly-crystalline cells and can continue for some time to supply lighting and pumping needs for irrigation and drinking water in villages. At present the average cost is about Rs.100 per watt but a cost range of 25 to 30 per unit is preferable.

Installation cost for Hydel Scheme = Rs. 55 to Rs.65/w.
Installation cost for Solar Scheme = Rs.1100/w, (20 times more than Hydel)

Leh District

No. of villages electrified with SPV units up to 1993 = 443 Units
Cost/per set = Rs. 20,000
Expected life = 20 to 25 years
Additional units proposed during 93-94 = 500 units

Wind Energy

The third alternative source of energy, Wind Energy, can be used for power generation or pumping water for drinking and irrigation purposes. So far three wind generators are installed in Leh area and are under test.

POWER DEVELOPMENT IN LADAKH
An Over-view

Jigmet Namgyal

SUMMARY

The primary source of power supply to Leh town and its immediate suburbs is the 4MW Stakna Hydel Power House, which utilises water from the Indus river and was commissioned in the year 1987. However icing problems prevent it functioning in mid-winter.

The other principal urban power sources at present are three Diesel Generators of about 1MW at Leh, Choglamsar and Kargil. Some villages in both Leh and Kargil districts have small Diesel Generating sets for evening hours only.

Some Micro and Mini Hydel Projects are under construction in both the districts of Leh and Kargil. Also electricity through Solar Photo Voltaic (SPV) arrays for lighting purposes is being provided to remote and inaccessible villages where other sources of energy are not possible.

******

The Ladakh region comprises two districts namely Leh and Kargil (which are also the two principal towns) and forms the northern frontiers of the state. The entire region is mountainous with a temperature ranging from +30 C to -30 C. In the year 1964, for the first time, electricity was made available to the people of Leh town by the commissioning of a 20 kw diesel generating set.

The primary source of power supply to Leh town and its immediate suburbs is the 4 MW Stakna Hydel Power House, which utilises the water of the Indus River and was commissioned in the year 1987. There is also a 1MW Diesel Generating Power House at Leh and a 1MW (derated capacity of 600 kw) at Choglamsar to supplement the power supply to the town in winter months.

The power supply to Kargil town is made available, during the evening hours only, from the 1MW Diesel Generating Power House at Kargil.

The power supply to a number of villages in both the Leh and Kargil districts is made available, during evening hours only, from isolated diesel Generating Sets. The installed capacity at present is as under:-

Name of Power House	Capacity
A. DISTRICT LEH	
1. Stakna Hydro-Electric Project	4000 kw
2. D.G. Station, Leh	1000 kw
3. D.G. Station, Choglamsar, Leh, 1000kw but derated	600 kw
4. Isolated Diesel Stations in various villages (see appendix)	943 kw
Total	6543 kw

B. DISTRICT KARGIL

1.	D.G. Station, Kargil	1600 kw
2.	Isolated D.G. Stations in various villages (see appendix)	1541 kw
Total		3141 kw

ON-GOING SCHEMES

Three Micro Hydel schemes, namely Sumur and Hundar in Nubra Valley and Basgo in Leh Block of District Leh, are under construction and are in an advanced stage of commissioning. The work on construction of 3MW Igo-Martselang Mini Hydel Scheme and 4.5MW Domkhar Micro Hydel Scheme has been started and is likely to take three years for completion. The projects under construction are as under:-

	Name of Project	Est. cost(Rs)	Capacity	Area to benefit
1.	Sumur Hydel Project	141,00 lakh[1]	100 kw	Nubra Block
2.	Hunder Hydel Project	261,00 lakh	400kw	,,
3.	Basgo Hydel Project	205,00 lakh	300 kw	Leh Block
4.	Igo-Martselang H. P.	1402,00 lakh	3000kw	Leh District
5.	Domkhar	1485,00 lakh	4500kw	,,
6.	Iqbal M.H. Project	2249,00 lakh	375 kw	Kargil
7.	Haftal	760 ,00 lakh	1000 kw	Zanskar
8.	Shakar-Chikten	370,00 lakh	1260 kw	Kargil District.
9.	Marpuchhu	225,00 lakh	300kw	Dras, Kargil Dist.

The following Hydro-Electric Projects are included for construction in the approved 8th Five Year Plan:-

1.	Tangtse	389,00 lakh	390 kw	Leh District
2.	Bogdang	228,00 lakh	200 kw	,,
3.	Kundog	169,00 lakh	100 kw	,,
4.	Dha Hanu	1200,00 lakh	3000 kw	,,
5.	Chutak	(in prep.)	12000 kw	Kargil
6.	Parkachik	,,	60000 kw	,,

NEW DIESEL STATION AT LEH.

The generation from Stakna Hydro Electric Project goes down during winter months due to low discharge and freezing problems in the canal. During the severe winter period when the freezing is acute, the Power House has to be shut-down due both to the non-availability of water and for the safety of the hydraulic structures and the machinery. As already stated above 1.6MW of Diesel Generating capacity is available in Leh to meet the power requirements of the people during winter months (for lighting purposes only) which is inadequate. Therefore, a new Diesel Generating Station which will have a generating capacity of 4MW has been planned at Choglamsar,

[1] 1 crore = 10,000,000; 1 lakh = 100,000

Leh, and construction has started. The equipment has been placed on order and has started coming up. The construction of the building has also commenced. Subject to availability of timely funds and cash, four units aggregating 2MW are proposed to be commissioned during the current working season. For this purpose an amount of Rs. 300.00 lakh is required.

STAKNA HYDEL PROJECT

The project was commissioned in the year 1987-88 with a generation capacity of 4MW at a cost of Rs.27.00 crore[1]. The generation from this power house has been increasing steadily and the generation figures during the last three years are as under:

1990-91	77.8 lakh units
1991-92	105.2 lakh units
1992-93	135.7 lakh units

The total generation so far from the date of commissioning is 537 lakh units and if we take the cost of generation to be the same as diesel generation at the rate of Rs.7 per unit, the total value of electricity generated till now comes to Rs. 37.6 crore with a present yearly generation worth Rs. 9.5 crore. This clearly indicates the performance of Stakna Hydel Project by any standard.

The project had its initial teething problems which is inherent in any such projects. Initially we had the problem of silting in the water conductor rendering the power house inoperative. We have procured a 0.75 cubic yard clamshell excavator for removal of silt from the desilting basin while water is flowing through the power canal. This has helped in reducing the silting of the canal and its consequent choking and we have been able to run the power house continuously without any shutdowns on account of silting during the last two years.

STAKNA HYDRO-ELECTRIC PROJECT

In the second phase of the Stakna Project provision has been kept for the installation of the third unit of 2MW. Provision for the installation of this unit has already been kept in the power house building, but power house machinery for this third unit is yet to be arranged. The works involves the construction of a balancing reservoir, balance penstocks and the erection of the generating unit. The provision has been kept in the 8th Five Year Plan.

RURAL ELECTRIFICATION

Out of total number of 112 villages in Leh District 52, 4

villages and 13 hamlets have been electrified ending 3/93. Similarly out of 129 villages in Kargil District, 82 villages and 29 Hamlets have been electrified ending 3/93.

ELECTRIFICATION BY SOLAR PHOTO VOLTAIC (SPV) SYSTEM

Provision of light by using a SPV Lighting System is meant to provide electricity to remote and inaccessible villages where conventional sources of energy are not availale. The scheme was started during the year 1990-91 and so far the progress achieved in various blocks of Leh District is as under:-

1990-91	30 units
1991-92	120 units
1992-93	293 units
Total	443 units

Orders for 700 units (500 units for Leh and 200 units for Kargil) have already been placed and are expected to be received during the current working season. These will be installed in both the Districts of Leh and Kargil.

SOLAR POWER HOUSES

In both the Districts of Leh and Kargil the population is widely distributed. There are large distances between habitations and topography of the area is such that hydel potential is not available in all the areas of the Districts. In view of the large distances and difficult terrain, extension of transmission lines is also not practicable. However both Districts are fortunate enough to have bright sun-shine all the year round with the sun at a high elevation angle. These conditions are suitable for power generation by a Solar Photo Voltaic System. Recently a 100 kw capacity Power House has been commissioned in Kalayanpur in Uttar Pradesh. Funds for a similar purpose are available in 8th Five Year Plan. It has been proposed to obtain an expert consultancy service for preparation of the feasibility report for installation of a Power House based on Solar Energy. This will provide expert advice and the latest technology. The proposal is already under consideration by the Government.

MEETING THE FUTURE DEMAND OF ELECTRICITY OF LEH TOWN AND THE NEARBY VILLAGES

The present demand of electricity of Leh town and the nearby villagers is of the order of 8 MW whereas the generation available both from Hydel and Diesel is hardly 5 MW. The town is under a heavy pressure of population increase due to the migration of people from the villages as well as an increase in the floating population of tourists.

The demand of electricity is thus increasing manifold. The demand could be met from a hydel site which is identified near Leh on the Zanskar river about 7 km upstream of Nimo. The discharge from the Zanskar river would be diverted through a tunnel and fall into the Indus river at Basgo village. The generation of 25 to 30 MW can be made available for 8 months of summer and 5 to 10 MW during the winter. Ladakhis and all their well wishers should propagate this idea and take it up with the government for early execution of the project.

APPENDIX

DIESEL ENGINED GENERATORS IN LEH & KARGIL DISTRICTS

DISTRICT LEH

		Capacity
1.	Hemis	18 kw
2.	Nimo	50 kw
3.	Saspol	50 kw
4	Khaltse	50 kw
5	Skurbuchan	50 kw
6	Chumathang	50 kw
7	Nyoma	50 kw
8	Lamayuru	50 kw
9	Diskit	125 kw
10	Turtuk	125 kw
11	Tingmosgang	125 kw
12	Tangtse (to be commissioned)	200 kw

DISTRICT KARGIL

1.	Saliskot	100 kw
2.	Sanku	200 kw
3.	Sangra	40 kw
4.	Panikar	100 kw
5	Silmo	40 kw
6.	Chiktan	96 kw
7.	Khangral	100 kw
8.	Shargol	100 kw
9.	Drass	200 kw
10.	Thasgam	40 kw
11	Pan-Dras	40 kw
12	Padum	100 kw
13	Sani	40 kw
14	Karsha	100 kw
15	Baletik	125 kw
16	Garkhon	60 kw
17	Hemiskot	60 kw

THE SOCIAL AND ENVIRONMENTAL COSTS OF THE GLOBAL ECONOMY
Lessons from Ladakh

Helena Norberg-Hodge
The Ladakh Project,
International Society for Ecology and Culture,
21 Victoria Square, Clifton, Bristol BS8 4ES, U.K.

Summary

Traditional ways of life in Ladakh and many other countries are being destroyed by conventional 'progress' and 'development', with their lure of riches and comfort for all. Direct or indirect subsidies from government or international aid result in local traditional products from staple food crops to specialised crafts being undercut and marginalised by large scale production elsewhere; control passes to national or multinational organisations; and local culture is homogenised with a global TV mediocrity.

Virtually every political leader today, in both the North and the South, believes that the goals of society are best met if the economy keeps growing. Most support the notion that continued growth can be achieved by internationalising the economy and liberalising trade. Around the world, this globalisation — which means tying ever more people and cultures into a single, centralised world economic system — is seen as a means of reviving ailing, bankrupt economies.

From a social and ecological point of view, however, this is a disastrous course. Rather than curing present problems, the globalisation of the economy will accelerate social and environmental breakdown. It will mean a dramatic increase in environmental pollution, a further erosion of family and community ties, and a marked weakening of real democracy. Instead, strengthening and diversifying local, regional and national economies should be high on the agenda of developed and developing countries alike.

My perspective is based on studying many societies at different levels of industrialisation. This has revealed the extent to which the complex interactions between technology and economics inherent in the industrial model affect not only the environment, but our culture and world view as well. I have lived and studied in America, where industrialisation has proceeded furthest; in Sweden, with its socialist variant of industrial society; in Innsbruck Austria, 25 years ago, when it was relatively uninfluenced by economic development; and in rural Spain, where Common Market trading policies have had a profound impact on rural life.

Most importantly, I have had the rare opportunity over the past two decades to observe firsthand the effects of development on Ladakh. The changes that occured there in this period are roughly equivalent to those that occurred over a period of 500 years or so in many other cultures. The situation in Ladakh thus can help to illustrate the impact of the West, from the conquistadors to colonialism and development, on other cultures.

Twenty years ago, life in Ladakhi villages was still based on the same foundations it had been for centuries. The economy was primarily based on subsistence farming, with trade limited to luxuries. Cultural practices (in particular, fraternal polyandry and monasticism) as well as an awareness of resource limits kept population within the bounds that the land could support. There was virtually no waste or pollution. Within the decentralised village structure the household was the centre of economic activity, and the status of women was high; in many cases they were the decision-makers. The old remained respected and productive members of society throughout their lives. Crime, unemployment and homelessness were essentially unknown. Thanks to an intimate, location-specific knowledge of their ecosystem, the Ladakhis had prospered, providing all their material needs, as well as beautiful works of art, drama and music, while having far more time for friends and leisure activities than the average Westerner.

The traditional way of life in Ladakh was certainly not perfect. However, it is clear that the changes wrought by development have not, on balance, been an improvement. As Ladakh is steadily tied into the global economy, the gap between rich and poor is widening; waste and pollution are rapidly increasing; the status of women is declining; the old are being forgotten and the young are growing ashamed of their own culture. A once self-reliant people is becoming increasingly dependent on imported resources over which they have no control, and is relying ever more upon a distant bureaucracy for needs once provided by their own community. By almost any meaningful measure, the quality of life is declining. And yet because of a reliance on narrow economic yardsticks, the destructive changes occuring in Ladakh are generally seen as mere side effects of the positive transformation called 'development.'

The promise of conventional development is that by following in the footsteps of the 'developed' countries of the world, the 'under-developed' countries can become rich and comfortable too. Poverty will be eliminated, and the problems of overpopulation and environmental degradation will be solved. This argument contains an inherent flaw, even deception. The fact is that the developed nations are consuming essential resources in such a way and at such a rate that it is impossible for 'underdeveloped' areas of the world to follow in their footsteps. When one-quarter of the world's population consumes three-quarters of the world's resources, and then in effect turns around and tells the others to do as they do, it is little short of a hoax. Development is all too often a euphemism for exploitation, a new colonialism. The forces of development and modernisation have pulled most people away from a sure subsistence and got them to chase after an illusion, only to fall flat on their faces, materially impoverished and psychologically disoriented. A majority are turned into slum dwellers, having left the land and their local economy to end up in the shadow of an urban dream that can never be realised.

Development and the corporate-led trend toward globalisation depend upon continuous government investments. They require the building-up of a large-scale industrial infrastructure, including roads, mass communications facilities, energy installations, and schools for specialised education. Among other things, this heavily subsidised infrastructure allows goods produced on a large scale and transported long distances to be sold at artificially low prices, in many cases at lower prices than goods produced locally. In Ladakh, the Indian government is not only subsidising roads, schools and energy installations, it is also bringing in subsidised food from India's breadbasket, the Punjab. The food arriving in lorries by the tonne is cheaper in the local bazaar than food grown five minutes walk away. Although Ladakh's local economy has provided enough food for its people for 2000 years, many Ladakhis no longer find it worthwhile to continue farming.

This same process is affecting not just food, but a whole range of products, from clothes to household utensils to building materials. Goods imported to Ladakh from distant parts of India can often be produced and distributed at prices far lower than those produced locally, again, because of a heavily subsidised industrial infrastructure. The end result of all this long-distance transport of subsidised goods is that Ladakh's local economy is being steadily dismantled, and with it the local community that was once tied together by bonds of interdependence.

This trend is exacerbated by other changes that have accompanied economic development. Traditionally, children learned how to farm from relatives and neighbours; now they are put into Western-style schools that prepare them for specialised jobs in an industrial economy. In Ladakh, these jobs are very few and far between. As more and more people are pulled off the land, the number of unemployed Ladakhis competing with each other for these scarce jobs is growing exponentially. What's more, the course of the economy, once controlled locally, is increasingly dominated by distant market forces and anonymous bureaucracies. The result has been a growing insecurity and competitiveness — even leading to ethnic conflict, and in 1989, violence — amongst a once secure and cooperative people. A range of related social problems has appeared almost overnight, including crime, family breakup and homelessness. And as the Ladakhis have become separated from the land, their awareness of the limits of local resources has dimmed. Pollution is on the increase, and the population is growing at unsustainable rates.

Economists would dismiss these negative impacts, which are not so easily quantifiable as the monetary transactions that are the goal of economic development. Yet the situation in Ladakh vividly illustrates the shortcomings of defining human welfare in terms of economic growth and its main indicator, GDP (Gross Domestic Product). In traditional parts of Ladakh, the standard of living is actually quite high when compared with most of the Third World. Yet because people provide for almost all their needs outside the cash economy, the GDP is virtually zero; Ladakh appears to be at the very bottom of the economic order, in dire need of economic development. In effect this means that no distinction is made between self-sufficient Ladakhi farmers and the homeless on the streets of New York. In both cases there may be no income, but the reality behind the statistics is as different as day and night.

In Ladakh and elsewhere in the Third World, farmers once grew a variety of crops and kept a few animals to provide for themselves, either directly or through the local economy. Now, development is encouraging these farmers to grow cash crops for distant markets. As a result, they are becoming dependent on forces beyond their control: huge transportation networks, oil and agro-chemical markets, the fluctuations of international finance. Over the course of time, inflation obliges them to produce more and more to secure the income that they now need in order to buy what they used to grow themselves. Throughout the world, development has thus displaced and marginalised self-reliant local economies in general, and small farmers in particular.

I should point out that it is not only the South that is affected by this process. The pressures of economic and technological change are bearing down even on the industrialised societies in a similar way; we too are being 'developed'. Today, even though only 2 or 3 percent of the population is left on the land, small farmers are still being squeezed out of existence; and even though industrialisation has pared the extended family down to a small nuclear unit, our economy is still chipping away at it. Technological advance is continuing to speed life up, while robbing people of time. Increased trade and ever greater mobility are furthering anonymity and a breakdown of community. In the West, these trends are labelled 'progress' rather than development, but they emanate from the same process of industrialisation that inevitably leads to centralisation, social degradation, and the wasteful use of resourccs.

'Progress' based on economic and technological development has reached an advanced stage in the West. Wherever we look, we can see its inexorable logic at work, replacing people with machines, local interdependence with global markets, country lanes with freeways, and the corner shop with a supermarket. Governments around the world — regardless of their political hue — are encouraging an acceleration in these changes through support for a globalised economy. Long-distance trade, in particular, receives heavy subsidies to maintain and expand networks of communication and transportation. Meanwhile, trade agreements like NAFTA, GATT and Maastricht, justified by the rhetoric of 'free trade', are leading to ever greater centralisation of economic and political power. Local communities are rapidly losing control over their own destinies, and even national governments are handing over control to supranational institutions such as the European Community, The World Bank, and now the WTO. Such organisations are so far removed from the people they are supposed to represent that they are incapable of responding to their diverse interests.

* * *

Even though the phrase 'think globally, act locally' is heard frequently these days, the thrust of development and progress is entirely in the direction of globalisation. Local cultures and economies are rapidly disappearing, taking animal and plant species with them. In the process, our very existence is threatened.

In the natural world, diversity is an inescapable fact of life. We are just beginning to discover how important even the most 'insignificant' insect or plant can be for our survival. The accelerating pace at which diverse species of life are being eradicated has, in fact, become a major issue. Cultural diversity is as important as diversity in the natural world and, in fact, follows directly from it. Traditional cultures mirrored their particular environments, deriving their food, clothing, and shelter from local resources. Even in the most developed parts of the world today, there are still remnants of local adaptation to diversity. In the American Southwest, for example, you find flat-roofed adobe houses, ideally suited to the extremes of the desert climate; in New England, houses are made of locally abundant wood, and have peaked roofs designed to shed the rain and snow. The cuisines of different cultures still reflect local food sources, from the olive oil prevalent in Mediterranean cooking to the oatmeal and kippered herring on the Scotsman's breakfast table.

The emerging world economy and the growing domination of science and technology are breaking down this natural and cultural diversity by remaking the cultures of the South so as to conform to a single monoculture. Both globalisation and development are based on the assumption that needs are everywhere essentially the same, that everyone needs to eat the same food, to live in the same type of house, to wear the same clothes. The same cement buildings, the same films and television programmes find their way to the most remote corners of the world. Across the world, "Dallas" beams into people's homes, and pinstripe suits are de rigeur. Lingonberry and pineapple juice are giving way to Coca Cola; woolen robes and cotton saris are being replaced by blue jeans; and yaks and highland cattle are disappearing in favour of Jersey cows. Virtually identical toy shops — in Ladakh, in Beijing, in remote mountain villages in Spain — sell the same blonde, blue-eyed Barbie dolls and Rambos with machine guns. Even language is being homogenised, since English is the lingua franca of the modern "global community".

The breakdown of cultural diversity throughout the South is accelerated by grossly distorted impressions of modern life. The predominant image is one of ease and glamour: everyone is beautiful, everyone is rich. People see the fast cars, the microwaves, and the video machines. Advertising and the media are telling them what to do, in fact telling them what to be : modern, civilised and rich. What isn't seen are the 'side-effects' of this way of life: the environmental deterioration, the psychological stress, the drug addiction, the homelessness. People who have been presented with only one side of the development coin are left vulnerable and eager for modernisation.

In this way, diverse cultures from Alaska to Australia are being overrun by the industrial monoculture. This is a tragedy of many dimensions. With the destruction of each culture, we are erasing centuries of accumulated knowledge. And as diverse ethnic groups feel their identity threatened, conflict and social breakdown almost inevitably follow.

Today, these trends are supported by government spending, a large portion of which is devoted to expanding transport and communication infrastructures, enlarging global markets and supporting the demands of large-scale producers. In Ladakh and throughout the developing world, money flows freely into huge projects aimed at increasing market transactions and boosting GDP. Heavy subsidies are available for huge dams and nuclear energy installations, television and radio facilities. Billions of dollars are poured into building roads, dams, fertiliser plants and airports, all of which serve to reinforce dependence on centralised systems. The pattern is the same in the industrialised nations as well. Government and industry continue to push towards larger scale, greater centralisation, and a further dependence on the multinational corporations which produce and deliver the goods that are traded world-wide.

* * *

Reversing these trends and solving today's social and environmental crises will require active steps towards decentralisation. This does not mean retreating into cultural or economic isolationism, but rather reducing the influence of powerful global economic forces so as to allow each region to nourish its own economy and its own traditions. Since extreme dependence has already been created on both national and international levels, it would be irresponsible to 'delink' economies from one day to the next. Countries in the North cannot, for example, suddenly halt their purchase of coffee or cotton from those countries in the South whose economies totally depend on such trade. But they can immediately begin supporting aid programmes that will enable people to provide basic needs for themselves - ensuring, for instance, that the production of food for local consumption has priority over exports to the West. Small and medium size producers the world over would be better off as a result. They would also benefit if their products did not have to compete with those shipped great distances via subsidised transport networks, and if support were given to developing technologies appropriate for local conditions, rather than labour-displacing, capital-intensive equipment suited to large-scale industry and agribusiness.

One of the most effective ways of supporting local economies would be to reduce unnecessary trade. We are currently transporting across whole continents and several oceans a vast range of products, from milk to apples to furniture, that could just as easily be produced in their place of destination. By reducing and eliminating subsidies for transportation, we would cut waste and pollution, improve the position of small producers, and strengthen local economies and communities in one fell swoop.

What exactly is 'local,' and what is 'necessary' as opposed to 'unnecessary' trade are issues that cannot be defined in absolute terms. But the crucial point is that the principle of heavily subsidised international trade is one that needs critical reassessment. The goal would not be to encourage narrow protectionism, but rather to allow for the sustainable and equitable use of natural resources worldwide. It is in robust, local-scale economies that we find genuinely 'free' markets, free of the corporate manipulation, hidden subsidies, waste, and immense promotional costs that characterise today's global market.

Parallel to economic decentralisation, the production of energy would need to be decentralised. This would be a positive step in both the North and the South, but because the energy infrastructure of most developing countries is still relatively limited, the widespread application of renewable energy technologies in these regions would be comparatively easy. Local communities and economies in the South would be better off if real support were given to small-scale projects based on locally available resources, such as village-scale hydroelectric installations, or solar ovens and water heaters for the household. Until now, however, such support has simply not materialised. Instead, the West has pushed its own industrial model, based on large-scale, centralised power production. One of the greatest scandals of development is that despite tremendous potential, not a single country in the developing world has managed to promote small-scale decentralised applications of solar energy on anything more than a token basis.

If the diverse cultures of the South are to survive the pressures leading towards global monoculturisation, another urgent requirement is a public information campaign to correct the incomplete and misleading images of the industrialised world. Information about the long-term effects of everything from powdered milk for babies to a dependence on fossil fuels tends not to reach the least developed areas of the world. The seductive images in the media and advertising that do arrive are not accompanied by warnings about toxic wastes, the erosion of farmlands, acid rain, or global warming. To reverse the pressures on people to join the wasteful consumer culture requires activities that we might term 'counter-development'.

The primary goal of counter-development would be to provide people with the means to make fully informed choices about their own future. Using every possible form of communication, from satellite television to storytelling, it should be publicised that today's capital- and energy-intensive trends are simply unsustainable. Ultimately, the aim would be to promote self-respect and self-reliance, thereby protecting life-sustaining diversity and creating the conditions for locally based, truly sustainable development.

At the same time, counter-development would promote and popularise a new, wider, and more humane definition of progress. It would highlight some of the innumerable local initiatives in the North that are exploring more sustainable alternatives. It would point to the viability of traditional systems as well as bringing information about new trends in agriculture: about permaculture, biodynamics, and the booming movement toward organic methods of cultivation. It would report on bioregionalism and local economic systems; it would publicize the windmills in Denmark and California, and the growing demand for acupuncture, homeopathy, and other nature-based systems of health care. It would make more visible the enormous interest around the world in environmental protection, soil conservation, and air and water quality.

For the North, strengthening local economies means shortening the links between producers and consumers. Grassroots initiatives are already springing up throughout the industrialised world aimed at supporting more localised economic activity. These range from local banks and currencies, to barter and local employment trading systems, to direct links between farmers and consumers through Community Supported Agriculture schemes. Such means enable communities in the North to reduce unemployment, cut back on pollution and waste, and enhance their connection with the natural world. They also indirectly help the cultures of the South, by allowing people to produce for themselves rather than selling their resources and labour to the North at cut-rate prices.

The stronger sense of community that stems from shorter producer-consumer links in turn has important psychological benefits. Recent research has made it clear that the rise in crime, violence, depression, even divorce, is to a very great extent a consequence of the breakdown of community. Conversely, children growing up with a sense of connection to their place on the earth and to others around them, in other words, children who are imbedded in a community, grow up with a stronger sense of self-esteem and healthier identities, thereby helping to solve many of today's most pressing social problems.

* * *

The momentum of development and progress, supported by massive investments from government and industry, are currently leading us towards a global monoculture, with potentially disastrous social and environmental consequences. A balance between the local and the global is clearly needed that can only be reached through a significant shift in direction. Today's trends put technology and the needs of the economy at the top of the agenda. If these are replaced by respect for nature and people, then diversity, both biological and cultural, will be an inevitable consequence.

CULTURE, HEALTH AND ILLNESS IN LADAKH

Tsering Norboo & Tsering Morup
Sonam Norboo Memorial Hospital, Leh, Ladakh

Summary
Medical problems must be approached from a holistic point of view, particularly when western medical practice is introduced into a society like Ladakh's with a strong tradition of alternative medicine. Health is more than physical fitness and includes mental and social contentment.

Overwhelmed by rapid advances in contemporary medical knowledge, a doctor trained in western medicine is often unable to recognise that health is not just an absence of disease but is influenced by social, cultural, economic, psychological and political factors. Health planners and doctors should find enough time to recognise the fascinating relationship between culture, religion and health. Health delivery systems can never be really effective unless these other factors are also considered simultaneously with prevention. It is the same as when much effort is being taken to rescue drowning people from a river and then resuscitating them; yet no one stops them being pushed into the stream higher up.

Today Ladakh finds itself in a precarious culture transition period. Some inherited values are being abandoned, others which should be discarded are being retained, yet at the same time, undesirable modern habits are being adopted. The results on people's health is bound to be disastrous. Whilst modern health care systems, including immunization, maternity and child welfare and efficient health delivery systems, together with well equipped district and referral hospitals are certainly important, the need for a healthy life style is easily neglected. The health related behaviour of an individual is influenced by his cultural background which includes knowledge, belief, morality and laws, as well as the habits he has acquired as a member of the society.

If we examine the influence of Ladakhi culture on health and illness from ancient times to the present, we shall perhaps appreciate that health is closely related to culture. In ancient Ladakh health was considered an ecological relationship between man and man; man and nature; and between man and the supernatural world. There were no doctors, but each village had at least one Amchi family, a member of which would practise Amchi medicine and be much respected. Besides, each householder was his own physician and cared for his family. Spiritual and religious leaders, folk healers and Amchis were much in demand and greatly revered. Many illnesses were attributed to witchcraft, sorcery or the evil eye, or to divine punishment, by gods, spirits or ancestral beings, as a result of sinful behaviour. In most cases, prayers and repentance rather than medicine seemed to cure both sin and sickness. The tools of Amchi medicine were mainly diet, a few painstakingly prepared herbal and mineral mixtures, hot spring bathing and branding (*tse-me* and *mem-bum*). Amchis in ancient Ladakh were in a way polymaths as they had to be proficient in astrology and they had to attain a certain degree of spiritual development to enable them to administer medicine accompanied by tantric rituals.

The Amchi system of medicine is believed to have been introduced in Ladakh by the famous Tibetan translator and philosopher *Rinchen Zangpo* in the tenth century A.D. It was Buddha who gave his teachings in the four principal Buddhist medical treatises "*Gyud-bzhi*" which were popular in Tibet. Some people believe that the Tibetan system of medicine predates Buddha and is about three thousand years old. Whatever the origin of Amchi medicine, it is intriguing to find in it a strong resemblance to the theory of causation of disease put forward by both Hippocrates (460-377 BC) and Aristotle (384-324 BC). They perpetuate the theory of disease in which there are four humours and four qualities. The humours were designated as blood, phlegm, white bile and black bile and people might therefore have sanguine, phlegmatic, choleric or melancholic temperaments. The four qualities were hot and cold, moist and dry. All matter was thought to consist of earth, air, fire and water. As in Amchi medicine, there is a religious background to Hippocratic medicine. This is evident in the Hippocratic Oath: "I swear by Apollo the healer, by Aesculapius, by health and all the powers of healing, and I call to witness all the Gods and Goddesses, that I shall keep this oath and I promise to the best of my ability and judgement ...." It is of interest in its appeal to the deities, particularly to those concerned with healing. The practice of appealing to the Gods and Deities by performing special prayer ceremonies still exists in modern Ladakh. "*gyagi, shenet dulzok, gumik, chasum tsezung*" are some of the prayers offered by monks when appealing to the Gods for the promotion of health. The resemblance between Hippocratic medicine and the Amchi theory of medicine amply demonstrates that in the history of ideas there are no monopolies by creed, nationality or any other artificial division of mankind. It also show how cultural beliefs are sometimes more powerful than facts.

While Hippocrates' theory of the causes of disease was later challenged, in the fifteenth and sixteenth centuries, a student of Amchi medicine should not miss the opportunity to study this subject in greater detail, for in Ladakh it has still not been seriously challenged. Recognising both the Hippocratic Oath and .the Amchi vows, western medicine and Amchi medicine in Ladakh are forging ahead in partnership and without rivalry. The Government policy to support the Amchi practice of medicine has definitely been a welcome move. The Leh Nutrition Project and the Save the Children Fund have played a big role in bringing the Amchis of Ladakh to a common forum by holding seminars and workshops. The last two decades of this century can certainly be called the renaissance period of Amchi medicine.

In societies where ill-health and other forms of misfortune are blamed on social causes (witchcraft, sorcery, and the evil eye) or on supernatural causes (Gods, spirits, and ancestral shades), religious folk-healers are particularly common. In Ladakh the cult of trance divination (*lhaba* or *lhamo*) practised by groups of folk-healers has been popular since ancient times. While such folk-healing practices have obvious shortcomings and dangers, they may have certain advantages in dealing with psycho-social problems. The flourishing practice of this cult in modern Ladakh, without the support of the Government or any other institution, is surprising. Does it reflect an increasingly insecure feeling in society? Is it part of the trend of modern society in general to look towards alternative medicine? Is it the result of the interaction of many varying cultures coming to live in close urban communities? All these developments and their relationship to the subject of trance divination and folk healing need thorough study by a keen student of anthropology.

Medicine, like any other discipline, is an art of civilization, flourishing best where it is well supported. The Moravian missionaries in the nineteenth century were perhaps responsible for introducing the Western style of medicine into Ladakh. From 1960 onwards, the Ladakhis were served by their own doctors trained in allopathic medicine. Immunization, family welfare, maternity and child welfare programmes have helped to reduce infant and maternal mortality to the present level. Although one may find much wanting in the District Hospital due to financial constraints, yet it is easily one of the best hospitals for the general public, and for the poor in particular. Dedication and a human approach to the patients have been the strengths of this hospital; modest contributions on the academic side include original research into environmental pneumoconiosis, koilonychia and the carotoid bodies at high altitude.

As clinicians practising in Ladakh, we have seen great changes in health, both for good and ill, within the Ladakhi community. While infectious diseases like smallpox, measles and whooping cough have been controlled, the progressive adoption of an unhealthy lifestyle has brought in the diseases of an affluent society. Today obesity, diabetes, coronary artery disease, gall-stones, cancer of the stomach, cervix and uterus and lung cancer are increasingly being diagnosed in Ladakh. Tuberculosis of the lung and extra-pulmonary tuberculosis continue to be big problems. The recognition of environmental pneumoconiosis has brought an awareness of the additional hazards of domestic fire pollution and environmental dust which hopefully will improve the respiratory health of the population. An anti-smoking campaign and preventive measures against environmental pollution require the total involvement of the community.

The probable relationship between the Ladakhis' high salt intake and the prevalence of hypertension, strokes and even cancer of the stomach is an example of the links between culture and ill-health. At least 12 - 15 cases of cancer of the stomach are diagnosed each year in a population of 80,000; the expected average would be 4 - 5 cases. Hypertension affects 16% of the adult population, one of the highest rates in the world, and stroke is the commonest cause of death. The fact that these diseases are particularly common in monks and the nomads of Changthang, whose consumption of salt tea is high, further supports the salt factor hypothesis.

There is world-wide epidemiological evidence to favour this association and a plausible scientific hypothesis to explain it. Since high salt intake in the form of salt tea has cultural sanction, it needs to be tackled at a socio-cultural level. We therefore beseech the many Government and non-government organisations which claim to concern themselves with culture, to initiate measures to convert this society to a low salt culture. One needs to realize that values and customs associated with ill-health are part of a wider culture and cannot be effectively tackled in isolation from it.

Viewed in a cultural context, the individual perception of symptoms such as pain varies from culture to culture. Ladakhi culture plays down the emotional expression and response to injury and tends to make light of its symptoms. This is in contrast to certain other cultures in which people in general expect an extravagant display of emotion in the presence of pain. Ladakhi women consider dysmennorhea, labour pains and the menopause as part of the business of being a woman, whereas in western societies analgesia is demanded for dysmennorhea and labour pains (epidural analgesia) and hormonal replacement therapy for the menopause. The stoicism, restraint and the playing down of symptoms in a society which minimizes the response to pain, and the unchecked expression of pain in a society which expects such disclosures, are two languages of distress, both of which may have a negative effect if a patient is receiving treatment from a clinician with a different cultural background. While Ladakhi patients might have their sufferings ignored as they continually underplay their symptoms, Italian or Kashmiri patients might be dismissed as "over-emotional" or "hypochondriacal" by a clinician from a cultural background which does not expect an emotional response. While evaluating people in pain, clinicians should be aware of the cultural influence.

The influence of culture on psychiatric illness is so profound that psychiatrists all over the world find difficulty in standardising diagnosis. Lack of hard physiological data, vagueness of diagnostic criteria, subjectivity and social and cultural influences are all factors responsible for the lack of consensus in diagnosing psychiatric diseases. In every society there is a spectrum between normal and abnormal social behaviour. The peculiar mourning behaviour in Ladakh where the female mourner expresses her grief in song and her solo singing is soon joined by other women in chorus has social sanction and is not considered abnormal behaviour, although a western-trained psychiatrist from a different culture may label this as mass psychotic behaviour.

In nonwestern societies such as Ladakh, mental illness is usually explained by spirit possession, witchcraft, the breaking of religious taboos or the capture of the patient's soul by malevolent spirits. This perspective carries the risk of neglecting the biological causes of mental illness such as brain tumour or dementia.

In primitive societies like Ladakh, illness whether somatic or psychological is considered a social event which intimately involves the patient's family, friends and community. The treatment consists mainly of ritual attempts to repair the social damage, to resolve the conflict causing the illness, to restore group cohesion and to integrate the patient in normal life. In this sort of cultural healing, mental illness seems to be more easily cured and far more short-lived. Patients are not exposed to the toxic effects of modern anti-psychotic, mood-stabilising anti-depressants and anti-anxiety sedative agents. Modern psychiatric treatment, in contrast to the Ladakhi style of cultural healing, serves to isolate the patient even further from society.

With the mad rush towards unplanned development, the social structure of Ladakh is threatening to collapse and as a result mental illness is bound to increase. The recent rise in the rate of suicide among young people is a warning sign of deteriorating mental health as Ladakhi society modernises.

In conclusion, we wish and pray that the elite group of Ladakhis, the well-wishers of Ladakh, and those Government and non-government organisations which take a keen interest in preserving Ladakhi culture, will use their committed leadership to help the community to prevent disease by maintaining the virtues of Ladakhi culture while discarding those elements within it which impede progress.

We are indebted to Margaret Mezzie, Dr Keith Ball and Francesca Ball for their assistance in preparing this paper.

ECONOMIC & CULTURAL LIFE OF THE FRONTIER REGION OF HIMACHAL PRADESH

Fateh Chand Negi
Research Fellow
Central Institute of Buddhist Studies,
Choglamsar, Leh Ladakh.

Kinnaur is located in the North-East of Himachal Pradesh and, because of its strategic position, it has special importance not only to Himachal but also to India as a whole. This region borders Tibet and western Uttar Pradesh. It is also an important place from the point of view of Buddhist religion and culture. Lotsawa-Rinchen-Zangpo of Radne, Guge, was the chief Lama who was responsible for spreading Buddhism in the Kinnaur region. It was mainly because of his efforts that about 108 stupas and vihara were built in the region extending from Kinnaur and Lahaul-Spiti to Ladakh.

The other important region of Himachal Pradesh is Lahoul and Spiti, including Ladakh, situated to the north of Lahoul. It is famous all over the world as an important Buddhist pilgrimage centre. Popular places of pilgrimage in the Lahoul valley are Dilburi and the marble statue of Avalokiteshvara at Triloknath. People in the Lahoul valley worship many other deities, particularly Gephang Maharaja. The practice of annual sacrifices to these deities is still prevalent. I am of the view that the young and up-coming generation should discourage this practice, because such cruel practices will not in any manner benefit us. The Buddha also spoke against such practices 2,500 years ago.

Although the caste system is a deplorable practice, it is still found in the society of Lahoul-Spiti and the Kinnaur valley. People of lower caste can not eat at the same table with the people of a higher caste. They can not even visit Gonpas. It is very regrettable that the caste division is also found in the traditional Buddhist societies of Kinnaur and Lahoul-Spiti. The Buddha fought against the caste system. It is because of this system that India strives unsuccessfully for real unity.

The Tibetan language is the only language in which the complete teachings of the Buddha are still preserved. Bhoti has been the traditional language of religion and culture in these frontier regions. From ancient times to the modern age, these frontier regions have kept intact the Buddhist culture of India in Himachal Pradesh. Thus the culture of Kinnaur and Lahoul Spiti is of special importance.

Farming has been the mainstay of the economy of these regions. Animal rearing is the other important economic activity. Pack animals are a popular means of transporting goods from and to the neighbouring areas. However roads have now been built connecting these regions to the other parts of the country and because vehicular transportation is now easily available, the business activities of the people have also increased. With this, cultural interaction with the people of other states has been possible. Since the opening up of these regions to foreign tourists last year, in 1992, more employment opportunities have been made available in the tourism sector.

SACRIFICIAL OFFERINGS TO LOCAL DEITIES IN LADAKH

Sonam Phuntsog
Achinatang, Purig, Ladakh

In '*A discourse on the early history of Tibet*' compiled by bsTan-'dzin rnam-dag, a former teacher of Smanri, it is said:-

"When Tibet first came into being, people came to settle near the four lakes around Mount Kailash, and depended for their livelihood on yaks, sheep and goats of the rocky slopes and snow mountains. At that time, a harmonious relation developed between people and animals, and the country was known as *gnyan yul*[1]. After that, empowered by the *klu*[2], pastures, forests and orchards came into existence, and people began living in river valleys. When they disturbed the environment, the *klu* caused misfortune. The land was known as the *klu na-ra seng-ngon*. After that, the *btsan*[3] came to power. They lived in crags, rocks and forests, and caused humans both harm and good. At that time, the practice of propitiating the local deities spread for the first time, and the country was known as the land of the red-faced ones."

When calamities occurred, the local deities were propitiated with sacrificial offerings. Since this tradition has no relation at all to Buddhist practice, it should be described as a local custom. This practice, which arose quite naturally as a local custom, is the very same as the one which survived/ in Ladakh until recent times.

This kind of practice spread among Ladakhi and 'Brog-pa[4] people alike. At the time of childbirth in a household, both the father and mother had to observe avoidances for a month.

As for the differences between the deities of the 'Brog-pa and central Ladakhis, at the time of marriage in central Ladakh and other villages, people must go to the place of local deities at night, whereas in the 'Brog-pa areas the local deities must be visited during the day. After the local deities have been welcomed with drumming and entertainment, offering scarves can be given. The 'Brog-pa worship *khyab 'jug* as their chief deity and they make five sacrifical offerings

1. i.e. the land of the *gnyan*: lit. wild sheep, but also kind of spirits.
2. earth/water spirits. (see P.Kaplanian "L'homme dans le monde surnaturel du Ladakh". *Recent Research in Ladakh 4*, 1995).
3. beings of the Middle World.
4. Tibetan term for nomads, but Ladakhi term for the settled people living around Da Hanu, Dards.

in a year to the male and female local deities: twice at New Year; once at *srub-lha*[5]; once at *sngo-la*[6]; and once in the eighth month of the Tibetan calendar. Although it is said that the 'Brog-pa regard both cows and ibex as deities, this is not true. Whereas the deities are pleased to see the ibex and are offered ibex horns after the hunt, they do not like beef, nor milk, nor butter, and these should not be given.

The seven sister deities worshipped by the 'Brog-pa people are: *shug-pa lha-mo* in Hemis Shupkachan; *brag-nag jo-mo* in Khalatse; *hang-la jo-mo* in Skyindiang; *gyak-ra jo-mo* in Domkhar ; *ur-bis jo-mo* in Urbis. The last is also the local deity of Tagmachig and Ledo. It is customary to make a sacrificial offering once a month to *phu-gkar jo-mo*. Six of the oracles of these seven local goddesses are Buddhist, and the oracle of *hag-nis jo-mo* is *sha-dkar drag-shos-pa'i ma-ha-mad* who is the oracle of Purig and Chigtan.

In 1896 the 36th Ladakhi king, bSod-rnam Nam-rgyal, invited 'Brug-pa rin-po-che and 'Bri-gung Chung-tshang chos-kyi blo-gros to Ladakh from Tibet. When Chung-tshang reached Skyurbucan in Sham, he was displeased by the monthly offering to the local deities. When he reached Lamayuru, he invited the oracle from Tagmachig who went into trance, and he asked "Is it sufficient to make sacrificial offerings to the local deities once a year?" The deity replied, "We deities subsist on flesh and blood, but on this occasion we cannot disregard the lama's order". After that, sacrificial offerings to local deities were made once a year, at the time of New Year. At that time, Chung-tshang chos-kyi blo-gros said that, instead of sacrificial offerings, incense should be given, and he composed a suitable offering prayer and along with the burning of incense added a prayer of atonement.

In 1943, having completed his studies, Ba-ku-la thub-stan mchod-nor came to Ladakh from Tibet, and began teaching religion. In 1944/5 he gave teachings to several villages and asked them to abandon the practice of sacrificial offerings to local deities. Although many people obeyed, the practice survived in a few remote villages. In 1960, rTogs-ldan bstan-pa'i rgyal-mtshan came to Ladakh from Tibet. He visited places like Lamayuru in Sham and elsewhere, and forbade the practice of sacrificial offerings. Many were able to give it up, but even then a few were left. In 1975, sKyabs-mgon che-tshang kun-bzang 'phrin-las lhun-grub came to Ladakh from Tibet. As a result of his repeated visits to 'Brog-pa areas like Dahanu, and his requests that sacrificial offerings be abandoned, since 1991 the custom of sacrificial offerings has been abandoned completely.

---

5. Harvest rites.
6. Greening of the mountains.

DISCRIMINATION IN LADAKHI SOCIETY
A Study of Mons & Bedas of Ladakh

Ali Mohmad Rather
Central Asian Studies, University of Srinagar

Summary

This paper describes the Mons and Bedas as cultural groups of Ladakh, their history in brief, and their position in the whole of Ladakhi society; they form approximately 2% of the total Ladakhi population. Mons and Bedas are Buddhists as well as Muslims and they are found in nearly all the villages of Ladakh, excluding Changthang and Zanskar. They are recognised as the professional musicians of Ladakh but are considered the lowest in the social hierarchy of Ladakhi society. This paper is based upon the research conducted for a M.Phil project entitled *Mons of Ladakh - an Ethnographic study.*

Mons and Bedas are two sub-cultural groups of Ladakh. It was stated in a recent report that the total population of Mons in Leh District is 873. They are all Buddhists and form 1.17% of the total population of Ladakh. Bedas are 319 in number. They are Buddhist as well as Muslims[1] and form 0.43% of the total population of Leh District. Mons and Bedas are the traditional musicians of Ladakh. We find a few odd families of Mons in each Ladakhi village.[2]

The term 'Mon' has been used for 'water dwellers' in the Tibetan language[3]. According to one view, the Mons are the original inhabitants of Ladakh. They are Aryan and settled there before the arrival of the Tibetans and the Dards. They are believed to have come from Karja in Himachal Pradesh and set up their dwellings in Ladakh[4]. S.S Gergan believes that the Mon or Rman people were of Austro-Asiatic origin .[5] The other view is that the Mons had come to Ladakh to spread Buddhism[6].

---

1. Tribal Census of Ladakh. 1991 Registrar Gen. of India. Report received through Supt. Archives, Leh, Ladakh.
2. Ribbach, S.H. 1940 *Drogpa Namgyal.* Repr. 1986, transl. John Bray as *Culture and Society in Ladakh.* Ess Ess. Pub. New Delhi. p.108.
3. Snellgrove, D. L. & T. Skorupski 1977, 1980 *Cultural Heritage of Ladakh.* Vikas Pub. New Delhi. Index.
4. Khan Hashmatullah Lucknowee. 1939 *Tareekhi-Jammu-wa-Maftoohati Maharaja Gulab Singh.* Lucknow. p.69.
5. Gergan, S.S. 1980 "Ladakh, the Land of Gumpas". In *Heritage of Kashmir.* Ed. Husnain, F.M. p.49.
6. Francke, A.H. 1981 *A History of Ladakh.* Summit Publishing, New Delhi. p.25.

Mons have been described as the rulers of Ladakh. It is opined that when the Mons arrived in Ladakh, they set up their government, the seat of which was at the village of Rgya and the ruler was called Gyapa cho who was also a member of the Mon group[7]. S.S.Gergan maintains that Leh was also the seat of the Mon king[8]. Mons have been called the great builders and artisans[9]. Various ruins such as the ruined castle of Rgya, the ancient palace of Sakti and Chemri villages, have been referred to as the constructions of Mons[10]. Francke writes that the various ruins of Zanskar, are remnants of the Mon civilization[11]. The famous statue of Chamba (Maitreya) which is twenty five feet high and carved in hard rock at Sanku and Mulbekh, are believed to be master pieces of Mon civilization[12]. However, the local traditions do not fully support the views of these researchers. The view that the Mons were the teachers of Buddhism, is not at all accepted by these traditions . Also the view that the Mons have ruled in any part of Ladakh is dismissed. It is however maintained that the Mons are Aryans and had migrated from Lahul, Spiti and Karja to Ladakh. It is also held that they inhabited Ladakh before the arrival of Buddhism there and they believed in Bon, the original religion of Tibet and Ladakh.

The word 'Beda' is derived from the Tibetan words *Be* and *da*. *Be* refers to separately and *da* means reside. So, Beda means to live separately. The local traditions maintain that the Bedas were the inhabitants of Lahul and had migrated to Ladakh, a long time after the Mons. All Muslim musicians are called Bedas. Muslim Bedas differ from Buddhist Bedas in many respects. They have permanent homes like the Mons; whereas Buddhist Bedas are wandering minstrels[13]. The Muslim Bedas own some land to give them subsistence; whereas the Buddhist Bedas sole means of livelihood is playing music. They go from door to door and beat their drums in front of houses and get a plate of flour and money in return[14]. The Muslim Bedas are believed to be descendants of a group of musicians (Kharmons) ,who came to Ladakh, with the Rgyal Khatoon of King Jamyang Namgyal of Ladakh

---

7. Khan Mashmatullah. op. cit. p.230.
8. Gergan, S.S. op. cit. p.150.
9. Ibid.
10. Kacho Sikander A. Khan. 1986 *Tareekhi-wa-Tamadu ni Ladakh.* KACHO, published Leh, Ladakh. p 94.
11. Francke, A.H. 1973 *Ladakh the mysterious land.* Cosmo Publishing. New Delhi. p.23.
12. Gergan, S.S. op. cit. p 160.
13. Shakspo, N. Tsering,. *Songs from the Himalayas.* Ladakh Ecological Development Group, Leh, Ladakh. p.7.
14. Ibid.

from Skardu[15].

The Mons and the Bedas are of great importance in Ladakhi Buddhist society. If you want to hear of the brave actions of king Kesar, it is the Mon musician who will tell you about them. If you have to arrange a wedding or any sort of entertainment, you must not omit to call the Mon drummer to sustain the enthusiasm of your guests, by beating his queer little kettledrum[16]. They are wanted at every social, religious and cultural function. No such function can take place in their absence .

In spite of all this, the Mons and the Bedas are the most despised people in the Ladakhi society. Common Ladakhis can not give any clarification to this lower social position of the Mons and Bedas. Francke believed that the Mons belonged to a nation different from Tibet and were conquered by the Tibetans and dominated, which lowered their social position[17]. There is a local tradition about the reason for the low social position of these people. According to this tradition, it is believed that before the arrival of Buddhism in Ladakh, the Mons were hunters and butchers. They continued these professions even after the spread of Buddhism. As Buddhism considers hunting and butchery vicious, hence the Mons too were considered low and vicious. Some local people regard their low economic position as the cause of their low social status.

There are some traditions observed by Ladakhi Buddhists to keep the social distance between a Mon and a non-Mon, which shows the social status of a Mon in Ladakhi society.

1. In any traditional gathering, whether it is social or religious, the seating arrangement follows a more or less rigid hierarchy, dependent upon the social status of the people there. They sit in a line with the terminal end of the line occupied by the Beda followed by the Mon.

2. The other people seated there have matting provided to sit on by the host, but no such matting is provided for a Mon or a Beda.

3. All the guests there with the exception of the Mon and the Beda are provided by the host with a cup, spoon etc. The Mons and Bedas have to bring their own.

4. All other persons seated there are provided with a small table called *tchok-tse* in front, on which to place the cups and the food.

---

15. Rizvi, Janet 1989 *Ladakh: crossroads of High Asia.* Oxford University Press, New Delhi.
16. Heber, A.R. & K.M. 1977 *In Himalayan Tibet and Ladakh.* Ess Ess Publications, New Delhi. p.24.
17. Ribbach, S.H. op. cit. p.108.

The Mons and the Bedas are strictly endogamous groups. The rule of endogamy is to be followed always. There is no incidence of any love marriage between a Mon or Beda and Bota. It is due to the fact that if a Bota marries a Mon or a Beda, he loses his own status in society. A Mon or a Beda cannot normally become a lama (i.e.a Buddhist priest) a status considered very holy and highly revered in the Buddhist society of Ladakh. However, there are two Mon Lamas, but due to social discrimination, they have migrated to Himachal Pradesh[18].

The case is entirely different for the Muslims of Ladakh. In Leh, the Muslim Bedas are on a par in status with the other Muslims but with some restrictions on inter-caste marriages. In Kargil district there is no such restriction, and we find Muslim Mons in the villages of Sakar, Chikthan, Fokar and Tambis, sometimes even having the same *phaspun*[19] as non-Mons. These Mon families are holding very good positions in their villages, unlike their co-group at Leh.

Now as far as the social structural consciousness among the Mons and Bedas is concerned, they are very conscious of their low status in the society. This awareness is more among the Mons than the Bedas. Hence most of the Mons do not like to be addressed as Mons. On visiting villages in and around Leh, it is difficult to locate Mon families. People do not refer to them as Mons but as 'artists'.

The question now arises as to whether they make any effort to change their social position. Certainly they do struggle to achieve this. As observed, they do send their children to schools to provide them with education and then they succeed in getting regular salaried jobs[20]. They are trying in this way to abandon their traditional profession of musician.

The Mons and the Bedas made a collective effort some years ago to bring about a change in the attitude of the Ladakhi Buddhists towards them. When H.H. The Dalai Lama (14th. Incarnation) visited Leh, a representative group of Mons and Bedas met him and presented their problem of social discrimination against them by the Ladakhi Buddhists. In response, His Highness, when addressing the audience, forbade people to continue their bad attitude to the Mons and Bedas.

All these efforts have proved useless so far and there has been no change in the attitude of the common Ladakhi Buddhist towards the Mons and the Bedas.

---

18. Rinpoche K. Tukdan, in response to this point, said at the Sixth Colloquium that these two lamas had been sent by him to Himachal.
19. *Phaspun* is a traditional social organisation at village level. It is a group of several families who cooperate in social activities
20. Shakspo, N.Tsering. op. cit. p.9.

KATHOG RIGZIN TSEWANG NORBU'S *(Kaḥ-thog-rig-'dzin Tshe-dbang-nor-bu)* diplomatic mission to Ladakh in the 18th century

Peter Schwieger
Im Kleefeld 16, 53639 Königswinter,
GERMANY

Summary

In 1734 the kingdom of Purig was separated from the kingdom of Ladakh. The relations between the two kingdoms became more and more strained. When there was already the danger of war the opponents turned to the seventh Dalai Lama to send a mediator to solve the conflict. Therefore in 1752 Tshe-dbang-nor-bu, a lama from Kaḥ-thog monastery in East Tibet, was sent to Ladakh. In 1753, at the end of extensive negotiations, the conflict was solved by the settlement of a detailed treaty between the two kingdoms.

In 1734 the kingdom of Purig was separated from the kingdom of Ladakh due to the influence of Zi-zi Khatun, the second wife of king Ñi-ma-rnam-rgyal (r. 1694-1729). She succeeded in her efforts to give her own son bKra-shis-rnam-rgyal a separate kingdom. bDe-skyong-rnam-rgyal, the first born son of Ñi-ma-rnam-rgyal and his first wife, was given the Ladakhi kingdom up to the Po-to-la (Fatu-la). bDe-skyong-rnam-rgyal died a few years later in 1739 and his son Phun-tshogs-rnam-rgyal followed him on the throne. The relations between uncle and nephew became more and more strained. In the end the opponents turned to the seventh Dalai Lama to send a mediator to solve the conflict. Therefore the Dalai Lama sent letters to the famous Tibetan Lama Tshe-dbang-nor-bu from Kaḥ-thog-monastery in East Tibet urging him to accept the diplomatic mission. Tshe-dbang-nor-bu was at that time in Nepal to organize the restoration of the Svayambhūnāth-Stūpa. In May 1752 Tshe-dbang-nor-bu started together with his companions his journey to Ladakh. He crossed the Tibetan-Ladakhi border in the beginning of September and travelled only a little bit further to the monastery of Vaṃ-le (Hanle) which should be - according to his decision - the place for the negotiations.

The knowledge we had about this subject up to now we owe to the basic works of Francke (1926), Gergen (1976), Petech (1977) and Tashi Rabgias (1984). Microfilms of copies of the whole and very long treaty, by which the conflict was settled in the middle of the 18th century allow us to take a much more detailed look at what happened in Ladakh during those troublesome years. The copies are from the collection of Reverend Gergan and from Lo Mustang in Nepal.

The mission of Tshe-dbang-nor-bu turned out to be a very difficult task. In spite of his hopes to solve the problems within three months the mission lasted until July 1753. Although both kings were informed about his coming in advance, he had to wait for the arrival of all participants until the second half of February 1753. I don't want to confuse you with all the ups and downs of the negotiations, which weren't always in proper order. I intend to give you a summary of what were the particular points in dispute and how they were settled in the end. A detailed study including an edition and translation of the treaty into German will be published soon.

Internal Tensions in the Kingdom of Ladakh

Kaḥ-thog-pa Tshe-dbang-nor-bu was first confronted with problems among the leading persons of the Ladakhi kingdom itself. The main cause was the poor mental health of king Phun-tshogs-rnam-rgyal. It is said that he was a clever boy in his childhood but then his mental health became worse and worse. And now the people were talking about him as someone who is crazy for weapons, whose actions are those of an empty brain and who is not able to forget his nurse. His nurse was indeed not only his permanent companion she was also pregnant during the negotiations in Vaṃ-le. The king lost his interest in government affairs. They were now managed by his mother, the rGyal-sras-rin-po-che and queen Kun-'dzoms.

The rGyal-sras-rin-po-che, also known under his prince-name Sa-skyong-rnam-rgyal and his monk-name Mi-pham 'Jam-dpal-rdo-rje, was the eldest son of king bDe-skyong-rnam-rgyal and the halfbrother of king Phun-tshogs-rnam-rgyal. According to custom he should have become king of Ladakh. But he neither got the kingship nor any property. Instead he was made a bla-ma in Hemis monastery. The chronicle says that this is attributed to the influence of Bu-khrid-dbang-mo, the mother of his halfbrother Phun-tshogs-rnam-rgyal. But in the treaty the rGyal-sras-rin-po-che himself sees the responsibility on the side of the Zi-zi Khatun, the mother of his uncle bKra-shis-rnam-rgyal and second wife of his grandfather king Ñi-ma-rnam-rgyal. As he tells us he was already sent away when he was still the only son in the castle. And Bu-khrid-dbang-mo is not at all characterized as a tricky person. Just the opposite she is shown as quite simple. You could make her believe that east is west and west is east because of her bodhisattva-disposition.

We get to know that the rGyal-sras-rin-po-che had on the one hand not the best relationship to his brother but that he had on the other so close connections with his brother's wife, queen Kun-'dzoms, that there were gossip about it in Mulbekh, the capital of Purig. By this he was very much offended.

The Conflict between Purig and Ladakh

The main conflict Tshe-dbang-nor-bu had to deal with was the one between the two kingdoms. Looking for its reasons we first of all have to talk about the Zi-zi Khatun whom we already mentioned. King Ñi-ma-rnam-rgyal had married her after the death of his first wife. She bore him a son named bKra-shis-rnam-rgyal and a daugther named bKra-shis-dbang-mo. The chronicle explains that due to her influence on the first born bDe-skyong-rnam-rgyal for whom she also had taken great care, her own son received the whole area of Purig as his kingdom.

In the treaty bKra-shis-rnam-rgyal tells us that at the time when the ruler of Kha-pu-lu in Baltistan sent his daughter Zi-zi Khatun to king Ñi-ma-rnam-rgyal as a bride it was promised that if she would give birth to a son he should receive the rule in the upper castle which implies the rule of the Ladakhi kingdom. bKra-shis-rnam-rgyal was not able to prove this by showing a document and the rGyal-sras-rin-po-che doubted it very much. As bKra-shis-rnam-rgyal explained it was because of the opposition of the Ladakhi people that his brother was given the rule over Ladakh and he himself received the rule over Purig. Anyhow both parties agreed on the fact that the division of the kingdom is to be traced back to the influence of the Zi-zi Khatun. But especially the Ladakhi party of the conflict blamed her also for other problems in the country while the king of Purig tried to justify her. It seems that one or two years after the Zi-zi rgyal-mo had come to Ladakh she had gained great personal power. And this power she had used especially in favour of her two children.

Bkra-shis-rnam-rgyal and the Kings of Zangs-dkar and He-na-ku

The next point we have to look at for an understanding of the whole conflict is the indistinct position of king bKra-shis-rnam-rgyal in relationship to the king of Ladakh and to the kings of Zangs-dkar and He-na-ku.

bKra-shis-rnam-rgyal saw himself not on the same level as the kings of Zangs-dkar and He-naku but more or less on the same as the king of Ladakh. The kingdoms of Zangs-dkar and He-na-ku were also separated from the kingdom of Ladakh but remained under Ladakhi sovereignty. The rGyal-sras-rin-po-che asked therefore who else than again the Zi-zi Khatun should be responsible for this claim of his uncle and what proof is the uncle able to show for the legality of his claim. But as in all the other cases bKra-shis-rnam-rgyal had no document to show. He even didn't present a witness. He just talked in general that there are still people who could prove his claim. He started to argue by relating stories from the time when the rGyal-sras-rin-po-che and Phun-tshogs-rnam-rgyal were still children, for example that his elder brother had charged him just before he died with the care for his children. This would clearly demonstrate that he was from the beginning on a higher position than the kings of Zangs-dkar and He-na-ku.

The rGyal-sras-rin-po-che on the other hand laid stress on the fact that up to bKra-shis-rnam-rgyal the kings and ministers of the Ladakhi kingdom always were in a position of higher rank compared to the kingdoms which were split off due to a partition of the inheritance.

As we see from the treaty of 1753 this claim of bKra-shis-rnam-rgyal brought him not only into conflict with the king of Ladakh but also with his small neighbour, the king of He-na-ku.

The Claim to the Areas of Spi-ti and Mkhar-bu

Another problem which put tensions on the relationship between Purig and Ladakh were the Ladakhi claims to the areas of sPi-ti and mKhar-bu, nowadays Bod Karbu. They were under the power of king bKra-shis-rnam-rgyal but the Ladakhis doubted the rightfulness of this possession.

The dispute about sPi-ti and mKhar-bu started after the enthronement of Phun-tshogs-rnam-rgyal. Obviously during the time of Ñi-ma-rnam-rgyal and bDe-skyong-rnam-rgyal bKra-shis-rnam-rgyal's possession of sPi-ti and mKhar-bu was no question at issue. Afterwards the Ladakhis enforced claims. But even most of the Ladakhi ministers thought that it would be better first to ask for mKhar-bu alone because for this demand they had the better arguments.

Of course bKra-shis-rnam-rgyal was not willing to cede the two areas. He said that they were given to him by his father and the fact that his brother didn't express any doubts would show his acceptance. But the Ladakhis answered him that bDe-skyong-rnam-rgyal died only four months after his father. Therefore no time was left for a demand.

Also in this case it was difficult for Tshe-dbang-nor-bu to examine the rightfulness of either bKra-shis-rnam-rgyal's possession or the Ladakhi's claim because again no document was shown to him. The only argument in favour of bKra-shis-rnam-rgyal was the lack of a public discussion during the time of Ñi-ma-rnam-rgyal and bDe-skyong-rnam-rgyal. This argument was sufficient for him to refuse the claims of Ladakh as unjustified.

The Disputed Tribute of the Nobles in Purig

The next point in dispute which the Ladakhis started to talk about was the tribute of the five jo-bo, the five leading noble families or dukes, of Purig. It was the custom that every new year those five nobles had to come personally to the big castle in Leh to deliver their tribute. The material value of this tribute obviously was of no great importance but it was considered as a proof of loyality. As stressed by the rGyal-sras-rin-po-che this ceremony was the uninterrupted custom since king Seng-ge-rnam-rgyal (r. 1616-1642) and was stopped in the times of bKra-shis-rnam-rgyal. But bKra-shis-rnam-rgyal's point of view was that already king Ñi-ma-rnam-rgyal gave up the custom and instead only the royal castle of Mulbekh had to deliver the annual tribute in Leh. And this the king of Purig was willing to do.

After a long discussion when bKra-shis-rnam-rgyal couldn't refuse any more a new regulation regarding the tribute, he still was not able to accept the personal appearance of the nobles in Leh. He based it on the unreliability of the nobles. The amount of the tribute was no real subject of the discussion. bKra-shis-rnam-rgyal even offered to give more than demanded. The Ladakhis should only give up the claim that the nobles have to appear personally in Leh.

The refusal of bKra-shis-rnam-rgyal sounds more reasonable when we hear that those nobles became the lords over many thousands of soldiers. Therefore it just seemed impossible to force them to a formal gesture of subordination. But in the opinion of Tshe-dbang-nor-bu the kingdom of Ladakh still had the power for a strong army even without the safe loyalty of the nobles from Purig. On the other hand the king of Purig had to rely on his nobles; otherwise he would be totally without an army. So in the end Tshe-dbang-nor-bu had sympathy for his position.

The Trouble about the Cattle from Purig

In Vaṃ-le the Ladakhis presented a whole list of complaints to discuss. One point in this list was the cattle which belonged to the king of Purig but for which he claimed the right to graze it on the pasture ground of Ladakh. The Ladakhis said that there were more than thousand animals. Undisputed among the opponents was the number of 22 herds of horses which were hended by bKra-shis-rnam-rgyal's herdsmen in Ladakh.

All this had its origin in a small herd of horses which were introduced by bSod-nams-rgya-mtsho, the first wife of king Ñi-ma-rnam-rgyal. At the end of the life of Ñi-ma-rnam-rgyal this herd was once again renewed. Obviously afterwards this herd of horses became the share of bKra-shis-rnam-rgyal. The number of horses was increased and also other kinds of cattle were added, but still he used the pastures in Ladakh. The Ladakhis of course felt it more and more as a burden. Furthermore they claimed the herds for themselves saying that bKra-shis-rnam-rgyal's possession was not according to the law. So they wanted him to drive his herdsmen back to Purig and to deliver the animals. What made a solution in this point more difficult was that bKra-shis-rnam-rgyal considered the number of the horses as a part of his reputation and that a reduction would be a humiliation.

The Fall of Minister Tshul-khrims-rdo-rje

One of the main troubles which arose during the reign of king Phun-tshogs-rnam-rgyal was the fall of the prime minister Tshul-khrims-rdo-rje. His fall also brought a lot of tensions in the relationship of the two kingdoms.

Tshul-khrims-rdo-rje stood in the succession of the nobles from rGya called the rGya-pa-jo-bo. How the trouble about Tshul-khrims-rdo-rje and his family arose is related in the treaty in detail from the Ladakhi point of view. According to them there was already in earlier times a saying in the royal family of Ladakh not to put someone of the rGya-pa-jo-bo in high offices of the government, because he would bridle the king and the whole country and ride on them. Then during the times of Ñi-ma-rnam-rgyal this advice was ignored. At that time bSod-nams-lhun-grub, the younger son of the rGya-pa-jo-bo, first had entered a monastery according to the traditional custom of hereditary succession. But then he gave up the life of a monk and became an official. Soon he was already appointed prime minister (bka'-blon). After that he only tried to grasp as much as possible from the king's power for himself and his sons. He and his son Tshul-khrims-rdo-rje were accused of having illegally taken possession of more than a third of all the land of the royal castle. It is told that at the end the family's possession of arable land was more than the double of the royal possessions.

According to the old customs of Ladakh and out of economic reasons up to that time, the elder son always inherited from the father the castle of the rGya-pa-jo-bo and the younger sons entered a monastery. Therefore always only one family of the rGya-pa-jo-bo developed. But when under Ñi-ma-rnam-rgyal the minister could dispose of the royal land at will, not even one of bSod-nams-lhun-grub's sons entered a monastery. Generously their father distributed the royal land to them. And it is said that he sent his daughters instead of the princesses to the jo-bo as brides. Even lies were spread that there existed an agreement according to which the power in the royal castle had been divided.

And in addition the Ladakhis blamed Tshul-khrims-rdo-rje for having been so cunning as to get bKra-shis-rnam-rgyal under his influence. During a drinking-bout Tshul-khrims-rdo-rje arranged a marriage between his daughter and the king of Purig. A promise was even made that this marriage would be insoluble. After that, king bKra-shis-rnam-rgyal sacrificed his nephews Phun-tshogs-rnam-rgyal and rGyal-sras-rin-po-che and the reputation of the Ladakhi kingdom to the interests of the minister, because he had no thoughts for anyone but his wife.

It is reported that finally, on the 15th of September 1750, the minister Tshul-khrims-rdo-rje was put on trial and found guilty. His two sons escaped to Hemis monastery where the rGyal-sras-rin-po-che granted them refuge. Because they didn't wish to lead a religious life they escaped again - this time to king bKra-shis-rnam-rgyal and her sister in Mulbekh. After that they were the source of quarrels.

What happened to Tshul-khrims-rdo-rje himself when he had been found guilty? As is clearly shown by the treaty he was not with the refugees in Hemis and Mulbekh. Although the treaty doesn't express it explicitly, it seems that he actually was put to death. And in his place his sons took over his interests and fought for them.

Of course bKra-shis-rnam-rgyal had another opinion about Tshul-khrims-rdo-rje and his family. For him the actions of the Ladakhis showed a lack of gratitude for the service which the rGya-pa-jo-bo had done for the kingdom of Ladakh. And he tried hard to present his marriage with Tshul-khrims-rdo-rje's daughter in another light, especially that the story of the drinking-bout was a total lie of the Ladakhis.

When the two sons of the minister fled from Hemis the Ladakhis tried to catch them by sending soldiers on the roads to Purig and Zangs-dkar. Then the Ladakhis tried to force their surrender from Mulbekh. Thanks to the bla-ma from Lamayuru who functioned as mediator and the objection of the rGyal-sras-rin-po-che, a war between Purig and Ladakh was prevented and the sons of Tshul-khrims-rdo-rje could stay in Mulbekh where they felt safe. But the trouble didn't stop. The Ladakhis considered their stay in Mulbekh as a danger. Therefore they were ordered to come to the castle in Leh at the 22nd of May 1752. As soon as they should see the castle they should proceed by successive prostrations. Of course they didn't obey and prefered to live without risking their lives. But the Ladakhis now refused to give them back their paternal land and property. The fear of the minister's sons was still there when the negotiations in Vaṃ-le were arranged. King bKra-shis-rnam-rgyal asked for a guarantee for himself and for Tshul-khrims-rdo-rje's sons before they were willing to come to Vaṃ-le. For sure they were a part of the reasons why Tshe-dbang-nor-bu had to wait such a long time for bKra-shis-rnam-rgyal to come.

The Involvement of Kashmir

Now let us try to reconstruct the events which led to the involving of Kashmir in the Purig-Ladakh conflict. We have to go back to the escape of the sons of minister Tshul-khrims-rdo-rje to Mulbekh and their pursuit by the Ladakhi soldiers.

Through these soldiers bKra-shis-rnam-rgyal saw a serious danger for his kingdom. He was afraid of an invasion. Regarding this the amount of soldiers must have been quite large. According to his statements in October 1750, less than a month after the fall of Tshul-khrims-rdo-rje, two armies marched towards Purig with the obvious intention to conquer mKhar-bu. Because bKra-shis-rnam-rgyal was informed just in time he was able to summon his fellowmen from mKhar-bu and about twenty additional men for the protection of the fort. Therefore the Ladakhi troops retired. But again new troops were summoned. As a reaction also in Purig the king called about 300 men for the protection of mKhar-bu and again 500 for Mulbekh itself. At that time the bla-ma from Lamayuru offered his service as mediator. The Ladakhi ordered the surrender of Tshul-khrims-rdo-rje's sons but bKra-shis-rnam-rgyal refused. Because the common people and the rgan-po wished good relationships between the two kingdoms the soldiers were withdrawn.

The Ladakhi denied that their soldiers retired because of being afraid of the few people in the fort of mKhar-bu. They said it would have been easy for them to conquer mKhar-bu if they really intended to do so. Their soldiers just wanted to catch the sons of Tshul-khrims-rdo-rje. Although some people on Ladakhi side pleaded for a conquest of Mulbekh the rGyal-sras-rin-po-che refused.

The next step in the conflict was the appearance of envoys from Kashmir about one month after these events. The Ladakhis maintained that bKra-shis-rnam-rgyal had called them but he himself affirmed that they were sent by the governor of Kashmir through his own decision. Anyhow the main reason for them to come was the fear of a threat for the trade-road through Purig and Ladakh. They first came to Mulbekh and by saying that they in any case have to listen to both sides they travelled further to Leh. In Leh they compiled a written agreement to settle the conflict between Purig and Ladakh and urged the Ladakhis to accept it already before it was presented to the king of Purig. Then they returned to Mulbekh in company with a representative of the dGe-lugs-pa-monasteries, a representative of the 'Brug-pa bka'-brgyud-pa and the phyag-mdzod of the royal castle as the representative of the rgan-gtso and the common people. They asked for good relationships and according to bKra-shis-rnam-rgyal's words also for sympathy for the young leading personalities in Ladakh who would not always make sound decisions. But the uncle was a mature person with patience and generosity. Therefore he should grant good and firm relationships between their kingdoms and put his seal on the agreement.

bKra-shis-rnam-rgyal first refused saying that a written agreement was not necessary because he never had the intention to damage the reputation of Ladakh. But in the end he signed the agreement after adding some modification to it regarding his rejection of the deliverance of the tribute by the jo-bo in Leh and his non-acceptance of a surrender of Tshul-khrims-rdo-rje's sons. Now he urged the Ladakhis once more to sign the agreement in the modified version.

The Ladakhis considered the envoys from Kashmir responsible for the modification because they had changed their mind in Mulbekh. In general they described the people from Kashmir as tricky by telling each party different words and versions.

Anyhow the agreement was not stable. Each side had its own justifications and blamed the opponents. According to the Ladakhis the reason was that the king of Ladakh was respected by the people from Kashmir as the actual king while bKra-shis-rnam-rgyal was treated as a minor king. For bKra-shis-rnam-rgyal the reason was some military actions of the Ladakhis in Baltistan where the fort of Shi-sgar was conquered which he explained as a preliminary action for the invasion of Purig. As a result bKra-shis-rnam-rgyal blocked the road to Kashmir pretending he was doing it because there would be the danger of the spread of epidemic diseases to his kingdom.

Danger of War

During the negotiations in Vaṃ-le, again and again speculations were discussed about the danger that soldiers would be sent from Kashmir as a support of one or the other party in the conflict. There was shown a letter from Kashmir addressed to the Ladakhis which bKra-shis-rnam-rgyal got in his hands by stopping the messenger in Purig. This letter said that two armies would arrive in September to beat Mulbekh and that therefore the Ladakhis also should summon their troops. As it turned out this letter was the answer to a message the Ladakhis had sent to Kashmir before they were informed about the coming of Kaḥ-thog-pa Tshe-dbang-nor-bu as the mediator. Afterwards such things didn't happen anymore. This was affirmed by the minister from Purig.

Whether the governor of Kashmir really intended to send troops to Purig or Ladakh is more than questionable, because of the weak state of the Moghul rule in Northern India in those times. Tshe-dbang-nor-bu was aware of this, but he was not totally sure about this question. Therefore he urged both kings to send letters to Kashmir telling that there is no need to send an army or any other people. Tshe-dbang-nor-bu also insisted on the opening of the Kashmir-Ladakh road as he didn't want to risk any provocation of Kashmir.

The Results of the Negotiations in Vaṃ-le

The Abdication Of Phun-tshogs-rnam-rgyal

Now let us take a look at the results of the negotiations in Vaṃ-le.

First of all the abdication of king Phun-tshogs-rnam-rgyal was confirmed. This had happened already on the first of December 1750 before the arrival of bKra-shis-rnam-rgyal. Instead of Phun-tshogs-rnam-rgyal his son Tshe-dbang-rnam-rgyal was enthroned. During his minority the rGyal-sras-rin-po-che was to function as regent.

bKra-shis-rnam-rgyal delayed his arrival in Vaṃ-le until the 22nd of February 1753, pretending always to have new reasons not to come. When he finally arrived Tshe-dbang-nor-bu had already waited for him more than five months. According to his statements this was a hard exercise of patience even for a yogin.

The Agreement with the Sons of Tshul-khrims-rdo-rje

An agreement with the two sons of Tshul-khrims-rdo-rje was also settled in Vaṃ-le and its points are stated in the treaty, although there existed a separate document compiled by Tshe-dbang-nor-bu and handed to the rGya-pa telling in detail what was granted to them by the Ladakhis.

To reach an agreement in this special conflict needed some pressure from Tshe-dbang-nor-bu towards the rGyal-sras-rin-po-che because he was not willing to give back to the rGya-pa any of their old land or property until they returned to the kingdom of Ladakh. But fearing for their lives the two brothers refused to settle in Ladakh. Everything else they agreed to do, like taking pledges of doing no harm to anyone of the royal family in Ladakh or confessing the evil deeds of their ancestors. The pressure was successful and the rGya-pa-brothers got back their paternal estate. Of course they didn't receive all the land and estates which were regarded as unlawfully gained. They took an oath not to do any harm to the people of the royal family of Ladakh. According to their wish the rGyal-sras-rin-po-che and queen Kun-'dzoms promised them that in future they could live in safety.

The Agreement between Purig and Ladakh

To facilitate his task Tshe-dbang-nor-bu at first agreed with both parties to fix an armistice of twelve years. But in the end it was the common wish to change it into a permanent agreement.

Tshe-dbang-nor-bu accepted the wish of both sides that there would be no necessity for new talks and discussions. So only a few supplements were added. The treaty which was fixed at the end of the negotiations contains the detailed record of proceedings based upon notes which Tshe-dbang-nor-bu had made during his time in Vaṃ-le, as well as the list of the single points which were settled.

According to this list, first it was agreed that sPi-ti and mKhar-bu are without any doubts part of the kingdom of Purig, further that the nobles of Purig deliver their annual tribute to the king of Purig who then personally gives every year the amount of eight dngul to the king of Ladakh.

16 of the total of 22 herds of horses of bKra-shis-rnam-rgyal shall be given back to the castle in Leh. The other herds he is allowed to graze on the pasture grounds of Ladakh like before.

The rights and the power of the king of He-na-ku are confirmed. And the king from his side promises not to do any harm to the reputation of the royal family of Ladakh.

As long as bKra-shis-rnam-rgyal has no son he shall accept Tshe-dbang-rnam-rgyal as his son. Should he still get a son with good mental health, this son shall become king in Mulbekh and then shall be the ally of Tshe-dbang-rnam-rgyal.

There shall be no difference for messengers from Kashmir and travelling traders regardless from which side they receive a passport. Leading persons shall receive a passport from the castle. Messengers from the king of Ladakh to the governor of Kashmir shall not be stopped in Mulbekh. The king of Purig has the right to send messengers to sPi-ti. If for this reason a passport from the castle in Leh is needed it should be given. The same is applied to messengers from Mulbekh who are sent to Tibet to do virtuous deeds at the holy places.

Disagreements between the two kings shall be settled by confidental talks and by the means of written contacts through messengers.

Ministers and rgan-gtso shall serve the king honestly. This means they also shall say the truth right away if the king is wrong. A wise minister encourages the harmony among the leading persons of the royal family. He isn't open to the influence of relatives and wives and is not motivated by the striving for possessions.

Except for demands for the usual taxes, travelling businessmen shall not be hindered or bothered. The traders from Kashmir had especially asked for such a gurantee. In accordance with this a guarantee for them was written on five copper plates.

In general everything which could harm the Buddhist religion should be avoided.

These are the main points, but some more are added:

1. The rGyal-sras-rin-po-che, his brother and queen Kun-'dzoms together with the king of He-na-ku and their family members shall take an oath to avoid any actions which could harm king bKra-shis-rnam-rgyal. Also the other way round bKra-shis-rnam-rgyal shall take an oath not to harm the lives of the rGyal-sras-rin-po-che, his brother and queen Kun-'dzoms and their family members.

2. The fixed agreement is complete and no open questions are left. No supplementary agreements were made by the kings, the queen or the rgan-gco.

3. The officials shall promote harmony and good relationship. The followers of Islam shall not be bothered. War with other kingdoms must be avoided especially because this threatens the buddhist religion.

4. Affirming this, all the parties concerned have taken an oath.

Apart from this detailed agreement the chronicle mentions only the confirmation of the rights of the kings from Zangs-dkar and He-na-ku. Regarding the king of Purig the result presented in the chronicle is misleading because it just says that there only shall be one king in one kingdom and further down it states that after the death of bKra-shis-rnam-rgyal both kingdoms shall be reunited. This is not what is said in the treaty itself. There the reunification is only to take place if bKra-shis-rnam-rgyal has no son who can follow him on the throne. But in the end the difference had not such a great meaning because bKra-shis-rnam-rgyal died without a son and his kingdom again became part of Ladakh.

Bibliography

FRANCKE, A.H. 1926, *Antiquities of Indian Tibet*, Vol. II, Calcutta.

GERGEN, YOSEB 1976, *Bla-dvags rgyal-rabs 'chi-med gter*, New Delhi.

PETECH, L. 1977, *The Kingdom of Ladakh*, Roma.

SCHWIEGER, P. 1991, *Die Hindernisse auf dem Weg zum Staatsvertrag zwischen Purig und Ladakh 1752/1753*, in: Tibetan History and Language, Studies dedicated to Uray Géza on his seventieth birthday (Wiener Studien zur Tibetologie und Buddhismuskunde, Heft 26), ed. Ernst Steinkellner, Wien, p. 435-440.

TASHI RABGIAS 1984, *History of Ladakh called the mirror which illuminates all: Mar-yul la-dvags-kyi sngon-rabs kun-gsal me-long*, Leh.

SOME WELL-KNOWN ADVENTURERS OF LADAKH

Abdul Ghani Sheik

Yasmin Guest House, Leh 194101, Ladakh.

Ladakh has produced some noted adventurers and enterprising mountaineers during the last three decades of the 19th. century and at the beginning of this century. They were employed by European travellers and explorers who undertook many expeditions to central Asia, Pamir and Tibet through Ladakh on political missions and for the purpose of exploration in those regions.

Among the Ladakhi adventurers, the names of Mohammed Issa, Galwan Rasul, Shukur Ali and Chhumbel are worth mentioning. With the exception of Chhumbel, all the others were Arghon Muslims of Ladakh. The Arghons served as caravan leaders, pony-men, coolies and orderlies for the European explorers.

There is a maxim that the high peaks of the Himalayas cannot be scaled without the co-operation of the Sherpas. The same maxim applies to the Arghons of those days. They bore the main brunt of the rigorous journey. The Arghons also spoke several languages.

Many Europeans have praised them in their books. Captain H.H.Deasy wrote:- 'For caravan work, the Arghons of Ladakh are most suitable, being immeasurably superior to the natives of Turkistan.' A.E.Ward expressed his observations in the following words:- 'Arghons are the best servants for distant travel being hardy and willing.'

Lord Dunmore paid tribute to the Arghons and Ladakhis in these words:

'There is not the slightest doubt that the men we have are the best pony-men in the world. They are the hardest workers I ever saw, with a thorough knowledge of their business. They are always cheery and generally sing when things look blackest.'

In his paper which Lord Dunmore read before the Royal Geographical Society, he said 'A better set of men, hardier or more willing, I have never met', while in the foreword of his book '*The Pamir*' he writes:

'It will ill become me to close this preface without paying a just tribute of praise to those excellent and hardworking Ladakhis, headed by Ramzan Ali who formed the personnel of the caravan and accompanied the expedition on foot for 2,200 miles crossing 69 rivers and 41 mountain passes, many of them being amongst the highest in the world.'

Referring to his travel to Tibet in 1908, Sven Hedin wrote (*Transhimalaya*):

'Some of the Ladakhis sing together to lighten the toil of themselves and the animals. They are as cheerful and contented as though they were going to a harvest festival.'

Besides Arghons, Ladakhi Buddhists were employed by the European explorers. They generally served as pony-men and porters.

Lord Dunsmore travelled to Pamir once in his life and gained worldwide fame from his book '*Pamir*'. Similarly, Younghusband travelled to central Asia and Tibet through Ladakh twice in his life and is ranked one of the most prominent explorers of the region.

Even though the above Arghon caravan leaders travelled with many Europeans, they are, by and large, unknown and their work is not appreciated. With the exception of Galwan Rasul none of them have left any records of their travels. A few explorers like Hedin, Younghusband and Lord Dunmore have praised them in their books, highlighting their roles and contributions.

There is no doubt that the basic motive behind the travel of an Arghon was an economic compulsion but the spirit of adventure and desire for globe trotting was also an important factor. Younghusband wrote in the preface of Galwan Rasul's book, *Servant of the Sahibs*:-

'These men love adventure just as much as their employers.'

The routes adopted by the European travellers to central Asia, Tibet and Pamir were dotted by inaccessible snowbound passes, inhospitable dreary plains and turbulent rivers. The journeys were very hazardous and full of risks. The travellers were under the perpetual threat of snowstorms and avalanches. Inclement weather was vexing. Hedin once recorded forty degrees below zero during his journey in Tibet. Sometimes highwaymen robbed the caravans of their goods.

Tibet was closed to foreigners and travellers had to face great hostility and resistance during their journeys there. Some noted explorers, Rhines, Dalgleish and others, lost their lives while encountering the native population. Sometimes caravans strayed from the paths and suffered untold hardships. The loss of pack animals was staggering. According to Dunmore, forty per cent of the pack animals collapsed on a single journey between Leh and Sinkiang. In one expedition, Hedin lost twenty nine horses and six mules from his total number of fifty eight horses and thirty six mules, with the result that a large quantity of provisions had to be left on the way and the members of the caravan had to face starvation due to the shortage of food.

Under such conditions even the most daring and determined

travellers were disheartened. Whilst crossing the Gobi desert Younghusband underwent many difficulties. He did not have a wink of sleep for many days which made him very miserable. According to his account, he cursed himself for undertaking the journey.

Ramzan Ali travelled from Leh to Srinagar on horseback in forty eight hours to convey an important message to the British Resident. It normally took fifteen days in those days. In order to protect himself from the jolting of the horse, he wrapped his body with cotton padded clothing and two horses were arranged for him at each station. According to Mr.E.Joldan, Qalam Rasul (also known as Baba Qalam) covered this distance in twenty four hours on horse-back. Mohammed Issa has claimed that once he had covered the journey from Leh to Sinkiang in ten days, whereas this journey normally took more than one month on horseback. One adventurous Arghon, Khoshal Ramzan, went to Sinkiang alone. The route between Leh and Sinkiang contains many high passes and bridgeless turbulent rivers.

These Arghon travellers were a cheerful, flamboyant and colourful lot. They were fond of music and dance. Qalam Rasul introduced the Dragon and Amban dances to Leh which became very popular in Ladakh. He had seen these dances in Kashghar. Qalam Rasul and his companions were also the prime movers behind the archery festival in Leh and they delighted their audience with their gimmicks and antics.

A caravan consisted of many interesting individuals. To cite one example, this is a description of Hedin's party. Tondup Sonam was a hunter and provided all the fresh meat. Hedin called him 'The Grand Court Hunt Man'. Rigzin was the jester who amused others with his wit. Mohammed Rahim Ali was the right hand man. Islam Akhon was the horse watchman. Tondup Gyalchan, a pony-man, was the storyteller. Every night he narrated an instalment of the lengthy epic of 'Gyalam Kesar' after a long and tedious journey during the day. Haji Ghulam Rasul was the cook for the caravan leader, Mohammed Issa. The seventy five year old Abdul Gafur was the oldest porter whereas Abdul was the youngest in the caravan at eighteen years old.

In Dunmore's team, Islam Junior was working as a pony-man as well as a tailor. Sidiq and Punchog were both pony-men and cobblers whereas Shukur Ali and Ghulam Rasul were pony-men and farriers.

Now I would like to give a brief description of these well-known adventurers.

Mohammed Issa served as the caravan leader for Carey, Younghusband, Dalgleish, Dutreiul de Rhines, Rawling, Ryder, Hedin and some other explorers. He had been caravan leader in the Lhasa campaign in 1903-4 under the leadership of Younghusband. For thirty years he had travelled in most parts off central Asia and was well acquainted with many parts of Tibet. He spoke Turki, Tibetan and Hindustani fluently.

In his book '*Transhimalaya*' Hedin mentioned Mohammed Issa with these words:

'He was a fine man, tall and strong as a bear with great power of endurance, reliable and honest and after a few day's journey with him, I found that my caravan could not have been entrusted to a better hand. He was always witty and amusing, always cheerful and ready for a joke and kept up the spirits of the rest in depressing circumstances.' Mohammed Issa died in June 1907 at the age of fifty three at Skadezang in Tibet, in the service of Sven Hedin.

The death of his caravan leader was a great shock to Hedin and he paid the following glowing tribute to the deceased in the Turki language at the small funeral ceremony:

'During all my journey, I had never had a more efficient, experienced and faithful caravan leader. He had maintained discipline in the caravan, been a father to men and taken the best care of the animals. He had been an excellent interpreter and had treated the natives with prudence and tact. By his happy, humorous disposition, he had kept all the others in good temper. In difficult situations he had always found the right way out. In unknown country, he had climbed passes and summits to look for the best route. He had always gone himself and not sent others. His memory would always be cherished and honoured among us; and he had always earned a great name in the exploration of Asia.' Hedin placed an inscription engraved on a stone on the grave of Mohammed Issa. At the end of this expedition, Hedin and six Ladakhis reached Simla on 16th. September, 1908. Viceroy Lord Minto and Lady Minto received them and Hedin related episodes of his travels before an audience of one hundred and fifty people. Among those present were the Commander in Chief, Lord Kitchener, a couple of Generals and the Rajas of Alwar and Gawalior. The Ladakhis wept when they parted from Hedin and Lord and Lady Minto remarked 'What faithfulness! What devotion! Their tears are more expressive than words.'

Mohammed Issa was deeply mourned by other explorers. In the Geographical Journal of April 1909, Rawling refers to him as follows:

'Having mentioned Saka-Dzong, let me break off one moment to pay a token of respect to the memory of that faithful servant of Sven Hedin who died here. Mohammed Issa was one of the finest characters it has been my fortune to be thrown with. Trustworthy and indomitable in his work, his knowledge of Asia was unequalled by any native.'

Galwan Rasul was also an adventurous traveller and a prominent caravan leader like Mohammed Issa. He travelled with different explorers when he was very young. In 1892 he went to Pamir with Lord Denmore. In 1895 after traversing difficult terrains in Tibet, he reached near to Lhasa together with the American explorer George Littledale. The same year he travelled to the Baltoro and Siachen glaciers in an expedition organised by Arthur Neve. In 1901, he went to central Asia on a hunting trip with Philips and Church and on their return to Leh he was offered a turban at a function by Philips in token of their appreciation of his services. He served with many other explorers including Younghusband, Martine, Professor Ronald Dixon. Dr. Filippo de Filippi and an American traveller Robert Brot.

It was on the persuasion of Robert Brot that Galwan Rasul wrote his autobiography entitled '*Servant of the Sahibs*' which describes his early life and some expeditions. He mentions his reasons for travelling as follows:

'My relations in Sinkiang were against my travelling. Offering financial help, they persuaded me to give up the hard life of a traveller, but I spurned their offer and told them that I find immense consolation in wandering.'

Younghusband described Galwan Rasul in these words:

'He is a very diligent, hardy and strong man. Any mountaineer will be proud of his great achievements. I have never seen such a man in all my life. He is clearly a popular singer and has also a great delight in banjo playing.'

Once when Dunmore's caravan strayed from the recognised road in Aksai-chin, Galwan Rasul succeeded in locating a new route through a ravine. This ravine is now known as Galwan Nullah. Dunmore has described Rasul as 'Old Francatelli'*.

Qalam Rasul was a contemporary of Galwan Rasul. It was said in Leh that Baba Qalam passed his entire life on horseback! he certainly travelled extensively in central Asia, China, Tibet and Baltistan. Our history teacher used to say:

'Had Baba Qalam been literate and written about his travels, his name would be taken with the eminent explorers of the world.'

When he was barely ten years old, a British Joint Commissioner at Leh employed him to graze his sheep and look after

---

* The reason is obscure. At one time Francatelli was chef to Queen Victoria (ed.).

his ducks.

Mr.E.Joldan, in his article '*Adventures of Baba Qalam*' wrote:

'Baba Qalam as a courier of the British Joint Commissioner covered the two hundred and forty miles between Leh and Srinigar on horseback in twenty four hours. Ponies were changed every five miles or so where men waited with fresh horses and a bonfire. As soon as the letter was given to him, he went to the nearby willow grove, cut a stout branch, peeled its bark, carefully slit a portion into two, placed the envelope in between and tied the two ends with string. He then hurried to the bath-room of the rest-house, tore a piece of red curtain and attached it to the stick. Selecting the fastest pony collected there for the Commissioner's party, he galloped towards Kashmir. The red cloth and the sealed envelope, plus the personality of the courier drew immediate attention everywhere on the way. He dashed back with the reply and delivered it at Spituk to the Joint Commissioner who gave him a pat on the back and a few rupees as Bakshish.'

Qalam Rasul is mainly remembered for his travels in central Asia with Major Malcolm and Captain Welby in 1896. He had a row with the latter and was forced to part company with the caravan. Qalam Rasul and his two companions ate grass, leather goods and the flesh of dead animals in order to survive. After experiencing great hardships, they reached China via Kashghar and eventually arrived back in Leh after three years. Their relatives had given up hope for their safe return and presuming them dead, had performed the funeral rituals.

Qalam Rasul was an excellent conversationalist and was also very witty. E.Joldan writes:

'Baba Qalam had several characteristics of a born storyteller; fluency of language, lucidity of description, modulation of voice, appropriate actions and an occasional dash of exaggeration here and there, without which one would be a dull story-teller. He could make others laugh but never did himself.'

Shukur Ali was also a contemporary of Qalam Rasul and Galwan Rasul. He was the first Ladakhi to cross the Mustagh Pass. Mustagh means mountain of ice. Younghusband dedicated a chapter to Shukur Ali in his book '*The Northern Frontier of Kashmir*' and also published his photograph. He wrote:

'Shukur Ali was the most faithful and my favourite of all servants. He was the most cheery, happy-go-lucky, easy-going man who ever proved a good servant in spite of his carelessness. Always laughing, always chaffing with the pony men or coolies, always loosing something vitally necessary, but always ready to do the hardest and most dangerous piece of work. When the crucial moment arrived, he was the only Ladakhi who dared to cross the Mustagh Pass with me.'

The Maharaja Rastap Singh awarded a medal and a certificate to Shukur Ali on the recommendation of Younghusband. He was also exempted from Begar or 'forced labour' practised at that time in Ladakh. About Shukur Ali, Sven Hedin observed:

'He was so unconsciously comical that one almost died of laughter as he opened his mouth, and he was my oldest acquaintance among this group of more or less experienced Asiatics.'

My paper would be incomplete without any reference to Chhumbel who hailed from Zangskar, and was the faithful companion to the Pandit explorers Nain Singh, Kishan Singh and Kalian Singh. The Pandit explorers were trained by the officials of British India to explore the uplands of central Asia and Tibet. They travelled in the disguise of pilgrims or members of the trade mission to Lhasa, (the Lopchag). To help them in their disguise, they carried a rosary and a prayer wheel like all good Tibetans. However, instead of the one hundred and eight beads normally carried, their rosaries had exactly one hundred and every tenth bead was marked with a bigger one. One bead was counted after one hundred paces, a large one marked one thousand. With due piety, the disguised Lamas murmured the Buddhist prayer 'om mani padme hum', turned the prayer wheel and dropped a bead to count the distance. The prayer wheel was fitted to take long strips of paper on which they jotted their journey notes. To hide their identity, the explorers worked under various pseudonyms.

Chhumbel and the explorers were in perfect harmony. He was true and faithful to the Pandit explorers throughout the hazardous journey enduring hardships cheerfully and willingly. Even in difficulties, he never divulged the secret of the explorers. When Pandit Kishan Singh was robbed by bandits in the Changthang and was deserted by another companion, Chhumbel stood firm. In the last stage of the journey, when Kishen Singh had run completely out of cash, Chhumbel took the begging bowl in his hand and followed his master. He suffered from frost-bite, sun-blindness and lost his toe, but he never deserted his master.

BIBLIOGRAPHY

In Tibet and Chinese Turkestan. H.H.P.Deasy. London. Unwin, 1901.
Servant of the Sahibs. Ghulam Galwan Rasul. Cambridge. Heffer, 1923.
Ladakh and its Adventurer Researchers [in Urdu]. A.G.Sheik. Tamir, Srinagar.
The noted Arghon Adventurers of Ladakh [in Urdu]. A.G.Sheik. Hammara Adah, Cultural Academy, Srinagar.
Indian Explorers of the 19th century. Indra Singh Rawat. New Delhi. Ministry of Information and Broadcasting, 1973.
Transhimalaya: Discoveries and Adventures in Tibet. Sven Hedin. London, Macmillan, 1909-13.
The Pamir. Lord Dunmore. London, 1893.
The Northern Frontier of Kashmir. Younghusband
Harvest Festival of Buddhist Dards of Ladakh & other essays. E.Joldan. Kapoor Bros., Srinagar, 1985.

ECOLOGY AND DEVELOPMENT in High Altitude Ladakh: a Conflicting Paradigm

Harjit Singh
Centre for the Study of Regional Development,
Jawaharlal Nehru University, New Delhi 110067, INDIA

Summary

Ladakh's remoteness and harsh environment resulted in a very distinct culture and economy. The agriculture in particular was highly specialised, while the practice of polyandry assisted in the stabilisation of population and land-holdings. The wars with Pakistan and China and the consequent large military presence and strengthened administration have brought major contacts with outside factors and forces, enhanced by the sudden rise in the number of tourists. The introduction of a cash economy has been accompanied by a dependence on imports of food and manufactures, a devaluation of traditional values, and the rise of new health and environmental hazards. To strike the best compromise between appropriate development and cultural and social conservation will be difficult.

Societies living in high isolated areas ordinarily develop socio-cultural and economic institutions in response to the requirements of the environment. Such regions are generally mountainous where rugged terrain restricts the area suitable for human habitation. Moreover, interaction of such areas with surrounding territories becomes difficult. Such regions, therefore, develop a strong regional identity which is generally different from other environmentally varied regions, but shows a strong imprint of local physical conditions. A serious situation arises when such areas are exposed to outside influences and to modern development. This puts traditional societies in sudden contact with very developed industrial societies. The process leads to major changes in the socio-economic set up. It forces the society to face difficult question of looking at traditional versus modern or indigenous versus exogenous. This also raises the uncomfortable issue as "no matter how attractive a traditional rural society may seem, its people cannot be denied the opportunity to enjoy the benefits of modern development"[1]. Leh district of Ladakh is typical of regions where environment is harsh and socio-economic and cultural practices and forms were evolved based on man's harmonious relationship with nature. This relationship faces serious stress today in the light of significant and sudden changes which came about in the region in the recent past. It, therefore, becomes important to understand the following to comprehend the dilemma that the society in Ladakh is facing today;

i) The environment and the traditional socio-economic setup reflecting the Man-Nature relations there.

ii) The factors and the nature of change and its spatial and temporal impact.

iii) Present day challenges faced by the society and the question of preservation of cultural heritage.

Ladakh, situated in the Trans-Himalayan region of India, is an elevated mountainous region. Nature expresses its harshness in the form of high altitude, rugged terrain and cold arid climate. The physiography and climate not only restrict the habitable area within the region but also put a serious constraint on its interaction with the outside world. Therefore, the society of Ladakh had a very limited interaction with other regions. It is, however,true that Ladakh was not a complete *cul-de-sac*. In fact, many important overland trade routes passed through this region linking Ladakh with Tibet, Central Asia, Kashmir and North Indian plains.[2] Many of these routes have been used by traders and nomads since early times. This significantly contributed towards the making of the culture of Ladakh. Ladakh gained transit significance where the traders coming from different parts of Asia met and exchanged their commodities and went back to their own places. This enhanced the importance of the region but the culture in no way was adversely affected to any significant level. The local socio - economic setup developed in response to harsh environment, based on pastoral nomadism in the higher parts and subsistence farming in comparatively lower areas.

The higher area located particularly in the eastern part of Ladakh popularly called Changthang is inhabited by the Changpas. The Changpas are pastoral nomads who have been traditionally rearing pashmina goats, sheep and yaks. The main products of the area include wool, meat, hides and yak tails. In fact, Changthang produces some of the finest wool in the world. These local products were partly used for self-consumption and some were exchanged with peasants living in the lower valleys for food grain. The larger part of these products was sold to outside traders in return of consumption items. Wool, hides, yak tails and borax were the main items of trade. The commodities bought in exchange included tea, sugar, utensils, coarse cloth, spices and jewellery etc. A barter system of exchange was prevalent. The traders from Kashmir generally had exclusive rights on the wool trade, particularly pashmina. The Kashmiri artisans had acquired the skill of weaving fine pashmina shawls. The Changpas made intense use of pastures in Changthang which were available during summer months. They traditionally moved to lower valleys during winters.

The environment is less harsh in lower parts of Ladakh. Here, the ecology permitted man to settle down and carry out simple farming in a few suitable pockets. Due to rugged terrain and cold arid climate, agricultural activity is possible only in areas which had the following specific features[3];

i) Relatively lower altitude where temperature is high enough for reasonable duration of time permitting seed to germinate and crops to mature.

ii) Gentler slope which could either be levelled or agricultural terraces could be cut.

iii) Availability of water for irrigation as the climate is arid. Whatever little precipitation (generally less than 10 cm. in a year) falls that mainly occurs during winter months when there is no agricultural activity. Therefore, farming is dependent on irrigation. It is done with the help of *kuls* (narrow channels) for which water is diverted in the higher reaches and taken to the fields.

iv) Adequate soil cover to sustain plant roots and provide essential nutrients. Large areas in Ladakh occur in the form of bare rocky surfaces.

The above mentioned conditions are met only in a few areas. These are associated with certain geomorphic features such as river terraces, glacio-fluvial fans and valley floor. Therefore, all agricultural settlements are confined to river valleys where the above mentioned geomorphic features are found. It is not surprising that the inhabited area is highly limited. It cover only 394 sq.km, i.e. slightly less than 0.5% of the total geographical area of the region which equals 82,665 sq.kms.[4] The cultivated area is even less and accounts for around 25 percent of the total inhabited land. Man settled down under these constraints and adopted self-subsistence farming (see diagram). Limited agricultural land is owned either by individual farmers or by the Gompas (Buddhist monasteries). Traditionally, it was tilled by the farmers themselves or by tenants particularly the land belonging to the Gompas.

Agricultural inputs have been simple in the form of non-mechanized agricultural tools. Ploughing is done using animal power especially of yak and dzo and irrigation through gravity by *kuls*. The farming involved intensive use of manual labour. Manure, made mainly of night soil and some animal dung, formed an important input. Part of the produce was kept as seed to be used for the next sowing. It shows very limited use of modern techniques and inputs such as improved varieties of seeds and chemical fertilizers etc. Labour intensive operations like sowing and harvesting were done with the help of community labour provided on a mutual exchange basis. Major crops grown included *grim* (naked barley), wheat, peas and *oal* (alfalfa). *Grim*, wheat and peas were roasted and ground to make *tsampa* - the staple diet. Some barley was fermented for making *chang* - the local light alcoholic drink. *Oal* is a fodder crop and is dried and preserved for winter use. Natural pastures are available only during summer months and animals have to be stall-fed during winter. All agricultural activity is confinied to summer and the growing season extends for about four to five months only in a year. Production, thus, is limited. It is, therefore, natural that most of the produce will be meant for self-consumption with limited agricultural surplus. Whatever surplus the farmers and the Gompas generated it was exchanged with the traders and the nomads.

Social structure was evolved tuned to the economic conditions and environmental compulsions prevalent in Ladakh. Good illustrations of such adaptations are depicted by the polyandry system of marriage and by the Gompa (Buddhist monastery). Traditionally, Ladakhi Buddhists had the practice where only the oldest son in the family would marry. His younger brothers generally not more than two would be the co-husbands of his wife. This system played an important role in this region having fragile eco-system and limited carrying capacity. It controlled the size of population on one hand and checked fragmentation of agricultural land on other. Property passed from the father to the oldest son and the younger sons had no right on the land. Since cultivable land is limited and land holdings small, it would become nonviable to cultivate if fragmented.

Similarly the Gompa, primarily a religious institution, emerged more like a "community centre".[5] They played an all encompassing role in the society of the region. Their significance has been notable in the local economy, cultural activities, local medicine (Amchi system), legal matters, traditional education and also in political spheres. Their role continues to be important in many of these aspects of Ladakhi life even today.

After having looked at the traditional socio-economic setup, it will be appropriate to see the nature and the factors of recent changes and their impact on the society and polity of Ladakh. As stated earlier, Ladakh due to its nodal location had been receiving traders from different parts of Asia. These traders bought food and some other local items from Ladakhis. The interaction of Ladakhis with the outside traders had very limited adverse impact on the culture of the region. The trade continued till late 1940s but after 1947 it started facing problems as the boundaries came to be defined more rigorously.

With trade becoming weaker, the interaction of Ladakh with Central Asia and Tibet declined. It, however, got enhanced with Kashmir. The boundary question gained a greater importance after the Indo-China border dispute of 1962. It was then, that the strategic significance of Ladakh was realised in a big way. This significance got further enhanced after the conflict with Pakistan in 1965 and 1971. It needs be mentioned that Ladakh is the only region of India which forms international border both with Pakistan and China. The Indian Army moved in a big way into Ladakh after 1962. Strategic consideration also led to the strengthening of local administration. Consequently, a number new offices were established in the region. This resulted in the coming in of many officers and other employees. The Leh-Srinagar highway was put on regular vehicular traffic in 1966. This further enhanced the interaction of Ladakh with Kashmir and through it with various other parts of India. Leh town emerged as an important market town dealing with all modern items of use.

The Indian Army and administrative personel also generated demand for items like vegetables etc. This had major impact on the self-subsistence farming and on land use. The peasants had been growing food grains mainly for self-consumption. The coming up of market at Leh town made it possible for farmers to change cropping pattern in favour of some market oriented crops like vegetables and fruits etc. The farmers started selling vegetables and fruits to the army and other officials. They could now buy food grains, brought from other parts of the country to the Leh market. However, this kind of change was noticed mainly in villages located near army settlements or close to Leh town. For example, the author observed that Saboo village situated near Leh supplied vegetables worth one hundred thousand rupees in 1972. In fact, vegetable farming was negligible in Ladakh till 1962. Besides, a lot of job opportunities came up for the local people. Army units like the Ladakh Scouts and other paramilitary forces such as Indo-Tibetan Border Police (ITBP) and the Indo-Tibetan Border Force (ITBF) were strengthened. This provided employment to many Ladakhis. The army also hired ponies to carry supplies to remote army posts. All this brought significant changes on the following lines;

i) Many Ladakhis started earning cash. It came from salaries as was the case with employees or by hiring out ponies etc. This changed the largely prevailing barter system to a money economy.

ii) Many of the items of consumption available in the army stores also became available to the locals. This changed their food habits. The consumption of items like rice, sugar, alcoholic drinks like rum etc., increased considerably.

iii) Exposure of Ladakhis significantly increased. It led to changes in their living style. For example pressure cookers, improved metal hearths, factory made clothes, glazed windows, patent leather shoes became common in Ladakhi households.

iv) Enhanced interaction resulted in Ladakhis realizing the importance of modern education and made available to them the allopathic system of medicine.

v) Traditional polyandry system of marriages declined. It may be mentioned here that polyandry system of marriage was banned through legislation in early 1950s in the Jammu and Kashmir State of which Ladakh is a part. The system persisted and started declining only in the 1960s and more importantly during 1970s.

The most important single factor of change in the socio-economic setup of Ladakh is tourism. It began in the region only in 1974. It must be remembered that earlier, Ladakh was a restricted area due to defence considerations. All non-Ladakhis including other Indians had to get a permit to visit the region.

Table I Tourist Arrivals at Leh (numbers of individuals)[6]

YEAR	**1974**	**1975**	**1976**	**1977**	**1978**	**1979**	**1980**
Foreign	551	650	4580	7692	9621	9834	13104
Domestic	27	128	253	265	876	621	1013
Total	578	778	4833	7957	10497	10455	14117
YEAR	**1981**	**1982**	**1983**	**1984**	**1985**	**1986**	**1987**
Foreign	13200	12786	12933	11785	12245	12828	13688
Domestic	1115	2936	2894	3063	3698	3683	4114
Total	14315	15722	15787	14848	15943	16511	17802
YEAR	**1988**	**1989**	**1990**	**1991**	**1992**	**1993**	**1994**
Foreign	16256	16074	6342	8014	13580	12918	15369
Domestic	8608	6664	396	1041	2438	1135	2080
Total	24864	22748	6738	9055	16018	14053	17449

Parts of Ladakh were opened to tourists in 1974. The rich cultural heritage, exotic land and Tibetan form of Lamaistic Buddhism started attracting tourists in a big way. The above table shows a rising trend in the number of tourists since 1974. Their number reached nearly to 25,000 tourists in 1988. Normally between 15 thousand to 20 thousand tourists visit Ladakh every year. The year 1988 was an exceptional one as Kal-Chakra function was performed by Dalai Lama in Ladakh. This attracted a large number of tourists that year. It may be mentioned that Ladakh also has very high potential for adventure tourism due to high mountains with snow covered peaks and vast unexplored areas. In fact, a survey conducted by the author in 1989 shows that nearly 12 percent of the total tourists visited Ladakh mainly for adventure tourism. It can be seen from the table that most of the visitors are foreign tourists. This created a more serious impact on the society due to greater economic and cultural distance between the tourists and the hosts. The number of tourists is again likely to go up soon because some of the hitherto restricted areas like Nubra and Changthang have been opened to tourists in 1994. Along with tourism, other infrastructure in the form of roads and schools have also been developed in Ladakh during the last three decades. A lot of tourists infrastructure came up in the form of hotels, restaurants and guest houses. It was observed by the author that Ladakh had no hotel or guest house till 1973. The only place of stay was P.W.D rest house and circuit house in Leh town basically meant for the visiting officials. However, there were thirty registered hotels and thirty - four guest houses in Leh town in 1989. Around eleven hotels belonged to the "A class" and were quite expensive. These hotels and guest houses had the capacity of 1,552 beds. It may be mentioned that tourism in Ladakh was developed suddenly in a haphazard manner, without considering its possible consequences on the local community and the environment. As expected, this kind of highly commercial activity was bound to have implications for the region which had weak economy but strong culture. The main considerations for tourism were to boost the economy and earn foreign exchange. The politico-strategic factor of showing greater links of the region with the rest of the country was another factor for the development.

Tourism and other developments which occurred in Ladakh during the last three decades significantly influenced the socio-economic structure. Some of these changes were positive in nature while other had negative impact. The major impacts can be seen in the economic and social spheres and also on environment. As mentioned earlier, Ladakh had a self-subsistence economy based on traditional agriculture and pastoralism largely following the barter system. The tourist and other outsiders generated demand for many local products such as vegetables, fruits, handicrafts and curios etc. Several shops selling these items were established especially in Leh Town. It may be known that many of these shops in Leh Town are run and owned by non-Ladakhis. Besides, the demand of local handicrafts did not lead to any significant rise in their production. In fact, a lot of items sold as local handicrafts are made in other places like Punjab and Delhi etc. The businessmen get a larger margin of profit in selling these rather than producing them locally. The demand of agricultural products led to changes in land use. The region which was producing mainly food grains for self-consumption also started raising crops meant for market. Ladakh is highly suitable for vegetable farming but as stated earlier, vegetable farming was negligible. It was because there was no market on the one hand and the first requirement of the peasants was food grains on the other. However, Leh Town became a market centre and other facilities developed in Ladakh. Now the locals could buy food grain from the market and sell vegetables there. This led to shift in the cropping pattern. An increase in area under vegetables to the tune of 34 per cent was registered during 1973-74 to 1985-86. In order to raise production, the farmers also started making use of some modern agricultural inputs in a big way. The use of chemical fertilizers, insecticides and pesticides was nearly unknown in the region. Traditionally, Ladakhi farmers made excellent use of night soil and animal dung as manure. A survey, conducted in 1988 of Saboo and Stok villages situated near Leh town, showed that more than 70 per cent farmers had started using chemical fertilizers. Many of them were also using improved varieties of seeds and other modern inputs. However, this made farming more resource intensive and some of the smaller farmers are finding cultivation to be unviable. A few cases of small farmers being marginalised in villages around Leh were noticed. They are either giving up farming in favour of jobs related to tourism or some have even started working as agricultural labourers. It is interesting to note that the Ladakhi society traditionally rested on cooperation. All labour intensive works like sowing, harvesting and house construction etc. were done on the basis of mutual exchange of labour. Most households owned some agricultural land. The category of agricultural labourer was nearly non-existent. Now, there is an increase in their number and agricultural labourers rose by 225 per cent during 1971-1981.

A decline is also noticed in the traditional arts and crafts. Now, these are produced mainly for selling purposes. Thus, these lack religious fervour and commitment as seen traditionally. Therefore, the quality of the products is quite poor. As stated earlier, many of these items sold as local products are imported from other places where these are mass produced. Recent changes, however, did provide a boost to the economy. A large number of jobs have been created in the recent past in hotels, offices, schools and in the army. Job opportunities also became available to the Ladakhi youths to work as tourist or trekking guides. All this raised the importance of modern education. Only 10.3 per cent people were literate in Leh district in 1961. The figure increased to 15.8 per cent in 1971 and again to 25.16 per cent in 1981. The growth in literacy, as expected, was much higher during 1971-81. In fact, the number of young boys and girls going for higher education to areas outside Ladakh also increased substantially in the recent times.

As mentioned above, Ladakh had a largely barter system but tourism brought commercialisation in a very sudden and quick way. This brought a lot of inflow of cash. It has been estimated "about Rs.8 million accounting for 17 percent of total tourist expenditure was incurred on food by the tourists in Leh in 1988".[7] These factors introduced various distortions in the Ladakhi society. In fact, in certain cases, Ladakhis were exposed more to foreign currencies like Deutsch mark, French frank, British pound, American dollar, Italian lira and Japanese yen than to the Indian rupee. This happened more during the initial stages of tourism when heaps of these currency notes could be seen on altars of the Gompas. The local people were seen to be comprehending prices and rates more in exchange rates of foreign currencies rather than in Indian rupee. In fact, some roadside beggars started flying to Leh from Chandigarh during tourist season. They found it more lucrative to beg from the foreign tourists.

Along with economy, the socio - cultural set up also underwent significant changes. One significant change was the sudden rise in population. The decadal growth rate of population in Ladakh has been less than 10 percent during 1901- 61. It rose to 19.1 percent during 1961-71 and phenomenally to 30.5 percent during 1971-81. The rise was mainly because many outsiders migrated to Ladakh to cater to the tourist needs and to man offices and provide services to the army. Along with it, the out- migration from Ladakh in search of jobs got checked in the light of opening up of new employment avenues there. Besides, local culture also got commercialised where traditional dances and drama came to be performed more in response to tourist demand on payment. These started losing their seasonal and occasional significance. The significance of the Gompas changed from that of a "community centre" playing role in all walks of Ladakhi life to that of a place of tourist attraction. Here tourist went by buying entry tickets and admired these more as "the relics of earlier culture". Fewer and fewer families started sending their young children to these monasteries to be ordained as monks. Some Lamas also began to get attracted to material comforts. However, those arts and crafts which have found new commercial values are progressing well under the changed situation. These include traditional dances, music and crafts of *thangka* (scroll) painting, mask making and the weaving of shawls and *pattus* (woven woollen strips).

As expected, with increasing exposure and rising awareness of locals their aspirations also rose. Surveys conducted at household level by the author in the villages show that most of the people wanted better transport facilities, electricity, loans, modern inputs for agriculture, food and fuel at subsidized rate. Moreover, most of them aspired for government jobs for their children. However, they were not very clear about the type of job they wanted. Many of them especially younger people were found to be overwhelmed by the glamourous life style of the tourists. This has brought about many disturbances in the social fabric of this region. The system which relied heavily on mutual cooperation without being conscious of religious or cultural differences has started facing serious stresses and strains due to limited opportunities and economic backwardness or lack of access to modern material comforts. In fact, the differences and identity on religious lines were in the foreground in the recent political disturbances. Such intolerance or differences were hitherto unknown in the region. Moreover, some economic prosperity which Ladakh witnessed in the recent past added to economic disparities because the distribution of benefits was highly uneven. Large share of these benefits accrued to the non-Ladakhis.

The development also affected the physical environment. Pressure on land and water resources increased especially in Leh town and areas visited by the tourists. Garbage disposal has become a serious problem. Contamination of water and soil can be seen in Leh town and also some air pollution is noticed due to heavy vehicular traffic. Water-borne diseases have now become quite common. It is, however, true that a large number of trees have been planted by the government, the army and the local people which have led to greening of certain areas. Somehow this afforestation which is normally taken as a panacea for the environmental conservation is viewed adversely by some people; many believe that the planting of trees have led to occurrence of rainfall during summer months which damages the buildings built in traditional style suitable for arid areas.

It may be mentioned that most of the developments discussed above have spatially varied influence. Mostly the impact is seen in and around Leh town, near army, administrative or tourist centres and along the Leh-Srinagar highway.

It can be concluded from the above discussion that the change during the last few decades has been quite dramatic and have significantly influenced the society and the environment of Ladakh. Some of the influences are perceived to be having positive role while others have negative impact. This raises the basic question of preservation of culture and a host of issues linked with it. It is true that many of us living in the oriental world are quite fond of glorifying the past and even referring to earlier times as golden era. However, it is also seen that no culture, however remote, remains static and there are always elements of dynamism in it. The importance and relevance of culture needs to be viewed with reference to the stage of development and in a particular time context. Besides, no culture is monolithic and invariably is made up of various elements, many of which outlive their relevance with the passage of time. Thus, the efforts need to be to strengthen the positive aspects of socio-economic setup. For every development or change a price has to be paid due to some of its adverse side effects. But, certainly going back into the past and recreate the earlier basis of society is neither possible nor feasible because the overall socio-economic situation undergoes a change and the context becomes different. The main role of a social scientist, therefore, is to sensitize the society about these changes and suggest ways of maximizing positive aspects of development and minimizing its harmful side effects. It is true that some societies, after attaining a very high level of material culture and of consumption, are genuinely propagating simpler living. But Ladakhis have a long way to reach that level. What are the good aspects of culture which need to be preserved on traditional lines? This is a big question mark. The decision needs to be left to the Laaakhis themselves. But the choice should be made in the presence of options of modern development and not under compulsion when these facilities are inaccessible to them.

REFERENCES

1. H.H. THE DALAI LAMA in Helena Norberg-Hodge *Ancient Futures - Learning from Ladakh*, Oxford University Press Delhi,1991, p.x.

2. For details see HARJIT SINGH "Evolution of space relations in a semi closed system - A Case Study of Ladakh", in *Our Cultural Fabric - Cultural Heritage of Ladakh*, Ministry of Education and Social Welfare, New Delhi,1978 P.P. 85-100

3. For details see HARJIT SINGH "Environmental Constraints on Agriculture in a Cold Desert" in *The Ecology Of Agricultural System* (ed. Noor Mohammed). Concept Publishers, Delhi, 1992 pp 79-91.

4. The figure includes the area under the illegal occupation of China.

5. For details see HARJIT SINGH "Territorial Organisation of Gompas in Ladakh in *Himalaya- Ecologie And Ethnologie* C.N.R.S. Paris, 1977 pp.351-370

6. Data for 1989-94 added from R.Gilham 1995 *The role of tourism within the modernisation of a non-industrial society: a sociocultural analysis of the changing structure of Ladakhi society*. Unpub. dissn., Business Sch., Univ. North London. The drop in 1990 was due to political unrest in Ladakh. [Ed.]

7. VIBHA SOOD: *Tourism and its Impact on the Socio-Economic Setup of Ladakh*. Unpublished M.Phil. dissertation submitted to Jawaharlal Nehru University, New Delhi, 1990.

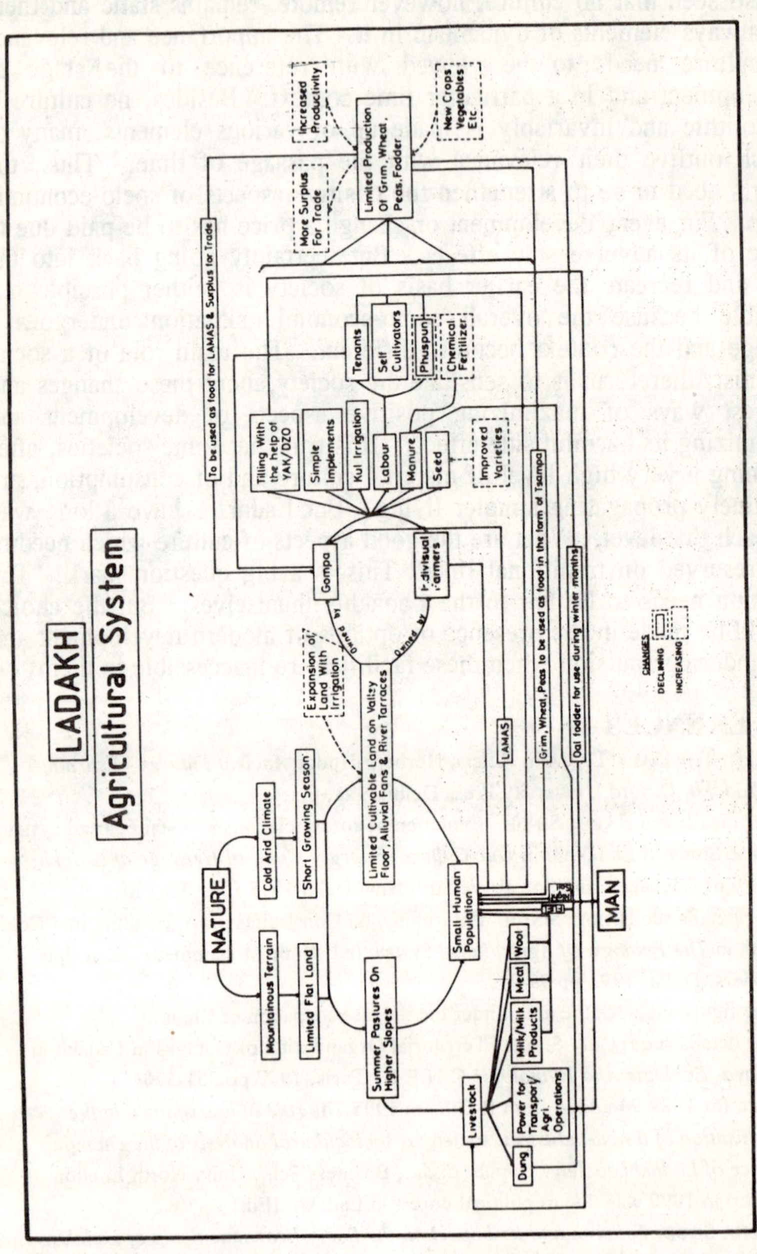

Harjit Singh Fig.1: LADAKH: Agricultural System

THE HOUSEHOLD, INTEGRATION AND EXCHANGE
Buddhists and Muslims in Nubra Valley

Smriti Srinivas
Sociology Unit,
Institute for Social & Economic Change,
Nagarbhavi P.O., Bangalore 560072, INDIA[1]

Summary
The internal organisations of two villages in the Nubra valley of northern Ladakh demonstrate a complex network of cross-cutting ties, so that persons allied in terms of one rule of association are separated by another. Families separated by religion (most are Buddhist but some are are Muslim) are nevertheless linked by vital interests in a common water-supply for irrigation. Despite recent political stresses between the Buddhists and Muslims, all households irrespective of religion participate equally in the administration of the village and take part in traditional rites affirming its identity. There is also a parallelism in the traditional inter-family groupings such as *phaspun*. The nature and composition of 148 households are described and tabulated.

The frontier region of Ladakh, now in Jammu and Kashmir state, became part of the Indian nation in 1947. It was added to the dominions of the ruler of Jammu, Gulab Singh in 1846, in agreement with the British, and throughout the 19th century was part of the "Great Game" between China, Russia, and Britain for possessions in Central Asia. Today it forms part of a militarily strategic tract between the nation-states of China, Pakistan and India. Four wars have been fought since Indian independence: with Pakistan in 1948, 1965 and 1971, and with China in 1962. In the last few years, the secessionist movement in Kashmir has also increased the importance of Ladakh to India for maintaining the integrity of the Indian union.

The presence of various routes across its area for trade, pilgrimage, war, etc., linking Ladakh with such areas as Central Asia, Tibet and Baltistan or Kashmir, and the movement of men and their cultural products from different regions until 1947 has made it a many-centred zone. The existence of various social groups in terms of language, religion, and ethnic origin, with differing cultural orientations leads to social conjunction and disjunction; political interests at the local and supralocal levels, between the region and Jammu and Kashmir state, are not allied, and opposition between forces at different levels makes it a locus of criss-crossing interests. Finally, it can be said that the local economy of the region's various

1. This paper is part of the work done for the author's Ph.D. thesis *Culture and community on the frontier; a study of Ladakh.*

communities is not fully integrated in the economy of the state, leading again to different sorts of pulls, ideologically and materially. In this article, taking the ethnographic case of the Nubra valley's villages, I will try and answer the question: What are the limits of the "community" in Nubra given the existential complexity of the region?

This question has to be answered in the background of my fieldwork in the valley, in 1989 and again between 1990-91. When the choice of the village, Tegar, was made, I had proceeded with the somewhat naive assumption that the community lay within the boundaries of the village. I began to live with a Buddhist family in Tegar, a village that contained a single family of Sunni Muslims. As the fieldwork proceeded, I learnt of the past year's tensions between the Muslim and the Buddhist communities in Ladakh as a result of certain political demands, primarily the demand for Union Territory status, and I learnt of the out-migration of Muslim families in some villages, and the existence of a social boycott between the two groups[2]. I decided that in order that I might understand how diverse religious groups inhabited the same space of the village and the nature of the interaction between them, I would live with a Muslim family for a while as well. In Tegar however, it was difficult to reside with a Muslim family for two reasons. Firstly, as the boycott was in force, my moving through the veil drawn between the Muslims and Buddhists in the village would create difficulties for me as an uneasy participant-observer in a time of strained relations, and for them, mutually suspicious, a certain restraint. Events had occurred in the village, and there existed confidential information to which I was privy which would have made my position extremely indelicate if I then went to reside with a Muslim family. Secondly, as there was only a single

2. The Ladakhis have been insisting since 1947 that Ladakh be included as part of the Indian state directly, on the grounds that with the withdrawal of British power from the sub-continent in 1947, the Treaty of Amritsar that had been concluded in the last century between the Dogras and the British making Ladakh a part of Jammu and Kashmir, was null and void. This demand gathered force in the 1980's, and one outcome of this agitation by the Ladakh Buddhist Association was that, especially from 1989 to 1992, the Ladakhi Muslims, especially Sunnis, came to be viewed as a symbol of domination and difference between Kashmir, whose coreligionists they were, and Ladakh. There has been a long standing perception that rule from Srinagar has been neglectful of Ladakh and Buddhists, but during this period, due to other local triggering factors, the Muslims settled in Ladakh itself, mainly Sunnis, were subject to a boycott by the Buddhists. Since the period of my fieldwork, the Indian government in 1993 offered to give Ladakh Hill Council status; Leh District accepted, but initially not Kargil District which is predominantly Muslim, and the boycott was lifted. By early 1995 this had still not been implemented but under the threat of further civil disturbances by all communities Hill Council status for the whole of Ladakh was gazetted on 9 May 1995.

family (since another family in the village had left since the boycott started and a son of a third family had converted to Buddhism very recently), I felt that I would not really be able to observe the practices of a Muslim community in some detail. So I arranged to move for a while to another village, this time across the river to Hundar, which had a large number of Muslims (of both sects) and Buddhists, in order to observe life from the "other side". I chose to live with a Sunni Muslim family since they were a stigmatised category, affected most by the boycott. Already the idea that a community was a coherent whole was beginning to be questionable. A shared residential space did not mean a shared perception of commonality, and a common practice of one sort could exist with another sort of practice that divided the same group.

The Nubra valley is an ecological niche within the administrative block of Nubra covering the valley of the Nubra and the Shyok rivers. Within this niche, the various villages work according to a particular agricultural calendar; this composite style of life is cross-cut however by differing ritual orientations. The history of Islam and Buddhism in Ladakh is a complex affair and there are present in various valleys, religious groups with differing allegiances. Thus the Buddhists in Tegar village where I did my fieldwork are largely Gelugpa and are locally associated to the main *gompa* (monastery) of the area i.e. Samstanling, while there are some families in a hamlet of the village who also belong to the Diskit *gompa*, both these *gompas* owning some land in the village[3]. What this means in practical terms is that the monthly ritual called the *lapsang* performed by each household and certain other rites will be performed by a monk of the order to which the household belongs.

---

3. Ladakhi terms are italicised in the text of this article, and their contextual meaning given as they were explained to me. Proper nouns are not, nor such words as "Sunni" or "Gelugpa", as they are generally understood. The reason they are not transcribed according to the rules of Tibetan grammar as tends to be the practice with most anthropologists working in Tibetan-speaking societies, is that the dialect in Nubra bears significant differences in vocabulary from the Tibetan dialect, and many words find no place in Tibetan-English dictionaries. To my knowledge, although there exists a standard Ladakhi dictionary and grammar, this is the dialect of Leh and increasingly one used by the press, and other media, in schools, etc. The colloquial language of Nubra differs from this also, and while both Tibetan and the Leh standard are considered to be "high" languages and prestigious, they are not the language of the common people of Nubra. There is the further danger that by transcribing it according to the rules of standard Ladakhi or Tibetan, Muslim speakers of colloquial Ladakhi, whose vocabulary contains words which are neither always Arabic in origin nor Tibetan, may be considered "outsiders". Rather than to participate in the hegemonic project of creating single,"pure" language, my position is that the language of Nubra,like its society, is a locus of cross-cutting ties.

Each village also has a *manekhang* (a temple), and the order with which it is associated appoints a monk there as a priest. Tegar has two *manekhangs* each with a priest of a different order. But all the major festivals of a monastery are attended by villagers of any religious affiliation, in the past also by the Muslims who took part in the fair and the festivities of a monastery event. The villages in the valley have *masjids* only where there are Muslim families in fairly large numbers. Tegar has no *masjid*, but Hundar, the other village where I did my fieldwork, has three: one belonging to the Sunnis, one to the Noorbakhshias and the third to a family which has adherents who are both Sunnis and Shias, although the current household head claims to be Sunni. The *masjids* and the *gompas* have ties with Leh as well as with other centres. The Gelugpa owes its allegiance to the Dalai Lama of Lhasa traditionally, while the Drugpa historically had close ties with the Dharmaraja of Bhutan. At present each *gompa* has its own sphere of influence in the villages around it, while the "royal" *gompa* of Ladakh i.e. Hemis, continues to be fairly important. The prevalence of both Shias and Sunnis, as well as Noorbakshias, who the local people say in the villages near Hundar where the sect is found in large numbers, is a hybrid between the Shia and Sunni sects, makes the orientation of Muslims a complex affair. For instance during *Ramzan*, the Sunnis in Hundar began their fast on the day that their Noorbakshia neighbours did, only to find that the *Imam* in Leh had not given a call for the fast. The Noorbakshias however continued to follow the dictates of the *Imam* of Skardu to whom they were customarily affiliated, although today a cease-fire line separates them. On the day of *Id* this kind of ambiguity was evident again for the fast was broken by the Noorbakshias a day earlier than the Sunnis, but the fact that large numbers of people were congregating in the *masjid* for the *Id namaaz* led the *Imam* of the Sunni *masjid* to celebrate *Id*' twice, once according to the calendar of Skardu and the Noorbakshias, and again according to the calendar of Leh (and Delhi) and the Sunnis. If this is the existential ambiguity of the region, how then is "community" to be defined? An examination of the sometimes turbulent history of the region also points to the diverse cultural ties of this area with others and the varied sources of customary cooperation and conflict between different groups.

A brief history of Nubra valley

There is very little information on the valley before the 14th century; but from the time of King Grags-pa-'bum-lde (1400-1440 AD) there are various historical references. The king's ambitious brother Grags-pa-'bum is said to have paid a visit to Nubra in the hope of seizing power. A local ruler, Nyi-ma-grags-pa, reigned there at that time and it is said that he assisted a Gelugpa exponent, Shes-rab-bzang-po, who came from the Leh valley to Nubra, where he built the monastery of Diskit, and installed a statue of Tsong-kha-pa,the founder of the Gelugpa sect. He also visited Charasa village near Tegar and installed another statue at the Dwensa temple. At the time of Blo-gros-chog-ldan (1440-70) who brought the whole of western Tibet under his reign, the Pan-chen Lha-btsun was born in Udmaru village in Nubra. He went to Tibet for his studies and at the completion of them, acted as the regent for the successor of the founder of Tashilhunpo monastery. In his old age, he returned to Nubra and passed away there, his remains being preserved in Charasa (Shakspo 1990).

In 1500 King Bkra-shis-rnam-rgyal, the first Rnam-rgyal king came to the throne in Ladakh. He had to face the troops of the famous invader from Central Asia, Mirza Haider, both in Nubra and around Leh. There was much bloodshed and the Hor (Turk) army was defeated. This event was significant in Nubra's history because after this, the area came under the king's rule, although the local nobles of Hundar and Diskit continued to have some power. The palaces of the two villages however were taken over and became the residences of the king of Ladakh. The king's son, Tshedbang-rnam-rgyal, came to the throne in 1530, and brought Skardu and Shigar under his rule; he planned to invade the Hor in Xinjiang but was persuaded to give up the idea by the people of Nubra who feared that trade with Yarkand would dry up. It is recorded that from the reign of the next king, Jams-dbang-rnamrgyal (1560-90), the people of Nubra began to pay a regular tribute to the king. At this time Muslims, mainly Shias, began to settle in Nubra. In the reign of Seng-ge-rnam-rgyal, the next ruler, the *gompa* of Hemis acquired land in Nubra, especially at Hundar, Charasa, and Yarma, becoming landlords to a number of households in these villages. Apart from becoming involved with a war with Khapalu in Baltistan and facing the combined might of the Baltis and the Moghuls, a war which he won, the king Bde-'ldanrnam-rgyal (1620-45) carved *mani* walls throughout his kingdom and appointed monks to recite the *mani tung chur* in Nubra as well as in other areas. The Rnam-rgyal kings seemed to have paid attention to religious matters; thus the king Nyi-ma-rnam-rgyal not only rebuilt the palace of Charasa, but also revered the relics of Panchen Lha-Btsun. The king, Tshe-dbang-rnam-rgyal, who came to the throne in the middle of the 18th century, offered Diskit *gompa* to the Rinpoche of Thikse and this arrangement has persisted to this day. He also went to war against the Balti invaders, and was assisted by Nang-gso-bkra-shis, a member of the leading family of Charasa, and for his successes presented him with land and other items. The king, Tshe-brtan-rnam-rgyal, who came to the throne in 1780, was said to have been a polyglot, and knew Yarkandi as well, and it is possible therefore that he lived in Nubra for some time (Shakspo 1990).

From the time of Tshe-dpal-don-grub-rnam-rgyal in the 1830's, when the traveller William Moorcroft visited Nubra, we find many accounts of Nubra and Ladakh attesting to the links of trade and religion of this region with others such as Central Asia, Tibet, Baltistan, Kashmir, etc. By the time the Dogra invasions in the early part of the 19th century were over, Ladakhi independence was coming to an end. The Dogras destroyed many monasteries and religious objects, besides destroying the authority of the kings. In Nubra, near Hundar, a village named after the Dogra king Pratap, came into existence populated by retainers and other servants of the Dogras, nearly all of whom were Muslims. The heads of the various monasteries and the monks tried to re-establish certain traditions: thus Tshul-khrims-nyi-ma founded the monastery of Samtanling near Tegar in 1834. It is the second largest *gompa* in Nubra with about 35 monks led by the incarnations of Tshul-khrims-nyi-ma, a Gelugpa *gompa* which lays emphasis on the observance of the Vinaya and has a far stricter discipline than other *gompas*. This event not withstanding, the forces of change were already set in motion by the events of the Great Game, and the continuous threat that was perceived by the rulers of India from Russia on the northern borders of Nubra. Trade did not however come to an end, and the routes to Central Asia passing also through Tegar towards the Karakoram pass, and between Nubra and Baltistan as well as Tibet, continued to be active. The locals supplied pasture for caravans and horses, and also some *begar,* forced labour, for travellers between the passes. It is said that some kind of tax was also collected by the government in kind and deposited at trading ind halting posts, for example, at Panamik. The Wazir and British officials occasionally toured this area in the summers.

The traffic on the travel routes, however, did abruptly halt when, in 1948, Nubra became a battle field, along with other parts of Ladakh, between Pakistan and India. When the enemy occupied Skardu and came as far as Skuru, about 20 km from Diskit, the Nubra guard was organised locally to resist the invaders (although some nobles and Buddhists fled, while some other Buddhists converted to Islam fearing that Nubra would be over-run by Pakistan) and villagers rallied with old matchlocks, grain, horses, and their men. The Pakistanis were driven back as far as Bogdang, 80 kms. from Diskit, almost purely due to local efforts. In 1971 Nubra again faced another attack, but this time there was an organised military set-up which recaptured some of the earlier occupied territories such as Thang, Turtuk, Taksi, etc. At the present moment, the borders of Nubra have been sealed militarily as both in the east and in the west, the Indian and the Pakistani armies confront each other. There is a huge army presence in the valley in a partly symbiotic relationship with the local people: the army buys vegetables from the villagers, uses its labour for building roads and for other construction activity, and also includes a sizeable number of the local men in the Ladakh Scouts regiment.

Administrative limits

After the inclusion of Ladakh in the Indian state, certain administrative boundaries have been created : first, the division of the region into two districts — Leh and Kargil —, with Zanskar, Dras and Suru, as parts of Kargil district, and Rupshu and Nubra as parts of Leh district. The political unit is composed of blocks. The block where I did most of my fieldwork is Nubra with its headquarters in Diskit. Towards the south and west lie the other blocks of Leh district: Leh, Khalatse, Nyoma and Durbuk. Nubra has an estimated 10,667 persons (all rural) according to the 1981 census, with 6 Gram Sabhas. It has one village electrified by water power, Diskit, and one village electrified by solar power, Tsati. The number of post offices in the area are five, plus one telegraph office, intending to cover 28 villages, but these facilities are extremely poor. Out of a total reported area of 11,936 hectares, the net cultivated area (which is the net irrigated area) was 1882 hectares in 1989-90. The current fallow area was 117 hectares, and the area not available for cultivation was 9634 hectares. The other uncultivated area was 882 hectares and waste land, 666 hectares. The main crops grown are wheat, grim, fodder, and mustard, and some orchards of apricot and apple trees. Only towards the line of actual control near Pakistan Occupied Kashmir do you have cherry, walnuts, grapes, etc., an area whose climate and mode of cultivation resembles Kargil. The number of plough animals are 2064; dairy animals, 3500; goats, sheep and rabbits, 27600; and poultry birds, 1756 (on 31.3.90). There are a few small scale industries (34) and some village skills like carpentry, weaving and blacksmithing. The valley is mainly oriented towards agriculture. There is a single agricultural cooperative marketing society for Nubra at Diskit which is affiliated to the central one at Leh, and it handles the marketing of vegetables, fodder, fruits, etc. from the village to the army. There is a single police station at Diskit with a Sub-Inspector and a constabulary, one primary Health Centre and 44 schools (primary, middle, and high) in Nubra. (All statistics are from SBI Annual Credit Plan 1990-91).

The two villages in which my fieldwork was done lie along the elbow formed by the main ridge of the Ladakh mountains and the Karakoram which meet at the Khardung pass. Hundar is located along the Shyok river; at the base of the Karakoram range is Tegar. The two villages, which derived their significance in the past from being on important routes, are now distinguished by being on the route to the sites of the conflict between India and Pakistan to establish fixed administrative jurisdictions — the Siachen glacier in the east and the Baltoro range in the west. Hundar has a middle school, as does Tegar, but neither has a bazaar, only dispersed shops situated on the highway. Most of the population is composed of those who work on land but each village has some occupational differences which will be discussed below.

A record first published in 1890 says of the village "Taghar" that it is a village in the Nubra district situated on the left bank of the Nubra river. It is a halting place on the summer route from Leh by the Karakoram and lies 18 miles below Panamik, and 7 miles above the junction of the Nubra with the Shyok. Barley and lucerne, apricot, willow, poplar and elm, are cultivated here. The river runs in divided streams over a wide bed of shingle and sand on which there are island patches of buckthorn and brushwood. It is frozen over in winter. It is the headquarters of the Nubra *kardari* and contains twenty houses (Gazetteer 1974:806).

Hundar, it states, lies on the left bank of the Shyok and lies about 7 miles below its junction with the Nubra river. It is a halting place on the route from the Nubra valley to Skardu. It is one of the most populous villages in Nubra with fine orchards of apricot trees. The village has about sixty houses, forty of which pay taxes. The inhabitants are said to possess seven horses, sixty-four horned cattle, and five hundred and fifty goats and sheep. A road from here leads up the Hundar stream dividing into two branches; one goes to Leh via the Thanglasgo pass, and the other to the Snimo and Likir valleys. The camping ground is in an orchard, and supplies are procurable (ibid.pp.366-7).

Today, Tegar has three hamlets; the one I resided in contains Buddhists and three Muslim families. However the third hamlet contains a separate *manekhang*, and it also contains families who form, in the eyes of villagers, another group. This hamlet also has a separate *Zimskang* i.e. a family distinguished by some act of bravery, social largesse, or duty to the king, which has been given that title in the past. It even has its own set of members for the village council in recent times (besides the fact that it spatially separated from Tegar by a few kilometres). These factors which lead one to conclude that it was included within the bounds of Tegar as a purely administrative measure. In this paper, when I refer to Tegar I mean only the first two hamlets with a population of about 93 households. Hundar has five hamlets, each with Buddhists and Muslims living together. The number of Muslim households is about 55, the total number of households in the village being about 200.

Cross-cutting ties

In my understanding, the household is the most basic unit of social life in the Nubra valley. It is the atom of organisation of production and consumption, reproduction and reciprocity in the community. It is differentially related to other households in increasing levels of integration. Levels of integration of social organisation occur through various modalities of exchange and practice within units - either exchange of work, men and women in marriage, ritual services, or the creation of political power. Such levels of integration and practice provide a way of analysing the community as a locus of cross-cutting ties.

There are three levels of integration in local life depending on the type of exchange or practice within each unit: the primary level of integration is the household composed of men and women related by consanguinity and affinity, labouring in the field and at the hearth, opposed to all other households in the village. The household exists in two forms minimally in Nubra: the *khangchen* (the big house) and the *khutu* (the small house) which indicate different stages in the developmental cycle of a family or group of interrelated households. There are groups of households in a village known by the same name, related patrilineally, matrilineally, and sometimes affinally, considered part of what I call the same "kin group". Out of these, the main house which holds the sacra of the family is called the *khangchen*. Within the household, the exchange of work between members and the gender and age based division of labour creates a domain of social life firmly anchored within the territory of the domestic group - the altar for Buddhists, and the hearth, the gardens and the fields owned by a household. In this individuated aspect, households are related to other categories of social life - the *chospun* (ritual siblings) of members of the household, the monk from the *manekhang* or the *gompa*, and the *imam* of the local *masjid*.

The secondary level of integration relates a household to other households in the village through diverse practices - the exchange of work through various kinds of work groups for harvesting, manuring, etc., involving different sections of the village or the whole village;

the ritual exchanges through the *phaspun* (a group of families in the village bound by the idiom of fictive kinship) among Buddhists and the agnatic group (usually) among the Muslims; and the practice of constituting power in the village. The secondary level of integration also includes the occupational division of the community in Ladakh into various ranked categories. Within the secondary level of integration, i.e. that which territorially indicates the domain of the village, also exists the division of the households in the village into two religious groups, as for instance was the case in daily practice during the social boycott.

The tertiary level of integration relates a household to other households by marriage, creating the category of the kindred. This level of integration occupies a domain greater than the village given the dominant practice of village exogamy. A household is also related to other households in political organisations of the Ladakh Buddhist Association and the Ladakh Muslim Association (LBA and LMA). This kind of integration relates Muslims and Buddhists, the town, Leh, and the villages politically, resulting in various sorts of cleavages and coalitions.

The idea that various levels of integration exist in a community is connoted by two words used locally for indicating space and place, and members of a group. *Yul* is a multi-vocal term and can indicate a hamlet, a village, a region, this world, the world of the gods or spirits, etc. The speaker using such a term normally uses it contextually depending on who he is speaking to. Thus two villagers of a valley may use it with reference to themselves and the other, as referring to a village or a hamlet as the case may be. A Kashmiri would be defined as belonging to *Kache-yul* in conversation with a Ladakhi when the issue of his place is discussed, and so on. The second term that is used to indicate that various levels of integration can exist is *pa* (people), used in such diverse contexts as *Kalon-pa* (people of the *Kalon* family), *Nubrapa* (people of Nubra), *Kache-pa* (people of Kashmir), etc. indicating that people can be members of many kinds of groups.

Within the space of this ecological niche in the Nubra valley, the inside and outside, and coalition and cleavage, are not absolute but contextually situated because integration occurs due to different social practices, and for any one unit leads to crosscutting ties. In British social anthropology (from the post-World War Two period until the late 1960's), particularly in the works of E.E.Evans-Pritchard, Gregory-Bateson, Max Gluckman and others, society was conceived of not as a consistent, organic structure premised only on fusion, consensus and societal homogeneity, but also on fission, conflict and cleavage. Different modes of relating structurally equivalent units — two households, two hamlets/villages, two cultural groups, men and women, etc.— were seen to create not a social system, but social fields. Further it was stated that:

> "....societies are so organised into a series of groups and relationships, that people who are friends on one basis are enemies on another. Herein lies social cohesion, rooted in the conflicts between men's different allegiances."
>
> (Gluckman 1960:4).

Two groups are seen not as facing each other as monolithic entities, but as implicated in criss-crossing networks of relations so that each position in the network becomes intercalary. Gluckman (1965) pointed out that in a society with cross-cutting ties, men allied in terms of one customary rule of association are grouped under a different rule with others who have a different ·allegiance under the first rule. A person's role or position can exist at many different levels and is not unitary because each social position or unit is the site of conflicting interests.

The issue therefore of how differences come to be articulated on a frontier such as Ladakh is related to this principle: because of boundaries of various kinds operating in Ladakh and multi-centredness, and because of levels of integration, cross-cutting ties of many types exist for social units and persons. These ties create alliance by one rule between social groups, cleavage by another, inscribing therefore variety in social existence as a mode of life. Distance and proximity are continually created or negated between units and roles, and dynamism is inherent in the way limits are worked out between them.

Ladakh has traditionally been seen as a homogeneous cultural area, primarily Tibetan Buddhist in character. The possibility of applying to it the concept that it is a site of cross-cutting ties with various levels of integration arises because it has slowly come to be recognised that Tibetan society was not centralized in political economy or society. Rather the figure of the spiritual lama/shaman possessing magical powers and the possibility of his intervention in social affairs, the existence of numerous Buddhist orders, the existence of networks of trade routes, etc. all made Tibetan society plural in character (Samuel, in press). Further, in the case of Ladakh itself, it has come to be recognised that there are, in its communities, various kinds of horizontal and vertical ties (for e.g. Dollfus 1989) as is the case with other frontier communities (for e.g. Aziz 1978).

Below is analysed the secondary level of integration of the community in the two villages; i.e. within the domain of the village.

The number and types of households in Hundar

According to the Bandobast (Land Settlement) for Hundar which I obtained from the office of the Assistant Commissioner at Diskit, in 1908 there were 53 houses whose owners were classified as owners of land, *malik*. Tenants appear only tangentially in the Bandobast since they were not tax payers and it was difficult for me to acquire details about the number of tenants. Out of these, 44 were Buddhists, 8 Muslims (1 *Balti* i.e. Shia Muslim, 2 *Arghuns i.e.* Sunni Muslims and 5 *Bedas* i.e. musicians who could be either Sunni or Shia but their origin indicating possibly that they were Noorbakshia), and 1 *Isahi* (Christian). Hemis and Chemrey *gompas* in the Leh valley and Diskit and Samstanling *gompas* in the Nubra valley were also owners of land. In addition, there were 7 other families who were tenants or servants. Table 3 indicates the Muslim families in the village, now grown into a large number of *khutus* from their original families (I was not able to trace the Balti household). I make a distinction here between a household and its members, *nangmi* in local terms (the family in sociological terms) and a group of *khangchens* and *khutus* descended from an ancestor in the village which I call a kin group. The villagers do not themselves have a term for this unity except to call them "the people of" a particular *khanochen* name, thereby indicating descent from it. I call it a kin group and not a descent group because they are formed bilaterally without strong patrilineal and matrilineal tendencies.

All of these families are considered to be Noorbakshia except the first who is Sunni. Besides these families there were 7 other families and their descendants who were not mentioned in the Settlement as *maliks* either because they were tenants and after the Land Reforms in India became owners in the post-1947 period or because they had other occupations when they settled in Hundar. (5) is a Sunni family, while (6) contains descendants who are both Sunnis and Noorbakshias. The original family in (7) was probably Shia but now most of the descendants are married into Sunni families. The others were considered to be Noorbakshias.

At the time of my fieldwork there were 11 kin groups of Muslims indicated in Table 1. The total number of households among the Muslims of Hundar at the time of my census was 55, counted as separate *tutbing* (smokes) in the villagers' enumeration i.e. as separate production and consumption units. They did not comprise a separate territorial area but tended to live in-between their Buddhist neighbours, sometimes in clusters and sometimes as solitary houses. There were 121 males and 118 females and the average household size was 4.35 souls. There were basically two types of households - **nuclear** and **composite**, though really part of different demographic stages of development of a household, the occurrence of impermanent accretions giving an appearance of greater diversity in structure and size. The **nuclear** household may be simple, consisting of husband, wife, and children, or **accreted**, consisting of those budding and declining accretions such as a son-in-law residing with his father-in-law, a widower/widow/divorcee living with a son/daughter, etc. The **composite** consists of a growing nuclear family at its broadest stage of development prior to division - either through parent and married children or through siblings. Table 1 categorises the Muslim households within these types and Table 3 analyses the Muslim households in detail.

The number and types of households in Tegar

According to the Bandobast for Tegar, in 1908 there were 38 households in all three hamlets classified as owners of land, *malik*. Out of these 37 were Buddhist and 1 was Sunni (*Arghun*). Diskit and Samstanling *gompas* were also holders of land. In the area that we consider to be Tegar for the purposes of this article the number of *malik* were 23. All the figures are given in tables 2 and 4. There were 17 kin groups, (1) to (17) in the table, numbering 69 households.

In addition there were about six kin groups, numbered (18) to (23) in Table 4, who may have been tenants in the past and now own some land. The total number of males is 228 and the total number of females was 197. There were 93 households and the average household size is 4.57. If the Muslim families are excluded, then the total number of males in Tegar, now all composed of Buddhist families, is 217 and the total number of females 191. The number of households is 89 and the average household size is 4.58. Tables 3 and 4 show details of all the households, including the three Muslim families - one composite family with a married son and other members, one nuclear family with husband, wife and children, and one with a widow and her two sons.

Grouping households together on the basis of their religious orientations suggests that the unity and the singularity of the household is cross-cut by other ties that integrate it within the territory of the village, i.e. at the secondary level. This kind of integration suggests other kinds of practices. These are of various kinds, but two such groupings must be mentioned here: first, the integration of the households in the village according to religion; and second, the integration of the villages into a hierarchical system of categories, basically occupational in nature.

Table 1: HUNDAR VILLAGE Types of Muslim Households

Type	Number
1. SIMPLE NUCLEAR	
Husband and wife group (old or young)	9
Husband, wife and children	31
2. ACCRETED NUCLEAR	
Widow and daughter	1
Widow alone	1
Widower man alone	1
Widower with married/unmarried children	2
Widower with adopted daughter	1
Widowed half sister with brother's family	1
Two unmarried brothers	1
Widow with married son	2
3. COMPOSITE	
Husband wife and at least one married son	4
Husband wife and at least one married daughter	1
TOTAL	55

Table 2: TEGAR VILLAGE Types of Households (90 Buddhist, 3 Muslim)

Type	Number
1. SIMPLE NUCLEAR	
Husband and wife group	4
Husband,wife and children	53
2. ACCRETED NUCLEAR	
Widow with married daughter	1
Widow alone	6
Widower alone	2
Widow with married son	2
Woman divorcee with daughters	1
Male divorcee with daughter	1
Widow with niece and her married son	1
Mother and son	2
Father and son	3
Unmarried man	1
Two brothers with elder's family	1
Widower with married daughter	3
Widow with daughters	1
Widow with two sons	1
3. COMPOSITE	
Husband, wife, children including at least one married son	7
Husband,wife,children including at least one married daughter	3
TOTAL	93

TABLE 3. HUNDAR VILLAGE: Census of Muslim households only

Ref.No.of Kin Group	No. of Households	Members M	Members F	Occupation	Adults M	Adults F	Children M	Children F
1	5	20	15	Farmer	1	7	12	7
				Teacher	2	1		
				Doctor	1			
				Shopkeeper	1			
				Driver	1			
				Govt. employee	2			
2	12	28	30	Farmer	8	13	14	17
				Musician	1			
				Soldier	5			
3	2	3	4	Farmer	2	2	1	2
4	2	5	7	Farmer	1	4	2	3
				Soldier	1			
				Labourer	1			
5	1	5	5	Farmer	2	3	2	2
				Merchant	1			
6	14	29	25	Farmer	2	16	14	9
				Shepherd	1			
				Moulvi/imam	2			
				Merchant	1			
				Soldier	5			
				Nurse		1		
				Teacher	1			
				Govt. employee	2			
7	2	1	3	Farmer	1	3		
8	3	9	5	Farmer	2	3	4	
				Teacher	1			
				Guard	1			
				Soldier	1			
				Servants		2		
9	3	6	7	Farmer	4	5	1	1
				Soldier	1			
				Servant	1			
10	1	2	2	Farmer	1	1		1
				Shepherd	1			
11	10	13	15	Farmer	11	9	2	6
Total	55	121	118		69	70	52	48

Average household size: 4.35

TABLE 4. TEGAR VILLAGE: Census of all households (90 Buddhist, 3 Muslim)

Ref.No.of Kin Group	No. of Households	Members M	Members F	Occupation	Adults M	Adults F	Children M	Children F
1	1	3	1	Farmer	1		2	
				Teacher		1		
2	2	7	8	Farmer	2	3	2	4
				Soldier	1			
				Teacher		1		
				Govt. employee	2			
3	3	12	7	Farmer	3	4	4	3
				Teacher	3			
				Driver	1			
				Contractor	1			
4	4	10	11	Farmer	6	5	2	6
				Soldier	2			
5	6	11	16	Farmer	7	11	2	5
				Lama	1			
				Govt. employee	1			
6	5	7	8	Farmer	3	6	1	2
				Lama	2			
				Soldier	1			
7	6	7	15	Farmer	4	7	2	7
				Labourer	1			
				Teacher		1		
8	2	4	3	Farmer		1	1	2
				Lama	1			
				Shopkeeper	1			
				Govt. employee	1			
9	10	21	16	Farmer	6	9	8	4
				Gov.t employee	3			
				Soldier		1		
				Driver	2			
				Travel agent	1			
				Teacher		3		
10	4	10	7	Farmer	5	6	5	1
11	5	13	8	Farmer	3	5	5	2
				Lama	1			
				Soldier	1			
				Teacher	2	1		
				Govt. employee	1			

TABLE 4 (cont.)

Ref.No.of Kin Group	No. of Households	Members M	Members F	Occupation	Adults M	Adults F	Children M	Children F
12	3	11	10	Farmer	3	3	5	5
				Lama	1			
				Nurse		1		
				Teacher		1		
				Soldier	1			
				Miller	1			
13	3	10	5	Farmer		3	6	2
				Govt. employee	2			
				Soldier	1			
				Nurse	1			
14	5	11	13	Farmer	3	6	4	5
				Soldier	4			
				Labourer		2		
15	1	5	4	Farmer	2	2	1	1
				Teacher		1		
				Nurse	1			
				Clerk	1			
16	6	21	16	Farmer	8	9	6	7
				Lama	2			
				Office messenger	2			
				Soldier	2			
				Shopkeeper	1			
17	3	7	3	Farmer	4	2	2	
				Soldier	1			
				Teacher		1		
18	13	33	25	Farmer	11	17	11	8
				Lama	3			
				Shopkeeper	3			
				Soldier	2			
				Teacher	2			
				Mason	1			
19	2	4	1	Farmer	2	1	2	
20	3	7	8	Farmer	5	4	2	3
				Labourer		1		
21	2	6	6	Farmer	1	4	3	2
				Soldier	2			
22	1	2	1	Farmer	2	1		
23	3	6	5	Farmer	2	3	4	2
Total:	93	228	197		148	126	80	71

Average household size:4.57 · Average without Muslim households: 4.58

The first kind of integration assumes some importance particularly in the background of the boycott of the Muslims, especially Sunnis, by Buddhists, and the LBA agitation which gathered momentum after 1989. This kind of separation is however not necessarily permanent and after February 1991, the social boycott in the villages was lifted so that effectively, one may assume that in terms of practice, if not in emotive content, this level of integration disappeared.

Households were hierarchically differentiated into various social categories in the village. The Land Settlement was one basis for the classification of social categories as well as the various land-owning households. The Land Settlement considered definitive is the one known as the Lawrence Bandobast. There is a mapping of two kinds of spaces in this Settlement: firstly the mapping of a social space which defines the various grades and sections of village society; secondly, the mapping of land into different categories, humanized for the purpose of subsistence and settlement. The placing of both these maps onto one another then results in a frame which defines both ownership in land (and transfers in ownership), and sources and items of revenue. The settlement also has details of livestock, mills, the distribution of water for irrigation purposes, etc.

The Bandobast for Tegar classified households according to the following categories: 1 household belonged to the *Kalon* category (Chief minister); 1 household was *Lonpo* (minister); 32 households were *Zamindars* (farmers; and one out of these was *Arghun*); 1 household was *Onpo* (astrologer); 2 households were *Shinkans* (carpenters); 1 household was *Mussalman* (Muslim); and 2 *gompas* held land - Diskit and Samstanling.

The Bandobast for Hundar classified the households into the following categories: 1 household belonged to the *Lonpo* category; 40 households were *Zamindars* (including 1 *Balti* household, 3 *Arghun* households, and one *Isahi*); 1 household was *Larje* (doctor); 2 households were *Gara* (blacksmiths); 5 households were *Mon* (musicians and carpenters); Diskit, Chemrey, Samstanling and Hemis *gompas* were landowners.

There is a further classification of land as that under settlement (houses and canals), *Abad-i-de*, and that which was government land (roads, market areas, gardens and Muslim cemeteries), *Khalsa Sircar*.

What is significant about this classification is that it is partly defined by religion, as for instance in the classification of certain households as *Isahi* or *Balti*, partly by social role or function, as *zamindar. larje. gara. onpo* etc., and partly by social status, the ***Kalons*** and the *Lonpos* being the highest in the social hierarchy and the *Mon* being the lowest. It is also defined partly by the ownership/tenancy polarity with the *gompas* and the *Sircar* being landlords and tenants being a sub-category under the landlords; it is defined occasionally by family name, for example *Kalon*.

By contrast Gokhale-Chatterjee (1987) and Mann (1972) describe Ladakhi society as being composed of ethnic groups; among the Buddhists, according to them, are included the *Botos* or Ladakhis (agriculturists), *Gara* (blacksmiths with some land), *Mon* (carpenters and musicians who have no land and only sell their labour); among the Muslims are the *Baltis* (Shias) and the *Arghuns* (of Kashmiri/Turkestani and Ladakhi parents) who are agriculturists and the *Beda* (wandering minstrels). Besides these there are the Changpas (pastoralists) and the Dards (agriculturists, a section of whom are Buddhists). Mann and Gokhale-Chatterjee do not see that social classification occurs in Ladakh not according to one dominant criterion, but according to various factors not all of which coalesce, as can be seen from the varied categories that the Bandobast uses to define the population. The actual position is that there are a number of criteria for classification — ethnic origins, territory, occupation, religion, rank, etc. which cross-cut each other.

The households in Tegar and Hundar present some disparities in wealth, occupation, prestige and influence. In the past there were ranked social groups sustained by rents and customary obligations. Gokhale-Chatterjee says that in the past society was classified into four different strata (including therefore the ethnic groups) in any local context: the royalty, including the king and ministers; the nobility; the peasants, who also supplied the revenue officers, the village headman, the temple guard, the master of the castle, the doctor, the astrologer and the oracle; and the outcastes, who included the blacksmiths, carpenters and musicians, and wandering minstrels (ibid.pp.459-461).

After the inclusion within the Indian state, the abolishing of the monarchial system (a process which began after the Dogra wars), and the Land Reforms, this system has altered. Only *gompas* were exempt from the act and continue to hold a large amount of land. The socio-economic processes of the Indian state have also created forces which resulted in new forms of social differentiation by creating bureaucratic offices, military positions of power, a commercial life which far exceeds in volume what existed previous to the closing of the borders and the traffic with Central Asia, Tibet, etc. A person can thus advance himself/herself by state patronage, through education, piety, commerce, and so on. Only the starting point of power is land and such paths as mentioned above which take men and women outside the settlement also bring strangers into it.

In the two villages, people tend to identify the following groups in terms of their occupations:

1. *Skutag* (old nobility, the upper strata, generally large landlords);
2. *Zingbatpa* (peasants);
3. *Mullahs*, *lamas* and *chomos* (religious persons);
4. *Mulazzim* (anyone connected with administrative work)
5. *Sepahi* (soldiers in the Indian army); and
6. *Mon, beda* and *gara* (the lowest rank).

The first and sixth form the clearest positions in the social hierarchy, being the highest and the lowest group. In the middle ranges, issues are more complex: for this differentiation is largely by occupation, past and present, and in the same household may be combined in a complicated form. It is not just relative wealth which decides, but also such factors as those with whom they are married or can marry. The monks are usually celibate, only some Drugpa monks marry. The other strata tend to form relatively endogamous groups - 2, 4, and 5 form one such group; the higher positions among 4 and 5 tend to form another such group with 1; 6 tends to be another group. This is less due to a formal rule then due to political, strategic and existential choices. These broad groups are complicated also by various sources of status and power today. In general it can be said that there are two systems of role positions currently that combine in a complicated fashion within a household and between households: given the considerable expansion in population and material resources, especially non-agricultural, it follows that if the classification given by Gokhale-Chatterjee is accurate, i.e. comprising of the royalty, the nobility, the peasant, and the outcaste (though we must include in this classification also the clergy who rank with the nobility or the peasants, depending on the rank of the monk), then this earlier role complex has been replaced by one that is far more complicated as indicated in the tables earlier for each household in the two villages.

Apart from the two modalities mentioned earlier i.e. according to religion and occupation, households within the secondary level of integration are grouped according to three other modalities. The first is the work group for all major occupations in the field; the second is the group which assists the household in life-crisis rituals called the "phaspun" in the case of the Buddhists and what I shall call the "iftarspun" in the case of the Muslims. These two — the work group and the ritual group — are not equivalent. The third is the minimum locus of political power — the village — which associates the household to all the other households in the locality and opposes it to other localities.

The work group

Within the limits of agricultural space and ecological time the village households organize themselves into fairly stable units for work. The smallest kind of work group is the household 'the unit of restricted simple exchange'[4]. The household is the locus of consumption and production and revolves around the axis of the hearth and the field made available by the joint efforts of the members. Day to day tasks in the field, such as watering, planting and transplanting vegetables, fencing, taking care of animals, collecting wood, etc., and in the house, such as cooking, spinning, etc., are done with certain basic tools which are owned by every household — the spade, the pick-axe, the hoe, the stove, the basket, and so on, requiring human labour.

But there are also tasks for which these do not suffice. Larger tools are pooled together by a stable group of various households composed of some kin and neighbours, or in the case of landlords, also including their tenants. These tools include the plough, the large winnowing plate, etc. used by what I shall call the extended group of simple exchange. Again there are tasks which involve all the households of the village for example, the cleaning of water channels, and involve 'the unit of complex exchange'. Since both fall within the territory of the village, they are a part of the secondary level of integration.

Men and women of the unit of simple extended exchange: (1) harvest mustard and barley; (2) plough and sow fields for mustard and barley; (3) take manure to the fields and (4) take animals to pasture.

Women of the simple extended exchange unit do the weeding of the large fields.

Men and women of the complex exchange unit (1) de-silt the water channels and (2) prepare the main canals for water for irrigation.

These groups are fairly stable over time although in the period 1990-91 the Muslims had organised themselves into a new grouping and had disassociated themselves from their Buddhist kin and neighbours due to the anti-Muslim boycott.

The phaspun

The *phaspun* includes kin groups that are not related by affinity since there is a custom that one cannot marry one's *phaspun*

---

4. These terms are used in the same sense as they were used by Terray (1972).

member. The *phaspun* is mutually exclusive and it becomes visible in its corporate form during life-crisis rituals of various sorts — birth, marriage, death, etc. They may belong to the same village or to adjoining villages although the importance of their presence makes it necessary that they do not belong to far-flung ones. They meet at a feast twice a year. Each *khangchen* of a kin group calls every other kin group of the *phaspun* for a grand meal in turns. The first occasion when this happens is during *shrupla* when the sickle is removed from the house for cutting grass in the fields. This usually occurs during the month *Dawa Tukpa* (mid-July to mid-August). On the 12th /13th day of *Dawa Tukpa* all households in the village go to the main sluice of their fields and pour *chang* into it in an act of consecration. They then cut a basket full of grass from the fringes of the field and bring it to the house. A ring of grass is made and tied to the main pillar of the house, usually in the kitchen which is simultaneously the axis mundi and the dwelling of the god of the house. This cutting is only symbolic and the main work of grass cutting begins on a day fixed by the village headman. The *phaspun* affirm their solidarity at a feast in the nights of *shrupla*. The other occasion on which they meet is during the New Year festival, *Losar*.

Some writers in the past have emphasized the common ancestor within a *phaspun* and assume that the *phaspun* is a clan, and its members blood relations. However it is my view that a clan is not an accurate description of the *phaspun* in this area. Firstly this society does not have strong patrilineal or matrilineal tendencies in the practice of kinship and it functions on a bilateral basis. Secondly, in terms of practice, it can be observed that it is not consanguinity that is the decisive criterion. According to Brauen (1980) the *phaspun* is a group of people belonging to more or less closely situated households who have reciprocal privileges and duties, the adoration of a mutual tutelary deity, and a jointly owned furnace for the dead in common. A *phaspun* contains about 4—6 households he states, although in the village of Tegar one observed many more kin groups and therefore many more households. Being a member is not bequeathed through males only; all children succeed to their father's *phaspun,* or in the case of uxorilocal *magpa* marriages, to that of their mother. Change in residence can also lead to a different membership. Thus blood relations can belong to different *phaspun*. The fact that at funerals it is the *phaspun* that takes care of all the funerary arrangements which are taboo to the blood relations proves that it is not consanguinity that is a decisive criterion, either patrilineal or matrilineal, but the idiom of fictive siblingship through the *phas-lha* that is decisive. The apex of the group is the *phas-lha*, which is a symbol of unity whose support is sought for prosperity and well-being; it is either a god or goddess. Brauen states that the Ladakhis are not in agreement over whether intermarriage is possible; there are indications that the rule of exogamy as now practised in the more distant areas of Leh was more strictly applied in the past. All these observations of Brauen's also apply to Tegar.

The *phaspun* duties included, in Tegar, assistance in life-crisis rituals since it is the *phaspun* who are supposed to stand by you in 'sorrow and happiness'; mutual support is expected in political disputes and occasionally, though it is not a rule, in agricultural work. There was some disagreement about whether Muslim households were also *phaspun* members. In Tegar there were seven *phaspuns* comprising of between 2-5 kin groups each and it is said that in the past the *Arghun* household used to be a member of a *phaspun*.

The iftarspun

The Sunni Muslims in Hundar (and I was given to believe this is the practice among the Noorbakshias as well) also have a group based on siblingship, although not fictive in the case of the *phaspun*. This group consists of a set of households related by ties of marriage and agnation, *khutus* of a given *khangchen* who meet primarily during the *iftar* (the evening meal that breaks the Ramzan fast daily). It is my understanding that this group which call the *iftarspun* also assists in the main rites of passage although I did not observe any cases. I call it thus because this is a group which can be observed according to the practice of meeting at *iftar*, though the people themselves do not have any name for it. It appears to be equivalent to the kin group. For e.g. they give assistance and participate in such rituals as the birth of a child, a boy's circumcision, death, etc.

On the fourth day after the death of a person, the Koran is read and 5 or 7 rotis and 150 gm of meat is said to be distributed to all the village households. Between the first and the fourth day, people in the area visit bringing a small quantity of barley flour and some money with them. Until the fourth day, food and water in the house of death are not ingested because of pollution. On the 40th day again the Koran is read because the *ruh* (spirit) is said to inhabit the house until then. After a year, *Lokhor*, about fifteen people gather and read the Koran to "give peace to the *ruh*"; food is distributed to all those gathered, and those who have prayed for the dead are paid a compensation of five rupees or so.

On the occasion of the birth of a child the *azan* is spoken into the child's ear. On the 7th day it is named, an occasion called *akhikat*. The naming takes place by a sort of lottery where pieces of paper holding various names are put into a container and a child is asked to pick one piece. A goat is slaughtered on this occasion and a part given to the mother to replace the milk and blood she has given to the baby. The rest is distributed to the poor and others.

On the day of the *sunnat* (circumcision), which is usually performed before a boy is 11-12 years old, relatives and friends, both men and women, go with incense, eggs, milk, and other gifts to give *mubarak* or greetings. Ritual scarfs are also exchanged.

On the occasion of marriage as well, the *iftarspun* is present. A lawyer is appointed to speak for the girl and two witnesses to vouch for the proceedings. In a separate room, the *imam* verifies the girl's acceptance of the proposal. The boy also gives his acceptance before a congregation. The *imam* reads out the *dua* (prayer) and ascertains the dowry. The *nikkah* ceremony takes place in the groom's house, or if it is a *magpa* marriage, in the bride's.

The *iftarspun* is usually a family consisting of brothers, father's brothers, sisters, etc. i.e. the branches of a *khangchen*, although it is my understanding that given the number of virilocal marriages among the Muslims in Hundar, it is usually a agnatic group. They meet by turns at *Ramzan*. In the period 1990-91 this group collapsed into the work group in the context of the Muslim boycott by the Buddhists. This coalescence is described below.

The calendar of agricultural work for a Muslim household is similar to the Buddhist one for the area. The ritual calendar is different but periodically at the completion of a cycle of festivity, the cycle of work provides a space and time in the ways of life of Buddhists and Muslims, of convergence. Besides the collective rituals such as *Id* there were those activities in the life cycle of individuals which involved also the *iftarspun*. Earlier the festive and ritual period and space also accommodated Buddhist neighbours and kin. In the period prior to 1990-91, there was an exchange of food, gifts, visits, etc. which ceased for that period. This was reflected in the work process as well. Hundar is divided into five geographical areas for the purpose of certain agricultural activities such as the cleaning of the canals, taking manure to the fields, etc., similar to the division of labour involved in Tegar. During 1990-91 they ceased to be a unit in all but the basic necessity i.e. the cleaning of the channel.

At the time of the agitation, the Muslims split into three groups in the village: Noorbakshias who sided with the Buddhists since they were excluded from the boycott; Sunnis who were intimidated by the threats and said they would support the LBA in its demands; and the Sunnis who opposed the LBA and were boycotted. This was in the period late-1989 onwards. But in late 1990, two movements occurred to change this grouping. All Sunnis came together as the LBA became more extreme in its approach and the Noorbakshias began to oscillate between the two groups. Towards mid-1991 when there was a possibility of elections being organised in Jammu and Kashmir, the LBA realised that it would not win the Congress-I ticket unless it attempted a rapprochement with the Muslims. Some Buddhist families began to borrow tools, animals.etc. from Muslims for work purposes and also began to buy goods from their shops, or travel in their vehicles which hitherto had ceased. In the meantime Muslims had begun to assist each other in work, meet for the Friday *jumma*, and form themselves into smaller work units for mutual assistance. When questioned, the Sunnis claimed that they formed one group as Muslims since they were a cohesive ritual and work unit although clearly in terms of origin and social and religious factors there were differences. The Sunnis were descendants of both Ladakhis and others — Kashmiri and Yarkandi traders, officials etc. - while the Noorbakshias were mainly tenants and servants of wealthy Buddhist families in Hundar who received land after the reforms.

But in 1990-91 the *iftarspun* and the work group for a Muslim household had tended to become unified, being linked to their Buddhist neighbours only in the most formal sense i.e. for the purpose of cleaning and regulating the water canals for which the labour and co-operation of the area's households was unavoidable. Prior to the boycott, the ritual and the work group were not identified. I do not know how far the current political reconciliation between Buddhists and Muslims from the end of 1992 has altered this situation.

The village

The minimal and customary unit of political power in the valley is the village. From a height, a village is usually a triangular patch fanning out towards the river. The only ecological constraint for the founding of a village is that there must be water in the form of a glacier-fed stream since Ladakh is a cold desert. Villages are usually found by the side of a major channel sharing water sometimes with a neighbouring settlement. In the case of Hundar, water was shared between three villages, while in the case of Tegar, it was shared with another two, the times of receiving water being fixed by custom and need. As a rule, villages in the area are either formed by the farming land being at the base of the settled area of the village as a whole or by it being around each household. Both fieldwork villages were of the first type. A village has a *manekhang* with a priest, a *Zimskang*, and sometimes a noble family, branches of a family in Leh.

In a purely spatial sense again, territories of villages are separated by large distances, especially in a region where the population is extremely thin and the inhabited area small, making a village easily identifiable. A number of villages also have "gateways" to them (hollow entrances standing in the middle of the road), though not all. A large enough cluster of households usually forms a separate village, identifiable, as we said, as a patch of green near a mountain stream.

In general, one may say that there are three components of political power in Tegar or Hundar:

(1) the village headman and his council;

(2) the symbolic unity of the village seen as a relationship of gods to man. or of men to their significant others;

(3) the material culture of the village, primarily in the form of the irrigation system and the arrangements for labour in agriculture.

All these are in turn affected by political institutions larger than the village which impinge on its internal affairs such as the LBA or the LMA, the administration in the form of the Assistant Commissioner, the District Commissioner and officials of the block, and the army, although in this article I will not deal with them.

(1) The representative of a village's political unity is the village headman, the *goba*, and the village council. In the past the position of the village headman may have been hereditary, the families of the nobles and the *Zimskang* also having de-jure political powers in addition to their being large landlords. This was largely customary, because power as such was not centralised, rather such nobles and petty chiefs had a great deal of autonomy, sending some gifts of tribute to the king in Leh and occasionally raising an army for him, but with the power to make or break him. The nobles and the *Zimskang* owned a large amount of land in the villages in an area as did the monastery, with a number of tenants, this itself being a source of great power. While relations within a village may have been oppressive, between the centre of the king and the local landlords, chiefs, ministers and monasteries, power seems to have been a site of centrifugal and centripetal forces rather than a clear-cut centralized system in which the clergy and the nobility were allied. (This is suggested by Samuel (1993) as well). In the present period, this power is considerably diminished both economically and politically, and the *goba* is chosen by rotation among the households for a period of two years. A male member of a household (the villagers admitting that it was rare that women become *goba*) is chosen at *Sakha*, the day ritually marking the beginning of an agricultural calendar, to be a *goba* for the next two years. A village council with six members or so is also chosen by

rotation every year. The village council and *goba* maintain authority for the period of their office by agreement on the part of the people. The exchange is equal and commensurate, and every household has a chance to assume authority, each household acceding to the power of a deputed representative for a defined period. The political power of the goba includes (a) the settlement of disputes in the village; (b) control over the fair distribution of water along with another person, the *churspon*, appointed for that purpose for that year; (c) mediation between the district authorities and the village; and (d) assumption of a leading role in some rites like *Losar*.

(2) The field of power in the territory of the village is constituted by many items: authority and obedience in the choice of the *goba*, the gods whose blessings must be invoked i.e. sacred beneficence, and work. This field of power is also constituted by the thoughts, actions and words of its members, all of which form the "life-force", *la*, of the community, embodied in the *yul-lha* (the god of the village or settlement) which is affected and affects the life-force of individual members. Thus a rise in the disputes in the village, a decline of morality, a lack of participation in work and ritual by some of the members, etc. is felt to affect this power. This last aspect is described from the Buddhist point of view although there exists an analogy between the concept of the *ruh* (spirit) and the *la* used by Muslims and Buddhists respectively. I do not know if the Muslims also subscribe to a belief of a community spirit although there does exist a sense that the individual and the social are inter-related intrinsically. I was however told that at Turtuk near the ceasefire line, a nearly completely Muslim village, the *yul-lha* is propitiated by Muslims. Bray (1991) cites a similar case at Khuksho in Purig.

The symbolic unity of the village as opposed to other villages, the internal field of power and well-being, is affirmed in the presence of the *lha* of the village settlement. Each settlement has a stone-cairn or *lhato* where the god is felt to dwell. Every year at *Jipa Chukshik*, the 11th day of the fourth month, the *yul*lha of Tegar has its annual *lapsang*. The 'waist band' of the *lhato* is replaced with a fresh one during the cleansing and *shukpa* (juniper incense) is burned, with organisers providing these items to the praying monks. These organisers belong to the entire village and two families take turns every year to be the officiants. Both men and women may be present. The *pumpa,* sacred little pots containing seeds, are removed from the body of the *lhato* and replaced. There is a direct relationship between the seeds, the agricultural crop for that year and the well-being of the village. If that year the seeds are not depleted in the pot, then it is read as an omen of good fortune and auspiciousness; otherwise some danger is felt to be augured for the village community. The *yullha* is also felt to be a protector of the community and propitiated if need be.

The second time when the boundaries of the village as a locus of power become visible is during *Losar*. This time the community of persons in the village is acknowledged by all groups in the yillage, although again in the context of the boycott, Muslims did not participate in the festivities as they had done in the past. The participation of the households in the village in its events, the exchange of gifts and visits, the assembly of the village men at a bonfire to burn the evil of the past year of the community, etc. affirms its boundedness and unity.

The third time is during the ritual called *Bumskor*, in *Dawa Tukpa,* the sixth month of the Buddhist calendar. This occurs at mid-point between sowing and reaping, when the sacred books of the monastery or *manekhang* are carried by the villagers on their backs in a path around the village. Men, women and children participate in charting the path that forms the limits of the village, including fields and houses.

These symbolic aspects of the village's boundedness are complex in nature: it can happen that a certain rite can come to be perceived as a rite of a particular group as was the case in the three occasions cited above, when it was felt by the Muslims in Tegar and Hundar that these were specifically Buddhist rites. In the past, the New Year festival also formed an instance of the unity of the village. Although it has achieved the status of a Buddhist festival, this idea of a festival to mark the winter solstice and view it as a rite of transition to a new period is common to a number of agricultural communities. Certainly there are a number of elements in the festival which are neither Buddhist nor Muslim but merely those of peasants; the monastery does not even participate in the round of feasting,drinking and games. Even if it is assumed that it was a Buddhist festival, the exchange of gifts and counter gifts ensured that the Muslims were also part of festivities marking the New Year; they visited the houses of their Buddhist neighbours to give *mubarak* and in turn were visited and greeted during such festivals as *Id*. It is possible that such an exchange has been resumed since the boycott has been called off.

(3) The material culture of the village as a factor in power situations in the village, including both Muslims and Buddhists, was most evident during the constitution of the complex unit of exchange which involves the labour of everyone within the bounds of the community for the purpose of the very conditions of their existence — the channelling of water through the canals for agriculture. The place of water systems in the constitution of unity and a decentralised system

of power has not really been addressed in the case of Ladakh. As explained in the earlier section, when the village community was under threat by the anti-Muslim boycott, its material unity nevertheless continued in a very basic sense due to the system of water management in Ladakh's villages.(I do not know of any instance during the boycott when water was denied to Muslim farmers, although there was one case in Hargam village when pasture was denied). In most villages in Ladakh, water systems encompass more than one village, their usage fixed by ancient custom and more or less continued during the Dogra rule and after 1947. As Gutschow (1993) has suggested, the analysis of water systems in various societies of the Tibetan ecological zone provides clues as to the practice of politics in these societies. Thus, in Tibet, water rights were adjudicated by a district official responsible to the Dalai Lama of Lhasa, and relatively centralised. In Ladakh and Zanskar, they were less centralised and managed by a village official in the former and by inter-household consensus in the latter. Disputes were also decided at the village level, rarely reaching higher authorities, and one may presume that this was true of most other conflicts. Gutschow points out that, similarly, power is not concentrated in Ladakh and Zanskar, but the tightness that the web of water management exercises creates both intimacy and control. Water has to be channelled to every field by a strict system of rotation and equality; everyone in the village keeps a strict watch on the usage of water and on each other so that although, as Gutschow suggests, the problems of distribution are complex, exploitation is rare. (see also Osmaston *et al*. 1994)

Conclusion

In this article I have tried to lay out the organisation of the "community" in two villages in Nubra valley, taking as a domain of description and analysis, the secondary level of integration, i.e. the territory of the village. The thesis of this article was that "community" can be understood as a locus of cross-cutting ties, so that persons allied in terms of one rule of association are separated by another. Roles are therefore not unitary in their enablements, but are premised on social variety. Further, by providing examples of Muslims and Buddhists in the valley, I have tried to show that there is a parallelism between their patterns of organisation, even though the current political situation has created a sense of separate identity.

References

AZIZ, Barbara N. 1978 *Tibetan Frontier Families*. New Delhi, Vikas

BRAUEN, Martin 1980 "The pha-spun of Ladakh " In Michael Aris,and Aung San Suu Kyi (eds) *Tibetan Studies in honour of Hugh Richardson* New Delhi, Vikas

BRAY, John 1991 "Ladakhi history and Indian nationhood" *South Asia Research*, Vol 11 No 2 115-133.

DOLLFUS, Pascale 1989 *Lieu de neige et de genévriers: organisation sociale et réligieuse des communautes bouddhistes du Ladakh*. Paris: Editions du CNRS

GAZETTEER OF KASHMIR AND LADAK 1974 First pub.1890, compiled under the direction of the Quarter Master General in India in the Intelligence Branch. Delhi:Vikas Publishing House.

GLUCKMAN, Max 1960 *Custom and Conflict in Tribal Africa*. Oxford: Basil Blackwell.

——— 1965 *Politics, Law and Ritual in Tribal Society*. Oxford: Basil Blackwell.

GOKHALE-CHATTERJEE, Sandhya 1987 "Stratification and change in contemporary Ladakhi society".In M.K.Raha (ed) *The Himalayan Heritage*. Delhi : Gian Publishing House, 456-468.

GUTSCHOW, Kim 1993 "The politics of water in three Tibetan societies: 'Lords of the fort','Lords of the water' and 'No lords at all'" This volume.

MANN R.S. 1986 *The Ladakhi: A Study in Ethnography and Change*. Calcutta: Anthropological Survey of India.

OSMASTON, H.A., J.FRAZER & S.CROOK 1994 "Human adaptation to environment in Zangskar". Chap.2 in *Himalayan Buddhist Villages; environment, resources, society and religious life in Zangskar, Ladakh*. Eds. J.H.Crook & H.A.Osmaston. University of Bristol, U.K. and Motilal Banarsidass, Delhi. 976p.

SAMUEL, Geoffrey 1993 *Civilized Shamans: Buddhism in Tibetan Societies*. Washington D.C.: Smithsonian Institution Press.

SHAKSPO, Nawang Tsering 1990 "Historical perspectives of Nubra in Ladakh" in L.Icke-Schwalbe and G.Meier (eds.) *Wissenschaftsgeschichte und Gegenwärtige Forschungen in Nordwest-Indien*. Staatliches Museum für Volkerkunde Dresden Forschungsstelle, 100- 106.

STATE BANK OF INDIA 1990 *Annual Credit Plan for Leh district, (1990-91)*. Manuscript of Lead Bank of State Bank of India, Leh.

TERRAY, Emmanuel 1972 *Marxism and "Primitive" Societies*. New York/London: Monthly Review Press (First published in French,1969).

THE WHEEL OF LIFE
The Cycle of Rebirth in Buddhism

Dr. Nawang Tsering
Central Institute of Buddhist Studies
Choglamsar, Leh 194101, Ladakh.

The Wheel of Life assumes great significance in Buddhist teachings. Its importance can be judged by the fact that a picture of the Wheel of Life is to be seen on the wall of all monasteries in the regions of the Buddhist Himalayas. The tradition of depicting the wheel of life in wall-paintings goes back as early as the Ajanta caves themselves. The obvious purpose of putting up the wheel of life on public entrances was to acquaint and educate the people about the theory of the endless process of reincarnation in Buddhism. The important thing shown in it is the cause of recurring life and once the cause is ascertained, it becomes easier for one to understand its remedy - a complete cessation of birth and suffering. Emancipation from the shackles of life and death is the primary aim of Buddha's teachings.

At any monastery, on the entrance gate, the first scene one's eyes capture is the wheel of life. A dreadful form, Yama "The Lord of Death", holds our entire existence in the firm grip of his jaws. This Lord of Death is the embodiment of impermanence. This wheel has three rings of lines: outer, middle and innermost. A pig, a cock, and a serpent, symbolizing ignorance or stupidity, animal desire and violent anger are shown within the innermost circle. The Buddhist concept of six realms of:- heaven or gods (*lha*), titans or demi-gods (*lta.mir*), animals (*dud.'gro*), hell (*dmyal.ba*) hungry-ghosts (*yi.dwags*), and humans (*mi*), are shown in the middle ring. Reincarnation may return us to any one of these realms, depending on our behaviour; one should endeavour to return as a human, for only thus can one hope for enlightenment and release from the wheel.

The greatest contribution of the Buddha is His invention of the Law of Causation known as Dependent Origination. The function of this law is expresed through the chain of twelve factors. These factors are shown in the outer circle of the ring. Although separate elements, these twelve factors are linked by the law of cansation. Any one factor of this chain of twelve factors is inevitably caused by the factor preceding it, and itself becomes the cause of the factors that follow.

1. **Beginningless Ignorance** is the first factor in the chain of 12 members of the wheel of life. As one sees, ignorance is represented by a blind woman. Due to her blindness she sees all as darkness; such is the state of ignorance which can not make any

distinction between what is desirable and what is not desirable, or what is meritorious and what is not meritorious. From ignorance grows the negative emotions like lust, anger, selfishness etc. And as long as ignorance exists, suffering continues to exist, giving birth to volition.

2. From ignorance arise emotional **Karmic** constructions, the 2nd factor in the chain of twelve factors. Karma is represented by a potter. He always keeps himself busy by molding clay pots, implying that every ordinary being keeps himself busy in the accumulation of various habitual reactions. A seed starts germinating as soon as necessary conditions are fulfilled with. In the same manner Karma works in creating a new life in the future.

3. Karmic constructions give rise to **Consciousness**. As one lamp lights another lamp, in the same manner one period of a consciousness is linked to another, thus creating a new-life. Such a re-incarnating consciousness is represented by a monkey. As a monkey leaps from one tree to another, the previous consciousness passes from its former position to a new position, and new life begins in the mother's womb.

4. Consciousness gives rise to **Name** and **Form**, the 4th factor in the wheel of life. This is represented by a raft or ship. In fact, name and form arise simultaneously with consciousness. Like a ship which travels from one shore to another shore, so mind and matter (name and form) also move from one life to the next.

5. Name and form give rise to the **Six Organs of Sense**, the 5th factor of the chain of twelve members. Sense organs are represented by an empty house, signifying their undeveloped state in the embryo.

6. Due to the sense organs **Human Contacts** arise, with a combination of objects, organs and movement. It is an awakening state, causing sense activities or sensory feelings.

7. This acute sensation gives rise to **Feeling**. The intensity of feeling is as acute as the piercing of an arrow to the eyes, the most sensitive part of a body. Feelings are of various kinds — both happiness and unhappiness. It is feeling that creates desire.

8. **Desire** is conditioned by feeling. Desire is a lust for desirable objects. Thus desire is represented by a drunkard. It is a cause affected by other factors too, just as a seed is stirred by moisture and manure etc.; in the same way desire leads to actual grasping of objects. Ignorance and desire are the two main causes and while the former is responsible for creating the present life, the latter creates future life.

9. Desire leads to **Grasping**. It is represented by a man

grasping a fruit. Desire is represented by feeling a fruit, but grasping is the actual handling of the fruit. Grasping also creates false views like 'my' and 'mine'.

10. The feeling of 'my and 'mine' gives rise to **Becoming**, that is desire for existence. Desire for existence is represented by a courting couple. The couple is in the process of accumulating more desire for existence in the present life.

11. Due to becoming, physical **Re-birth** takes place in the world. Such birth is represented by the conception of a baby.

12. Due to birth, **Old age, death, disease** etc. follow. In reality, death commences in the embryo and thus birth and death are simultaneous in Buddhist metaphysics. Such is the working of the wheel of life which revolves endlessly round and round.

References

1. Phar-phgi, p.558.
2. The Taftvasangrala of Shantaraksita, tr. Ganganatha Jha, V.I, p.1.
3. The Buddha and His teaching by Narada Maha Thara, p.240.

****

The twelve factors (nidanas) of conditioned causation (pratityasamutpada)

English	Sanskrit	Tibetan
1. Beginningless Ignorance	avidyā	ma.rig
2. Karmic Formations	saṃskāra	'du.byed
3. Consciousness	vijñāna	rnam.ses
4. Name & Form	nāma-rūpa	min.gzugs
5. The Six Senses	sadāyatana	skye.mched
6. Contact	sparśa	reg.pa
7. Feeling	vedana	tshor.ba
8. Desire	tṛṣṇā	sred.pa
9. Grasping, Clinging	upādāna	len.pa
10. Becoming	bhava	srid.pa
11. Rebirth (Reincarnation)	jāti	skye.ba
12. Old Age and Death	jārā-maraṇa	rgas.sis

Note. I am indebted to John Crook for the table above, which supplements the text. There is a more detailed account by Zara Fleming in *The Middle Way*, 66, 4. p.223 (Feb.1992). Ed.

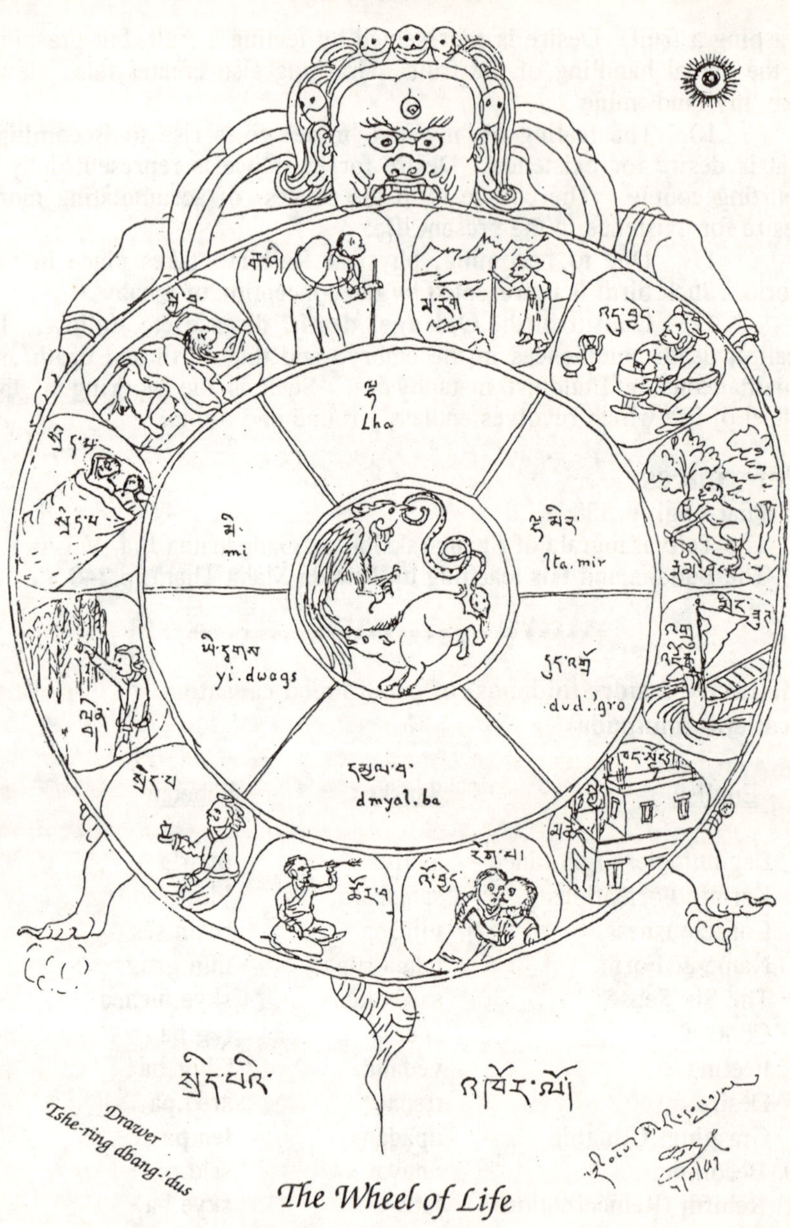

The Wheel of Life

A COMPARATIVE STUDY OF SALVATION IN CHRISTIANITY AND BUDDHISM.

Lobzang Tsewang.
Lecturer in Comparative Philosophy,
Central Institute of Buddhist Studies,
Leh Ladakh.

Abstract

Everybody wishes to achieve a state of perfect peace where there will be no suffering. Such a state is recognised to be 'salvation' in both Buddhism and Christianity. To attain salvation is considered to be the ultimate aim of human life in both Buddhism and Christianity. The question raised here is "Is it really possible that such a salvation can be attained?" It is very difficult to convince some modern people, there is no doubt that if any one strives to attain it by adopting the right methods, it is possible to succeed. Both Buddhism and Christianity teach the pathway leading to salvation.

All over the world people are living in distressed conditions; there is no place for them in human society. They are afflicted by many problems related to either the mind or the body and they are forced to struggle against horrible situations. They are still hoping to escape from this damnation and are endeavouring from time to time to find a way how to solve these problems. As a matter of fact, the external means of material comforts are not sufficient to generate lasting peace and happiness; they depend, exclusively, upon the inward revolution. Therefore as Narada Maha Thera says; "Real happiness is found within and is not to be defined in terms of wealth, power, honours or conquests."[1]

In a similar way Dr. Radha Krishnan says; "Jesus demands inward renewal and inner change. The Kingdom of Heaven is not a place but a state of mind."[2] In the same manner Lord Buddha also says in the Sutra; "Buddha evolves from the good mind so, one must salute one's own mind."[3] In short, in the view of both Buddha and Christ, bondage and salvation depend upon the state of the mind and in order to create a state of perfect peace, one should endeavour to cure the inner ailment. This is the central teaching of both Buddha and Christ.

---

1. Narada Mahathera; The Buddha and His Teachings. P 179
2. Dr. Radha Krishnan; Recovery of Faith. P 115
3. Buddha; Sutra.

BONDAGE

This disastrous situation forces us to explore the real source of suffering. According to Christianity the so called 'original sin' is considered to be at the root of all human suffering. This sin was committed by Adam, the for-father of mankind. He disobeyed the Divine authority, ate the forbidden fruit and strayed from God's will. As a result of this he lost God's love and grace. He was deprived of his sanctuary and driven out of Paradise. Thus he became mortal and would have to bear final punishment for his sins on the day of Judgement. The Bible says; "You must not eat the fruit of that tree; if you do, you will die the same day."[4] Professor Tiwari also says; "Adam's sin, the original sin, is sin for every man and that sin is the main cause of human suffering."[5]

If the original sin is the root cause of human suffering, then the following questions arise. Why did Adam commit the sin? How was it transmitted to all mankind?

According to Christianity man is made by God in his own image. It signifies that man has been chosen to help in the building of the Kingdom of Heaven all over the world. This is the main purpose of God's creation. Man is endowed with an immortal soul, intelligence and free will. The spirit of man is called the candle of the Lord. It differentiates man from other animal creations. Free will plays an important role in all human activities.

The first humans, Adam and Eve, lived in the garden of Eden. However the devil in the form of a snake tempted them to eat the fruit of the forbidden tree. He criticised the restrictions that God had placed on Adam and Eve and explained the benefits of eating the fruit. The Bible says; "That's not true; you will not die. God said that because he knows that when you eat it you will be like God and know what is good and what is bad."[6] With this provocation, the evil attitudes, i.e. pride, lust, etc. sprang into their minds. At the same time they misused their free-will, plucked the forbidden fruit from the tree and ate it. In doing so they defied God's command and committed the first sin. Professor Tiwari says; "Here two factors in a combined fashion became responsible for evil - The devilish provocation of Satan and the utter mis-use of the free will granted to them."[7]

The gene is the medium through which the original sin is transmitted from Adam to all the succeeding human race. Thus man is

---

4. The Bible; Genesis, ch.2, v17.
5. K.N. Tiwari; Comparative Religion. P 139.
6. The Bible; Genesis, ch.3, vv4-5.
7. K.N. Tiwari; Comparative Religion. P 140.

born with certain evil taints, i.e. lust, anger, jealousy and so on. It is obvious that a young baby expresses his anger when he does not get his milk. Professor D. Smith says; "The sin that all men committed when Adam sinned; as his death made all men mortal, likewise his sin made men sinful."[8] Similarly Denny also says; "The guilt of the first transgression is reckoned in its consequences upon all the races represented by the first transgressor. But apart from their own sin, all are not regarded as sinners but made sinners also through the inheritance of the nature of itself inclined only to live."[9]

The sanctity of the human soul is distorted by committing the original sin. As a result man falls down from Paradise and becomes subject to death. The soul does not perish with the physical death, but has to wait to be resurrected at the Day of Judgement.

The bondage is nothing more than a strange human phenomenon which is explained by Christianity as the state of original sin or the fallen state. Antony states; "In the case of religious liberation, nobody has a clear idea as to the state of 'Slavery' or 'Bondage' from which the victim has to be liberated. A Christian would refer to it as original sin, the devil, the fallen state or Hell."[10]

A Christian believes in the one life theory and has no room for the concept of the pre-existence of the soul. That is why, in a Christian's view, the human being is newly created by God at the time of conception. If this is the case, it would be difficult to posit the evil passions which grow in the newly created mind or soul and the original sin, committed by Adam, could not be transmitted to the succeeding generations. If the original sin belongs exclusively to the body, it would not be the main obstruction to salvation, as the body dissolves into dust at the time of death. The body will not endure along with the immortal soul and consequently it cannot be justified that the original sin is the main impediment from entering the Kingdom of Heaven.

According to Buddhism all problems start from ignorance, the mental defilement. That is how every person has the conception of 'I'. It ignores the real nature of 'I' and mistakenly thinks 'I' exists on its own or independently. In fact this is not so. A person has an intense attachment towards his relatives due to holding this conception, and does all sorts of evil deeds for their benefit. If anyone harms his relatives or their property he becomes angry and hates them. As a result he is gripped with the three poisons: ignorance, attachment and

---

8. D Smith; The Teaching of the Catholic Church. P 338.
9. Denne; James Husting Encycl. of Religion and Ethics. V5, P 705.
10. Antony; Buddhism and Christianity; their inner affinity.

hatred. Hence Chanrakirti says; "Homage to that compassion for migrators who are powerless like a bucket travelling in a well, although initially adhering to a self as an 'I' and then generating attachment for things; 'This is mine'."[11]

When one becomes a slave of the three poisons, many kinds of negative motivations arise in the mind. They encourage the person to perform evil deeds whenever the circumstances are suitable. Any action remains in the active form for a short period and it leaves a deep impression upon the mental continuum when it loses its intensity. It lives in a potent form until its fruit ripens. No action is completed without begetting its fruit and it waits for a suitable occasion to blossom. Hence Lord Buddha says;

> *"All actions for a hundred aeons,*
> *Remain unexhausted, condition and time*
> *Find, all sentient beings,*
> *Have to experience their fruits."*[12]

There is nothing in the world which would exempt a being from suffering, because everything is the product of Karmic forces. The so-called external world is composed of atoms and the force in the atom which either attracts or repels things, comes from the Karma. The moving force in the atom is inserted by the conscious mind and therefore the evolution and involution of the world depends upon Karmic energy. Vasubhandu says; "The different world systems are originated by the Karma."[13] In other words, in the outside world nothing exists individually because the universe is a simple process of the inter-connected activities of the mind and matter. A single object is nothing more than a mental illusion. Saint Nagar Juna says; "For them (the Hungry ghosts) even the moon is hot in the summer, while the sun is cold in the winter. The trees become fruitless and the rivers dry up when they looked upon them."[14] In the same way Acharya Shanttideva says; "The burning iron base is created by whom? From where to the crowded women come? Buddha says 'That all the things come out of the evil mind'."[15]

Some modern scientists also support this fact. Wigner asserts that it is impossible to give a description of quantum mechanical

---

11. Chandrakirti; Madhyamikavatra.
12. Lord Buddha; Sutra.
13. Vasubhandu; Abhidharma.
14. Nagarjuna; A Friendly Letter. St.95
15. Shantideva; A Guide to the Bodhisattva's Way of Life. Ch.5, St.15.

processes without explicit reference to consciousness. Sir James Jen makes the assertion that the mind may be the creator and governor of the realm of matter. Jack Sarfatti also states an idea of the utmost significance for the development of the psycho-energetic system is that the structure of matter may not be independent of consciousness.[16]

All Buddhist schools unanimously accept that Karma is endowed with a tremendous potency which produces everything to be found in this mundane world. Do not hope to receive real peace and happiness through utilising worldly things or lusting for worldly comforts which eventually result in frustration.

The sentient being is imprisoned in the wheel of life and suffers incessantly. The wheel is comprised of twelve links and one has to revolve through the circle until liberation is achieved, as one's psycho-physical perpetual process starts from ignorance. Wherever one lives in the world, one has to cross each miserable stage in turn. Among the twelve conditions, ignorance, craving, and clinging are afflictions, action and existence are deeds, and the other seven are sufferings. As long as nescience is ingrained in one's mind there is no hope to receive real peace and happiness, only trouble and mental anguish. That is why action rises out of nescience and then one can gradually rise through all the other conditions. Lord Buddha says; "When this is, that arises, for instance out of ignorance action arises."[17] In the same way Nagarjun says; "If there is birth, then a very great heap of suffering ensues, such as sorrow, disease, old age, frustration, fear of death etc."[18]

SALVATION

In Christianity salvation means when man is saved from his present fallen status. In other words it is when man is able to regain his original status when he had eternal fellowship with God. The first man, Adam, lost his original status by sinning and through him, all mankind became sinners and subject to death. Because of this it became necessary for mankind to attain salvation from sin and punishments. One must ascend from mortal to immortal status. William L. Reese says; "From the Latin 'salare' (to save) the Christian term for that state in which man is redeemed, reconciled to God."[19]

In a word salvation means renewal and in order to attain salvation one must get inner positive change. Man's inward nature is

---

16. C.F. Michael Talbot; Mysticism and New Physics. P 35-36.
17. Nagarjuna; A Friendly Letter. St.11.
18. Buddha; The Rice Seedling Sutra.
19. William L Reese; The Dictionary of Philosophy and Religion. P 506

distorted with numerous evil attitudes; viz: anger, lust, anxiety and so on. Professor Antony says; "Through his insight into concrete human nature, Christ clearly saw that many people were unable to accept adult responsibility in life and act as free noble beings, because they were continually thwarted by feelings of inner anxiety and despair."[20]

These kinds of inner faults are major impediments to salvation. Salvation is not given from the outside and will evolve from the human's inner core. That is why one must purify one's mind through wiping out the mental evils. Dr. Radna Krishnan says; "It is the attainment of truth which makes for freedom or liberation. Jesus refers to inner perfecting, the possible evolution of man."[21]

The *'summum bonum'* of mankind is to transform into a spiritual being. He lives in Paradise with a divine body which never decays. He is free from sins and sufferings and enjoys perfect peace and bliss in fellowship with God. This state is called eternal or immortal life. Hughes says; "God's ultimate purpose is the creation of a moral universe of free self conscious beings, who shall live in loving fellowship with him, and shall do his will gladly and spontaneously."[22] In the same way F. Antony says; "The Kingdom refers primarily to the qualitativeness of the life of an individual who has evolved from a childish behaviour to an adult one."[23]

The so-called salvation is the realization of resurrection in the Kingdom of Heaven. The resurrected body is spiritual, and not a material one. His original stainless nature is revived on the Day of Judgement and he becomes qualified to live in the Garden of Eden, the spiritual abode. In other words he achieves membership in the Kingdom of God.[24]

In Buddhism, the **Nirvana** is the supreme goal, the *'summum bonum'* of human life. In this state all the miserable conditions are irrevocably extinguished. When Nirvana is achieved, the person feels real inner peace and tranquillity which cannot be expressed in human language. The so-called Nirvana is nothing more than an inner transition from being impure to being pure. It is possible for everyone because the contamination in the mind is not static, but springs up from the prevailing conditions. In the changing circumstances it will get an obstruction to sustain it; the root cause of which is ignorance. There is a vigorous antidote to this which is the wisdom of emptiness

---

20. F. Antony; Buddhism and Christianity; their inner affinity P 120
21. Dr. Radha Krishnan; Recovery of Faith. P 106
22. Hughes
23. F. Antony; Buddhism and Christianity; their inner affinity. P 120
24. K.N. Tiwari; Comparative Religion. P 144

and when such wisdom develops in the mind, the ignorance automatically collapses. That is why both of them observe the same object and conceive the result is opposite ways. The great logician Dharma Kirti says; "One does not permanently exist, whose cause is the victim of obstruction."[25]

The term Nirvana consists of two component words i.e. *Nir* and *Vana*. *Nir* is the negative particle and *Vana* means weaving. *Vana* is interpreted as meaning the three poisons which link between the previous and the next life. As a result a person is bound to revolve in the endless cycle of birth and rebirth. The term Nirvana thus makes sense as being the state when a person escapes from the cycle of birth and death, when the afflictions and Karmic forces cease to operate in a proper way. [26]

Some say the word Nirvana is comprised of two different words. i.e. *Nir* and *Vata*. *Nir* means out and *Vata* stands for wind; and the suffix *Ta* is changed to *Na*. Thus the word Nirvana gives a sense of blowing out or cooling off. The real meaning of Nirvana then becomes to blow out the flames of the three fold poisons i.e. lust, hate and delusion. A sense of the complete extinction of the individual can not be drawn. Dr. Radha Krishnan says; "The word Nirvana literally means blowing out or cooling. Blowing out suggests extinction, cooling suggests not a complete annihilation, but only the dying out of hot passion."[27]

Hinyana Buddhism believes the *Pari Nirvana* or *Nirupadehsesa* is nothing less than the utter extinction of the beginningless process of aggregates. With the dissolution of the body of the *Arahat*, all feelings and experiences become cool, just as the oil lamp extinguishs itself when the oil is exhausted. Nothing remains as a residue after the passing away of a Buddha or an Arahat No Arahat is transformed into a certain purified state when he dies and no half-way house giving shelter is perceived between existence and non-existence. *Nirupadhesesa* means the complete cessation of everything that pertains to the aggregates. Hence this idea is expressed in Udana;

"The body broke up, perception ceased,
All feelings cooled, all formation stilled,
Consciousness disappeared."[28]

---

25. Dharmakirti; Pramanavartika. Chp.2.
26. Narada Thera; Buddha and His Teaching. P 288
27. Dr. Radha Krishnan; Indian Philosophy. Vol.1 P 447
28. Piyadasi Thera; The Buddha's Ancient Path. P 71

The living being is nothing but a mere conflux of mind and matter. No 'I' self or soul is found among the aggregates which is able to enter Nirvana. In this fluctual process everything undergoes change and nothing remains the same for two consecutive moments. The life process consists of the procession of the co-ordinated energies, e.g. Klesa and Karma. When one achieves Nirvana all the energies completely cease. Satkari Mookerjee says; "The Sautantrikas conception of Nirvana therefore, has nothing to distinguish it from that of the Therevada, as both these schools regard Nirvana not as an annihilation of passion and impurities alone, but of consciousness also. Nirvana is a blank and a void."[29]

In Mahayana Buddhism, Nirvana is the complete cessation of afflictions.(Klesa) When an Arahat has passed away his contaminated (sasrava) psycho-physical aggregates become utterly extinct and he achieves nerupdhisesa Nirvana. This never means he becomes blank at his death as his purified mental continuum survives for ever. H. H. The Dalai Lama says; "But the basic, ultimate, innermost subtle consciousness will always remain. It had no beginning nor will it have to end."[30] Moreover the Arahat has to enter the Mahayana system to attain perfect enlightenment. His mind is still tainted with certain subtle defilements which can not be eliminated by practising the Hinyana path. He is compelled to adopt the Boddhisattva's path and yet has not developed great compassion and the Bodhicitta etc. Without the co-ordination of the Bodhicitta, wisdom is defunct and the Arahat is unable to attain Buddhahood. To attain perfect enlightenment he must get unified meditation of wisdom and method.

MEANS TO SALVATION

We find various methods to lead to salvation described in the scriptures. I would like to explain some of those which seem the most important. I have to consider that in order to attain salvation there needs to be two essential factors viz: To remove obstacles and to develop favourable conditions. Keeping these points in mind, I will explain the means to salvation.

In Christianity prayer is an essential path to salvation. The teachings of Christ emphasise the importance of prayer to obtain a living relationship with God. Jesus says; "Your Father already knows what you need before you ask him. This, then, is how you should pray."[31] Penance is an effective means to cleanse the soul tainted with

29. Satkari Mukarjee; The Buddhist Philosophy of Universal Flux. P 268
30. Dalai Lama; The Bodh Gaya Interview. P 46
31. The Bible; Matthew, ch.6 vv.8-9.

past faults, and is a necessary one to demonstrate penitence. It is a struggle against evil passions. Adolphe Tanquerey says; "Penance is defined as a supernatural virtue, allied to justice which inclines the sinner to detest his sin because it is an offence against God, and to form the firm resolve of avoiding sin in the future and for atoning for it."[32]

Love is the basic lesson of Christianity. Man restores the broken relationship with God and receives grace through genuine love. One should love God as well as fellow beings with all one's heart. The Bible says; "For the whole law is summed up in one commandment: Love your neighbour as you love yourself."[33] To regain the divine nature in man he must purify his soul with atonement bringing him into unique oneness with God. He can then share in the glory and fullness of God's grace and love. The Bible says; "God offered Him, so that by his sacrificial death He should become the means by which people's sins are forgiven through their faith in Him."[34] Nobody can attain salvation without Christ's intervention as man's effort alone is insufficient to restore the broken relationship between man and God. Man can only be saved from sin through Christ's crucifixion. As a substitute Christ suffers for one's sins and brings us to God. Hence the cross becomes the means to create the sinless humanity. The Bible says; "For Christ died for sins once and for all, a good man on behalf of sinners, in order to lead you to God."[35] God's grace is essential for salvation because in its absence salvation is impossible. Personal efforts should not be neglected as it is only through both the Grace of God and the individual effort that the seeker is able to realise salvation. The Bible says; "For it is by God's grace that you have been saved through faith. It is not the result of your own efforts, but God's gift, so that no one can boast about it."[36]

In Buddhism ignorance is the root cause of all the troubles and sufferings. Unless such a nescience is demolished, nobody can achieve the final peace and happiness. A false view of self is an impediment and envelops the essential purity of the mind. The mind has the nature of being empty of an inherent existence and the defilements are only there temporarily. Hence it is said that the mind's nature is clear light. If one develops its antidote, the wisdom, it automatically diminishes and the trainee then hopes to achieve

---

32. R.S. Shrivastava; Comparative Religion. P 140
33. The Bible; Galatians ch.11 v.6.
34. The Bible; Romans ch.3 v.25
35. The Bible; First Epistle of Peter. ch.3 v.18.
36. The Bible; Ephesians ch.2 v.8.

perfect enlightenment. Dharmakirti says;

> *"The mind's nature is a clear light,*
> *All the defilements are Adventitious."*[37]

Ignorance is nothing more than a false notion e.g. ''I am, and this is mine'. It causes many false ideas, i.e. greed, aversion, likes and dislikes and so on. Because of them one fails to see things as they are and they conceal the real nature of things. They make one perceive things with delusion; permanence in impermanence, satisfaction in dissatisfaction, self in non-self, beauty in repulsion etc. Because of these delusions one delights in one's own experiences and rejects feelings of disgust towards them. These types of false views attach one to the five aggregates and cause one to revolve in the cycle of birth and death. Ignorance, which is the main obstruction to liberation, has to be dispelled to enable the evolvement of right understanding. Liberation from the cyclic existence will eventually be achieved if the mind develops right understanding and is detached from taints. Hence Nagarjuna says; "When the notion of an *Atman*, self or soul ceases, the notion of mind also ceases, and one becomes free from the idea of I and Mine."[38]

We find extensive descriptions of the Buddha-nature in Lankavatra and Utter Tantra. It refers to the innate purity of the mind. Even now we also have Buddha-nature. The purity is the essential calibre of the mind. In exact terms the inner most luminous mind is called the Buddha-nature. No distinction is found between the mind of Buddha and all sentient beings in the Buddha-nature and because of this, all sentient beings can evolve up to Buddha level. The defilements can not penetrate the inner core of the mind and pollute it, it simply shrouds the clarity of the mind. When the fog of the taint subsides, then the Luminous mind emerges in its original form and is called the **Truth body**. Maitreya Nath says;

> *"The grace is permeated from Buddha,*
> *The innermost nature of beings are the same,*
> *The sentient beings have the potency to become perfect*
> *Every one is endowed with the essence of Buddha."*[39]

---

37. Dharmakirti; Pramanavartika ch.2.
38. Nargarjuna; Madhyamaka Karika; ch.18 v.2.
39. Maitriya Nath; Uttertantra ch.1.

The unified practice of wisdom and method, consisting of altruistic attitude, compassion, Bodhicitta etc., is indispensable to achieve Buddhahood. Under the influence of these methods, Buddha and Bodhisattva evolve to benefit others while expecting no reward. Dharmakirti says; " All the efforts are made for others."[40].

On the other hand wisdom is a specific component of the **truth body** of Buddha and that is why the major obstruction to attain the **truth body** is the misconception of self which must be first dispelled. The unified practice of method and wisdom is generally held to be the essential path to achieve Buddhahood. Nagarjuna says;

> *"Thus these two collections cause*
> *Buddhahood to be attained*
> *So, in brief, always rely*
> *Upon merit and wisdom."*[41]

In brief there are similarities between Buddhism and Christianity as both explain the salvation and bondage of sentient beings. However the nature of salvation is explained in different ways; according to Buddhism salvation is not a place, but a state of mind; in Christianity it is a place i.e. the Garden of Eden or Paradise. Both agree that to reach that state the human mind must be purified first.[42]

---

40. Dharakirti; Pramanavartika ch.2
41. Nagarjuna; Precious Garland. ch.3 st.213.
42. While this paper mainly sets out traditional Roman Catholic Christian dogma, numerous points (especially the concept of 'original sin') are at variance with current Protestant doctrine. Ed.

HEALTH ACTIVITIES IN LEH DISTRICT, LADAKH

Stanzin Tondup
Chief Medical Officer, Leh District

Leh — the largest district not only in J&K state but also in the whole of India — was inhabited (1981 census) by a disproportionately small population of 68,380 with a sex ratio of 886f/1000m and an area of 44,000 sq.km. The estimated population in 1991 was 89,000 at a density of 2 persons per sq.km., 87% of the population being rural.[1] The decennial population growth is recorded as 32 % during 1971-81, as compared to 30% for the state of Kashmir. The crude birth rate of the district is 33% whereas the crude death rate is 8%.

The environment

Being cradled inside the lofty Himalayan Mountain ranges, the major part of the district is inaccessible, mountainous, remote and isolated. Leh is one of the coldest and most elevated inhabited regions in the world with altitudes ranging from 2,800 metres to 5,900 metres above sea level. The district combines the conditions of both erratic and desert climates with wide diurnal and seasonal fluctuations with temperatures ranging from 30°C in summer, to -30°C during the winter.

Health

During pre-Independence there used to be one mobile doctor for the region including Skardo. In the early fifties there was one centre each in Leh and Kargil with the services of one doctor.

1. The Census of India recorded a sex ratio of 1010f/1000m in 1961 and 1012f/1000m in 1971. The sudden change to 886f/1000m in 1981 was due to a disproportionate increase in the number of males, presumably by immigration. Between 1921 and 1961 the decennial population growth averaged only 6.5%. In 1961-71 it was 19% for both females and males. In 1971-81 it was 24% for females, but 40% for males. The estimated 1991 population figure of 89,474 appears to have been derived from a projection of the 1981 census population at the same mean growth rate, so is unreliable. Figures from various sources for the area of Leh tehsil/district differ, partly because of differing inclusion of disputed boundary areas. Data from *Statistical Hand-Book, District Leh, 1982-83*. Directorate of Economics & Statistics, Planning & Development Dept., Srinagar. (Ed.)

In 1979 the district of Leh and Kargil was divided into two districts and there were 88 health institutions of various categories functioning in the Leh district. These have been increased to 172 institutions ranging from the District Hospital to a sub-centres as on August 1993. Out of 112 inhabited 'census villages', 96 have been provided with basic facilities and the remaining 16 villages have to be covered by the end of the century, if we are to meet the optimistic WHO target of "Health for All by 2000 AD". 30 hamlets have also been covered and 82 still need to be covered.

The following National Goals have been set for 2000 AD:

1. Reduction of the Infant Mortality Rate to below 60 per 1000 live births.
2. To raise the expectation of life at birth to 64.
3. To reduce the crude death rate to 9 per 1000.
4. To reduce the crude birth rate to 21 per 1000.
5. To achieve a net Reproduction Rate of one.

To move towards these goals and to improve medical facilities, the department, besides getting assistance with the district plan and the centrally sponsored schemes, is getting much help from the non-governmental organizations, such as the Leh Nutrition Project (LNP), the Ladakh Ecological Development Group (LEDeG) and the Ladakh Environmental Health Organisation (LEHO). These also help patients who require financial assistance for heart surgery etc. that has to be performed out of the J & K state at hospitals such as A.I.I.M.S.[2] (Delhi) and P.G.I.[3] (Chandigarh). LEHO is particularly concerned with countering the high incidence of silicosis due to inhaling dusty air.

L.N.P supports the department in improving the health services in several ways e.g:-

1. Providing measles vaccine for the whole district.
2. Supplementing costly TB medicines.
3. Providing dietary/medicine grants to poor patients admitted through the specialists concerned.
4. Supplementing medical and teaching equipment to the Sonam Norboo Memorial (SNM) Hospital and the AMT[4] School attached to it.

---

2. All India Institute for Medical Services
3. Post-Graduate Institute
4. Auxiliary Medical Training School

5. Helping to improve the paediatric services of the hospital.
6. Helping to construct an improved design of heated labour and operation room, especially for the winter.
7. Help in giving training refresher courses and workshops to the various levels of health workers to improve their understanding and skill and to tackle the health and management problems peculiar to this part of the country.

The Amchi System

The Amchi system of treatment is one of the oldest in the history of Ladakh, and the system is still very popular especially among the rural population. To keep alive and to boost this system of treatment, the department engages amchis on the government staff roll, on an honorarium basis at present. The department has got 40 amchis whose services have been kept especially in remote and inaccessible villages. These amchis are being supervised by a Chief Amchi at Headquarters. The department, every year, organises hot water therapy camps at the hot springs of Panamik, Chumathang and Demjok etc.

Since 1987, the Leh district has been brought under the purview of U.I.P.[5] under which a comprehensive package of immunization coverage against the six killer diseases was supposed to be provided to the eligible children. Since all the MCH[6] and Family Welfare programmes are target oriented and ongoing schemes, it needs a continuous thrust. Achievement of high level coverage in a given year does not make any sense unless it is ensured that the same services are made available to the children born subsequently. Excessive target levels can lead to a backlash if either the coverage or the quality is allowed to decline.

The achievements under MCH during the year 1992-93 and in the first quarter of 1993-94 are as follows:

	DPT[7]	Polio	BCG[8]	DT[9]	Measles
1992-93	1672	1566	1679	368	1568
Ending 6/93	427	407	435	105	412

Common ailments-in Leh

5. Universal Immunisation Programme
6. Maternal & Child Health
7. Diptheria, Pertussis (whooping cough) & Tetanus vaccine
8. Tuberculosis vaccine
9. Diptheria & Tetanus vaccine

A. Respiratory Tract Infections: these form almost 60% of the total diseases because of the severe winter, high altitude and dusty atmosphere during the winter. People live in the common kitchen with an open fire exposed to the smoke.
B. Rheumatic Heart Diseases.
C. Gastro-intestinal Tract Infections.
D. Worm infestations.

Aims and objects

Most people think that health is a mere absence of disease but in reality it consists of well-being in body, mind and spirit, in order to be able to give one's best to society. People like to be living in healthy surroundings, in a place where they can trust each other, work together to meet daily needs and share in times of difficulties and joy. The objectives are of the following categories:

1. Curative.
2. Preventive.
3. Promotive.

If ordinary people are provided with clear information regarding health education, they can prevent and treat most common health problems in their own home and often better than can a doctor. Medical knowledge should not be the guarded secret of a select few but should be freely available for every one.

Brief description of Blocks

The district of Leh consists of five blocks as follows:-

1. **Nubra** — with its headquarters at Deskit, consists of 28 census villages and 30 hamlets with a population of 10,667, and is situated to the North of the District at a distance of 118 km from the district headquarters, across the Khardongla pass which is difficult to approach during winter due to the snowfall on this highest motorable road in the world. The inhospitable terrain and the hilly areas make it difficult to approach the villages, thus the people of Nubra need to have every basic facility available at the village level itself. The department of Health and Family Welfare has laid much emphasis on providing facilities to the remotest corners and at present is having 29 health institutions of various categories established for the benefit of the residents of the block.

2. **Nyoma** — Situated to the south of Leh at a distance of 160 km is a block consisting of 16 inhabited and one uninhabited census

village and 17 hamlets. The majority of this population is nomadic and is the fourth largest block with a population of 7,320. Because of the scattered population and difficult access it needs special attention in providing health facilities. At present the department has got 38 institutions of various categories established there.

3. **Khalsi** — Situated to the west of Leh, at a distance of 96 kms, with Khalsi village as its headquarters. The block has 24 census villages and 26 hamlets with a population of 13,287. This block has been provided with 36 health institutions of various categories to render medical facilities to the inhabitants.

4. **Leh** — Leh block, consisting of 38 census villages and 22 hamlets, and having the town of Leh as its headquarters, is one of the better known areas with 33,573 inhabitants. This area also has a big influx of tourists and migrant labourers etc., especially during the summer season, which forces the department to have every facility available. 49 institutions of various categories have been established including the only hospital in the district. The hospital has been provided with some specialised facilities such as an X-Ray machine, ultrasound laboratory etc.

5. **Durbuk** — Situated across the second highest road in the world ("Changla"), Durbuk is part of a block consisting of only 5 census villages and 17 hamlets with the smallest population of 3,533. It lies to the east of the district headquarters, Leh, at a distance of 118 kms. This block is the toughest and the coldest and borders Tibet and China. In view of the topography, inaccessibility and other aspects of the area, the department has provided all the five census villages and seven hamlets with medical facilities.

Construction Programme

During the current financial year the department has got the following construction programme:

1. A casualty block at the SNM Hospital, Leh.
2. A sub-district hospital at Nubra.
3. A dispensary building at Tagar/Sumoor.(Nubra.)
4. Renovation of the Primary Health Centres at Nyoma and Khalsi.

In addition to the above items a token amount has been earmarked for a central heating system at the SNM Hospital, Leh.

Further, under the India Population Project VII, the department has proposed 20 sub-centres to be constructed during the current financial year, four in each block. During 1992-93 twenty sub-centre buildings have been constructed, most of which have been taken over by the department from the Rural Engineering Department.

Shifting of patients

We are responsible for the necessary arrangements for transferring serious patients from remote places like Skiu-Markha, Lingshed, Hunderdok and Korzok where there are no jeepable roads, and in the year 1992-93 we have made a requisition to the Airforce Authority for twenty helicopter sorties for the transfer of patients.

Future Plans

As mentioned earlier, 17 villages and about 82 hamlets have yet to be provided with medical facilities. The department has a proposal to reduce the work load of the only hospital in the district which is located at Leh, by upgrading the Primary Health Centres in Nyoma and Khalsi to sub-district hospital status. This proposal has been submitted to the government. This will enable the inhabitants of these blocks to have major/minor treatment at the block headquarter itself.

The department also lays emphasis for providing the improved equipment for the hospital and the public health centres and much has been done in this regard. During 1992-93, apparatus worth several lakhs[10] has been purchased and procured for the SNM Hospital, Leh. The ambulance services are being made more efficient too.

In view of the importance of the area geographically and the climatic conditions of the district, it is essential that the district SNM Hospital in Leh should be raised to the status of a provincial level hospital and it is intended to submit this proposal to the government for consideration.

10. One lakh is Rs.100,000

ལ་དྭགས་སུ་སངས་རྒྱས་ཀྱི་

བསྟན་པ་དར་ཚུལ།

འཇམ་དབྱངས་རྒྱལ་མཚན།།

la dwags su sangs rgyas kyi bstan pa dar tshul

'jam dbyangs rgyal mtshan

THE INTRODUCTION OF BUDDHISM INTO LADAKH

Jamyang Gyaltsen

Summary

Although it is said that the site of Lamayuru gonpa was blessed by Nima Gunpa in about 550 BC, the first clear introduction of Buddhism was under King Kanishka of Kashmir in about 130 AD. In the 8th century Padma Sambhava spread the Tantric teachings of the Old Tradition, from which developed the Nyingmapa sect, now represented only by Tak-Tak gonpa. In the 11th century Naropa, Marpa and Milarepa started the Kagyupa sect, founding Hemis, Stakna and other important gonpas. Also in the 13th century the Saskyapa sect spread from Tibet, but Matho is the only gonpa now remaining in this tradition. In the 15th century Tsonkhapa and his disciples of the Gelugpa sect founded the great monasteries of Ganden, Sera, Drepung and Tashi Lhunpo in Tibet, and with the aid of King Dragpa Bumde this sect spread widely in Ladakh founding many important gonpas such as Spituk.

Also see p.117-120

ལ་དྭགས་སུ་སངས་རྒྱས་ཀྱི་བསྟན་པ་དར་ཚུལ།

གང་སྐུ་མཚན་དང་དཔེ་བྱད་རྒྱན་གྱིས་སྤུད་

གང་གསུང་ཡན་ལག་དྲུག་ཅུའི་དབྱངས་དང་ལྡན།།

གང་ཐུགས་སྤངས་རྟོགས་མཐར་ཕྱིན་ཆོས་ཀུན་མཁྱེན།།

ཀུན་མཁྱེན་རྒྱལ་བ་རྣམས་ལ་བདག་ཕྱག་འཚལ།།

ཡི་མེད་ཆོས་ཀུན་གསལ་ལེར་རབ་གཟིགས་ནས།།

ཤེས་བྱའི་གླིང་ལ་མངའ་དབང་སྒྱུར་བ་པོ།།

ཐུབ་པ་མཆོག་གི་རྒྱལ་ཚབ་དགེ་སྦྱོང་ཆེ།།

བསྟན་པ་འཛིན་སྐྱོང་སྤེལ་མཁས་གང་དེར་འདུད།།

ཡི་དག་གཉུག་མའི་གནས་ལུགས་ཇི་བཞིན་གཟིགས།

ཤེས་རབ་མཆོག་གིས་རྒོལ་ངན་རྩད་ནས་འཇོམས།།

ཐབས་ཚུལ་བཟང་པོས་ལེགས་བཤད་འདོམས་མཁས་པའི།།

མཁས་མཆོག་བླ་མ་རྣམས་ནི་ཕྱག་གི་ཡུལ།།

ས་འཛིན་དཀར་པོས་ཡོངས་བསྐོར་མང་ཡུལ་འདིར།།

ས་ལེ་སྦྲམ་ལྟར་རིན་ཆེན་ཐུབ་པའི་བསྟན།།

ས་ཕྱོགས་ཀུན་ཏུ་ཇི་ལྟར་དར་བའི་ཚུལ།།

ས་གསུམ་འགྲོ་བའི་དོན་དུ་སྤེལ་ལ་སྤྲོ།།

ཞེས་མཆོད་པར་བརྗོད་པའི་ཚིག་གིས་སྔོན་བསུས་ཏེ་གང་གླིང་བར་བྱ་བ་ནི། མང་ཡུལ་ལྗོངས་འདིར་མཉམ་མེད་བུ་རམ་ཤིང་པའི་ལུང་རྟོགས་ཀྱི་བསྟན་པ་རིན་པོ་ཆེ་དེ་ཉིད་ཇི་ལྟར་དར་ཞིང་རྒྱས་པའི་སྐོར་ཡིན་ལ་དེ་ཡང་ཐབས་མཁས་ལ་ཐུགས་རྗེ་ཆེན་པོ་དང་ལྡན་པ། འགྲོ་བ་རྣམས་

ཀྱི་མ་འདྲེས་པའི་མཛའ་བཤེས་ཆེན་པོ། ཞི་བ་དང་བདེ་བའི་ལམ་བཟང་སྟོན་པ་ལ་འགྲན་ཟླ་དང་བྲལ་བའི་སྟོན་སངས་རྒྱས་དེ་ཉིད་ལུམྦི་ནི་ཚལ་དུ་སྐུ་བལྟམས། རྡོ་རྗེ་གདན་གྱི་སྒྲོ་ལ་མངོན་པར་རྫོགས་པར་སངས་རྒྱས། ཝཱ་ར་ཎཱ་སཱིའི་དྲང་སྲོང་ལྷུང་བ་རི་དྭགས་ཀྱི་ནགས་སུ་སྡོན་ལྔ་དང་མི་ར་གྱུར་པ་སྐུས་ཀྱང་མ་བསྐོར་པའི་ཆོས་ཀྱི་འཁོར་ལོ་བསྐོར་བར་མཛད། ལྷ་སྡེ་བཟང་པོ་ལ་སོགས་པའི་སྐལ་ལྡན་གྱི་གདུལ་བྱ་དཔག་ཏུ་མེད་པའི་དོན་མཛད། ཆོས་ཀྱི་ཕུང་པོ་བརྒྱད་ཁྲི་བཞི་སྟོང་བསྟན། མཐར་དགུང་ལོ་བརྒྱད་བཅུར་ཕེབས་ནས་རྩྭ་མཆོག་གྲོང་དུ་གདུལ་བྱ་རྟག་འཛིན་ཅན་རྣམས་ཆོས་ལ་བསྐུལ་བའི་ཕྱིར་དུ་སྐུ་མྱ་ངན་ལ་འདས་པའི་ཚུལ་བསྟན་པར་མཛད། འོད་སྲུང་། ཀུན་དགའ་བོ། ཤཱ་ནའི་གོས་ཅན། ཉེར་སྦས། དྷི་ཏི་ཀ། ནག་པོ་དང་ལེགས་མཐོང་ཆེ་བ་བཅས་སྟོན་པའི་གཏད་རབས་བདུན་གྱིས་བསྟན་པ་ཚུལ་བཞིན་དུ་བསྐྱངས།

ཀུན་དགའ་བོའི་སློབ་མ་ཉི་མ་གུང་པ་ལྔ་བརྒྱ་བྱུང་། དེ་དག་གི་གཙོ་བོ་ནི་ཉི་མ་དགུང་པ་ཆེན་པོའམ་རྒྱ་དབུས་པ་ཆེན་པོ་ཞེས་གྲགས་སོ། འདི་ནི་ཕྱི་ལོའི་སྔོན་ལོ་༥༥༠ ཙམ་གྱི་དུས་སུ་ཡིན། ཉི་མ་གུང་པ་ཆེན་པོ་དེ་ཉིད་རྫུ་འཕྲུལ་གྱིས་ཀཤྨཱིར་དུ་ཕེབས། ཀླུ་གནས་པའི་མཚོ་འགྲམ་དུ་བཞུགས། ཀླུའི་རྒྱལ་པོ་ཨེ་རུ་ཌ་སོགས་བཏུལ། ཉི་མདགུང་པ་ཉིད་བཞུགས་པའི་དུས་སྐབས་སུ་ཀཤྨཱིར་གྲོང་ཁྱེར་ཆེན་པོ་དགུ་དང་། རི་བོར་གྱི་གྲོང་མང་པོ་དང་། རྒྱལ་པོའི་ཕོ་བྲང་གཅིག་དང་། གཙུག་ལག་ཁང་བཅུ་གཉིས་དགེ་འདུན་ཤིན་ཏུ་མང་པོ་དང་བཅས་པས་ཡུལ་བརྒྱན་པར་གྱུར་ཏེ། ༡ ཁ་ཆེའི་ཡུལ་དུ་གུར་

ཀུམ་་གྱི་སྐྱེ་གནས་ཀྱིས་ཁྱབ་པར་མཛད། དེ་དུས་དགྲ་བཅོམ་པ་དེ་ཉིད་ལ་དྭགས་ཀྱི་གཡུང་དྲུང་ན་དང་དཔེ་ཐུབ་བར་དུའང་རྫུ་འཕྲུལ་གྱིས་ཕེབས། གཡུང་དྲུང་གི་མཚོ་རལ་ས་གཞི་བྱིན་གྱིས་བརླབས།

ཕྱི་ལོ་༡༣༥་ནས་རྒྱལ་པོ་ཀ་ནིཀའི་རྒྱལ་སྲིད་འཛིན། ཁོང་གིས་ཀཤྨིར་དུ་སྲིད་དབང་སྒྱུར་དུས་ནང་པའི་ཆོས་དང་ནང་པའི་དགེ་སློང་ནམ་མཁའི་སྐར་ཚོགས་བཞིན་དུ་འཕེལ། དེ་ཡང་ཀཤྨཱར་གྱི་སྙན་ངག་དང་རྒྱལ་རབས་ཀྱི་མཁས་པ་ཆེན་པོ་ཀལ་ཧན་གྱིས༔

རྒྱལ་པོ་ད་མོ་དར་གྱི་རྗེས་སུ་ཧུཥྐ་ཛུཥྐ་དང་ཀ་ནིཥྐ་བྱ་བའི་རྒྱལ་པོ་གསུམ་བྱུང་། དེ་དག་གིས་རང་རང་གི་མིང་དང་མཐུན་པའི་གྲོང་ཁྱེར་རེ་བཏབ། དེ་ཡང་ཧུཥྐ་པུར་ཛུཥྐ་པུར་དང་ཀནིཥྐ་པུར་བཅས་ཡིན། རྒྱལ་པོ་དེ་གསུམ་གྱིས་ཀཤྨིར་དུ་མཆོད་རྟེན་དང་དགོན་པ་མང་པོ་བཞེངས། ཡོད་པ་དེ་ཡང་ཀཤྨིར་གྱི་རྒྱལ་རབས་རཛ་ཏ་རངྒི་ཎི་ ༣ ཞེས་པ་མཁས་དབང་ཀལ་ཧན་གྱིས་མཛད་པ་དེ་ནས་གསལ་པོར་རྟོག་ཐུབ། དེ་ལ་བརྟག་ན་ཀ་ནིཥྐས་ལ་དྭགས་སུའང་མཆོད་རྟེན་དང་དགོན་པ་བཏབ་ཡོད་པར་མངོན། ལྷག་པར་དུ་ཟངས་དཀར་སནའི་ཀ་ནི་མཁར་ན་ཆོས་རྒྱལ་དེ་ཉིད་ཀྱིས་བཞེངས་པར་མཛད་པའི་མཆོད་རྟེན་ཀ་ནི་ཀ་ཞུ་བཞིན་ད་སྣའང་གསོད་ནམས་གསོག་པའི་ཞིང་དུ་བཞུགས་ཡོད། དེ་ལྟ་ན་ཕྱི་ལོ་༡༣༠་ཙམ་ནང་ལྗོངས་འདིར་སངས་རྒྱས་ཀྱི་བསྟན་པའི་དབུ་བརྙེས་ཡོད་པ་གསལ་པོར་རྟོགས་ཐུབ། གཞན་ཡང་གཏེར་རི་རུ་ཆོས་རྒྱལ་མྱ་ངན་མེད་ཀྱི་དུས་སུ་བཞེངས་པའི་མྱ་ངན་མེད་ཀྱི་མཆོད་རྟེན་ཞུ་བཞིན་ད་ལྟའང་མཇལ་རྒྱུ་ཡོད། དེ་དག་ལ་བརྟག་ན་ཕྱི་ལོའི་གོང་དུ་སངས་རྒྱས་ཀྱི་བསྟན་པ་དར་མེད་ནའང་

བརྒྱ་ཕྲག་དང་པོ་གཉིས་པའི་ནང་དུ་དར་ཡོད་པ་ལ་ཐེ་ཚོམ་གང་ཡང་མི་འདུག།

གཞན་ཡང་ཀ་ནིཥྐ་ཡར་ཀྱིན་དང་ཁོ་ཏན་ཡང་དབང་དུ་བསྡུས། ༣ དེ་ལ་བརྟག་ན་ཀ་ནིཥྐ་ལ་དྭགས་སུའང་ཕེབས་ཡོད་པར་མངོན། དེ་དུས་སྐར་རྡོ་དང་འགྲིལ་སྒྲིད་སོགས་ལའང་སངས་རྒྱས་ཀྱི་བསྟན་པ་ཉི་མ་ཤར་བ་ལྟར་དར་ཡོད་པས། ལྡོངས་འདིར་དར་མེད་པའི་རྒྱུ་མཚན་གང་ཡང་མི་སྣང་།

༡ ཏཱ་རཱ་ནཱ་ཐའི་རྒྱ་གར་ཆོས་འབྱུང་། ལྷཱ་ཁའི་པར་མ ཤོག་གྲངས་༡༣

༢ རཱ་ཛཱ་ཏཱ་རྒྷི་ཎི་ཁག་དང་པོ ཤོགས་བཅད ༡༦༨ ༦༩ ༧༠ པར་གསལ།

༣ པྲཱ་ཙཱིན་རཱད་ཥཔ ཏཐཱ་བོདྡྷ་དྷ་རྨ ཤོག་གྲངས་༣༧༣

བརྒྱ་ཕྲག་དགུ་པ་བདུན་པའི་ནང་དུ་ཀ་ཤྨཱིར་དུ་གན་དྷ་རཱ་ལུགས་ཀྱི་རྡོ་སྐུ་བཟོ་རྒྱུའི་སྲོལ་ཤུགས་ཆེན་པོ་དར། དེ་བཞིན་ལ་དྭགས་སུའང་རྡོ་སྐུའི་བཟོ་རྒྱུའི་སྲོལ་ཚུགས། དེའི་རྟགས་མཚན་ནི། ད་ལྟའི་དངུལ་འབེབས་ཀྱི་རྒྱལ་བ་བྱམས་པ། སངས་སྐུའ་བྲག་ལ་བརྐོས་ཡོད་པའི་སྐུ་བརྙན།། སྐར་རྡོ་སོགས་སུ་བྲག་ལ་བརྐོས་ཡོད་པའི་སྐུ་བརྙན་མང་པོ་ད་ལྟའང་སྔོན་དུས་ལྡོངས་འདིར་སངས་རྒྱས་ཀྱི་བསྟན་པ་དར་ནས་སྐུ་བརྙན་དེ་དག་ལ་ཕྱག

མཆོད་འབུལ་མཁན་དང་དད་པ་དག་སྣང་བྱེད་མཁན་མང་པོ་ཡོད་པར་འཆད་བཞིན་ཡོད།

དེས་ན་ལ་དྭགས་ལྗོངས་འདིར་སངས་རྒྱས་ཀྱི་བསྟན་པ་ཕྱི་ལོ་བརྒྱ་ཕྲག་གཉིས་པའི་ནང་དུ་དར་ཡོད་པ་གསལ་པོར་རྟོགས་ཐུབ། འོན་ཀྱང་ཆོས་རྒྱལ་གྲགས་པ་འབུམ་ལྡེ་དང་སེངྒེ་རྣམ་རྒྱལ་སྐབས་ལྟར་དར་ཁྱབ་ཆེན་པོ་རང་མ་བྱུང་།

ཕྱི་ལོ་བརྒྱ་ཕྲག་བདུན་པའི་ནང་དུ་ཆོས་རྒྱལ་སྲོང་བཙན་སྒམ་པོས་ཐུ་མི་སཾ་བྷོ་ཊ་སོགས་རྒྱ་གར་དུ་བརྫངས། སཾ་བྷོ་ཊས་བྲམ་ཟེ་ལི་པི་ཀ་ར་དང་ལྷ་རིག་པའི་སེངྒེ་སོགས་མཁས་ཤིང་གྲུབ་པ་བརྙེས་པའི་སློབ་དཔོན་མང་པོ་བརྟེན་ནས་ལེགས་སྦྱོར་གྱི་སྒྲ་དང་། ནང་དོན་རིག་པ་སོགས་ལ་སློབ་སྦྱོང་མཐར་ཕྱིན་པར་མཛད། ཡིག་རིགས་མི་འདྲ་བ་མང་པོ་སྦྱངས། ལྷག་པར་དུ་ལཉྫ་དང་ཝ་རྟུ་ཕྱིས་ཕྱིན་པར་ཁོང་དུ་ཆུད་པར་མཛད་ནས་སླར་བོད་དུ་ཕེབས། བོད་ཡིག་གི་དབྱངས་གསལ་གྱི་ཡི་གེ་རྣམས་གསར་དུ་བཙམས། མ་ཆད་པཱ་ཎི་ནིའི་སྒྲའི་བསྟན་བཅོས་དང་མཐུན་པའི་བོད་སྐད་ཀྱི་སྒྲའི་རྣམ་གཞག་སྐོར་ལ་བསྟན་བཅོས་ཆེན་པོ་བརྒྱད་མཛད།

བརྒྱ་ཕྲག་བརྒྱད་པའི་ནང་དུ་ཆོས་རྒྱལ་ཁྲི་སྲོང་ལྡེའུ་བཙན་གྱིས་ཨོ་རྒྱན་གྱི་སློབ་དཔོན་ཆེན་པོ་པདྨ་འབྱུང་གནས་དང་མཁན་ཆེན་བོ་དྷི་སཏྭ་རྣམ་གཉིས་ཀྱིས་བཀའ་བཀོད་མཛད་པ་ལྟར་ཕྱི་ལོ་༨༠༩ ལོར་བསམ་ཡས་མི་འགྱུར་ལྷུན་གྱིས་གྲུབ་པའི་གཙུག་ལག་ཁང་བཞེངས། བཻ་རོ་ཙ་ན་སོགས་ལོ་ཙཱ་དང་། ཛྙཱ་ཀི་རྟི། བི་མ་ལ་མི་ཏྲ། ཤཱནྟི་གརྦྷ་དང་ཀ་མ་ལ་ཤཱི་ལ་

སོགས་རྒྱ་གར་གྱི་པཎྜི་ཏ་མང་དུ་བྱོན་ནས་སངས་རྒྱས་ཀྱི་བསྟན་པ་ཉི་མ་ཤར་བ་ལྟར་དར་རྒྱས་བྱུང་།

ཕྱི་ལོ་༨༠༧་ལོར་གླང་དར་མས་བོད་དུ་སངས་རྒྱས་ཀྱི་བསྟན་པ་བསྣུབས། ཐུ་མིས་མཛད་པོའི་སྒྲའི་བསྟན་བཅོས་བརྒྱད་ལས་སུམ་ཅུ་པ་དང་རྟགས་འཇུག་གཉིས་མ་གཏོགས་མེར་བསྲེགས།

ཕྱི་ལོ་༨༤༣ ལོར་བོད་ཀྱི་རྒྱལ་ཁབ་ཆེན་པོ་སིལ་བུར་འཐོར། དེ་དུས་སྐྱིད་ལྡེ་ཉི་མ་མགོན་ཁྲིངས་ལོག་གི་འཇིགས་པས་མང་ཡུལ་ལ་དྭགས་ཕྱོགས་སུ་ཕེབས་དགོས་བྱུང་། ལོ་གསུམ་བརྒྱ་ཞི་བདུན་བོད་སིལ་བུར་ལུས། དེ་ནས་དཔལ་ས་སྐྱའི་དཔོན་རབས་ཉེ་ཤུས་བོད་ཀྱི་ཆབ་སྲིད་ལོ་དགུ་བཅུ་གོ་དགུ་བར་དུ་བསྐྱངས། དེ་ནས་བཟུང་ཕྱི་ལོ་ ༡༨༤༨ བར་སྐྱ་སེར་སྲིལ་མས་བོད་ཀྱི་ཆབ་སྲིད་ཆོས་བཞིན་དུ་བསྐྱངས། འོན་ཀྱང་བོད་ཡོངས་ལ་དབང་སྒྱུར་བའི་རྒྱལ་པོའི་བརྒྱུད་པ་དག་གིས་ན་དབང་བསྒྱུར་མ་ཐུབ།

ཕྱི་ལོ་ ༡༠༠༨ ནས་བསྟན་པ་ཕྱི་དར་གྱི་འགོ་ཚུགས། སྨད་དང་སྟོད་ནས་འདུལ་བའི་བསྟན་པ་རིམ་བཞིན་དར། སྐྱིད་ལྡེ་ཉི་མ་མགོན་གྱི་སྲས་ཆུང་བ་ལྡེ་གཙུག་མགོན་ལ་སྲས་འཁོར་རེ་དང་སྲོང་ངེ་ཞེས་པ་གཉིས་བྱུང་། འཁོར་རེ་ལ་སྲས་དེཝ་རཱ་ཛ་དང་ནག་རཱ་ཛ་ཞེས་པ་གཉིས་བྱུང་། ...གསུམ་རབ་ཏུ་བྱུང་སྲོང་ངེ་ལ་སྲས་ཞི་བ་འོད། བྱང་ཆུབ་འོད་དང་འོད་ལྡེ་གསུམ་བྱུང་། འདི་དག་བཅོམ་ལྡན་འདས་ཀྱི་ཆོས་ལ་ཧ་ཅང་གི་དད་མོས་ཆེ་བ་རྗེས་སུ་འཁོར་རེ་ཡབ་སྲས་གསུམ་རབ་ཏུ་བྱུང་། ཆོས་འཁོར་རེ་ལ་ཡེ་ཤེས་འོད་ཞུའོ། ཡེ་ཤེས་འོད་ཀྱིས་རྒྱ་གར་ནས་ཇོ་བོ་རྗེ་དཔལ་ལྡན་ཨ་ཏི་ཤ་གདན་ཞུ་ཆེད་རང་གི་སྐུ་སྲོག་ཀྱང་གར་ལོག་གི་རྒྱལ་པོ་ལ་སྤྲད། །འོན་

ཀུང་ཁོང་གི་ཐུགས་བསྐྱེད་སྨོན་ལམ་བཟང་པོའི་བཀའ་དྲིན་ལ་ཆ་བོ་བྱུང་ཚུབ་འོད་ཀྱིས་ཇོ་བོ་རྗེ་དཔལ་ལྡན་ཨ་ཏི་ཤ་རྒྱ་གར་ནས་བོད་དུ་གདན་ཞུས། སྐབས་དེར་ལོ་ཆེན་རིན་ཆེན་བཟང་པོས་ལ་དྭགས་སུ་ལྷ་ཁང་བརྒྱ་རྩ་བརྒྱ་དང་མཆོད་རྟེན་བརྒྱ་རྩ་བརྒྱད་མང་ཡུལ་གྱི་ཉར་མ་གུ་གེའི་ཁ་ཙེ་གོ་ཁར་པུ་ཧྲངས་ཀྱི་མཐོ་ལྡིང་བཅས་སུ་བཞེངས་སུ་བཤད་སྒྲུབ་ཀྱི་བསྟི་གནས་དགོན་པ་བཏབ་ནས་བཤད་སྒྲུབ་ཀྱི་བྱ་བའི་འཁོར་ལོ་རབ་ཏུ་སྤེལ། དེར་བརྟེན་ལ་དྭགས་ཀྱི་ལྗོངས་འདིར་སངས་རྒྱས་ཀྱི་བསྟན་པ་ཆེས་ཆེར་དར། ཕྱི་ལོ་༨༧༥ ཙམ་ནང་སྐྱིད་ལྡེ་ཉི་མ་མགོན་གྱིས་སྟོད་མངའ་རིས་ལ་དབང་བསྒྱུར། སྲས་གསུམ་འཁྲུངས། ཆེ་བ་ལྷ་ཆེན་དཔལ་གྱི་མགོན། བར་པ་བཀྲིས་མགོན་དང་། ཆུང་བ་ལྡེ་གཙུག་མགོན་བཅས་ཡིན། དང་པོས་མང་ཡུལ་གཞུང་དང་བར་པས་གུ་གེ་པུ་ཧྲངས། ཆུང་བས་ཟངས་དཀར་སྤྱི་ཏི་སོགས་ལ་མངའ་མཛད། ལྷ་ཆེན་དཔལ་གྱི་མགོན་གྱིས་ཞལ་དུ་ཕྱི་ལོ་༡༠༠༠ ཙམ་ནང་མཁར་བརྩིགས། འདི་ནི་ལ་དྭགས་གཞུང་དུ་འགོ་མ་རང་བརྩིགས་པའི་མཁར་ཡིན། ཁོང་གིས་རྒྱལ་སྲིད་ཆོས་བཞིན་དུ་བསྐྱངས་སོ།།

ཕྱི་ལོ་༡༡༡༠ ཙམ་ལ་ལྷ་ཆེན་རྒྱལ་པོས་ཀླུ་འཁྱིལ་དུ་དགོན་པ་བཞེངས། དགེ་འདུན་གྱི་སྡེ་བཙུགས། དེ་དུས་ཇོ་བོ་རྗེ་ནས་བརྒྱུད་པི་བཀའ་གདམས་པའི་ཆོས་བརྒྱུད་འཛིན་པའི་དགོན་གནས་ཤིག་ཡིན་ནོ།།

རྙིང་མའི་ཆོས་བརྒྱུད་དང་དེ་ལ་དྭགས་སུ་དར་ཚུལ།

གསང་བ་སྔགས་ཀྱི་ཐེག་པ་ལ་སྔ་འགྱུར་དང་ཕྱི་འགྱུར་གཉིས་སུ་ཕྱེ་ནས། སྔ་མ་ལྟར་ཉམས་བཞེས་མཛད་པ་རྣམས་ལ་རྙིང་མ་པ་ཞེས་གྲགས། དེ་ཡང་བརྒྱ་ཕྲག་བདུན་པའི་ནང་དུ་ཆོས་སྐྱོང་བའི་རྒྱལ་པོ་སྲོང་བཙན་སྒམ་

པོའི་སྐུ་དུས་སུ་རྒྱ་གར་རྒྱ་ནག་བལ་ཡུལ་སོགས་ནས་བྱོན་པའི་པཎྜི་ཏ་རྣམས་དང་ཐུ་མི་སམ་བྷོ་ཊ་སོགས་ཀྱིས་འཕགས་པ་ཐུགས་རྗེ་ཆེན་པོཨི་མདོ་རྒྱུད་མང་པོ་ཞིག་སཾསྐྲྀཏའི་སྐད་ནས་བོད་སྐད་དུ་བསྒྱུར། རྒྱལ་པོ་རང་ཉིད་ཀྱིས་དེ་དག་གི་ཚིག་དོན་མ་ལུས་པ་ཐུགས་སུ་ཆུད་པར་མཛད་ནས་སྐལ་པ་དང་ལྡན་པའི་སློབ་མའི་ཚོགས་ལ་གསང་སྔགས་ཞི་ཁྲོའི་ལྷ་རྣམས་ཀྱི་གདམས་ངག་མང་དུ་བསྟུལ། དེ་ལ་བརྟེན་ནས་དུས་དེར་དངོས་གྲུབ་ཐོབ་པའི་གང་ཟག་ཀྱང་མང་དུ་བྱུང་། དེ་ནས་བཟུང་སྟེ་མིས་ཨག་ཚོམས་ཡན་ཆད་ལ་གསང་བ་སྔགས་ཀྱི་སྒོར་ཉམས་ལེན་མཛད་མཁན་མང་པོ་བྱུང་།

ཆོས་རྒྱལ་སྲོང་བཙན་གྱིས་བོད་ཀྱི་ཡུལ་གྲུ་ཀུན་ལ་ཡི་གེ་དྲུག་མ་འདོན་པའི་སྲོལ་བཙུགས། བརྒྱ་ཕྲག་བརྒྱད་པའི་ནང་དུ་རྒྱལ་པོ་ཁྲི་སྲོང་ལྡེའུ་བཙན་གྱི་སྐུ་དུས་སུ་མཁན་ཆེན་བོ་དྷི་སཏྭ་དང་སློབ་དཔོན་པདྨ་སྐལ་ལྡན་རྣམས་ལ་རྣམ་འགྱུར་བླ་ན་མེད་པ་གཙོ་བོར་གྱུར་པའི་དབང་བསྐུར། རྒྱུད་བཤད། གདམས་ངག་གནང་། ཆོས་གཏེར་དང་ནོར་གྱི་གཏེར་བཏོན་ནས་གསང་སྔགས་ཀྱི་དམ་ཆོས་ཟབ་མི་དེ་ཉིད་ཤིན་ཏུ་དར་ཞིང་རྒྱས་པར་མཛད།།

སྐབས་དེར་དར་བའི་རྒྱུད་ནི། གསང་བ་འདུས་པ་དང་། ཟླ་གསང་ཐིག་ལེ་སོགས་ཏནྟྲ་སྡེ་བཅོ་བརྒྱད་དུ་གྲགས་པ་རྣམས་ཡིན། ཉམས་ལེན་གཙོ་བོ་ནི་སྒྲུབ་པ་ཆེན་པོ་བཀའ་བརྒྱད་ལ་བྱས།། དེ་ལྟ་བུའི་གསང་སྔགས་ལ་ཉམས་ལེན་མཛད་ནས་རྗེ་འབངས་ཉེར་ལྔ་སོགས་གྲུབ་པ་བརྙེས་པའང་མང་དུ་བྱུང་།

སྙིང་མའི་ཆོས་བརྒྱུད་ལ་དྲགས་སུ་དར་ཚུལ།

བརྒྱ་ཕྲག་བརྒྱད་པའི་ནང་ཨོ་རྒྱན་སློབ་དཔོན་པདྨ་སཾབྷ་ཝ་མང་ཡུལ་ལྗོང་འདི་ཉིད་ཀྱི་ཟངས་དཀར། གསེར་ཁྲི། ཕོ་དཀར་རྫོང་སོགས་སུ་ཕེབས་ཏེ་གྲུབ་པ་མཛད་པ་དང་ཆབས་ཅིག་ས་གཞི་རྣམས་ཀྱང་བྱིན་གྱིས་བརླབས་པར་མཛད། དེ་དུས་ལྗོང་འདིར་གསང་སྔགས་རྙིང་མའི་དབུ་བརྙེས། ཕྱི་རིམ་བཞིན་དར་རྒྱས་བྱུང་ཡང་སྐབས་གཅིག་ལ་ཉམས་ཆགས་ཆེན་པོ་བྱུང་། དེ་ལྟར་བྱུང་ཡོད་པ་ཡང་ད་ལྟ་སྟུམ་ར་རུ་ཡོད་པའི་དགོན་པོ་ཁག་དང་གཞན་ཡང་དགོན་པ་དགའི་ལྡེབས་རིས་སོགས་ནས་གསལ་པོར་ཤེས་ཐུབ། ཕྱིས་ཕྱི་ལོ་ ༡༩༣༠ ཙམ་ནང་གྲུབ་ཐོབ་པདྨ་འཕྲིན་ལས་ཨོ་རྒྱན་པདྨའི་སྒྲུབ་གནས་ཁྱད་པར་ཅན་དེར་སྒྲུབ་པ་སྙིང་པོ་མཛད་ཀྱིན་བཞུགས། དེ་ནས་བཟང་ཁོང་གི་སློབ་མ་སྤུ་འགྱུར་བྱུང་གཏེར་གི་ཆོས་བརྒྱུད་འཛིན་པའི་འདུས་སྡེ་ཟམ་མ་ཆད་པར་བྱུང་དང་འབྱུང་བཞིན་ཡན་ནོ།། གསེར་ཁྲི་རུ་སྤྲག་ཐོབ་དགོན་པ་གསར་དུ་གཏབ། ངུར་སྨིག་གསུམ་ལྡན་གྱི་འདུས་པའི་སྡེ་བཙུགས། ཆོས་རྫོགས་པ་ཆེན་པོ་ལ་ཐོས་བསམ་སྒོམ་སྒྲུབ་མཛད་མཁན་གྱི་གང་ཟག་མང་དུ་བྱུང་། དེ་ལྟ་བུའི་བརྒྱུད་པ་བཟང་པོའི་རྗེས་སུ་སློབ་པའི་དུས་སྡེ་སྦྱིན་བདག་དང་བཅས་པ་ད་བར་མི་ཉམས་གོང་འཕེལ་ངང་བཞུགས་ཡོད།

བཀའ་བརྒྱུད་ཀྱི་ཆོས་བརྒྱུད་དང་དེ་ཉིད་ལ་དྲགས་སུ་དར་ཚུལ།

ཆུ་འགོ་གངས་ལ་ཐུག་པ་ལྟར་བཀའ་བརྒྱུད་ཀྱི་བརྒྱུད་པའི་སྲོལ་གཏོད་པར་མཛད་པོ་མར་པ་ཆོས་ཀྱི་བློ་གྲོས་དེ་ཉིད་ནི་ཕྱི་ལོ་༡༠༡༣ ལོར་ཡབ་མར་པ་དབང་ཕྱུག་རྡོ་རྗེ་དང་། ཡུམ་རྒྱ་མོ་ཟ་མདོ་སྡེ་གཉིས་ཀྱི་སྲས་སུ་

འབྲུངས། དགུང་ལོ་ནར་སོན་ནས་མདོ་སྔགས་ཀྱི་གཞུང་རྣམས་ལ་སློབ་སྦྱོང་ལེགས་པར་མཛད། རྒྱ་གར་དུ་ཐེངས་གསུམ་ཕེབས། གྲུབ་པའི་དབང་ཕྱུག་དཔལ་ནཱ་རོ་པའི་ཞབས་ལ་གཏུགས། འཁོར་ལོ་བདེ་མཆོག་དང་གསང་བ་འདུས་པ་སོགས་ཀྱི་རྒྱུད་སྡེ་དང་སྨིན་བྱེད་དབང་དང་། སྒྲོལ་བྱེད་གདམས་ངག་མང་དུ་གསན། གཞན་ཡང་བླ་མ་བརྒྱ་ཙ་བརྒྱད་བསྟེན་ནས་མདོ་དང་སྔགས་ཀྱི་གཞུང་ལུགས་རྒྱ་མཚོ་ལྟ་བུ་ཐུགས་སུ་ཆུད་པར་མཛད། སླར་བོད་དུ་ཕེབས་ཏེ་བསྒྱུར་བཤད་ཀྱི་མཛད་པ་ཕྲིན་ལས་རླབས་པོ་ཆེ་མཛད། གསུང་ལས་སྐྱེས་པའི་སློབ་མ་གྲངས་མེད་བྱོན། དེ་རྣམས་ཀྱི་ནང་ནས་མཆོག་ཏུ་གྱུར་པ་ནི་བཀའ་ཆེན་བཞི་ཡིན། དེ་དག་ནི།

༡ འཕོ་བ་རྒྱ་མཐོངས་ཁ་ཕྱེ་བའི་ནང་ནས་བྱ་འཕུར་བ་ལྟ་བུའི་བཀའ་བབས་ནི། དོལ་གྱི་མཚུར་སྟོན་དབང་པོ།

༢ རྒྱུད་བཤད་ཐབས་ཀྱི་ཨན་ངག་ཨུ་ཏིག་བསྟར་ལ་བརྒྱུས་པ་ལྟ་བུའི་བཀའ་བབས་ནི། གཞུང་གི་རྔོག་སྟོན་ཆོས་རྡོར།

༣ འོད་གསལ་མུན་ནང་དུ་སྒྲོམ་མེ་སྦར་བ་ལྟ་བུའི་བཀའ་བབས་ནི། གཙང་རོང་གི་མེས་སྟོན་ཆེན་པོ།།

༤ གཏུམ་མོ་ཤིང་བསྐམས་བཤགས་པ་ལ་མེ་སྦར་བ་ལྟ་བུའི་བཀའ་བབས་ནི། གུང་ཐང་གི་མི་ལ་རས་པ་བཅས་ཡིན་ནོ།།

དང་པོ་གསུམ་གྱིས་རྒྱུད་བཤད་པའི་སྲོལ་གཙོ་བོར་བཟུང་། བཞི་པ་རྗེ་མི་ལ་ནི་གྲུབ་པའི་དབང་ཕྱུག་གི་སར་གཤེགས་ཏེ་སྒྲུབ་བརྒྱུད་ཀྱི་བསྟན་པའི་རྒྱལ་མཚན་འཛིན་ནས་སློབ་མ་མང་དུ་བསྐྲུན་པར་མཛད། སློབ་མའི་གཙོ་བོ་རྗེ་རས་ཆུང་པ་དང་། དྭགས་པོ་ལྷ་རྗེ་རྣམ་གཉིས་བྱུང་ངོ།།

རས་ཆུང་པ་རྒྱ་གར་དུ་ཐེངས་ཁ་ཤས་ཕེབས། ལུས་མེད་མཁའ་འགྲོའི་ཆོས་སྐོར་ལྷག་མ་ཀུན་བོད་དུ་སྤྱན་དྲངས། རས་ཆུང་སྙན་བརྒྱུད་སོགས་ཀྱི་མན་ངག་རྣམས་ཁོང་རང་ནས་དར་བ་ཡིན་ནོ།།

དྭགས་པོ་ལྷ་རྗེ་བསོད་ནམས་རིན་ཆེན་གྱིས་ཕྱི་ལོ་༡༡༥༣ ལོར་དྭགས་ལ་སྒམ་པོ་ཞེས་པའི་དགོན་སྡེ་ཞིག་ཕྱག་བཏབ། ཁོང་ཆུང་དུས་སུ་བྱ་ཡུལ་བ་དང༌། ལྕགས་རི་གོང་ཁ་བ་སོགས་བཀའ་གདམས་ཀྱི་བླ་མ་མང་དུ་བསྟེན་ནས་སྦྱངས་པ་མཐར་ཕྱིན་པར་མཛད། ཕྱིར་རྗེ་བཙུན་མི་ལ་ལས་གདམས་པ་མང་དུ་གསན། བཀའ་ཕྱག་ཆུ་བོ་གཉིས་འདྲེས་ཀྱི་གདམས་ངག་སློབ་མའི་ཚོགས་ལ་སྤེལ་བར་མཛད་དོ།།

བཀའ་བརྒྱུད་ལ་ཆེ་བཞི་དང་ཆུང་བ་བརྒྱད་དུ་གྲགས། དེ་ལས་ཆེ་བ་བཞི་ནི།

༡ དྭགས་པོ་བཀའ་བརྒྱུད།

༢ ཚལ་པ་བཀའ་བརྒྱུད།

༣ ཀརྨ་བཀའ་བརྒྱུད།

༤ ཕག་གྲུ་བཀའ་བརྒྱུད་བཅས་དང༌།

འབྲུག་པ་དང་འབྲི་གུང་བཀའ་བརྒྱུད་སོགས་ཆུང་བ་བརྒྱད་བྱུང་བ་ཡིན་ནོ།།

དེ་ལྟར་སྒྲུབ་བརྒྱུད་ཀྱི་བསྟན་པ་འཛིན་སྐྱོང་སྤེལ་བར་མཛད་པའི་སྐྱེས་ཆེན་ལྷ་ལམ་ཡངས་པའི་རྒྱ་སྐར་བཞིན་བྱོན་ནས་བསྟན་པ་དང་འགྲོ་བའི་དོན་དཔག་ཏུ་མེད་པ་མཛད་བཞིན་ཡིན་ནོ།།

ལ་དྭགས་སུ་བཀའ་བརྒྱུད་ཀྱི་བསྟན་པ་དར་ཚུལ།

དེ་ཡང་ཕྱི་ལོ་ ༡༠༧༠ ཙམ་ནང་གྲུབ་པའི་དབང་ཕྱུག་ཆེན་པོ་དཔལ་ནཱ་རོ་པ་ཀ་ཤྨཱིར་ནས་ལ་དྭགས་གཡུང་དྲུང་དང་ཟངས་དཀར་དུ་ཕེབས་ནས་ས་གཞི་བྱིན་གྱིས་བརླབས། གང་གི་སློབ་མའི་མཆོག་གྱུར་བླ་མ་མར་པ་མཆོག་ཟངས་དཀར་དུ་ཕེབས་ནས་མར་པ་གླིང་བཏབ། ཕྱི་ལོ་ ༡༡༠༠ ཙམ་ནང་སྒྲུབ་བརྒྱུད་ཀྱི་བསྟན་པ་མང་ཡུལ་ལྗོངས་འདིར་དར་བའི་དབུ་ཚུགས། དེ་ནས་རྒྱལ་པོ་བཀྲིས་མགོན་ ༡༣༣༥ ༡༣༥༠ གྱི་ཆབ་སྲིད་སྐྱོང་བའི་སྐབས་སུ་རྒྱལ་བ་རྩོད་ཆང་པ་མགོན་པོ་རྡོ་རྗེ་ལ་དྭགས་སུ་ཕེབས། དེ་མི་ རྩོད་ཆང་། དབྱིབས་དགུའི་དགོན་པ་དམར་བཟངས་ མང་སྤྲོ་དང་གསེར་ཁྲིའི་སྐྱིད་ཕུག་དགོན་སོགས་སུ་སྒྲུབ་པ་ཉམས་ལེན་མཛད། དེ་མི་སོགས་སུ་གྲུབ་སྡེ་རི་ཡང་ཙུགས། དོན་དུ་ཕྱི་ལོ་ ༡༣༣༠ ཙམ་ནང་ལྗོངས་འདིར་སྒྲུབ་བརྒྱུད་ཀྱི་བསྟན་པ་ཞིགས་པར་དར། སྟག་ཚང་ངག་དབང་རྒྱ་མཚོ་མ་ཕེབས་གོང་དུ་ལ་དྭགས་ཀྱི་གཤམ་སྟོད་ཀྱི་ཡུལ་གྲུ་མང་པོ་མ་ཚད་ཞིང་ཉིད་བར་དུ་བཀའ་བརྒྱུད་ཀྱི་བསྟན་པ་འཛིན་པའི་དགོན་སྡེ་དང་། དགེ་འདུན་བཞུགས་ཡོད་པར་མངོན། སྟག་ཚང་ཟངས་དཀར་ནས་ཧེ་མི་དང་དེ་ནས་ཨ་ལྕི་རུ་ཕེབས། དེ་ནས་བ་མགོ་རུ་རྒྱལ་པོ་སེངྒེ་རྣམ་རྒྱལ་དང་ཡུམ་རྒྱལ་ཁ་ཏུན་གཉིས་ཀྱིས་ཕེབས་བསུ་ཞུས། དེ་དུས་བ་མགོའི་མཁར་གྱི་ཕྱམས་ཁང་དུ་བཀའ་བརྒྱུད་ཀྱི་དཀོར་གཉེར་བཞུགས་ཡོད་པ་སྟང་ཚང་ཁོང་རང་གི་རྣམ་ཐར་ནས་གསལ།

རྒྱལ་པོ་སེངྒེ་རྣམ་རྒྱལ་ ༡༥༩༠ ༡༦༣༠ གྱིས་བླ་མ་སྟག་ཚང་དབུ་བླར་བསྙེན། མཆོད་ཡོན་ཉི་ཟླ་ཟུང་གིས་ཧེ་མི་བྱང་ཆུབ་བསམ་གླིང་། ཕྱན་ལེ་དགོན་རྫི་རུ་རུ་བཀྲིས་མཐོང་སྨོན། དགོན་སོགས་ཕྱག་བཏབ་པར་མཛད།

རྒྱལ་པོས་ལ་དྭགས་གང་པོ་ནས་གྲྭ་ཁྲལ་བསྡུས། ཡུལ་ལྗོགས་ཚང་མ་ནས་ས་གཞི་དང་སྦྱིན་བདག་མང་པོ་བླ་མ་སྣག་ཚང་ལ་ཕུལ། དེ་ལ་བརྟེན་ནས་ལ་དྭགས་སུ་སྒྲུབ་བརྒྱུད་ཀྱི་བསྟན་པ་ཉི་མ་ཤར་བ་ལྟར་དར་རྒྱས་བྱུང་། བཀའ་བརྒྱུད་ཆུང་བརྒྱུད་ཀྱི་ནང་ནས་འབྲུག་པ་བཀའ་བརྒྱུད་ཟེར་བཤད་པ་ལྟར་ཕྱི་ལོ་༡༣༣༠ ཙམ་ནང་དར། རྒྱལ་པོ་བཀྲིས་རྣམ་རྒྱལ་༡༥༠༠ ༡༥༣༠ གྱིས་སྐུ་དུས་སུ་ཆོད་རྗེ་འདན་མ་ལ་དྭགས་སུ་ཕེབས་ནས་འབྲི་གུང་བཀའ་བརྒྱུད་ཀྱི་བསྟན་པ་སྤེལ། འབྲུག་པ་ལ་ སྟོད་འབྲུག སྨད་འབྲུག་བར་འབྲུག་དང་ལྷོ་འབྲུག་བཅས་བཞི་ལས་ལྷོ་འབྲུག་གི་བརྒྱུད་པ་ནི་ཆོས་རྗེ་ཐུགས་འཛིན་ལ་དྭགས་སུ་ཕྱི་ལོ་ ༡༥༨༨ ནང་ཕེབས། སྟག་སྣ་དང་ཐུགས་སུ་དགོན་པ་བཏབ་པ་ནས་དར་འགོ་ཚུགས་ནས་ད་ལྟ་བར་ལྗོངས་འདིར་ལྷོ་འབྲུག་གི་བརྒྱུད་འཛིན་དགོན་སྡེ་ཁག་དང་སྤྲུལ་སྐུ་དང་འདུས་སྡེ་བཅས་དར་ཞིང་བཞུགས་ཡོད། ཕྱི་ལོ་༡༩༨༧ ནང་བཀའ་བརྒྱུད་ཆེ་བ་བཞིའི་ཡ་རྒྱལ་ཀརྨ་བཀའ་བརྒྱུད་ཀྱི་བསྟན་པ་ཡང་ལྗོངས་འདིར་དར་འགོ་ཚུགས། རོང་མ་ཧེ་དགོན་པ་དང་ལྷུག་ཚལ་ཀརྨ་སྒྲུབ་བརྒྱུད་གླིག་ག་ཆོས་སྡེ་གཉིས་སུ་དགོན་འཛིན་བླ་སྤྲུལ་རེ་དང་དགེ་འདུན་གྱི་སྡེ་དར་རྒྱས་ངང་བཞུགས་ཡོད།

དེ་ལྟར་གོང་དུ་ཞུས་པ་ལྟར་ད་ལྟ་མང་ཡུལ་ལྗོངས་འདིར་བཀའ་བརྒྱུད་ཀྱི་བསྟན་པ་དྲི་མ་མེད་པ་དེ་ཉིད་འཛིན་སྐྱོང་སྤེལ་བར་མཛད་པའི་བླ་སྤྲུལ་རྣམ་པ་དང་འདུས་སྡེ། འཚོ་བ་ཚུལ་བཞིན་འབུལ་བའི་སྦྱིན་བདག་བཅས་ཀྱིས་སྒྲུབ་བརྒྱུད་ཀྱི་བསྟན་པ་རིན་པོ་ཆེ་ལ་ཞབས་འདེགས་ཞུས་དང་ཞུ་བཞིན་པ་ཡིན་ནོ།།

དཔལ་སྐྱའི་ཆོས་བརྒྱུད་དང་དེ་ཉིད་ལ་དྭགས་སུ་དར་རྒྱལ།

༧ གསང་སྔགས་གསར་མའི་སྲོལ་འཛིན་འཁོན་དཀོན་མཆོག་རྒྱལ་པོ་དེ་ཉིད་ཕྱི་ལོ་ ༡༠༣༨ ལོར་ཡབ་ཤཱཀྱ་བློ་གྲོས་ཀྱི་སྲས་སུ་འཁྲུངས། དགུང་ལོ་ནར་སོན་ནས་འབྲོག་མི་ལོ་ཙཱ་བ། བ་རི་ལོ་ཙཱ་བ་དང་། རྨང་ལོ་ཙཱ་བ་སོགས་མཁས་གྲུབ་གཉིས་ལྡན་གྱི་བླ་མ་མང་དུ་བསྟེན་ནས་གསང་སྔགས་གསར་མའི་ཆོས་འཁོར་མང་དུ་གསན་ཞིང་ཉམས་བཞེས་མཛད།

ཕྱི་ལོ་ ༡༠༩༡ ལྕགས་ལུག་ལོར་ས་དཀར་པོ་སེངྒེའི་བཞིན་རས་འདྲ་བའི་ལོགས་སུ་སལུའི་སྨན་ལྗོངས་ཀྱི་རྡོ་རྗེ་གདན་ཆེན་པོ་དཔལ་སསྐྱའི་ཆོས་གྲྭ་ཆེན་པོ་དེ་ཉིད་ལྷར་བཅས་སྐྱེ་རྒྱུ་རྣམས་ཀྱི་བསོད་ནམས་ཀྱི་དཔལ་དུ་ཕྱུག་བཏབ་པར་མཛད། ས་ཞིའི་མིང་ཆོས་དང་གང་ཟག་ལ་ཐོགས་ནས་གང་གི་ཆོས་བརྒྱུད་ལ་སསྐྱ་དང་དེ་རྒྱལ་བཞིན་དུ་འཛིན་སྐྱོང་སྤེལ་བར་མཛད་པའི་གང་ཟག་རྣམས་ལ་སསྐྱ་པ་ཞེས་གྲགས། དེ་ཡང་རྗེ་བཙུན་ཆེན་པོ་གྲགས་ལ་རྒྱལ་མཚན་གྱིས༔

ས་དཀར་པོ་སེངྒེའི་གདོང་པ་འདྲ། །
དཔལ་ལྡན་སསྐྱ་སེངྒེའི་ལུས། །
འགྲོ་དྲུག་གི་བསམ་པ་འགེངས་པ་པོ། །
ཛོ་རྡོ་རྗེ་འཆང་གི་བཞུགས་གནས་ཡིན། །

ཞེས་བསྟོད་ཅིག་བསྔགས་པར་མཛད་དོ།། འཁོན་དཀོན་མཆོག་རྒྱལ་པོ་དེ་ཉིད་ཀྱི་སྲས་སུ་ཕྱི་ལོ་༡༠༩༣ ལོར་གངས་རི་ར་བའི་མགོན་པོ་འཕགས་པ་འཇིག་རྟེན་དབང་ཕྱུག་དེ་ཉིད་མིའི་ཟོལ་གྱིས་བྱོན། མཚན་དུ་དཔལ་བརྩེ་བ་ཆེན་པོ་ཀུན་དགའ་སྙིང་པོ་གསོལ། རྗེ་བཙུན་དམ་པ་དེ་ཉིད་

ཀྱིས་རིག་པའི་ལྷ་མཆོག་འཇམ་པའི་དབྱངས་བསྒྲུབས་པས་ཟླ་བ་དྲུག་ན་གྲུབ་སྟེ་ཞལ་གཟིགས། ཞེན་པ་བཞི་བྲལ་གྱི་གདམས་ངག་གནང་། དེ་ནས་ས་སྐྱའི་ཆུ་འགྲ་འབར། མལ་ལོ་ཙཱ་བ་དང་སུ་རྟངས་ལོ་ཆུང་སོགས་ཟླ་མ་དུ་མ་བསྟེན་ནས་མདོ་སྔགས་ཀྱི་ཆོས་ཚུལ་མཁའ་ཡས་པ་ལ་གསན་སྦྱངས་མཛད། ལྷག་པར་དུ་ཞང་དགོན་པ་པ་ནས་དཔལ་ལྡན་བེ་ཧྭ་པའི་བཞེད་གཞུང་གསུང་ངག་རིང་པོ་ཆེ་ལམ་འབྲས་བུ་དང་བཅས་པའི་མན་ངག་རྣམས་གསན་ནས་གངས་ཅན་གྱི་ལྗོངས་འདིར་ལམ་འབྲས་ཀྱི་སྲོལ་ལེགས་པར་གཏོད་པར་མཛད།

རྗེ་བཙུན་བསོད་ནམས་རྩེ་མོ་དང་གྲགས་པ་རྒྱལ་མཚན་རྣམ་གཉིས་གྱིས་ཀྱིས་དར་ཞིང་རྒྱས་པར་མཛད། ས་པཎ་ཀུན་དགའ་རྒྱལ་མཚན་དང་འགྲོ་མགོན་ཆོས་རྒྱལ་འཕགས་པ་རྣམ་གཉིས་ཀྱིས་གངས་རིའི་རབས་བསྐོར་བའི་སྐྱིད་ལྗོངས་འདི་ཉིད་དཔལ་ལྡན་ས་སྐྱའི་ཆོས་སྲིད་ཀྱི་གདུགས་དཀར་པོའི་གྲིབ་མ་སྐམ་པོའི་།འོག་ཏུ་དབང་དུ་བསྡུས་ཏེ་ཤིན་ཏུ་དར་ཞིང་རྒྱས་པར་མཛད། དཔལ་ས་སྐྱའི་རྗེ་བཙུན་གོང་མ་ལྔ་ཞེས་པའི་མཚན་སྙན་གྲགས་འཛིན་མའི་ཁྱོན་ལ་ཡོངས་སུ་ཁྱབ། འདི་དག་གིས་རྒྱལ་བའི་བསྟན་པ་ལ་ལྷག་པའི་བྱ་བ་དཔག་ཏུ་མེད་པ་མཛད།

རྗེ་བཙུན་གོང་མ་རྣམ་པ་ལྔ་པོ་དེ་དག་གི་བསྟན་པ་མ་ལུས་པ་ཕྱོགས་མཐར་དུ་གསལ་བར་བྱེད་པའི་བསྟན་སྐྱོང་གི་སྐྱེས་བུ་ཆེན་པོ་བགྲང་གིས་མི་ནུས་པ་བྱོན་ཞིང་ལྷག་པར་དུ་འཛམ་གླིང་བྱང་ཕྱོགས་ཀྱི་ནོར་འཛིན་དགའ་མའི་དཀྱིལ་འཁོར་ཀུན་ཏུ་ཉི་མ་དང་། ཟླ་བ་ལྟར་ཡོངས་སུ་གྲགས་ལ་རྒྱལ་བ་དགྱེས་པའི་འཕྲིན་ལས་འཆད་རྩོད་རྩོམ་གསུམ་ལ་བག་ཆ་བ་དང་བྲལ་

བའི་མཁས་པ་ཡོངས་ཀྱི་འཁོར་ལོ་སྒྱུར་བ་ཀུན་དགའ་རྣམ་པ་གཉིས་ཏེ་ངོར་ཆེན་ཀུན་དགའ་བཟང་པོ་དང་ཛོང་པ་ཀུན་དགའ་རྣམ་རྒྱལ་གཉིས་བྱོན། ངོར་ཆེན་གྱིས་ཕྱི་ལོ་ ༡༦༣༥ ལོར་ངོར་དགོན་པ་དཔལ་ཨེ་ཝཾ་ཆོས་ལྡན་བཏབ། ཛོང་པས་ཕྱི་ལོ་ ༡༦༧༦ ལོར་ངོར་གོང་དཀར་རྡོ་རྗེ་གདན་གྱི་ཆོས་གྲྭ་བཏབ་ནས་ཕྱིར་རྒྱལ་བའི་བསྟན་པ་རིན་པོ་ཆེ་དང་བྱེ་བྲག་ཏུ་དཔལ་སསྐྱའི་ཆོས་བརྒྱུད་དེ་ཉིད་ཡར་ངོའི་ཟླ་སྟར་རྒྱས་པར་མཛད།

ཕྱིས་སུ་དཔལ་ས་སྐྱའི་ཆོས་བརྒྱུད་འཛིན་པའི་མཁས་པ་ལྷ་ལམ་ཡངས་པའི་སྐར་ཚོགས་ལྟར་མང་དུ་བྱོན་པ་རྣམས་ཀྱི་ནང་ནས་མདོ་ལ་མཆོག་ཏུ་མཁས་པ་གཡག་ཕྲུག་སངས་རྒྱ་དཔལ་དང་རོང་སྟོན་ཤེས་བྱ་ཀུན་རིག ཡང་ན་རེད་མདའ་བ་གཞོན་ནུ་བློ་གྲོས་ཏེ་གཡག་གཞོན་རྣམ་གཉིས་དང་། སྔགས་ལ་མཁས་པ་ངོར་ཆེན་ཀུན་དགའ་བཟང་པོ་དང་ཛོང་པ་ཀུན་དགའ་རྣམ་རྒྱལ་ཏེ་ཀུན་དགའ་རྣམ་གཉིས། མདོ་སྔགས་གཉིས་ཀ་ལ་མཁས་པ་ཀུན་མཁྱེན་གོ་བོ་རབ་འབྱམས་པ་བསོད་ནམས་སེངྒེ་དང་། གསེར་མདོག་པཎ་ཆེན་ཤཱཀྱ་མཆོག་ལྡན་ཏེ་གོ་ཤཱཀ་རྣམ་གཉིས་ཏེ་དྲུག་ལ་ས་སྐྱ་པའི་བསྟན་འཛིན་གངས་ཅན་མཛེས་པར་བྱེད་པའི་རྒྱན་དྲུག་ཅེས་གྲགས།།

མཁས་པའི་དབང་པོ་གཡག་གཞོན་རྣམ་གཉིས་ཀྱི་སྐུ་རིང་ལ་གདན་ས་ཆེན་པོ་དང་ བྱང་ངམ་རིང་གི་ཆོས་སྡེ་སོགས་སུ་གྲྭ་ཚོགས་ཆེན་བཅོ་བརྒྱད།[༡] འཆད་པ་དང་རྩོད་པའི་སྒྲོལ་རྒྱ་ཆེན་པོ་གཏོད་པར་མཛད་ནས་མཁས་པའི་དབང་པོ་མང་པོ་བྱུང་། དེ་དག་གིས་གཞུང་འགྲེལ་རྨད་དུ་བྱུང་བ་དུ་མ་མཛད། འཆད་རྩོད་རྩོམ་གསུམ་ཐོས་བསམ་སྒོམ་དང་མཁས་

བཙུན་བཟང་གསུམ་ལྡན་པའི་སྐྱེས་ཆེན་མང་དུ་བྱུང་བའི་ཐུགས་རྗེ་དང་བཀའ་དྲིན་ལ་གཞུང་ཆེན་བཅོ་བརྒྱད་ཀྱི་འཆད་ཉན་ལེགས་པར་དར་ནས་ད་སྔའི་བར་དུའང་དཔལ་ས་སྐྱའི་མདོ་སྔགས་ཀྱི་བཤད་བཀའ་གཞན་ལ་ངོམས་སུ་ཆོག་པ་ཡོད་དོ།།

ལ་དྭགས་སུ་ས་སྐྱའི་ཆོས་བརྒྱུད་དར་ཚུལ།

དེ་ཡང་ཕྱི་ལོ་ ༡༣༧༨ ལོར་འགྲོ་མགོན་ཆོས་རྒྱལ་འཕགས་པས་རྒྱ་ནག་སེ་ཆེན་རྒྱལ་པོས་དབུ་མཛད་པའི་དབང་པ་ཉི་ཤུ་རྩ་ལྔ་ལ་ལན་གསུམ་གྱི་བར་དུ་ས་སྐྱ་པའི་ཁྱད་ཆོས་དཔལ་ཀྱི་རྡོ་རྗེའི་དབང་ཡོངས་སུ་རྫོགས་པར་བསྐུར་པས། ཧོར་གྱི་རྒྱལ་ཁམས་སུ་རྡོ་རྗེ་ཐེག་པའི་དབུ་བརྙེས་པ་ཡིན་ཞིང་། དེའི་དབང་ཡོན་དང་པོ་ལ་བོད་ཁྲི་སྐོར་བཅུ་གསུམ་ཕུལ། དབང་ཡོན་བར་མའི་སྐབས་སྟོན་པ་ཐུབ་པའི་དང་བོ་ལ་ལྷའི་དབང་པོ་བརྒྱ་བྱིན་གྱིས་ཆོས་ཀྱི་འཁོར་ལོ་བསྐོར་བར་ཕུལ་པའི་ཆོས་དུང་དཀར་པོ་རྒྱང་དུ་གྲགས་པ་དེ་ཉིད་ཕུལ། དབང་ཐ་མའི་དབང་ཡོན་དུ་རྒྱའི་མི་ཡུར་ཆེན་པོ་ཕུལ། ཐེར་སྒྲང་དར་མའི་རྗེས་སུ་ཁེང་

༡ ཤཀྱའི་གདུང་རབས་ངོ་མཚར་བང་མཛོད། མི་རིགས་དཔེ་སྐྲུན་ཁང་གིས་པར་མ་ཤོག་གྲངས་ ༡༥༩

ལོག་སྐབས་བོད་སིལ་བུར་གྱུར་ཡོད་པ་དེ་ཉིད་སླར་ཡང་གོང་བུ་གཅིག་ཏུ་གྱུར། དེ་དུས་བོད་ཁམས་ཡོངས་ལ་དཔལ་ས་སྐྱ་པའི་བསྟན་པ་ཆེས་ཆེར་དར་ཁྱབ་བྱུང་། དེ་ལ་དཔག་ན་ཕྱི་ལོ་ ༡༣༠༠ ཙམ་ནང་མང་ཡུལ་ལྗོངས་འདིར་དཔལ་ས་སྐྱ་པའི་ཆོས་བརྒྱུད་དེ་ཉིད་དར་འགོ་ཚུགས། འོན་ཀྱང་ཁྱབ་བརྡལ་ཆེན་པོ་ཞིག་མ་བྱུང་། ཕྱིས་ཕྱི་ལོ་ ༡༩༣༠ ནང་

མཁས་གྲུབ་གཉིས་ལྡན་གྱི་སྐྱེས་བུ་ཆེན་པོ་དྲུང་པ་རྡོ་རྗེ་དཔལ་བཟང་ས་སྐྱ་ནས་བླ་ཆབ་ཏུ་མང་སྤྲོ་ཕེབས། དེ་དུས་ཆོས་རྒྱལ་གྲགས་པ་འབུམ་ལྡེས་ལྗོངས་འདིར་མངའ་དབང་སྒྱུར་བཞིན་ཡོད་པས་ཁོང་གིས་སྦྱིན་བདག་མཛད་ནས་མང་སྤྲོར་དགོན་པ་ཤ་གླིང་ཆོས་འཁོར་ཞེས་པ་གསར་དུ་བཏབ། དགེ་འདུན་གྱི་སྡེ་བཙུགས། དེ་བཞིན་སྐྱིད་མང་དང་། སྤྱི་ཏི་རུའང་དགོན་པ་འདུས་སྡེ་དང་བཅས་པ་བཏབ། དེ་ནས་བཟུང་མང་ཡུལ་ལྗོངས་འདིར་དཔལ་ས་སྐྱའི་ཆོས་བརྒྱུད་འཛིན་པའི་འདུས་སྡེ་སྦྱིན་བདག་དང་བཅས་པ་དར་རྒྱས་བྱུང་'' འོན་ཀྱང་རྒྱལ་པོ་འཇམ་དབྱངས་རྣམ་རྒྱལ་གྱི་སྐུ་དུས་སུ་སྦལ་ཏིའི་དམག་གིས་དགོན་པ་བཅོམ། དགོན་བདག་ལྷ་མ་དང་ཡུལ་མི་མང་པོ་ཞིག་ལ་རྒྱ་ནོར་སོགས་བཀལ་ཏེ་སྦལ་ཏིའི་ཡུལ་དུ་ཁྲིད། དེ་ནས་མང་སྤྲོ་དགོན་པར་ཉམས་ཆགས་ཆེན་པོ་བྱུང་། ཕྱིས་རིམ་བཞིན་གསོས་ནས་ད་ལྟ་ལྗོངས་འདི་ས་བསྟན་ཉམས་པ་སོར་ཆུད་དང་མི་ཉམས་གོང་འཕེལ་གྱི་བགྱི་བ་བཟང་པོ་ལ་བརྩོན་བཞིན་དུ་མཆིས་སོ།།

དགེ་ལུགས་ཀྱི་ཆོས་བརྒྱུད་དང་དེ་ཉིད་ལ་དྭགས་སུ་དར་ཚུལ།

༡ དེ་ཡང་ཁམས་གསུམ་ཆོས་ཀྱི་རྒྱལ་པོ་འཇམ་མགོན་བླ་མ་བློ་བཟང་གྲགས་པ་དེ་ཉིད་མདོ་ཁམས་ཙོང་ཁའི་ཡུལ་དུ་ཡབ་ཀླུ་འབུམ་དགེ་དང་ཨུམ་ཤིང་མོ་ཨ་ཆོས་གཉིས་ཀྱི་སྲས་སུ་ཕྱི་ལོ་ ༡༣༥༧ ལོར་སྐུ་བལྟམས། སྐུ་ན་ཆེར་ཕེབས་ནས་གངས་ཅན་ལྗོངས་སུ་དར་ཡོད་པའི་མདོ་སྔགས་རིག་གནས་ཀྱི་གཙུག་ལག་རྒྱ་མཚོ་ལྟ་བུ་ལ་གསན་སྦྱངས་མཐར་ཕྱིན་པར་མཛད། ཐོས་དོན་དཔྱོད་པ་དང་སྒོམ་པའི་སྒོ་ནས་ཐུགས་ཉམས་སུ་བཞེས། སྐུ་ཚེའི་སྨད་དུ་འགྲོ་དོན་དང་འཕྲིན་ལས་བླ་ན་མེད་པར་རྒྱས། ཕྱི

ལོ་༡༩༡༣ ལོར་ལྷ་ལྡན་ཚོ་འཕྲུལ་གྱི་དུས་ཆེན་སྨོན་ལམ་ཆེན་མོ་བཙུགས། ཕྱི་ལོ་ ༡༩༡༣ ལོར་འབྲོག་རི་བོ་དགའ་ལྡན་རྣམ་པར་རྒྱལ་བའི་གླིང་ཕྱག་བཏབ། བསླབ་གསུམ་ངུར་སྨྲིག་འཆང་བའི་དགེ་འདུན་གྱི་སྡེ་བཙུགས། གནས་མིང་ཆོས་དང་གང་ཟག་ལ་ཐོགས་ནས་རྗེའི་བསྟན་པ་དང་དེ་འཛིན་གྱི་འདུས་སྡེ་ལ་དགའ་ལྡན་པའམ་དགེ་ལུགས་པ་ཞེས་གྲགས།

དེ་ནས་བཟུང་རྗེའི་སློབ་མ་ཡང་སློབ་རྗེས་འབྲངས་བརྒྱུད་པ་དང་བཅས་པ་ལ་དགེ་ལུགས་ཞེས་སྙན་པའི་གྲགས་པ་འཛིན་མའི་ཁྲོན་ད་དབྱར་གྱི་ཛ་སངས་ལྟར་ཁྱབ། དེ་ཉིད་ཀྱི་གསུང་ལས་སྐྱེས་པའི་སློབ་མ་གྲངས་ལས་འདས་པ་བྱུང་བ་རྣམས་ཀྱི་ནང་ནས་མཆོག་ཏུ་གྱུར་པ་ནི། རྒྱལ་ཚབ་དར་མ་རིན་ཆེན། མཁས་གྲུབ་དགེ་ལེགས་དཔལ་བཟང་། ཐམས་ཅད་མཁྱེན་པ་དགེ་འདུན་གྲུབ། འདུལ་འཛིན་གྲགས་པ་རྒྱལ་མཚན། འདུལ་འཛིན་བློ་གྲོས་སྦས་པ། སྟོད་སྨད་ཀྱི་བྱང་སེམས་ཤེས་རབ་བཟང་པོ་གཉིས་བཅས་ཡིན་ནོ།།

རྗེ་དགེ་འདུན་གྲུབ་ཀྱིས་ཕྱི་ལོ་ ༡༤༤༧ ལོར་བཀྲིས་ལྷུན་པོའི་ཆོས་སྡེ་ཆེན་པོ་ཕྱག་བཏབ། དེ་བཞིན་འཇམ་དབྱངས་ཆོས་རྗེས་ཕྱི་ལོ་ ༡༤༡༩ ལོར་དཔལ་ལྡན་འབྲས་སྤུངས་ཀྱི་ཆོས་སྡེ་དང་། བྱམས་ཆེན་ཆོས་རྗེས་ཕྱི་ལོ་ ༡༤༣༩ ལོར་སེ་ར་ཐེག་ཆེན་ཆོས་གླིང་བཏབ་པར་མཛད་ནས་སྡོམ་པ་གསུམ་ལྡན་གྱི་ཐུགས་རྒྱུད་ལེགས་པར་ཕྱུག་པའི་འདུས་སྡེའི་རྒྱ་མཚོ་ཆེས་ཆེར་འཕེལ། དེ་དག་གི་མཐུ་ལ་བརྟེན་ནས་ད་ལྟའི་བར་རྒྱལ་བའི་བཀའ་དང་དེའི་དགོངས་འགྲེལ་དང་བཅས་པ་ལ་ཐོས་བསམ་སྒོམ་གསུམ་འཆད་རྩོད་རྩོམ་གསུམ་གྱི་རྒྱུན་བཟང་འགྲོ་བའི་དཔལ་དུ་ད་ར་ཞིང་རྒྱས་པ་དང་།

ལྷག་པར་དུ་རྗེའི་གསུང་རབས་ཀྱི་སྙིང་ཁུ་བྱང་ཆུབ་ལམ་གྱི་རིམ་པ་དང་། སྔགས་རིམ་ཆེན་མོ་སོགས་ཀྱི་འཆད་ཉན་སྒོམ་སྒྲུབ་རྣམ་པར་དག་པའི་སྒོ་ནས་མདོ་སྔགས་ཟུང་འབྲེལ་གྱི་བསྟན་པ་རིན་པོ་ཆེ་ནོར་འཛིན་ཡངས་པའི་ཁྱོན་དུ་དར་རྒྱས་བྱུང་དང་འབྱུང་བཞིན་ཡིན་ནོ།།

ལ་དྭགས་སུ་དགེ་ལུགས་ཀྱི་ཆོས་བརྒྱུད་དར་ཚུལ།

གོང་དུ་བཤད་པ་ལྟར་ཕྱི་ལོ་ ༡༤༡༣ ལོར་རྗེ་བླ་མས་དགའ་ལྡན་རྣམ་པར་རྒྱལ་བའི་གླིང་བཏབ། དེ་དུས་མང་ཡུལ་ལྗོངས་འདིར་ཆོས་ཀྱི་རྒྱལ་པོ་གྲགས་པ་འབུམ་ལྡེ་མངའ་དབང་སྐྱོར་བཞིན་ཡོད་པ་ཡིན། རྒྱལ་པོ་འདིས་ཕྱི་ལོ་ ༡༤༠༠ ནས ༡༤༤༠ བར་དབང་བསྒྱུར་བར་མཛད། དེ་དུས་རྗེ་བླ་མ་དེ་ཉིད་ཀྱིས་རང་གི་ཤངས་ཁྲག་ལ་གྲུབ་པའི་ཚེ་དཔག་མེད་ཀྱི་སྐུ་བརྙན་དེ་བྱ་བྲལ་བ་གཉིས་ལ་བསྐུར་ནས་འདི་ག་མང་ཡུལ་ལྗོངས་ཀྱི་ས་སྐྱོང་གྲགས་པའི་མཚན་ཅན་ནམ་ཡང་ན་ ལྡེའི་ཕྱག་ཏུ་ཕུལ། ངའི་བསྟན་པ་རྒྱས་པའི་རྟེན་འབྲེལ་ཡོད་གསུངས་ནས་བསྐུར་པ་དེ་ཉིད་རྒྱལ་པོའི་ཕྱག་ཏུ་འབྱོར་པ་དང་། རྒྱལ་པོ་ཤིན་ཏུ་དགྱེས། འཇམ་མགོན་བླ་མ་ཙོང་ཁ་པ་ཆེན་པོའི་རིང་ལུགས་དྲི་མ་མེད་པའི་བསྟན་པ་རིན་པོ་ཆེ་དེ་ཉིད་ཅིས་ཀྱང་དར་བ་ཞིག་བྱེད་དགོངས་ཏེ་རྒྱལ་པོ་སྦྱིན་བདག་དང་བླ་མ་ལྷ་དབང་བློ་གྲོས་ཀྱི་ཐུགས་ཁུར་བཞེས་ནས་ཕྱི་ལོ་ ༡༤༡༥ ལོར་དཔེ་ཐུབ་ཀྱི་རི་མགོར་དགོན་པ་དགའ་ལྡན་དར་རྒྱས་གླིང་བཏབ། དེ་བཞིན་སྟོད་བྱང་སེམས་ཤེས་རབ་བཟང་པོས་ཕྱི་ལོ་ ༡༤༣༠ ཙམ་ནང་སྟག་མོ་རྩེ་ལྷ་ཁང་སེར་པོར་གྲགས་པ་དེ་ཉིད་ཕྱག་བཏབ་ནས་གཞི་གསུམ་གྱི་སྒྲོལ་བཙུགས་པར་མཛད། དེ་བཞིན་བྱང་སེམས་ཀྱིས་ལྷུམ་རའི་བདེ་སྐྱིད་དགོན་དང་ཟངས་དཀར་གྱི་

དཀར་ཤ་བྱམས་པ་གླིང་། དགོན་མོ་ཆེ་དང་ཕུག་དལ་དགོན་སོགས་སུ་གཞི་གསུམ་གྱི་སྲོལ་བཙུགས་པར་མཛད། ལྷུམ་རའི་དབེན་ས་རུ་ལྷ་ཁང་གཅིག་དང་རྟེན་གཙོང་རྒྱལ་བ་ཙོང་ཁ་པའི་སྐུ་བརྙན་བྱིན་རླབས་ཀྱི་གཟི་འོད་འབར་བཞིན་ཡོད་པ་དེ་ཉིད་བཞེངས། གང་ལྟར་ཕྱི་ལོ་ ༡༩༧༥ ནས་བཟུང་མང་ཡུལ་ལྗོངས་འདིར་རི་བོ་དགའ་ལྡན་པའི་ཆོས་བརྒྱུད་འགྲོ་བའི་བདེ་སྐྱིད་ཀྱི་དཔལ་དུ་དར་རྒྱས་བྱུང་དང་འབྱུང་བཞིན་ཡིན་ནོ།།

....

༄༅། །ལ་དྭགས་རྒྱལ་རིམ་ཡོན་བདག་རྣམ་ལྔ།[1]

བ་མགོ་བྱམས་པ་རྣམ་གསུམ།

རྩོམ་པ་པོ། བློ་བཟང་འཇམ་དཔལ།

la dwags rgyal rim yon bdag rnam lnga
ba mgo byams pa rnam gsum

rtsom pa po
blo bzang 'jam dpal

THE FIVE ROYAL PATRONS AND THREE MAITREYA IMAGES IN BASGO

by

Lozang Jamspal
606 W. 116th Street,
New York, N.N.10027, U.S.A.

Summary

Three Maitreya images and their temples were constructed in the sacred Basgo valley of Ladakh by the Kings Takpa Bumde, Tshewang Namgyal, Jamyang Namgyal & his Queen Khatun - the Balti Princess, and King Sengge Namgyal in the period 1450-1650 C.E. Although in neglected condition, the extraordinarily beautiful images and mural paintings within the temples are still visible and are very important from cultural and artistic viewpoints. The temples and their contents are in immediate need of preservation to protect them from collapse due to erosion. The author earnestly asks for patrons to help in this restoration project.

The author clarifies and corrects the statements of previous Western and Ladakhi scholars on the chronology of the construction and patronage of these temples, and the reigns and lifetimes of the five main patrons. Two appendices are based on incidents in the life of one patron and a Basgo hero. See also p.139-156

བློ་བཟང་འཇམ་དཔལ་ Lozang Jamspal

༄༅། །ལ་དྭགས་རྒྱལ་རིམ་ཡོན་བདག་རྣམ་ལ།[1]

བ་མགོ་ཁྲམས་པ་རྣམ་གསུམ།

འབྲི་པོ། བློ་བཟང་འཇམ་དཔལ་

བྲིས་ཀྱི་དོན་བསྡུས།

བ་མགོ་ཡུལ་ལུང་དང་། རྒྱལ་རིམ་ཡོན་གྱི་བདག་པོ་གྲགས་པ་འབུམ་ལྡེ་དང་། ཚེ་དབང་རྣམ་རྒྱལ་དང་པོ། འཇམ་དབྱངས་རྣམ་རྒྱལ། རྒྱལ་མོ་ཁ་ཏུན། རྒྱལ་པོ་སེང་གེ་རྣམ་རྒྱལ་བཅས་ཀྱི་ངོ་སྤྲོད་མདོར་བསྡུས་དང་། དེ་དག་གིས་རྒྱལ་སྲིད་དབང་བའི་དུས་སྐབས་གཏན་འབེབས། དེ་རྣམས་ཀྱིས་བཞེངས་པའི་རྒྱལ་བ་བྱམས་པ་ལྷ་ཁང་ཆེན་མོ་དང་། བྱམས་ཆུང་ལྷ་ཁང་དང་། གསེར་སྒྲུངས་ལྷ་ཁང་རྣམ་གསུམ་སྟེ། གཙུག་ལག་ཁང་འདི་རྣམས་ཀྱི་ལེགས་པར་གྲུབ་པའི་སྐུ་འདྲ་ཀུན་དང་། ངོ་མཚར་ཆེན་པོ་དང་ལྡན་པའི་ལྡེབས་རིས་རྣམས་ནི། ལ་དྭགས་ཡོངས་ཀྱི་སྤྱི་རྫས་ཡིན་པ། དད་པ་དང་ལྡན་པ་རྣམས་ལ་ཕྱག་དང་མཆོད་པ་འབུལ་བའི་ཕྱིར། རྟེན་བཟང་པོ་དང་། མར་ཡུལ་ལོ་རྒྱུས། སྤྲོལ་ཆགས་བཟང་པོ། བཟོ་རིག་སྐོར་ལ་འཚོལ་སྒྲུབ་བྱེད་པ་པོ། སློབ་གཉེར་པ་དང་། མཁས་པ་ཀུན་ལ་སློབ་སྦྱོང་གི་ཕྱིར་དུ་ཡང་། གཞི་རྟེན་བཟང་པོ་ཡིན་ཀྱང་། ལོ་མངས་རིང་ནས། འདི་ཀུན་གྱི་ཉམས་གསོའི་ཕྱིར་མཐུན་རྐྱེན་མེད་པས། ད་ལྟ་འདི་ཀུན་རྡིབ་པ་ལ་མངོན་དུ་ཕྱོགས་པར། སངས་རྒྱས་པའི་རྗེས་འཇུག་རྣམས་དང་། མི་རིགས་ཀྱི་ཆགས་སྲོལ་བཟང་པོ་ལ་དགའ་བ་རྣམས་ཀྱིས་གཏོང་སེམས་ཆེན་པོས། བྱིན་རླབས་ཆེ་བ་དང་། ངོ་མཚར་ཆེ་བའི་རྟེན་འདི་རྣམས་ལ་ཞིག་གསོའི་ཕྱིར། གྲོགས་མཛད་པར་ཞུ་བ་བཅས་སོ། །

---

1 ཆོས་རྗེ་སྟག་ཚང་རས་པའི་རྣམ་ཐར་དང་། པཎ་ཆེན་བློ་བཟང་ཡེ་ཤེས་ཀྱིས་མཛད་པའི། **ལམ་རིམ་བླ་བརྒྱུད་རྣམ་ཐར་པདྨ་དཀར་པོའི་ཕྲེང་བ།** སོགས་སྔོན་གྱི་ཡི་གེ་རྙིང་པ་རྣམས་སུ། **ལ་དྭགས་**ཀྱི་ཚབ་ཏུ། **ལ་སྟགས་**ཞེས་འབྱུང་ངོ་། །

བ་མགོ་ཡུལ་གྱི་ངོ་སྤྲོད་

ལ་དྭགས་ཀྱི་རྒྱལ་ས་རྙིང་པ། བ་མགོའམ་བ་སྒོའི་ཡུལ་ལྗུང་། ལོ་རྒྱུས་རྒྱལ་རབས་ལ་གལ་ཆེན་པོ་ཡིན། ཡུལ་ལྗོངས་འདི་ཡི་རིང་ཚད་ལ་དཔག་ཚད་གསུམ་ཙམ་དང་། ཞིང་དུ་སྐབས་འགར་ཞིང་ཆེ་བ་དང་། སྐབས་འགར་ཞིང་ཆུང་། ཡུལ་གྱི་མགོ་དང་མཇུག་ཞིང་ཆེ་བ་ཡོད། ཡུལ་གྱི་སྟོད་ན་གངས་རི་དཀར་པོའི་ཆུ་དང་། ཆུ་མིག་གི་ཆུ་འདྲེས་མ་བསིལ་ཞིང་དྭང་བ་ལ་སོགས་པ་ཡན་ལག་བརྒྱད་ལྡན་གྱི་[2]ཆུ་རྒྱུན་ལྷུང་ལྷུང་དུ་འབབ། ལྗུང་པའི་ལོགས་ཀུན་སྔང་དང་། གད་པ་དང་། བྲག་རི་མཐོན་པོས་བསྐོར། ཤར་གྱི་སྐྱབ་ཁང་དུ་མ་ཡོད་པའི་རི་བོ་ཆེན་པོ་ངང་པ་སོགས་རི་བོ་མཐོན་པོ་མང་པོ་བརྗིད་ཆགས་ཤིང་། གཅིག་གིས་གཅིག་ལ་འགྲན་པ་བཞིན་དུ་གནམ་སྟོན་པོར་སྙེགས་པའི་རི་རྩེ་ཀུན་སྤྲིན་དཀར་པོས་དཀྲིགས་པ་རྒྱང་རིང་པོ་ནས་མཛེས་པར་སྣང་། ལྷག་པར་བྱང་ཕྱོགས་ཀྱི་རི་བོ་དམར་སེར་ཀུན་རྗེ་བཙུན་འཇམ་དཔལ་དབྱངས་དང་། དབུས་ཀྱི་རི་བོ་དཀར་སྐྱ་ཀུན་ཐུགས་རྗེ་ཆེན་པོ་སྤྱན་རས་གཟིགས་དབང་ཕྱུག་དང་། ལྷོ་ཕྱོགས་ཀྱི་རི་བོ་སྔོ་ནག་ཀུན་དཔལ་ཕྱག་ན་རྡོ་རྗེ་སྟེ། འཕགས་པ་རིགས་གསུམ་མགོན་པོའི་ངོ་བོར་བསྒོམ་ཆོག་པ་ཡོད། ལྗུང་པའི་སྨད་ན་ཆུ་བོ་སེང་གེ་ཁ་འབབ་ཆུ་ཞེས་པའི་གཙང་པོ་ཆེན་པོ། ཤར་ནས་ནུབ་ངོས་ལ། ལྷ་ཡི་རི་བོ་དེ་དག་དང་ཡུལ་ལྗུང་གི་སྐུ་རྟེན་རྣམས་ལ་མཆོད་པ་འབུལ་བའི་ཚུལ་དུ་འབབ། དབྱར་གྱི་ཆུ་འཕེལ་བའི་དུས་སུ་ཆུ་བོ་དེ་ར་ངར་སྒྲ་ཅན་གྱི་ཆ་རླབས་དཔྱིབས་སྣ་ཚོགས་པ་གྱེན་དུ་འཕྱུར། སྟོན་ཀ་དགུན་ཀ་དཔྱིད་ཀའི་དུས་སུ་ཆུ་བོ་དེ་བཻཌཱུརྱ་སྔོན་པོ་ཞུས་པ་ལྟ་བུ་སྔོ་འཁྱུག་འཁྱུག་ཏུ་འབབ། དབྱར་དུས་ཀླུངས་ན་གྲོ་དང་། ནས་དང་། སྲན་མ་ལ་སོགས་པའི་འབྲུ་སྣ་ཚོགས་ཀྱི་ལྗང་པའི་རླབས་ཆེན་སྔོ་ལྡེམ་ལྡེམ་དུ་བྱེད། ཙུ་ལི་དང་ཀུ་ཤུའི་སྡོང་པོ་མང་པོར་འབྲས་བུ་གཡུར་གཡུར་དུ་ཟ། ལྕང་མ་དང་དབྱར་པ་མཛེས་ཤིང་ཡིད་དུ་འོང་བས་ཡོངས་ཡོངས་སུ་གཏམས། རྒྱ་ལམ་གྱི་ལོགས་རྣམས་སུ་བྱིན་རླབས་ཅན་གྱི་མཆོད་རྟེན་བརྒྱ་ཕྲག་ལོངས་པ་ཚར་ཚར་དུ་དངར་ཞིང་། དད་པ་དང་ལྡན་པའི་འགྲུལ་པ་ཀུན་

---

2 བསིལ་དང་ཞིམ་དང་ཡང་དང་འཇམ། །དྭང་བ་དང་ནི་དྲི་ང་མེད།
འཐུང་ན་ལྟོ་དང་མགྲིན་པ་ལ། །མི་གནོད་ཡན་ལག་བརྒྱད་ལྡན་ཆུ། །

ཞེས་**ཆོས་མངོན་པ་མཛོད**་ཀྱི་འགྲེལ་པ་གྲགས་པའི་བཤེས་གཉེན་གྱིས་མཛད་པ་ལ་གསལ་བ་བཞིན་ནོ། |

ལ་བསོད་ནམས་གསོག་པའི་ཞིང་མཆོག་དམ་པར་བརྟན་བརྟན་པར་བཞུགས་ཤིང་མཛེས་མཛེས་པར་སྣང་བ་འདི་ན་གྲོང་པ་ཁྲིམ་ཚང་བརྒྱ་དང་ལྔ་བཅུ་ལྷག་ཙམ་དང་། མི་གྲངས་ཕལ་ཆེར་བརྒྱད་བརྒྱ་ལྷག་ཙམ་ཡོད་པའི་དཔག་ཚོད་ཡིན་ནོ། །

ལྷག་པར་དུ། ཡུལ་ལུང་གི་དཀྱིལ་ཙམ་གྱི་ཤར་ངོས་ཀྱི་གད་པའི་སྟེང་ན། ཕུར་གྱི་རྒྱལ་པོའི་མཁར་ཞིག་རལ་གྱི་གྲུང་བལྟ་བ་ལ་ཡ་མཚན་པ་དང་། རྗེ་བཙུན་བྱམས་པ་མགོན་པོའི་སྐུ་བརྙན་གསུམ་གྱི་གཙུག་ལག་ཁང་རྙིང་སོང་གསུམ་མཆིས། དེ་དག་ཀུན་ན་ཕུར་གྱི་བཟོ་བོ་མཁས་པ་རྣམས་ཀྱིས་བཞེངས་པའི་སྐུ་འདྲ་བྱིན་རླབས་ཅན་དང་། རྒྱལ་བའི་བཀའ་འགྱུར་རིན་པོ་ཆེ་དང་། བསྟན་འགྱུར་[3]ཀྱི་པོ་ཏི་རིན་ཐང་བྲལ་བ་མང་པོ་དང་། ལྟ་བས་མི་ངོམས་པ་ཡིད་དུ་འོང་བའི་ཕུར་གྱི་ལྡེབས་རིས་མང་པོ་བཞུགས་པ་དེ་རྣམས་ཀྱི་བཞེངས་པ་པོའི་ཡོན་གྱི་བདག་པོ་ནི། རྒྱལ་པོ་གྲགས་པ་འབུམ་ལྡེ་དང་། ཆེ་དབང་རྣམ་རྒྱལ་དང་པོ། དེའི་སྐུ་མཆེད་འཇམ་དབྱངས་རྣམ་རྒྱལ། དེའི་བཙུན་མོ་རྒྱལ་མོ་ཁ་ཏུན། དེའི་སྲས་སེང་གེ་རྣམ་རྒྱལ་རྣམས་ཡིན་པར་རྒྱལ་རབས་དང་རྣམ་ཐར་དག་ན་གསལ་ལོ། །

གྲགས་པ་འབུམ་ལྡེ།

རྒྱལ་པོ་གྲགས་པ་འབུམ་ལྡེའི་བྱུང་དུས་ནི། ཕྲན་ཙ་ཀེ་ཡིས། ༡༥༠༠ ནས་ ༡༥༥༠ བར་དུ་ངོས་འཛིན། བཀྲ་ཤིས་རབ་རྒྱས་ཀྱི་བཞེད་པ་ཡང་འདི་དང་མཐུན།[4] རྒྱལ་རབས་དང་ལོ་རྒྱུས་འབྲི་བ་པོ་གཞན་དག་གིས་རྒྱལ་པོ་འདི་ནམ་བྱུང་བའི་ལོ་དུས་སྐོར་ལ་བྲིས་པ་མ་མཐོང་། །གང་ལྟར་ཡང་རྒྱལ་པོ་འདིའི་དུས་ལ། ལ་དྭགས་ཀྱི་རྒྱལ་ས་ལྟེ་བ་ནི། རབ་བརྟན་ལྷ་རྩེ་སྟེ། བ་མགོའི་མཁར་ཡིན།[5] རྒྱལ་པོ་འདི་ལ་བུ་བྲལ་བ་གཉིས་དང་མཉམ་དུ་རྗེ་ཙོང་ཁ་པའི་ཐུགས་བརྟགས་དང་། ཕྱག་རྟགས་འཁོར་པ་ཡིན་ཞེས་བཤད་ཀྱང་། དེ་ཉིད་བདེན་པ་ཡིན་པར་མི་

---

3 བཀའ་འགྱུར་བྲིས་མ་ཆ་ཚང་བ་ད་ལྟར་ཡང་བཞུགས་ཤིང་། བ་མགོ་པ་ཡུལ་པས་ལོ་རེ་རེ་བཞིན་དུ། ཡུལ་དུ་གདན་འདྲེན་ཞུས་ཏེ། གྲྭ་པ་དགེ་འདུན་པ་དང་མི་སྐྱ་ཀློག་ཤེས་པ་རྣམས་ལ་བསྙེན་བཀུར་གྱིས་ཀློག་ཏུ་འཇུག།

4 རབ་རྒྱས། ཤོག ༡༣༣།

5 དེ་ཉིད་ཀྱི་ ཤོག ༡༣༧།

སྣང་སྡེ།[6] རྗེ་ཙོང་པ་ཆེན་པོ། རབ་བྱུང་བདུན་པའི་ས་ཕག་ལོར། སྤྱི་ལོ་ ༡༤༡༩། སྐུ་ཞིང་ལ་གཤེགས། དེ་ནས་ཕལ་ཆེར་ལོ་བཞི་བཅུ་ལྷག་ཙམ་གྱི་རྗེས་སུ་ཐམས་ཅད་མཁྱེན་པ་རྗེ་དགེ་འདུན་གྲུབ་ཀྱིས་། གཙང་བཀྲ་ཤིས་ལྷུན་པོར་གསེར་ཟངས་ཀྱི་བྱམས་པའི་སྐུ་འདྲ་བཞེང་ཕྱིར། འབུལ་སྡུད་བྱེད་པར་དགེ་བཤེས་བློ་བཟང་ཞེས་པ་བྱང་ཆུབ་སེམས་དཔའི་བརྟུལ་ཞུགས་ལ་གནས་པ་ཞིག་ཡོད་པ་དེ་གྲོགས་མཆེད་གཉིས་མངའ་རིས་[7]སྟོད་ལ་འབུལ་སྡུད་ལ་བཏངས། དེའི་དུས་ཁོང་རྣམས་ལ་མངའ་རིས་རྒྱལ་པོ་ཇོ་བོ་གྲགས་འབུམ་ལྡེ་ཞེས་བྱ་བས་སྣང་མང་པོ་རི་བའི་གཡུ་མོ་ཆེས་ཐོག་དྲངས་འབུལ་བ་མང་པོ་དང་། གཞན་ཡང་དེ་ཕྱོགས་ཀྱི་བུ་སློབ་སྦྱིན་བདག་རྣམས་ཀྱི་དད་འབུལ་བསམ་གྱིས་མི་ཁྱབ་པ་དང་བཅས་ཏེ། རབ་བྱུང་བརྒྱད་པའི་ལྕགས་མོ་སྦྲུལ་ལོར། སྤྱི་ལོ་ ༡༤༨༧། སྔོན་དུས་ཉེས་སྐྱོན་མེད་པར་འདིར་སླེབས་[8]ཞེས་ **རྗེ་དགེ་འདུན་གྲུབ་ཀྱི་རྣམ་ཐར་**ན་གསུངས་སོ། [9] ཡེ་ཤེས་རྩེ་མོས་གྲགས་འབུམ་ལྡེ་ལ་མངའ་རིས་རྒྱལ་པོ་ཇོ་བོ་གྲགས་འབུམ་ལྡེ་ཞེས་བྲིས་པ་ནི། མར་ཡུལ་ལ་དྭགས་སྔོན་དུས་སུ་མངའ་རིས་བསྐོར་གསུམ་གྱི་ནང་ནས་གཅིག་ཡིན་པ་ལྟར་བདེན་པའི་གསུང་ངོ་། །

བྱ་བྲལ་བ་འདི་གཉིས་ཀྱིས་དང་པོ། ལྷུམ་ཏྭ་ར། གྲགས་འབུམ་སྡེ་རྒྱལ་པོ་ཆུང་བ་མཐའ་ཅིས་མཛད་ཀྱང་དོན་དག་མ་གྲུབ། ཧྲེང་ན་གླི་ར། གྲགས་པ་འབུམ་ལྡེ་སྡེ་རྒྱལ་པོ་ཆེ་

---

6 ཡོ་སེབ། ཤོག་ ༣༤༨།

7 བོད་ཀྱི་རྒྱལ་པོ་ཉི་མ་མགོན་དབུས་གཙང་ནས་མངའ་རིས་སུ་ཐེབས། དེ་ཡི་སྟོད་ཀྱི་མགོན་གསུམ་ཞེས་པ་སྲས་གསུམ་ཡོད་པ་གཅིག་གིས་མར་ཡུལ་ཏེ་ལ་དྭགས་བཟུང་། གཞན་གཉིས་ཀྱིས་པུ་རངས་དང་། ཞང་ཞུང་བཟུང་ཞེས་**བུ་སྟོན་ཆོས་འབྱུང་**སོགས་ན་གསལ་ཞིང་། དེ་དག་གིས་བསྐྱངས་པའི་ཡུལ་ཀུན་ལ་མངའ་རིས་སྐོར་གསུམ་ཞེས་མིང་བཏགས་ཀྱང་། ཕྱིས་སུ་མར་ཡུལ་དང་མང་ཡུལ་གྱི་དབྱེ་བ་དབུས་གཙང་པ་དག་གིས་ཕྱི་མ་ཤེས་པར། མར་ཡུལ་ལ་མང་ཡུལ་ཞེས་བྲིས་པ་དེ་ཉིད་**ཆོས་རྗེ་སྟག་ཚང་རྣམ་ཐར་**དང་། **བཻ་སེར་**སོགས་དཔེ་ཆ་ཆེན་རྣམས་སུ་ཡང་ནོར་བ་ཤོར་འདུག་པས། མར་ཡུལ་གྱི་གཞོན་ནུ་རྣམ་དཔྱོད་དང་ལྡན་པ་རྣམས་ཀྱིས་འདི་འདྲའི་ཡིག་ནོར་རིགས་ལ་བག་ཡོད་པར་མཛོད་ཅིག མར་ཡུལ་ནི་ལ་དྭགས་དང་། མང་ཡུལ་ནི་བལ་པོ་དང་བོད་ས་མཚམས་ན་མཆིས་སོ། །

8 ཡེ་ཤེས་རྩེ་མོ། མདུན་ཤོག ༣༧།

9 རབ་རྒྱས་ཀྱིས་རང་གི་རྒྱལ་རབས་སུ་རྒྱལ་པོ་གྲགས་འབུམ་ལྡེ་དང་། རྒྱ་པ་ཇོ་བོས་ཀྱང་འབུལ་ཆེན་ཕུལ་བར་མངོན་བྲིས་ཡོད་པ། **དགེ་འདུན་གྲུབ་ཀྱི་རྣམ་ཐར་**ལ་ཁུངས་བཏུགས་པ་ཡིན་ན། ཁོང་རང་གིས་རྗེ་དགེ་འདུན་གྲུབ་ཀྱི་རྣམ་ཐར་ལེགས་པར་གཟིགས་མེད་པ་དང་། གཞན་བོད་སྐད་ལ་གོ་བ་མེད་པ་ཞིག་གིས་བཤད་པ་འགོད་པར་སྣང་། ཡེ་ཤེས་རྩེ་མོ་གོང་གསལ་ཤོག་གྲངས་ལ་གཟིགས།

བ་མཇལ། རྒྱལ་པོས་ཀྱང་རྣལ་འབྱོར་པ་གཉིས་ལ་དད་པ་ཆེན་པོས་བསྙུ་བ་མཛད་དོ། །10
ལ་དྭགས་རྒྱལ་རབས་ན་གསལ་བ་ལྟར། གྲགས་འབུམ་ལྡེ་ཡིས་གླི་ཏྲ་དེའུ་སེར་པོའི་སྣང་ལ་བཀྲ་
ཤིས་འོད་འཕྲོ་ཞེས་པའི་མཆོད་རྟེན་ཆེན་མོ་བཞེངས། འདི་དང་ཉང་སྟོད་རྒྱལ་རྩེའི་དཔལ་
འཁོར་དགོན་དུ་བཞུགས་པའི་སྐུ་འབུམ་མཆོད་རྟེན་ཆེན་མོ་གཉིས་བཟོ་དབྱིབས་བྱད་ཀྱི་ཚུལ་མཐུན་པ་
ཡོད་པས། གང་རུང་གཅིག་གིས་གཅིག་ལ་དཔེ་ཡི་བསམ་བློ་འཁྲིར་ཏེ། བཞེངས་པ་ཡིན་
པར་བདག་ལ་དབྱིན་ཡུལ་པ་རྒྱལ་རབས་ལ་མཁས་པ། ནེ་ཨིལ་ ཏལྷཊ་མཆོག་གིས་བྲིས་།
རྒྱལ་རྩེའི་མཆོད་རྟེན་ཆེན་མོ་དེ། ཕྱི་ལོ་བརྒྱ་རབས་ ༡༤༣༧ ལོར་བཞེངས་པ་ཡིན་ནོ། །11

དེ་ཡང་སྡེ་སྲིད་སངས་རྒྱས་རྒྱ་མཚོས་**བེ་ཌཱུ་སེར་པོ**ར། རྒྱལ་མཁར་རྩེ་བ་བདག་
པོ་རབ་བརྟན་ཀུན་བཟང་འཕགས་དང་། མཁས་གྲུབ་ཆོས་རྗེ། ༡༣༨༥ ནས་ ༡༤༣༨ བཞུགས་
པ། མཆོད་ཡོན་ཟུང་གིས་རྒྱལ་རྩེའི་དཔལ་འཁོར་དགོན་ཕྱག་བཏབ་པ་དང་།12 གཞན་ཡང་
བེ་སེར་དུ། མཁས་གྲུབ་རྗེ་སློབ་མ། གསང་ཕུ་བ་ལྷ་དབང་བློ་གྲོས་ཀྱིས་དཔེ་ཐུབ་དགོན་པར
ཞིག་གསོ་མཛད་པར་གསུངས། དེས་ན་རང་རེས་འདི་ལྟར་དཔག་ཚོད་བྱ་ནུས་ཏེ། བླ་
མ་ལྷ་དབང་བློ་གྲོས་ཀྱིས་རྒྱལ་རྩེ་མཆོད་རྟེན་མཇལ་ནས་ངོ་མཚར་དུ་འཛིན། རྟིང་ན་མར་ཡུལ་
དུ་ཕྱིན། ཇོ་བོ་གྲགས་པ་འབུམ་ལྡེ་ལ་ཞལ་བཀོད་མཛད་དེ། རྒྱལ་རྩེའི་མཆོད་རྟེན་དང་
མཚུངས་པའི་གླིའི་ཏྲའུ་སེར་པོའི་སྣང་ལ་མཆོད་རྟེན་བཀྲ་ཤིས་འོད་འཕྲོ་ཞེས་པ་འདི་ཉིད་བཞེངས་པར་
མཛད་དོ། །

གྲགས་འབུམ་ལྡེ་སྐུ་གཤེགས་པའི་རྗེས་སུ། དེའི་སྲས་བློ་གྲོས་མཆོག་ལྡན་པས་བླ་མ་
ལྷ་དབང་བློ་གྲོས་ཀྱི་སྦྱིན་བདག་མཛད། ནུབ་ཕྱོགས་པ་རྒྱལ་རབས་སྨྲ་བར་མཁས་པ་པེ་ཏེ་ཙ་དང་།
རང་རེ་མར་ཡུལ་པ་རྒྱལ་རབས་སྨྲ་བར་མཁས་པ་བཀྲ་ཤིས་རབ་རྒྱས་གཉིས་ཀྱིས། རྒྱལ་པོ་བློ་
གྲོས་མཆོག་ལྡན་པས་བཀྲ་ཤིས་ལྷུན་པོར་རྒྱལ་བ་དགེ་འདུན་གྲུབ་ལ་འབུལ་ཆེན་ཕུལ་ཏོ། །ཞེས་

10 ཕྱཀྲ་ཀི། ཤོག ༣༦ དང་ ༩༡། ཡོ་སེབ། ཤོག ༣༤༤ དང་། ༣༤༥། རབ་རྒྱས།
ཤོག ༡༣༣ དང་། ༡༣༤།

11 བོད་རྒྱ་ཚིག་མཛོད་རིའུ་མིག ཤོག ༣༣༤༧།

12 སྡེ་སངས་རྒྱས་རྒྱ་མཚོ། ཤོག ༣༤༤།

བྲིས་པ་དེ་དག་གི་ཁུངས་གཏུག་ས་ནི། **བེ་ཊ་རུ་སེར་པོ་ན།** **མང་ཡུལ་**13**སྐྱོད་པའི་རྒྱལ་པོ་བློ་གྲོས་མཆོག་ལྡན་པས་མཁས་པ་ལྷ་དབང་བློ་གྲོས་ཀྱི་སྤྱིན་བདག་མཛད།** **གཙང་དུ་རྗེ་བླ་མའི་ཡང་སྲིད་གོང་མ་དགེ་འདུན་གྲུབ་ལ་འབུལ་ཆེན་ཕུལ།**14 ཅེས་པའི་རབ་བྱེད་འདི་ཉིད་ཡིན་པར་མངོན། ངེད་ངོས་ཀྱི་གོ་བ་ལྟར་ན། རབ་བྱེད་འདི་ཡི་བརྗོད་པ་ཕྱི་མ་དེ་ཉིད་དག་པོ་རང་མེད་པར་སྣང་། ཅིའི་ཕྱིར་ཞེར་ན། རྗེ་དགེ་འདུན་གྲུབ་ཀྱི་སྐུ་ཚེའི་དུས་སུ། བོད་ཀྱི་ཆོས་ལུགས་མང་ཆེ་བར་བླ་མའི་ཡང་སྲིད་སྤྲུལ་སྐུ་ངོས་འཛིན་པའི་སྲོལ་མེད་པས། རྗེ་དགེ་འདུན་གྲུབ་ལྷ་བུ་སྐུ་ཡོན་མཛད་པ་བསམ་གྱིས་མི་ཁྱབ་པ་ཡང་སྤྲུལ་པའི་སྐུ་ཡིན་ཞེས་ངོས་འཛིན་ཞུས་མེད། འོན་ཀྱང་རྗེ་དགེ་འདུན་གྲུབ་མྱ་ངན་ལས་འདས་པའི་རྗེས་སུ། སྤྱི་ལོ་ ༡༩༧༥ ལ་གཙང་རྟ་ནག་ཏུ་གྲོང་པ་ཞིང་པ་ཞིག་ལ་བུ་ཚ་རྟགས་མཚན་ངོ་མཚར་ཅན་ཞིག་བྱུང་པ་དེ་ཉིད་རྗེ་དགེ་འདུན་གྲུབ་ཀྱི་ཡང་སྲིད་སྤྲུལ་སྐུར་ངོས་འཛིན་ཞུས་ཏེ་མཚན་ལ་དགེ་འདུན་རྒྱ་མཚོ་ཞེས་གསོལ། འདི་ཉིད་དགོངས་ལོ་བཅུ་གཅིག་ནས་བཅུ་དགུ་བར་དུ་བཀྲ་ཤིས་ལྷུན་པོར་བཞུགས་ཏེ། སློབ་སྦྱོང་མཛད། དགོངས་ལོ་བཅུ་དགུ་སྐབས་སུ། འབྲས་སྤུངས་སུ་བྱོན། སྤྱི་ལོ་ ༡༥༠༨ ཙམ་ལ་བོད་དབུས་གཙང་ཡོངས་ལ་ཆོས་གསུང་བ་ལ་ཡུལ་ལུང་མང་པོར་ཕེབས། དེའི་དུས་སུ་སླར་ཡང་བཀྲ་ཤིས་ལྷུན་པོར་གདན་འདྲེན་ཞུས་ཏེ། ལོ་ཁ་ཤས་དེར་བཞུགས་སོ་ཞེས་གསལ་ལོ། །15

དེས་ན་གོང་གསལ་**བེ་སེར་**གྱི་རབ་བྱེད་དེ་ལ། **གཙང་དུ་རྗེ་བླ་མ་སྐུ་གོང་མ་དགེ་འདུན་གྲུབ་ཀྱི་ཡང་སྲིད་རྗེ་དགེ་འདུན་རྒྱ་མཚོར་འབུལ་ཆེན་ཕུལ།** ཞེས་ཞུས་དག་བྱེད་ན་འགྲིག་གམ་མི་འགྲིག་བློ་གྲོས་ཀྱི་རྩལ་དང་ལྡན་པ་རྣམས་ཀྱིས་བརྟག་དཔྱད་མཛོད།།

གཞན་ཡང་རྒྱལ་པོ་བློ་གྲོས་མཆོག་ལྡན་དང་། རྒྱལ་པོ་བ་གན་གཉིས། སྤྱི་ལོ་བརྒྱ་རབས་བཅུ་དྲུག་པའི་མགོ་སྟོད་ཙམ་བྱུང་བའི་ཁུངས་གཞན་ཞིག་ཀྱང་མཐོང་། སྤྱི་ལོ་ ༡༥༣༣ ལ། ཧོར་གྱི་དམག་དཔོན་མིར་ཛ་ཧི་དར་ཞེར་བས་མགོ་འཁྲིད་བྱས་པའི་ཧོར་དམག་ལ་དྭགས་ལ་སླེབས། འདི་ཡི་ལོ་རྒྱུས་སྐད་རིགས་གཞན་མ་ཞིག་ཏུ་བྲིས་པ་ན་ཛ་བོ་བློ་གྲོས་མཆོག་ལྡན་དང་། ཛ་བོ་བ་གན་ཞེས་བྲིས་ཡོད་ཀྱང་། ཡུལ་དུས་མི་མཚུངས་པ་དང་། བྲིས་མི་གསལ་བའི་དབང་གིས།

13 མང་ཡུལ་ཞེས་པ་མ་དག། མར་ཡུལ་ཞེས་དག་པའོ། །

14 རྒྱ་མཚོ། ཤོག ༣༨༠།

15 ཡ་རབས་ཀྱང་། / **དྭ་ལའི་བླ་མའི་རྣམ་ཐར།** ཤོག ༣༨།

ལ་དྭགས་རྒྱལ་རབས་ན་གསལ་བའི་རྒྱལ་པོ་བློ་གྲོས་མཆོག་ལྡན་དང་། རྒྱལ་པོ་བ་གན་ཡིན་པ་མི་སྲིད་དོ་ཞེས་ ཕྲན་ཙ་ཀེ་དང་། པེ་ཏེ་ཙ་[16]གཉིས་ཀྱིས་བྲིས་ཀྱང་། དེ་རྣམས་ཀྱིས་གདན་འབེབས་བྱས་པའི་དུས་ཚོད་ལས། རྒྱལ་པོ་གྲགས་འབུམ་ལྡེ་སོགས་ཀྱི་རྒྱལ་སྲིད་བསྐྱངས་པའི་དུས་ཚོད་ལོ་ངོ་བཞི་བཅུ་ལྷག་ཙམ་གྱི་རྟིང་ན་བྱུང་བ་ངེས་པས། གོང་གསལ་ལ་དྭགས་ཀྱི་ཇོ་བོ་གཉིས་རྒྱལ་པོ་བློ་གྲོས་མཆོག་ལྡན་དང་། རྒྱལ་པོ་བ་གན་གཉིས་ཡིན་པར་ཐག་གཅོད་ཐུབ་པ་ཡིན་ཅིང་། དེའི་དུས་ལ། རྒྱལ་པོ་ལ་ཇོ་བོ་ཞུ་བ་ཡོད་པ་ནི། པཎ་ཆེན་ཡེ་ཤེས་རྩེ་མོས། རྒྱལ་པོ་གྲགས་པ་འབུམ་ལྡེ་ལ། མངའ་རིས་རྒྱལ་པོ་ཇོ་བོ་གྲགས་འབུམ་ལྡེ་ཞེས་ཞུས་པ་ལྟ་བུ་ཡིན་ནོ། །

དེར་མ་ཟད་ཁུངས་གཞན་མ་ཞིག་ཀྱང་མཐོང་སྟེ། སྤྱི་ལོ་བརྒྱ་རབས་བཅུ་བདུན་པའི་འགོ་ཙམ་ལ་བཙུན་པ་འགྱུར་མེད་བདེ་ཆེན་གྱིས་བརྩམས་པའི་**གྲུབ་ཐོབ་ཆེན་པོ་ཐང་སྟོང་རྒྱལ་པོའི་རྣམ་ཐར་དུ།**

> **རྡོར་གྱི་ཁ་གནོན་ལ་གྲུབ་ཐོབ་ཆེན་པོ་ཆེ་རློམ་གདང་བའི་དཔོན་སློབ་ཉི་ཤུ་མར་ཡུལ་དུ་བྱོན། མར་ཡུལ་སྟོད་སྨད་ཀྱི་རྒྱལ་པོ་གཉིས་མངོན་ཤེས་དང་རྫུ་འཕྲུལ་གྱིས་ཚོད་པ་ཤི་བར་མཛད། མར་ཡུལ་ན་གཞིས་པབ་པའི་སྟོད་རྡོར་སྟོང་ཁྱེར་དྲུག་ཅུ་ཙམ་ལ། མ་ཎིའི་ལུང་གནང་། . . . [17]རྡོར་དམག་ཁྲིལ་གྱིས་གནོན་པའི་ཐུགས་དམ་མཛད་པས། རྡོར་ཡུལ་དུ་བྱི་བའི་ཆར་ཕབ་འབྲུ་བཟླག་པས་མུ་གེ་དང་ནད་ཡམས་ཆེན་པོས་སྟོད་རྡོར་གྱི་དམག་དཔུང་ཁ་བ་ཅན་གྱི་རྒྱལ་ཁམས་ལ་འཇུག་པའི་གོ་སྐབས་མེད་པར་མཛད་དོ།** །[18]

གདམ་རྒྱུད་འདི་ཉིད་གང་པོ་ལོ་རྒྱུས་ལྡན་པ་མ་ཡིན་རུང་། འབྲི་བ་པོ་འདི་ཡིས་མར་ཡུལ་སྟོད་སྨད་ཀྱི་རྒྱལ་པོ་གཉིས་མཐུན་པོ་མེད་པ་དང་། མར་ཡུལ་དུ་རྡོར་དམག་བྱུང་ནས་གཞིས་ཕབ་པར་བཤད་པ་རྣམས་ལོ་རྒྱུས་ལྡན་པ་ཡིན་པ་དང་། མིད་ཏི་དར་གྱི་ལོ་རྒྱུས་སུ།

---

16 ཕྲན་ཙ་ཀེ། དེབ་གཉིས་པ། ཤོག ༡༠༡ ༡༠༣ དང་། པེ་ཏེ་ཙ། ཤོག ༣༥ དང་། ༣༧།

17 . . . རྟགས་འདི་ནི་ཚིག་གཞན་ཡོད་པ་འདིར་མ་བྲིས་སོ་ཞེས་པའི་དོན་དག་ཡིན།

18 བདེ་ཆེན། ཤོག ༣༠༩

ཇོ་བོ་བློ་གྲོས་མཆོག་ལྡན་དང་། ཇོ་བོ་བ་གན་གཉིས་ཞེས་གསལ་ཡོད་པ་ནི་གྲགས་པ་འབུམ་ལྡེའི་སྲས་བློ་གྲོས་མཆོག་ལྡན་དང་། གྲགས་འབུམ་གྱི་སྲས་བ་གན་19གཉིས་ཕོ་ན་ཡིན་པར་སེམས་ཤིང་། རྒྱུ་མཚན་དེ་དག་ལ་བརྟེན་ནས། གྲགས་འབུམ་ལྡེའི་རྒྱལ་སྲིད་ཕལ་ཆེར་ཕྱི་ལོ་ ༡༤༥༠ ནས་ ༡༤༨༠ ཙམ་གྱི་དབར་ལ་ཡིན་པའི་དཔག་ཚོད་བྱས་སོ། །

ཚེ་དབང་རྣམ་རྒྱལ་དང་པོ་

རྒྱལ་པོ་ཚེ་དབང་རྣམ་རྒྱལ་དང་པོ་ནི། རང་གི་ཨ་ཁུ་བཀྲ་ཤིས་རྣམ་རྒྱལ་གྱི་ཚ་བོ་ཡིན། ལ་དྭགས་རྒྱལ་རབས་ན། འདི་ལ་སྤྲུལ་པའི་རྒྱལ་པོ་ཞེས་ཞུ་བ་ལྟར་ན། ངོ་མཚར་དུ་འཕགས་པ་ཞིག་བཞུགས་པར་ངེས། གཙུག་ལག་ཁང་མང་པོ་བཞེངས་ནས། སངས་རྒྱས་ཀྱི་བསྟན་པ་མེས་པོ་རལ་པ་ཅན་ལྟ་བུ་ཞིག་བྱེད་དགོས་དགོངས་ཀྱང་། སེམས་ཅན་གྱི་བསོད་ནམས་ཀྱི་ལས་ཟད་པས། རྒྱལ་པོ་འདི་ཆུང་དུས་སྐུ་ཚེ་ལས་འདས་སོ། །20རྒྱལ་པོ་འདི་ཡི་དུས་སུ། བ་མགོ་བྱམས་པ་ཆེན་པོའི་ལྷ་ཁང་འདིའི་ལྡེབས་རིས་ཡོངས་རྫོགས་བཞེངས་པ་ཡིན་ན། འདུ་ཁང་གི་ནུབ་ངོས་ལྡེབས་རིས་དེ་རྣམས་ཀྱི་རྟེན་གཙོ་བོ་ལྟ་བུར་རྒྱལ་བ་ཙོང་ཁ་པ་བཞུགས་པ་དང་མཉམ་དུ་དགེ་ལུགས་པའི་བླ་མ་ལྷ་ཚོགས་མང་དུ་བཞུགས་པའི་རྒྱུ་མཚན་གྱིས་རྒྱལ་པོ་འདི་ཉིད་དགེ་ལྡན་པའི་རྗེས་འཇུག་ཡིན་པར་སེམས། དེ་ཙུག་ཡིན་ན། བཞེངས་པའི་ལོ་ཁ་ཤས་རྟེང་ན། ཕལ་ཆེར་སྐུ་མཆེད་ནུ་བོ་འཇམ་དབྱངས་རྣམ་རྒྱལ་གྱི་དུས་སུ། ལྷ་ཁང་འདི། འབྲུག་ལུགས་ལ་ཕུལ་པ་ཡིན་པར་ངེས།

འདིའི་དུས་སྐབས་སྐོར་ལ། ཀ་རྗིང་ཟླམ་གྱིས། འདི་ཉིད་ ཕྱི་ལོ་ ༡༥༧༠ ཙམ་ལ་རྒྱལ་པོར་གྱུར་པ་དང་། ཕྱི་ལོ་༡༦༠༠ སྐུ་ཚེ་ལས་འདས་པ་བྲིས།21 ཕྲན་ཙ་ཀེ་ཡིས། རྒྱལ་པོ་འདིའི་སྲིད་དབང་། ཕྱི་ལོ་ ༡༥༣༣ ནས་ ༡༥༦༠ བར་ཡིན་པ་ངོས་འཛིན།22 ཡོ་སེབ་ཀྱིས། ཕྱི་ལོ་ ༡༥༦༨ ཙམ་ལ་འདི་ཉིད་སྐུ་ཚེ་འདས་པར་བྲིས་ཡོད་ཀྱང་། འཕྲུངས་ལོ་

---

19 **ལ་དྭགས་རྒྱལ་རབས་**སུ། གྲགས་པ་འབུམ་གྱི་སྲས་སྦ་ར་དང་། དེའི་སྲས་བ་གན་ཡིན་པར་བཤད་ཀྱང་། དུས་སྐབས་ལ་བརྟག་གཞིགས་བྱས་ན། ཡིག་ནོར་གྱིས་དེ་ལྟར་བྱུང་བར་ཤེས།

20 ཕྲན་ཙ་ཀེ། དེབ་གཉིས་པ། ཤོག ༣༧།

21 ཀ་རྗིང་ཟླམ། ཤོག ༣༡༨།

22 ཕྲན་ཙ་ཀེ། དེབ་གཉིས་པ། ཤོག ༡༠༥།

དང་། རྒྱལ་པོར་གྱུར་པའི་ལོ་དུས་མ་བྲིས།23 རབ་རྒྱས་ཀྱིས། འདི་ཡིས། ཕྱལ་ཆེར་སྤྱི་ལོ་ ༡༥༣༠ ནས་ ༡༥༨༠ བར་དུ་རྒྱལ་སྲིད་ལ་དབང་བ་བྲིས་སོ། །24

འདི་དག་ཀུན་གྱི་ནང་ནས། ཀརྫིང་སྣམ་གྱི་བཞེད་པ་དེ་ཉིད་ཆེས་བདེན་པ་ཡིན་པ་ནི། རྗེ་སྟག་ཚང་རས་པ་དང་། རྒྱལ་པོ་འཇམ་དབྱངས་གཉིས་ཞལ་འཛོམས་པའི་ལོ་དུས་འོག་ཏུ་བཀོད་པ་ལས་ཤེས་ཐུབ་བོ། །

འཇམ་དབྱངས་རྣམ་རྒྱལ་

འཇམ་དབྱངས་རྣམ་རྒྱལ་ནི། ཇོ་བོ་ཆེ་དབང་རྣམ་རྒྱལ་གྱི་ནུ་བོ་ཡིན། ཟངས་དཀར་དུ། ཆོས་རྗེ་སྟག་ཚང་མཇལ་དུས། ང་ཡང་འབྲུག་པའི་སྦྱིན་བདག་ཡིན། བསྟན་པ་ལ་དགོངས་ཏེ། མར་ཡུལ་དུ་ཕེབས་ཞེས་བླ་མ་སྟག་ཚང་རས་པ་ཆེན་པོར་ཞུ་བ་ནན་ཏན་མཛད། ཆོས་རྗེས་ཀྱང་ཨུ་རྒྱན་གནས་བསྐོར་ནས་ལོག་སྐེ་འཁོར་བ་དང་། འབྱོན་པའི་ཞལ་བཞེས་མཛད། དེ་ནས་རྒྱལ་པོ་འདི་ཉིད། ཕྱལ་ཆེར་སྤྱི་ལོ་ ༡༨༡༥ ཙམ་ཞིག་ལ། སྐུ་ཆེ་མ་ཟིན་པར་མངོན་ཏེ། ཆོས་རྗེ་དེ་ཉིད་ལ་དྭགས་མར་ཡུལ་དུ་བྱོན་པའི་སྐབས་སུ། རྒྱལ་པོ་འདི་དང་མཇལ་བའི་གཏམ་རྒྱུད། ག་ན་ཡང་མི་སྣང་། །རྒྱལ་པོ་འདི་ཡིས་བ་མགོ་རུ་གསེར་སྤྱངས་བྱམས་པ་བཞེང་བའི་མགོ་བཙམས་ཀྱང་མཐར་མ་ཕྱིན་པར་ལུས་པ་དེ་སྲས་སེང་གེ་རྣམ་རྒྱལ་གྱི་དུས་སུ།ལེགས་པར་གྲུབ་པ་འོག་ན་གསལ་ལོ། །

ཀརྫིང་སྣམ་གྱིས། འདི་ཡི་སྲིད་སྐྱོང་དུས། ཕྱལ་ཆེར་སྤྱི་ལོ་ ༡༨༠༠ ནས་ ༡༨༣༠ བར་དང་།25 ཕྲནཙཀེ་ཡིས། ༡༥༨༠ ནས་ ༡༥༩༠ བར་དུ་ངོས་འཛིན་བྱས།26 རབ་རྒྱས་ཀྱི་བཞེད་པ་འདི་དང་མཐུན་ནོ། །27

འདིའི་སྐོར་ལ་ཡང་། ཀརྫིང་སྣམ་ཉིད་ཆེས་བདེན་པ་ཡིན་ཏེ། ཟངས་དཀར་དུ་རྣལ་འབྱོར་གྱི་དབང་ཕྱུག་སྟག་ཚང་རས་པ་དང་། རྒྱལ་པོ་འདི་གཉིས་མཇལ་དུས་སྤྱི་ལོ་ ༡༨༡༣

---

23 ཡ་སེལ། ཤོག ༣༥༥།

24 རབ་རྒྱས། ཤོག ༡༥༥།

25 ཀ་རྫིང་སྣམ། ཤོག ༣༣༣།

26 ཕྲནཙ་ཀེ། དེབ་གཉིས་པ། ཤོག ༡༠༨།

27 རབ་རྒྱས། ཤོག ༡༨༣།

ནས ༡༥ གང་རུང་ཞིག་ལ་ཡིན་དགོས། ཅིའི་ཕྱིར་ཟེར་ན། རབ་བྱུང་བཅུ་གཅིག་པའི་ཆུ་གླང་ལོར། སྤྱི་ལོ་ ༡༦༡༣། ཆོས་རྗེ་སྟག་ཚང་བོད་དབུས་ནས་འཁོན། ཤིང་ཡོས་ལོར། སྤྱི་ལོ་ ༡༦༡༥། ཟངས་དཀར་ནས། ཨོ་རྒྱན་གྱི་ཡུལ་ཕྱོགས་སུ་ཕེབས་གྲུབས་མཛད་ཅེས་**རྣམ་ཐར་**ན་གསལ་ལོ། །28

རྒྱལ་མོ་ཆེན་མོ་ཁ་ཊྭན་

རྒྱལ་མོ་ཁ་ཏུན་གྱི་མཚན་དངོས་མ་ནི་ཅི་ཡིན་ངེས་མ་ཟིན། ཁ་ཏུན་ཟེར་བ་ནི་ཧོར་ཡུལ་ནུབ་ཕྱོགས་ཀྱི་སྐད་དུ། ཇོ་བོ་དཔོན་པོ་དག་གི་བཙུན་མོ་ལ་འབོད་པའི་དོན་ཡིན་འདུག། དཔེར་ན་རྒྱལ་པོ་ལ་ཁན་ཟེར་བ་ལྟ་བུ། ཧོར་གྱི་ཚིག་འགའ་ཤས་རྒྱ་གར་ནུབ་ཕྱོགས་སུ། ད་ལྟ་ཡང་བཀོལ་བ་ཡོད། རྒྱལ་མོ་འདི། སྐར་མདོའི་ཇོ་བོ་ཨ་ལི་མིར་གྱི་སྲས་མོ་ཡིན། ཡབ་ཨ་ལི་མིར་གྱིས་གཡོ་སྒྱུའི་འཆར་གཞི་བཏིངས་ཏེ། རྒྱལ་པོ་འཇམ་དབྱངས་རྣམ་རྒྱལ་ལ་བག་མར་བཏང་སྟེ། མིས་པོ་དམ་པ་ཡོ་སེབ་ཀྱིས། རྒྱལ་མོ་ཁ་ཐུན་རང་ཉིད་འཆི་བའི་བར་དུ་རང་གི་ཨིས་ལམ་གྱི་ཆོས་ལུགས་སུ་གནས་པ་དང་། གླིའི་མཁར་འོག་དང་། གཏིང་སྒང་མཁར་གྱི་ཉེ་འདབས་དང་། ལྷུམ་རྣ་རྣྟ་དར་བཅས་ཡུལ་གནད་ཆེ་སར་མས་ཇིད་གསུམ་བརྩིགས་སོ། །29 ཞེས་པ་ལྟར་ན། ད་ལྟ་བྱམས་ཆུང་བཞུགས་པའི་ཁང་པ་འདི་ཡང་མས་ཇིད་ཕྱིར། བརྩིགས་པར་ཤེས། འོན་ཀྱང་རྒྱལ་མོ་ཁ་ཏུན་རང་གི་སྐུ་ཚེ་རྫོགས་པོར་ཨིས་ལམ་གྱི་ཆོས་ལུགས་ལ་བཞུགས་པ་དེ་ནི་བདེན་པར་མི་སྣང་སྙེ། ལ་དྭགས་ལ་ཕེབས་ཏེ། ལོ་ཁ་ཤས་རིང་ལ་ཨིས་ལམ་གྱི་ཆོས་ལུགས་ལ་བཞུགས་ཀྱང་། དེའི་རྗེང་ན། རྒྱལ་མོ་རང་གི་ཐུགས་འདོད་ཀྱིས་ནང་པར་གྱུར་པར་མཐོང་སྙེ། བ་མགོ་མཁར་དུ། ཆོས་རྗེ་སྟག་ཚང་རས་པ་བྱོན་སྐབས་སུ། **རྒྱལ་མོ་ཁ་ཏུན་དང་མི་དབང་སེང་གེ་རྣམ་རྒྱལ་སྐུ་མཆེད་ཀྱིས་དད་གུས་ཀྱི་རིམ་གྲོས་བསྙེན་པར་གྲུབ་ལུགས་ཀྱི་ཚེ་དུའི་དབང་སོགས་འབུལ་བ་མཛད།**30 ཅེས་ཆོས་རྗེ་དེ་ཉིད་ཀྱི་**རྣམ་ཐར་**ན་གསལ། གལ་

28 ཀུན་དགའ། **རྒྱབ**ཤོག ༣༠།

29 ཡོ་སེབ། ཤོག ༦༣༡

30 ཀུན་དགའ། རྒྱབ་ཤོག ༣༦།

དེ་རྒྱལ་མོ་འདི་ནང་པར་གྱུར་མེད་ན། ཆོས་རྗེ་སྟག་ཚང་ལྷ་བུ་འཇིག་རྟེན་ཆོས་བརྒྱད་[31]སྤྱངས་པའི་གྲུབ་ཐོབ་ཆེན་པོས། མཆོག་གསུམ་ལ་སྐྱབས་འགྲོ་མེད་པའི་གང་ཟག་ལ་གསང་སྔགས་ཀྱི་དབང་བསྐུར་བར་མཛད་པ་ག་ལ་སྲིད། དེས་ན་རྒྱལ་མོ་ཆེན་མོ་འདི་ཉིད་ནང་པར་གྱུར་ནས། མས་རྗེད་དེའི་ནང་། རྗེ་བཙུན་བྱམས་མགོན་གྱི་སྐུ་འདྲ་དང་། ཕྱིབས་རིས་སུ་རྗེ་བཙུན་བློ་བཟང་གྲགས་པ་དང་། གསང་བདེ་འཇིགས་གསུམ་སོགས་བཞེངས་པར་མཛད། དེ་ར་མ་ཟད་གསེར་ཟངས་ཀྱི་བྱམས་པ་བཞེངས་ནས་གྲུབ་དུས་ཕྲ་རྒྱན་ཡོངས་རྫོགས་རྒྱལ་མོ་ཆེན་མོ་འདི་ཡིས་དད་པས་ཕུལ།[32] གཞན་ཡང་བྱམས་ཆུང་ལྷ་ཁང་དུ་དགེ་ལུགས་པའི་ལྷ་ཚོགས་བཞུགས་པ་དང་། རྒྱལ་མོ་འདི་ཉིད་སྐུ་ཆེ་འདས་པའི་རྗེས་སུ། དགེ་ལུགས་པའི་བླ་མ་པཎ་ཆེན་ཆོས་ཀྱི་རྒྱལ་མཚན་ལ་བསྔོ་རྟེན་རྒྱ་ཆེན་པོ་ཕུལ་སྣང་དང་། **ཆོས་རྗེ་སྟག་ཚང་གི་རྣམ་ཐར་དུ།** བསྔོ་རྟེན་བྱུང་བ་དང་། རྒྱལ་མོ་འདི་ཉིད་སྐུ་གཤེགས་པའི་སྐོར་ལ། ཅང་བྲིས་མེད་པ་ལ་དཔགས་ན། འདི་ཉིད་དགེ་ལྡན་པའི་རྗེས་འཇུག་ཡིན་ཅིང་། སྤྲུལ་ནོར་བུ་རྣམ་རྒྱལ་གྱི་ཕྱོགས་པ། དགེ་ལུགས་པའི་ཕྱོགས་འཐེན་མཛད་དེ། སྤྲུལ་སེང་གེ་རྣམ་རྒྱལ་མཆོད་ཡོན་ལ། མོས་པ་ཆེ་བ་རང་མེད་པ་ཡིན་ནམ་སྙམ་པ་བདག་རང་གི་རྣམ་པར་རྟོག་པ་ཡིན། རྗེ་ལྟར་ཡིན་ན་ཡང་། རྒྱལ་མོ་ཆེན་མོ་འདི་ཉིད་འགྲོ་བ་སེམས་ཅན་ལ། བྱམས་པ་དང་སྙིང་རྗེ་ཐུགས་ལ་མངའ་ཞིང་། མཛད་སྤྱོད་བཟང་པོ་བཞུགས་པར་བརྟེན། སྐྱེ་བོ་ཀུན་གྱིས་ཀྱང་། དད་གུས་ཀྱིས་བཀུར་ཅིང་། རྗེ་བཙུན་མ་སྒྲོལ་དཀར་གྱི་སྤྲུལ་པ་ཡིན་། ཞེས་ངོས་འཛིན་ཞུས་པ་རྒྱལ་རབས་སྒྲ་བ་ཀུན་གྱིས་གླེང་ངོ་།
།[33]

---

31 འཇིག་རྟེན་ཆོས་བརྒྱད་ནི། དཔལ་མགོན་འཕགས་པ་ཀླུ་སྒྲུབ་ཀྱིས།
འཇིག་རྟེན་མཁྱེན་པ་རྙེད་དང་མི་རྙེད་དང་།
བདེ་དང་མི་བདེ་སྙན་དང་མི་སྙན་དང་།
བསྟོད་སྨད་ཅེས་བགྱི་འཇིག་རྟེན་ཆོས་བརྒྱད་པོ།
བདག་གི་ཡིད་ཡུལ་མིན་པར་མཉམ་སྙོམས་མཛོད།
ཅེས་**བཤེས་པའི་སྤྲིངས་ཡིག** ཚིགས་བཅད་ཉི་ཤུ་ཙ་དགུ་པ་ལ་གསུངས་པ་བཞིན་ནོ།

32 ཀུན་དགའ། རྒྱབ་ཤོག ༣༠།

33 ཕྲན་ཚ་ཀ། དེབ་གཉིས་པ། ཤོག ༣༤། ཡོ་སེབ། ཤོག ༣༥༦། རབ་རྒྱས། ཤོག ༡༥༧།

སེང་གེ་རྣམ་རྒྱལ་

སྤྲས་སེང་གེ་རྣམ་རྒྱལ་ནི། ཡབ་འཇམ་དབྱངས་རྣམ་རྒྱལ་སྐུ་ཚེ་འདས་པའི་རྗེས། རྒྱལ་པོར་མངའ་གསོལ། རྒྱལ་པོ་ཆེན་པོ་འདིའི་དུས་སུ། ཡབ་རྒྱལ་པོས་འགྱོན་པར་ཞུ་བ་ཕུལ་ཡོད་པ་བཞིན། ཡོནྟལ་འགྱུར་གྱི་དབང་ཕྱུག། ཆོས་ཀྱི་རྗེ་སྟག་ཚང་རས་པ་ཆེན་པོ། སངས་རྒྱས་བསྟན་པ་རྒྱས་པ་དང་། འགྲོ་བ་སེམས་ཅན་གྱི་བསོད་ནམས་ཀྱི་ཞིང་མཆོག་དམ་པའི་ཕྱིར། མར་ཡུལ་དུ་བྱོན། དེ་ཡང་ཐོག་མར་རྒྱ་དང་། ཤེལ་དུ་བྱོན། དེ་ནས་ཨ་ལྕི་ཆོས་འཁོར་མཇལ་བར་ཕེབས། ལོག་ལམ་དུ་བ་མགོར་ཞབས་ཀྱི་པད་མོ་བཀོད། བྱམས་པའི་དགོན་གཉེར་ལ། འབྲུག་པའི་དགེ་སློང་ཁ་ཅིག་ཡོད་པ། དེར་ཞག་བཞུགས་མཛད་པ་ན། ཡུམ་རྒྱལ་མོ་ཁ་ཏུན་དང་། སྐུ་མཆེད་ནོར་བུ་རྣམ་རྒྱལ་དང་ལྷན་ཅིག་ཏུ། རྒྱལ་པོ་འདི་ཡིས། ཆོས་རྗེ་སྟག་ཚང་རས་པ་ཆེན་པོ་ནས། དབང་ཁྲིད་ལྷབས་ཀྱི་ཆོས་འབྲེལ་ཐོག་མར་ཞུས། སྟག་ཚང་རས་པ་ཆེན་པོ་དེ་ཉིད་ལ་དྭགས་སུ་ལོ་ངོ་བཞི་ཙམ་བཞུགས་ནས། རབ་བྱུང་བཅུ་གཅིག་པའི་ལྕགས་སྤྲེལ་ལོར། སྤྱི་ལོ་ ༡༦༣༠། དབུས་གཙང་ལ་ཕེབས་ཀྱང་། སེང་གེ་རྣམ་རྒྱལ་དང་། ནོར་བུ་རྣམ་རྒྱལ་སྐུ་མཆེད་ནང་ཕན་ཚུན་མི་མཐུན་པར་བཞུགས་པ་ལ་ནང་སྲིག་མཛད་པའི་ཕྱིར། སླར་ཡང་དབུས་གཙང་ནས་མར་ཡུལ་དུ་བྱོན། དེ་ནས་བཟུང་སྟེ། མི་ཡི་དབང་པོ་འདི་ཡིས་བླ་མ་སྟག་ཚང་རས་པ་ཆེན་པོ་དེ་ཉིད་རང་ཉིད་ཀྱི་རྩ་བའི་བླ་མར་བསྟེན་ནས་ཆོས་ཕྱོགས་ཀྱི་མཛད་པ་རྒྱ་ཆེན་པོ་མཛད་ཅིང་། རབ་བྱུང་བཅུ་དྲུག་པའི་ཆུ་རྟ་ལོར། སྤྱི་ལོ་༡༦༩༣། གངས་རིའི་ཕྱོགས་སུ། སོག་པོ་ཨོ་རོད་ཀྱི་དམག་ལྔ་བརྒྱ་ཙམ་འོངས་པ། དེ་དག་ཕྱིར་ལོག་འདེད་པའི་ཕྱིར། མངའ་རིས་ཕྱོགས་ཀྱི་དམག་མགོར་ཕེབས། དམག་ལས་རྒྱལ་ཏེ། སླེ་རུ་ལོག་ཕེབས་སྐབས་སུ། ཧྣན་ལེ་རུ། ཆོས་རྗེ་སྟག་ཚང་རས་པའི་ཞབས་ཀྱི་པདྨ་ཟླ་བ་གཅིག་གི་ཡུན་དུ་བསྟེན། སྨིན་གྲོལ་གྱི་ཆོས་ཀྱི་བདུད་རྩིས་ཚིམ་པར་གྱུར། སྐུ་ཚེ་འདི་ཡི་མཛད་པ་ཟིན་ཏེ། སྐུ་ཚེ་ལས་འདས། སྐུ་སྤུར་གསང་ཐབས་ཀྱིས་སླེའི་མཁར་དུ་གདན་ཞུས། སྐུ་ཕུང་མི་ལྷར་ཕུལ་པ་སོགས་རྗེས་ཀྱི་དགེ་བའི་བྱ་བ་རྣམས་ལེགས་པར་བསྒྲུབས་སོ། །[34]

---

34 ཀུན་དགའ། མདུན་སོག ༩༠།

རྒྱལ་པོ་འདི་ཡི་སྲིད་དབང་སྐྱུར་བའི་དུས་ནི། ཀཧྲིང་ཟླམ་གྱིས། ཕལ་ཆེར་ སྤྱི་ལོ་ ༡༨༣༠ ནས་ ༡༨༧༠ བར་དུ་ངོས་འཛིན་པ་དང་།35 ཕྲནཙ་ཀེ་ཡིས། སྤྱི་ལོ་ ༡༥༩༠ ནས་ ༡༨༣༥ བར་དུ་དང་།36 ཡོ་སེབ་ཀྱིས། སྤྱི་ལོ་ ༡༥༨༧ ནས ༡༥༩༨ བར་དུ་དང་།37 སླེལལ་གྲོ་བེ་དང་། སྐོ་རུ་པ་གཉིས་ཀྱིས། འབྲུངས་ལོ་དེ། སྤྱི་ལོ་ ༡༥༧༠ དང་ གྲོངས་ལོ་དེ་ ༡༨༦༣ ལ་ཡིན་པ་དང་།38 རབ་རྒྱས་ཀྱིས་། སྤྱི་ལོ་ ༡༥༩༠ ནས་ ༡༨༣༠ བར་དུ་ངོས་འཛིན་མཛད་དོ། །39

འདི་དག་ཐམས་ཅད་ཀྱི་ནང་ནས། སྲིད་དབང་ལ་མངའ་གསོལ་བའི་དུས་སྐབས་དེ། ཀཧྲིང་ཟླམ་ཉིད་ཕལ་ཆེར་འཐད་པར་མཐོང་ཞིང་། གྲོངས་པའི་ལོ་དུས་སྐོར་ལ་ནི་ཁོང་གིས་ཀྱང་ཚོད་འཕྱིགས་མི་འདུག། སླེལལ་གྲོ་བེ་དང་སྐོ་རུ་པ་སྐི་གཉིས་ཀྱིས། གྲོངས་པའི་ལོ་དེ། **ཆོས་རྗེ་སྟག་ཚང་གི་རྣམ་ཐར་**ན་གསལ་བ་བཞིན། འཐད་པ་དང་ལྡན་ཡང་།40 འབྲུངས་པའི་ལོ་དུས་དེ་ནི་འཐད་ལྡན་དུ་མ་མཐོང་ངོ་། །

བྱམས་པ་ལྷ་ཁང་ཆེན་མོ་

བ་མགོའི་མཁར་གྱི་ལྷ་ཁང་དེ་དག་གི་ནང་ནས། བྱམས་པའི་ལྷ་ཁང་དེ་རྙིང་ཤོས་དང་། རྒྱལ་རབས་ལོ་རྒྱུས་དང་། ཆགས་སྤྱོལ་བཟང་པོའི་ཤེས་རིག་ལ། གལ་ཆེན་པོ་ཡིན། འདིར་རྗེ་བཙུན་བྱམས་པའི་སྐུ་འདྲ་ཆེན་མོ། ཐོག་ཚད་གསུམ་པ་བྱིན་རླབས་ཀྱི་འོད་འཕྲོ་བ་དང་། འདུ་ཁང་གི་སྒོ་ལོགས་ཀྱི་ལྡེབས་རིས་སུ། བཅོམ་ལྡན་འདས་རྡོ་རྗེ་སེམས་དཔའ། དེ་ཡི་གཡས་གཡོན་དུ་རྗེ་བཙུན་མ་སྒྲོལ་མ་དཀར་ལྗང་། རྒྱལ་ཆེན་བཞི། གཞན་ཡང་ཞི་བ་དང་དྲག་པོའི་ལྷ་རྣམས་བཞུགས། ནུབ་ངོས་ཀྱི་ལྡེབས་རིས་སུ། དུས་གསུམ་སངས་རྒྱས། རྗེ་ཙོང་ཁ་པ་

---

35 ཀ་ཧྲིང་ཟླམ། ཤོག ༣༣༦།

36 ཕྲནཙ་ཀེ། དེབ་གཉིས་པ། ཤོག ༡༠༤།

37 ཡོ་སེབ། ཤོག ༣༥༩ དང་ ༣༤༨།

38 སླེལྷ་གྲོ་བེ་དང་། སྐོར་རུ་པ་སྐི་ ཤོག ༤༨།

39 རབ་རྒྱས། ཤོག ༡༧༤།

40 ཀུན་དགའ། མདུན་ཤོག ༦༠།

ལ་བཀའ་གདམས་གསར་མའི་བླ་བརྒྱུད་ཀྱིས་བསྐོར་བ། ཤར་ངོས་ཀྱི་ལྡེབས་རིས་སུ། རྒྱལ་བ་རྡོ་རྗེ་འཆང་། སྟོན་པ་ཐུབ་པའི་དབང་པོ། མཁས་གྲུབ་ཆེན་པོ་འབྲུག་པ་པདྨ་དཀར་པོ།41 འཕགས་པ་སྤྱན་རས་གཟིགས་ལ་སོགས་པ་བཞུགས་ཤིང་། ཤར་ངོས་ཀྱི་ལྡེབས་རིས་རྣམས། ལྡེབས་རིས་གཞན་གཉིས་ལ་བལྟོས་ཏེ། བྲིས་རགས་པ་དང་། ཚོན་རྩི་མདངས་ཞན་པས། དུས་གཞན་ཞིག་ལ་ལྷ་བྲིས་པ་གཞན་གྱིས་བཞེངས་པ་ཡིན་པར་མངོན། གཞན་ཡང་སློབ་དཔོན་ཆེན་པོ་པད་མ་འབྱུང་གནས་དང་། གྲུབ་ཆེན་མི་ལ་རས་པ་སོགས། ཕྱིས་སུ་བཞེངས་པ་བཞུགས། ནུབ་ངོས་ལྡེབས་རིས་ཆེན་མོ་ཀུན་གྱི་འོག་ཏུ། སྟོན་པ་སངས་རྒྱས་ཀྱི། མཛད་པ་བཅུ་གཉིས་དང་། ལྷོ་སྒོ་ཕྱོགས་ཀྱི་ལྡེབས་རིས་ལྷ་སྐུ་རྣམས་ཀྱི་འོག་ཏུ། རྒྱལ་བློན་རྣམས་དང་། བཙུན་མོ་རྣམས། འབངས་དྲུང་འཁོར་རྣམས་ཀྱིས་གུས་བཀུར་ཞུ་ཚུལ་དང་། རྩེད་མོ་འབྱུལ་བ་སོགས་ཀྱི། དགའ་སྟོན་ཚོགས་པའི་བྲིས་གཟུགས་མཆིས། །

འདིར་ཆོས་རྒྱལ་ཆེན་པོ་ཚེ་དབང་རྣམ་རྒྱལ་བཞུགས་སོ་ཞེས་ཡིག་གཟུགས་དང་དག་ཆ་ལེགས་པ་རང་མེད་པ་ཞིག་བྲིས་འདུག། གོང་དུ་གསལ་བ་བཞིན་རྗེ་ཙོང་ཁ་པའི་བྲིས་སྐུ་གཙོ་བོར་བྱས་ཏེ། བཞུགས་པ་ལ་དཔགས་ན། གཏིང་མོ་སྒང་གི་བྱམས་པའི་ལྷ་ཁང་བཞིན་དུ། དེའི་དུས་འདི་ཡི་དཀོན་གཉེར་དགེ་ལུགས་པ་ཡིན་ཀྱང་། རྒྱལ་པོ་འཇམ་དབྱངས་རྣམ་རྒྱལ་གྱི་དུས་སུ་འདི་ཡི་དཀོན་གཉེར་ལ་འབྲུག་ལུགས་ཀྱི་གྲྭ་པ་བཞུགས་པ་**ཆོས་རྗེ་སྟག་ཚང་རྣམ་ཐར་**ན་གསལ།

གང་ལྟར་ཡང་འདི་ཉིད་ནམ་བཞེངས་པ་དང་། སུས་བཞེངས་པའི་སྐོར་ལ། ལོ་རྒྱུས་སླ་བ་པོ་རྣམས་ལ་བཞེད་ཚུལ་མི་འདྲ་བ་འདུག། ཕྲན་ཙཀཱ་ཡིས། རྩིགས་པའི་ལྡེབས་རིས་ལ། རྒྱལ་པོ་ཚེ་དབང་རྣམ་རྒྱལ་དང་པོ་དང་། དེའི་སྐུ་མཆེད་གཉིས་སོགས་སྐུ་འཁོར་ལྷན་རྒྱས་དང་བཅས་པའི་བྲིས་གཟུགས་དང་། དེའི་འོག་ཏུ་ཡོད་པའི་མཆན་བྱང་དང་བཅས་པ་ལ་གཞིར་བཟུང་སྟེ། གཙུག་ལག་ཁང་འདི། རྒྱལ་པོ་ཚེ་དབང་རྣམ་རྒྱལ་དང་པོས་བཞེངས་པར་བཤད།42 རང་རེའི་ལ་དྭགས་ཀྱི་རྒྱལ་རབས་སླ་བ་བཀྲ་ཤིས་རབ་རྒྱས་ཀྱིས། ལ་དྭགས་པ་ལ་ཉེ་བར་མཁོ་

41 གྲུབ་པའི་དབང་ཕྱུག་འདི་ཉིད། རབ་འབྱུང་དགུ་པའི་མེ་ཕག་ལོར། སྤྱི་ལོ་ ༡༥༢༧། སྐུ་འཁྲུངས། རབ་བྱུང་བཅུ་པའི་ཆུ་འབྲུག་ལོར། སྤྱི་ལོ་ ༡༥༩༢། སྐུ་མྱ་ངན་ལས་འདས་སོ། །

42 ཕྲན་ཙཀཱ། དེབ་དང་པོ། ཤོག ༥༦་དང་༥༧།

བའི་གདམ་རྒྱུད་གསལ་ཞིང་འཇེབས་པ་དུ་མས་གདམས་པ། རིན་པོ་ཆེའི་རྒྱན་ལྟ་བུ། རྣམ་དཔྱོད་དང་ལྡན་པ་རྣམས་ཀྱི་མགྲིན་པར་རྒྱན་དུ་གདག་པར་འོས་པ། **མར་ཡུལ་ལ་དྭགས་ཀྱི་སྟོན་རབས་ཀུན་གསལ་མེ་ལོང་དུ།** བྱམས་པ་འདི་ཉིད། སྤྱི་ལོ་བརྒྱ་རབས་བཅོ་ལྔ་པའི་ནང་དུ།རྒྱལ་པོ་གྲགས་པ་འབུམ་ལྡེས་གཉིང་མོ་སྒང་གི་བྱམས་པ་བཞེངས་དུས་སུ་བ་མགོའི་བྱམས་པ་འདི་དང་། གླིའི་བྱམས་པ་རྣམས་ཀྱང་བཞེངས་པ་ཡིན་ཞེས་བྲིས།43 འོན་ཀྱང་གཉིང་སྒང་བྱམས་པ་བཞེངས་བ་པོའི་སྐོར་ལ། ལ་དྭགས་ཀྱི་རྒྱལ་རབས་ལ་གཅེས་སྤྲས་ཀྱིས་འཚོལ་སྒྲུབ་མཛད་པ་པོ་མིས་པོ་བསོད་ནམས་ཚེ་བརྟན་ཡོ་སེབ་ཀྱི་བཞེད་པ། རབ་རྒྱས་ཀྱི་བཞེད་པ་དང་མི་མཐུན་པ་མཆིས། ཁོང་གིས་གཉིང་མོ་སྒང་གི་བྱམས་པ་དེ་གྲགས་པ་འབུམ་ལྡེ་རྒྱལ་པོ་ཆེ་བས་བཞེངས་པ་མ་ཡིན་པ། གྲགས་པ་འབུམ་རྒྱལ་པོ་ཆུང་བས། ཙོང་ཁ་པའི་ཐུགས་བརྟགས་ལ་བརྟེན་ནས་བཞེངས་པར་བཤད་ཀྱང་། བདེན་པར་མི་སྣང་སྟེ། གྲགས་པ་འབུམ་གྱིས་ཙོང་ཁ་པའི་བང་ཆེན་བྱ་བྲལ་བ་གཉིས་པོ་དང་ཐུག་ཕྲད་མཛད་མེད་པ་དེ་**ལ་དྭགས་རྒྱལ་རབས་**རང་ན་གསལ་བས་སོ། །

དེས་ན་རབ་རྒྱས་ཀྱི་བཞེད་ཚུལ་དེ་བདེན་པ་ཡིན་ན། བྱམས་པའི་ལྷ་ཁང་དེ་གོང་གི་ཕྲན་ཙ་ཀའི་བཞེད་ཚུལ་དེ་ལས། ལོ་བརྒྱ་འཁོར་སྔོན་དུ་གྲུབ་ནས། ལྡེབས་རིས་ངོ་མཚར་ཅན་དེ་ཀུན། རྒྱལ་པོ་ཆེ་དབང་རྣམ་རྒྱལ་ལམ་གྱི་དུས་སུ་ལྷོ་ངོས་དང་། ནུབ་ངོས་ཀྱི་ལྡེབས་རིས་རྣམས་བཞེངས་པར་ངེས་ཤིང་། ཤར་ངོས་ཀྱི་ལྡེབས་རིས་དེ་རྣམས་ནི་ཕྱིས་སུ་བཞེངས་པར་མངོན་ཏེ། ལྡེབས་རིས་རྩིག་ལོགས་གཞན་གཉིས་པོ་ལས་དཔགས་ཏེ། འདི་ཡི་ཚོན་རྩི་ཞན་པ་དང་རི་མོ་ཀུན་ཀྱང་རགས་པར་སྣང་། །སླེལྷ་གྲོ་བེ་དང་། སྐར་རྩྭ་སྐེ་གཉིས་ཀྱིས་ཀྱང་། ཆོས་རྗེ་འབྲུག་པ་པདྨ་དཀར་པོའི་བྲིས་སྐུ་བཞུགས་པའི་རྒྱུ་མཚན་གྱིས། ལྡེབས་རིས་འདི་ཕྱིས་སུ། སླར་ཡང་སྐྱར་དུ་བསྐྱུན་པ་ཡིན་པར་བྲིས་སོ། །44

རབ་རྒྱས་ཀྱིས་བྲིས་པའི་གྲགས་འབུམ་མཆན་ཅན་རྒྱལ་པོ་རྣམ་གཉིས་དང་གཤམ་ཕྱོགས་སྐུ་གསུང་ཐུགས་རྟེན་ལ་སྐུ་མཆེད་གཉིས་ཀས་དད་གུས་ཞུ་ཚུལ་གྱི་ཉིང་དོན་གཤམ་གསལ་ལྟར་ཡིན་འདུ

---

43   རབ་རྒྱས།   ཤོག   ༡༣༣།

44   སླེལྷ་གྲོ་བེ་དང་།   སྐར་རྩྭ་སྐེ་   ཤོག   ༨༥།

སྐུ་ཚེའི་སྐྱོད་དུ་གྲགས་འབུམ་ལྡེས་ལ་དྭགས་གཤམ་སྟོད་གཉིས་ཀར་མངའ་དབང་མཛད་ཀྱང་། ཕྱིས་སུ་གྲགས་འབུམ་ གྱིས་གཤམ་ཕྱོགས་མངའ་དབང་འཕྲོགས་ཤིང་། རྒྱལ་པོར་གྱུར་ཏེ་གཤམ་ཕྱོགས་ཀྱི་སྲིད་ལེགས་པར་བསྐྱངས། ཆོས་རྒྱལ་གྲགས་འབུམ་ལྡེས་བཞེངས་པའི་རྗེ་བཙུན་བྱམས་པ་དང་། རྙེད་པའི་འཕགས་པ་སྤྱན་རས་གཟིགས་རྣམ་གཉིས་ལ་གྲགས་འབུམ་གྱིས་ཀྱང་དད་མོས་དག་སྣང་ཆེན་པོ་མཛད་དོ། །45

གཉིང་མོ་སྒང་གི་བྱམས་པ་དང་། བ་མགོའི་བྱམས་པ་དང་། གླིའི་བྱམས་པ་རྣམས་ཀྱི་ལྡེབས་རིས་སོགས་ལ་མཉམ་བསྡུར་བརྟག་དཔྱད་ཞུ་འོས་ཀྱང་། གཉིང་མོ་སྒང་དང་། གླིའི་བྱམས་པའི་ལྷ་ཁང་གི་སྔར་གྱི་རྟིག་པ་ཀུན་ད་ལྟ་ཞིག་ནས་མེད། བ་མགོའི་ལྷ་ཁང་གི་རྟིག་པ་མ་ཞིག་པར་ལུས་པ་ནི། ཤར་དང་། ནུབ་དང་། བྱང་གི་ཕྱོགས་ཀུན་ལ་ཕྱིས་སུ་རྟིག་པ་གཞན་བསྐོར་ནས་བརྩིགས་པ་དེ་ཡི་རྐྱེན་གྱིས་ཡིན་པར་སེམས།46 གཉིང་མོ་སྒང་བྱམས་པའི་ལྷ་ཁང་དེ། སྤྱི་ལོ་ ༡༩༨༣ ནས་ ༡༩༨༥ བར་དུ། གསར་དུ་བཞེངས་པར་སྔར་གྱི་ལྡེབས་རིས་དག་མཐའ་དུ་མེད་ཀྱང་། རྗེ་བཙུན་བྱམས་པའི་སྐུ་བརྙན་ནི་སྔར་གྱི་དེ་རང་ཡིན་པ། ད་ལྟར་ཡང་མ་ཉམས་པར་བཞུགས། སྐུ་བརྙན་དེ་ཉིད་དང་། འདུ་ཁང་འོག་མའི་ཐོག་གི་རི་མོ་མི་ཏོག་གི་དཀྱིལ་འཁོར་དེ་ཀུན་དང་། བ་མགོ་བྱམས་པའི་སྐུ་བརྙན་དེ་དང་། ཐོག་གི་མི་ཏོག་གི་དཀྱིལ་འཁོར་ཀུན་ལ་མཉམ་སྡུར་མཛད་དེ། དེ་དག་ལྷ་བཟོ་པ་གཅིག་གིས་བཞེངས་པ་ཡིན་ནམ་མ་ཡིན། བཟོ་རྩལ་སྐོར་ལ། རྣམ་དཔྱོད་དང་ལྡན་པ་རྣམས་ཀྱིས། བརྟག་དཔྱད་མཛད་ཐུབ་པའི་གཞིར་བཞུགས་སོ། །47

---

45 རབ་རྒྱས། ཤོག ༡༣༨ དང༌ ༡༣༥ སྤྱན་རས་གཟིགས་ཇོ་དཀར་ལ་གྲུབ་པ་འདི་ཉིད་ད་ལྟར་བཞུགས་ཤིང་། བྱིན་རླབས་ཀྱང་ཆེ་བར་བརྩིའོ། །

46 ནེ་ཤིལ་ ཇོ་ལྷན། ཁོང་གིས་བ་མགོའི་མཁར་འགོག་དང་། དགོན་པ་ཀུན་གྱི་རྟིག་པའི་སྐོར་ལ་བྲིས་སོ། །

47 །སྣེལླ་གྲོ་བེ་དང་། སྐོར་རུཔ་སྐེ་ཤོག ༡༠༨། གཉིང་སྒང་གི་བྱམས་པའི་སྐུ་བརྙན་དེ་ཉིད་ཤིན་ཏུ་མཛེས་པ་དང་། འདུ་ཁང་འོག་མའི་ཐོག་གི་རི་མོ་མི་ཏོག་གི་དཀྱིལ་འཁོར་ཀུན། སྔར་གྱི་རི་མོའི་གྲས་འདི་ཁོ་ན་ལུས་ཡོད་པ། དེ་དག་གི་དབྱིབས་བཀོད་སྣང་ས་དེ་དག་ལ་ལྟ་དུས། བ་མགོའི་བྱམས་པའི་ལྷ་ཁང་གི་རི་མོའི་བཀོད་སྣང་ས་དེ་སེམས་ལ་འཆར་རོ། །ཞེས་བྲིས་སོ།

ལ་དྭགས་རྒྱལ་རབས་སུ་རྒྱལ་པོ་གྲགས་པ་འབུམ་ལྡེས་བ་མགོ་རུ་བྱམས་པ་བཞེངས་པ་མི་གསལ་ཀྱང་། འདི་ལྟར་གསལ་ཏོ།

**གྲགས་འབུམ་ལྡེས། བློ་ལ་སོགས་པར་མངའ་མཛད་ནས། རྒྱ་མ་ཕྱག
རྗེས་སུ་གཙུག་ལག་ཁང་མང་པོ་[48]བཞེངས་ནས། རྒྱལ་བ་བྱམས་པ་
མགོན་པོ་དགུང་ལོ་བརྒྱད་པའི་ཚད་དང་། གཡས་གཡོན་གཉིས་སུ་
འཇམ་དབྱངས་ཕྱག་ན་རྡོ་རྗེ་གཉིས་ཐོག་ཚད་རེ་བཞེངས། གཙུག་ལག་ཁང་
བཞེངས་ནས་རྗེ་བཙུན་བྱམས་པའི་སྐུ་འདྲ་སོགས་བཞེངས། ལོགས་བྲིས་
རྣམས་ལ་བདེ་བར་གཤེགས་པ་རྣམས་ཀྱི་འདྲ་སྐུ་དང་། འཇིག་རྟེན་
བརྟན་བཞག་དང་། རང་ཉིད་མོས་པའི་ལྷ་རྣམས་ཚང་བ་དང་། ལྷ་
ཁང་སུམ་བརྩེགས་མཐོ་ལྡིང་[49]གི་དཔེ་རུ་བཞེངས། །**

འདི་བཞིན་དམར་པོ་ཞེས་པའི་ཚིག་དེ་མ་དག་པ་དང་། མང་པོ་ཞེས་པའི་ཚིག་དེ་དག་པ་ཡིན་ན། རབ་རྒྱས་ཀྱི་བྲིས་པ་དེ་བདེན་པར་སྣང་ངོ་། །བ་མགོ་བྱམས་པའི་ལྷ་ཁང་ལ་གོང་གསལ་གྱི་མཚན་ཉིད་ཚང་སྟེ། བྱམས་པའི་གཡས་གཡོན་གཉིས་ན་བྱང་ཆུབ་སེམས་དཔའི་འདྲ་སྐུ་ཐོག་ཚད་རེ་བཞུགས་པ་**འཇམ་དབྱངས་དང་། ཕྱག་ན་རྡོ་རྗེ**་དང་། **བདེ་བར་གཤེགས་པ**་གསུམ་དང་རྗེ་ཙོང་ཁ་པའི་འདྲ་སྐུ་ནུབ་ངོས་ཀྱི་ལྡེབས་རིས་ལ་བཞུགས་པ་དང་། རྡོ་རྗེ་སེམས་དཔའ་དང་རྗེ་བཙུན་མ་སྒྲོལ་དཀར་དང་། སྒྲོལ་ལྗང་སོགས་ལྷོ་ངོས་ཀྱི་ལྡེབས་རིས་ལ་བཞུགས་པ་སོགས་**རང་ཉིད་མོས་པའི་ལྷ**་དང་། **འཇིག་རྟེན་བརྟན་བཞག**་ཅེས་པ་རྒྱལ་བློན་འཁོར་བཅས་ཀྱི་བཞུགས་གྲལ་ལ་གོ་བ་སླངས་པ་ཡིན། དེ་མིན་ཚིག་འདིའི་དོན་བདག་གིས་ངོ་རྟོགས་མ་སོང་། འདི་རྣམས་འོལ་ཚོད་ཀྱིས་བྲིས་པ་ཡིན་གྱི། ཁུངས་ཐུབ་པས་བྲིས་པ་མ་ཡིན། མཁྱེན་པའི་སྤྱན་རས་ཡངས་པ་རྣམས་ཀྱིས་ཕྱིས་སུ། འཚོལ་སྒྲུབ་མཛད་དེ། ཇི་ལྟར་ཡིན་པ

---

48 ད་ལྟའི་དཔེ་ཆ་དག་ཏུ་དམར་པོ་ཞེས་གསལ་ཀྱང་། དབྱིན་ཡུལ་ལན་དོན་དུ་ཡོད་པའི་དཔེ་ཆ་དེའི་ནང་མང་པོ་ཞེས་བྲིས་པ་དག་པ་ཡིན་པའི་རྩིས་བྱས། འདིར་མང་པོ་ཞེས་བཀོད་པ། བདེན་པ་ཡིན་མིན་ངེས་པ་མེད། བརྟག་དཔྱད་མཛོད།

49 ལྷ་བླ་མ་ཡེ་ཤེས་འོད་ཀྱིས་བཞེངས་པ་**དེབ་ཐེར་སྔོན་པོར**་གསལ། དེབ། ཤོག ༨༩

གདན་ལ་འབེབས་པར་མཛོད། ལྷ་ཁང་སུམ་བརྩེགས་ཞེས་པ་ནི་ཐོག་ཚད་གསུམ་གྱི་མཐོ་ཚད་ཡོད་པས། སུམ་བརྩེགས་ཞེས་པ་ཡིན། དཔེར་ན་ཨ་ལྩི་སུམ་བརྩེགས་ལྷ་ཁང་ལ་སྙིང་འོག་གཉིས་མ་གདོགས་མེད་ཀྱང་། སུམ་བརྩེགས་ཟེར་བ་ལྟ་བུ་ཡིན་ནམ་སྙམ། རྒྱུ་མཚན་དེས་ན། གྲགས་འབུམ་ཕྱིས་བཞེངས་པའི་ཕྱིབས་རིས་རྣམས་ལ་ཆར་ཆུ་སོགས་ཀྱིས་ཞིག་སྐྱོན་སོང་སྟེ། སྔར་གྱི་ཕྱིབས་རིས་དང་འདྲ་བ་བྱས་ཏེ། ཆོས་རྒྱལ་ཆེ་དབང་རྣམ་རྒྱལ་གྱི་དུས་སུ། ཕྱིབས་རིས་སོ་མ་བཞེངས་པ་ཡང་ཡིན་སྲིད། ཤར་ངོས་ཀྱི་ཕྱིབས་རིས་རྣམས། འཇམ་དབྱངས་རྣམ་རྒྱལ་སོགས་ཀྱི་སྐབས་སུ་བཞེངས་པ་ཡིན་པ། འཚོལ་སྒྲུབ་བརྟག་དཔྱད་ཀྱི་གཞིར་གནས་སོ། །

དབྱིན་ཡུལ་པ་མཁས་པ། སྨིཐ་གྲོབ་དང་། སྐོ་རྩབ་སྐྱི་གཉིས་ཀྱིས་བྱམས་པ་གཙུག་ལག་ཁང་སྐོར་ལ་འདི་ལྟར་བྲིས་ཏེ།

རྗེ་བཙུན་བྱམས་པའི་སྐུ་འདྲ་འདི་མཛེས་ཤིང་། ཡིད་དུ་འོང་བ་བཞུགས། ཨ་ལྩི་ཆོས་འཁོར་དམིགས་བསལ་བྱས་པའི་རྗེང་ན། གཙུག་ལག་ཁང་འདི་ཉིད་རྙིང་ཤོས་ཡིན་པ། མཁས་པ་རྣམས་ཀྱིས་མཉམ་བསྡུར་ལྟ་རྟོག་བྱེད་ཐུབ་པའི་གཞིར་བཞུགས། དོན་སྙིང་པོ་ནི། རྟེན་དང་བརྟེན་པར་བཅས་པའི་གཙུག་ལག་ཁང་ངོ་མཚར་ཆེ་ཞིང་། ཟླ་དུ་བྱུང་བའི་ཁྱད་ཆོས་དང་ལྡན་པ་ཞིག་སྟེ། ཕལ་ཆེར་ལོ་ངོ་གསུམ་བརྒྱའི་རིང་ལ་སུས་ཀྱང་། ལག་པས་གནོད་པ་བསྐྱལ་མེད་པར་བཞུགས་ལ། བཟོ་བོའི་ཆ་ནས་བཤད་ན། འདི་དག་ཐུན་ལེགས་པ། དབྱིབས་འགོད་སྣང་ས་མཚུངས་པ། ཚོན་རྩི་འབྱུག་སྣང་ས་ཆ་སྙོམས་པ་བཅས་གསལ་པོར་མངོན་ཐུབ། འདུ་ཁང་གི་ཐོག་དེར་ཡང་། མེ་ཏོག་གི་དཀྱིལ་འཁོར་དང་། སྔགས་ཀྱི་ཡིག་འབྲུ་རྣམས་ཀྱི་དཀྱིལ་འཁོར་གསལ་ལ། གཟི་རྗིད་དང་ལྡན་པ་ཡིད་དུ་འོང་བ་མང་པོས་ལེགས་པར་བརྒྱན་པ་བཅས་བཞུགས་སོ། །50

50 སྨིཐ་གྲོབ་དང་། སྐོ་རྩབ་སྐྱི། ཤོག ༩༦།

བྱམས་ཆུང་ལྷ་ཁང་

མཁར་གྱི་རྒྱ་སྒོའི་སྙིང་ཙམ་ན། བྱམས་ཆུང་ལྷ་ཁང་ཞེས་པའི། ལྷ་ཁང་རྙིངས་པ་ཞིག་བཞུགས།
གཙུག་ལག་ཁང་འདིའི་ཕྱི་ལོགས་ཀྱི་བཟོ་དབྱིབས་དེ། ཐལ་དེའི་མས་ཇིད་ལྷ་བུར་སྣང་།[51]
རྒྱལ་མོ་ཁ་ཏུན་རང་ཉིད་ནང་པར་གྱུར་པའི་རྗེང་ན། གསེར་སྤྱངས་བྱམས་པ་གྲུབ་པའི་སྔོན་དུ།
མས་ཇིད་དེ་ཉིད་རྗེ་བཙུན་བྱམས་པའི་ལྷ་ཁང་དུ། རྒྱལ་མོ་རང་ཉིད་ཀྱི་ཐུགས་ཀྱི་ཐུགས་འདོད་
བཞིན་དུ་བསྒྱུར་ཏེ། དེའི་ནང་དུ། རྗེ་བཙུན་བྱམས་པའི་སྐུ་འད་འདི་དང་། ཡིབས་རིས་
ཙ་མཚར་ཅན་ཀུན་བཞེངས། ཉི་མའི་མདངས་འཕོག་པ་མེད་པའི་རྐྱེན་གྱིས། སྤྱིར་བཏང་།
སྐུ་འདྲ་ཞལ་བྱང་ལ་གཟིགས་པ། བཞེང་སྲོལ་མེད་ཀྱང་། ཁང་པ་བརྩིགས་ཟིན་པའི་དབང་གིས།
འདིར་བྱམས་པའི་སྐུ་བརྙན་དེ་ཞལ་བྱང་ལ་གཟིགས་དགོས་པ་བྱུང་། འདིར་རྒྱལ་བ་བྱམས་པ་སྐྱིལ་
ཀྲུང་དུ་བཞུགས། ཡིབས་རིས་སུ་འཇམ་མགོན་བླ་མ་ཤར་ཙོང་ཁ་པ་ཆེན་པོ་དང་། དཔལ་
གསང་བ་འདུས་པ། བདེ་མཆོག་འཁོར་ལོ་སྡོམ་པ། དཔལ་རྡོ་རྗེ་འཇིགས་བྱེད། དགེ་ལུགས་
པའི་སྲུང་མའི་གཙོ་བོ། དམ་ཅན་ཆོས་ཀྱི་རྒྱལ་པོ་ལ་སོགས་པ། ལྷ་བྲིས་ངོ་མཚར་ཆེ་བ་དང་ལྡན་
པ་རྣམས་བཞུགས་པ། ཞིག་གསོའི་ཕྱིར། མཐུན་རྐྱེན་མེད་པས། ད་ལྟ་ལྷ་ཁང་འདི་ཉིད་
འཇོལ་བ་ལ་མངོན་དུ་ཕྱོགས་པས། ལྷ་ཁང་འདི་ལ། ཅི་མགྱོགས་ཉམས་གསོ་ཞུ་དགོས་པར་
འཚལ་ལོ། །[52]

གསེར་སྤྱངས་གཙུག་ལག་ཁང་

ཡབ་རྒྱལ་པོ་འཇམ་དབྱངས་རྣམ་རྒྱལ་གྱི། རྒྱལ་བ་བྱམས་པའི་སྐུ་འདྲ་བཞེང་བའི་རྩིས། གར་
ལོག་གི་དམག་ལ་སོགས་པས། དུས་མ་བདེ་བས་མཐར་མ་ཕྱིན་པར་ལུས་པ། ཡབ་ཀྱི་
དགོངས་རྫོགས་ཕྱིར། རྒྱལ་པོ་སེང་གེ་རྣམ་རྒྱལ་སྐུ་གཞོན་ནུའི་དུས་སུ། སླར་བཟོ་སྐྲུབ་པར་
བཀའ་གྲོས་ཏེ། ནག་བརྟུངས་ཙམ་གྲུབ་ཡོད་པར། ཆོས་ཀྱི་རྗེ་སྟག་ཚང་རས་པས་བགེགས་སྒྲོད་

---

51 རབ་རྒྱས། ཤོག ༡༥༧།

52 ཀླུ་གྲོ་བེ་དང་། སྒོར་རུཔ་སྒོ་གཉིས་ཀྱིས་འདིར་སྐལ་བཟང་སྒྲོལ་མའི་མཚན་ཡོད་པའི་ཡིག་བྲིས་ཡོད་པར་བཤད་པ་ནི། ན་ཞིང་བདག་གིས་བཙལ་ཀྱང་མ་རྙེད།

མཛད། གསེར་སོགས་ཞུལ་རྒྱུར་ལུས་པ་ལ་མཐུན་རྐྱེན་རྣམས་བསྒྲིགས་ཏེ། བཟོ་པ་ཀུན་བོས་པར་མཛད། རབ་བྱུང་བཅུ་གཅིག་པའི་ཆུ་ཁྲི་ལོར། སྤྱི་ལོ་ ༡༦༣༣། བཟོ་བཙམས་པའི་འགོ་ཚུགས། སྐུ་གསེར་ལ་ཞོ་ལྔ་བརྒྱ་ལས་ལྷག་པ་དང་། རྒྱལ་མོ་ཁ་ཏུན་གྱིས་ཕྲ་རྒྱན་རྣམས་ཕུལ། ཆུ་ཕག་ལོར། སྤྱི་ལོ་ ༡༦༣༣། རྗེ་བཙུན་བྱམས་པའི་སྐུ་བརྙན་མཆར་ལ། གཟི་བྱིན་ཅན་དེ། གཙུག་ལག་ཁང་དང་བཅས་པ་ལེགས་པར་བཞེངས་གྲུབ། ཆོས་རྗེ་སྟག་ཚང་རས་པས་དབུ་གཙོས། གྲྭ་པ་དང་སྒྲུབ་པ་བརྒྱ་ཕྲག་གིས། འཁོར་ལོ་སྡོམ་པའི་སྒོ་ནས་རབ་གནས་མཛད། རྒྱལ་བློན་དྲུང་འཁོར་སྟོང་ཕྲག་ཙམ་དང་། བཟོ་རིག་པ་བརྒྱད་ཅུ། ཉེ་སྐོར་ཡུལ་མི་བརྒྱ་ཕྲག་བཅུ་གཉིས་ཙམ་འཛོམས་ཏེ། ཚོགས་འཁོར་འབུལ་བ་ལ་སོགས་པ། རབ་གནས་དགའ་སྟོན་རྒྱ་ཆེན་མོ་མཛད་དོ། །53

འདིར་གསེར་སྐུ་བྱམས་པ། ཐོག་ཚད་གཉིས་ཙམ་ཡིན་པ། གཟི་འོད་འབར་བ་བཞུགས། ཞིབས་རིས་རྣམས་སུ། རྣམ་པར་སྣང་མཛད། མི་སྐྱོད་པ། རིན་ཆེན་འབྱུང་ལྡན། འོད་དཔག་མེད། དོན་ཡོད་གྲུབ་པ་བཅས་རྒྱལ་བ་རིགས་ལྔ་དང་། རྒྱ་མཐོང་དུ། དཔལ་བཀའ་བརྒྱུད་པའི་བླ་བརྒྱུད་རྒྱལ་བ་རྡོ་རྗེ་འཆང་དང། གྲུབ་ཆེན་ཏེལློ་པ་དང་ན་རོ་པ། མར་པ་ལོ་ཙ་བ་ཆོས་ཀྱི་བློ་གྲོས། རྣལ་འབྱོར་གྱི་དབང་ཕྱུག་མི་ལ་རས་པ་ལ་སོགས་པ་དང་། འདུ་ཁང་དུ། བཀའ་འགྱུར་བྲིས་མ་ཆ་ཚང་དང་། སེང་དམག་གིས་བརླག་གཏོར་བཏང་བའི་ལྷག་ལུས། པོ་ཏི་མང་པོ་གསེར་དང་། དངུལ་དང་། ཟངས་ལ་སོགས་པ་རིན་པོ་ཆེའི་རིགས་བཏུལ་བའི་སྣག་ཚས་བྲིས་པ་བཞུགས། གཟིམ་སྒོའི་ལོགས་སུ། སྲུང་མ་དཔལ་ལྡན་ལྷ་མོ་གསུང་འབྱོན་མ་དང་། སྙིང་གི་སངས་གཡབས་སུ། སངས་རྒྱས་ཀྱི་མཛད་པ་བཅུ་གཉིས་སོགས་ཞིབས་རིས་ངོ་མཚར་དང་ལྡན་པ་རྣམས་བཞུགས་སོ། །

དགེ་སྦྱོར་བོད་བསྐྱལ་ཞུ་བ

གོང་གསལ་སྐུ་གསུང་ཐུགས་རྟེན་རྙིང་པ། ངོ་མཚར་ཅན་འདི་ཀུན། ལ་དྭགས་ཡོངས་ཀྱི་སྤྱི་རྫས། ཁྱད་པར་དུ་འཕགས་པའི་གྲས་ཡིན་པ་འདི་དག། ཆར་ཆུ་དང་། ལྷུང་དྲག་གིས་རྩ་མེད་དུ་བརླག་པའི་དུས་འདིར། བ་སྒོ་པ་དད་པ་དང་ལྡན་པ་མང་པོས་དྭངས་བླངས་

53 ཀུན་དགའ། རྒྱབ་ཤོག ༣༠།

ཀྱིས་སྐྱོང་སྐྱོབ་ཞུས་ཏེ། དེང་དུས་གནས་སྐབས་ཆ་རྐྱེན་མ་འབྱོར་ཙམ་ཡོད་ཀྱང་། ཕྱོགས་ཡུན་རིང་ཙམ་བརྟན་པའི་ཞིག་གསོ་བྱེད་པ་ལ། བ་མགོ་པ་ཙམ་མ་ཡིན་པ། དགོན་བདག་ཏེ་མི་དགོན་པས་དབུ་གཙོས། ལ་དྭགས་ཀྱི་མི་མངས་ནང་ནས། རྣམ་པར་དཔྱོད་པའི་མཁྱེན་པ་དང་ལྡན་པ་དག་གིས། སངས་རྒྱས་དང་། བྱང་ཆུབ་སེམས་དཔའི་བྲིས་འབུར་གྱི་སྐུ་བརྙན་ངོ་མཚར་ཅན་འདི་རྣམས་ལྷུང་དྲག་དང་། ཆ་རྐྱེན་ངེབ་པ་ལས། ཐབས་མང་པོའི་སྒོ་ནས་སྐྱོང་སྐྱོབ་བདག་པོ་མཛད་དགོས་པར་འཚལ་ལོ། །

རྟེན་འདི་རྣམས་ཀྱི་ཞིག་གསོ་ཡི། ཞལ་འདེབས་མཚོན་བྱེད་དུ། ཕྱི་ལོ་ ༡༩༨༣ ལ་ངེད་ཀྱི་གྲོགས་པོ་བཟོ་བོའི་སློབ་དཔོན། མོ་རིས་ལོ་ཕྱི་མཆོག་གིས་ཞལ་འདེབས་ཕུལ་ཏེ། བྱམས་པའི་ལྷ་ཁང་དུ་འགྲོ་ལམ་ཞིག་རལ་གྱུར་པ། སླར་ཡང་ལམ་དེ་ཉིད། གད་པའི་ནང་ལ། བརྩིགས་ཐུབ་པ་དང་། དེའི་རྟེང་ནས། གཙུག་ལག་ཁང་གི་ཐོག་ཀ་ནས་ཆར་ཆུ་མི་འཛག་པའི་ཕྱིར། ཐོག་ཀ་བརྟན་པོར་བྱེད་པ་ལ། ངེད་རང་ངོས་ནས་ཀྱང་། ཞལ་འདེབས་ཕྲན་བུ་འབུལ་ཐུབ་པར་དགའ་བ་ཆེན་པོ་བྱུང་། དད་ལྡན་བ་མགོ་པ་ཀུན་གྱིས་རང་གི་དྭང་བླངས་ཀྱིས། ཉམས་གསོས་ལ་འབད་བརྩོན་མཛད་པ་ལ། རྗེས་སུ་ཡི་རང་བཅས་གུས་པ་བློ་བཟང་འཇམ་དཔལ་གྱིས། ཕྱི་ལོ་ ༡༩༩༣ ཟླ་བ་ ༧ ཚེས་ ༣༠ ལ་བྲིས་པ་དགེ་བར་གྱུར་ཅིག།

དེ་བཞིན་ན་ཞིང་གི་ལོར་རི་པིན་དུ་སྐུ་འཁྲུངས་པ་རྗེ་བཙུན་བྱམས་པ་ལ་དད་པ་དང་ལྡན་པ་བཙུན་མོ་ཏེ་དེ་ཀོ་ཕྲ་ཡ་མན་མཆོག་ནས་ཀྱང་བྱམས་པའི་གཙུག་ལག་ཁང་འདི་ཉིད་ཀྱི་ཉམས་གསོ་ཞུ་བའི་ཕྱིར་ཞལ་འདེབས་ཕུལ་པས་བ་མགོ་པ་རྣམས་ཀྱིས་ཉམས་གསོ་དྭང་བླང་གང་ནུས་ཞུ་བཞིན་པ་ལ་དགའ་བ་སྐྱེད་དོ། །

བྲིས་འདི་ཉིད་ལ་ ༡༩༩༥ ལོར་སླར་ཡང་ཞུས་དག་དང་འཕྲི་སྣོན་ཅི་རིགས་པ་བྱས་སོ། །

རྩར་དུ་ལུས་པ་དང་པོ་

རབ་འབྱུང་བཅུ་གཅིག་པའི་ལྕགས་རྟ་ལོར། སྤྱི་ལོ་ ༡༦༣༠། རྩ་མུ་རྟེ་འབངས་གྱིན་ལོག་གིས་གུ་གེ་འགྲོག་ཀུན་རྒྱལ་པོ་སེང་གེ་རྣམ་རྒྱལ་ལ་ཕུལ།54 ལོ་དེ་ར་རྗེ་རྟོད་ཚང་པའི་གནས་རྟེ་མིར་གཙུག་ལག་ཁང་སྐྲུབ་སྟེ་དང་བཅས་པ་བཏབ།55

རབ་བྱུང་བཅུ་གཅིག་པའི་ཆུ་སྤྲེལ་ལོར། སྤྱི་ལོ་ ༡༦༣༣། རང་ཉིད་དགུང་ལོ་ང་དགུ་པའི་སྐབས་སུ། སྟག་ཚང་རས་པ་ཆེན་པོ་བོད་དབུས་གཙང་དུ། ཕེབས་རྩིས་མཛད་ཀྱང་། རྒྱལ་པོ་སེང་གེ་རྣམ་རྒྱལ་གྱིས་ཕེབས་སུ་མ་བཅུག།56 དེ་ནས་ལྕགས་ཡོས་ལོར། སྤྱི་ལོ་ ༡༦༥༡། ཆོས་དབྱིངས་སུ་གཤེགས་སོ། །

ལྕགས་སྟག་ལོར། སྤྱི་ལོ་ ༡༦༥༠། སེང་གེ་རྣམ་རྒྱལ་སྲས་རྒྱལ་པོ་བདེ་ལྡན་རྣམ་རྒྱལ་སྙིང་ཞལ་སྲས་བློན་དྲུང་རིགས་བསྡུས་བཅས། ཆོས་རྗེ་སྟག་ཚང་སྐུ་མདུན་དུ། རྒྱལ་བུའི་མཚན་ཞུ་བར་ཕེབས། རྒྱལ་བུར་བདེ་ལེགས་རྣམ་རྒྱལ་ཞེས་མཚན་གསོལ།57 ཡང་ལོ་འདིར་སེང་གེ་རྣམ་རྒྱལ་བཙུན་མོ་རྒྱལ་མོ་སྐལ་བཟང་སྒྲོལ་མ། དབྱི་གུ་བརྒྱུད། ཉི་མ། ལྷན་ལི་ནས་ཟངས་དཀར་དུ་བྱོན། དེར་སྐུ་གཤེགས། ཤེལ་དཀར་པོ་བྲང་དུ་སྤུར་དྲུང་བར་སྤྱལ།58

དགའ་ལྡན་ཚེ་དབང་གིས་སྟེ་ཁྲིད་པའི་སོག་པོ་དང་བོད་དམག་གིས་བ་མགོའི་མཁར་བསྐོར་ནས་ལོ་ངོ་གསུམ་ལུས་པ། སྤྱི་ལོ་ ༡༦༨༡ ནས་ ༡༦༨༣ བར་ལ་ཡིན་དགོས།59

---

54 དེ་ཉིད་ཀྱི་ མདུན་ཤོག་ ༣༣།

55 དེ་ཉིད་ རྒྱབ་ཤོག་ ༣༣།

56 དེ་ཉིད་ རྒྱབ་ཤོག་ ༣༥།

57 དེ་ཉིད་ མདུན་ཤོག་ ༤༨།

58 དེ་ཉིད་ རྒྱབ་ཤོག།

59 **བོད་རྒྱ་ཚིག་མཛོད་ཆེན་མོ།** ཤོག་གྲངས། ༢༣༧༠ དང་། ཡོ་སེབ། ཤོག་གྲེ་ ༤༢༢ དང་ ༤༢༢ །

བཟུར་ལུས་གཉིས་པ་

སེང་དམག་གིས་བ་མགོའི་མཁར་གཏོར་བཤིག་དང་། ཤིན་ཏུ་ནས་འཕངས་པ་ནི། གསེར་གྱི་གླིགས་བམ་རྣམས་གཏོར་བཤིག་བྱས། གསེར་ཟངས་བྱམས་པའི། ཕྲ་རྒྱན་ཀུན་བཀོག་སྟེ། གསེར་དངུལ། གཡུ། བྱུ་རུ། མུ་ཏིག རག ཟངས་སོག་རིན་པོ་ཆེ་རིགས་ཏ་སྐལ་མང་པོ་ཇམ་མུ་རུ་བཀལ། ཡིག་དཔོན་ནམ་མཁའ་དཔལ་60སོགས་ཀྱིས་བྲིས་པའི། བཀའ་བསྟན་གླེགས་བམ་མང་པོ་གླེའི་དམག་སྐར་ཀྱི་ལྷ་དང་། གཞན་སེང་པའི་ཁང་པ་བརྩིགས་པའི་ཐོག་ཀུན་ལ་སྦྱར་རྩེ་སྲི་ལབ་ཚབ་ཏུ་བརྒྱབས།61

དེ་དུས་དབང་ཅན་དང་དབང་མེད་ཐུག་སྟེ། བ་མགོ་པ་སོགས་ལ་དྭགས་པ་ཉམས་ཆུང་ཀུན་གྱིས། སེང་པ་བཙན་དབང་ཅན་ཟོ་ར་ཝར་གྱི་ཅི་ཟེར་སྒྲུབ་དགོས་པ་བྱུང་། བ་མགོ་བཀའ་བློན་ནོ་ནོ་བསོད་ནམས་ཞེས་པའི་དཔའ་བོ་ལ་ཡང་། ནང་སེམས་ན། དགྲ་ལན་ལེན་པའི་དམ་བཅའ་ཡོད་ཀྱང་། སྐབས་ལ་མ་བབ་གྱི་བར་དུ། ཟོ་ར་ཝར་ཅི་ཟེར་ཉན་དགོས་ཀྱང་། སྐབས་ཐོབ་པ་ན་ཞུམ་པ་མེད་པར་སེང་པའི་དམག་དཔོན། ཟོ་ར་ཝར་ལྷ་པའི་ལམ་དུ་གཏོང་བ་པོ་ནི། ནོ་ནོ་བསོད་ནམས་ཡིན་ཞེས་པ་དང་། པཎ་ཆེན་བསྟན་པའི་ཉི་མ་ (༡༧༨༡ ནས་ ༡༨༥༣) ཞབས་ཀྱིས་སེང་པའི་དམག་དཔོན་དེ། ནོ་ནོ་བསོད་ནམས་ཀྱིས་འདུལ་ཐུབ་པའི་སྐབས་ལ་གཟིགས་ནས། ནོ་ནོ་དེ་ལ་བྱང་ཤམ་ལྷ་ལའི་ཞིང་བཀོད་ཀྱི་ཞལ་ཐང་ཞིག ཕྱག་རྟགས་ལ་བསྐུར་བར་མཛད་དེ། སེང་པའི་དམག་དཔུས་གཙང་དུ་མ་སླེབ་པ། ཁྱོད་ཀྱིས་བྱོས་དང་། ངེད་ངོས་ནས། ཁྱེད་ཞིང་དེར་སྐྱེ་བར་ཡིད་སྨོན་བྱེད། ཅེས་གསུངས་པའི། གསང་བའི་ཕྱག་བྲིས་བསྐུར་པའི་གཏམ་བརྒྱུད། བདག་གིས་རང་གི་དགེ་བའི་བཤེས་གཉེན། མང་རྒྱུ་པ་དཀའ་ཆེན་མཐར་ཕྱིན་ཞབས་ལ་སོགས་པ། བཀྲས་ལྷུན་གྲྭ་པ་རྒན་པོ་འགའི་གསུང་རྒྱུན་ལ་ཐོས། གཞན་ཡང་གཞིས་ཀ་རྩེ་རུ་ནོ་ནོ་བསོད་ནམས། པཎ་ཆེན་བསྟན་པའི་ཉི་མའི་སྐུན་གསལ་ཡིན་པ་དང་། ཁོང་ལ་དྭགས་ནང་ཚང་དྭན་ནས། སེམས་པ་མི་སྐྱེ་བའི་ཕྱིར། ཀུན་སྐྱོབ་གླིང་ཟེར་

60 དཔལ་ལྡན། ཤོག་ ༡༠༨-༡༡༧།

61 ཡོ་སེབ། ཤོག་ ༥༦༨།

བའི་སྐྱིད་ཚལ་ནང་དུ། ཤ་ག་རན་པོ་ལོ་རྩེ་ས་གསར་དུ་བསྐྲུན་པ་དང་། ཀུ་ཤུའི་སྡོང་པོ་བཙུགས་པ་སོགས། ནོ་ནོ་བསོད་ནམས་ལ་གཅེས་སྤྲས་ཆེན་པོ་མཛད་པར་མངོན་ནོ། །

ནོ་ནོ་བསོད་ནམས་ཀྱི་མི་མདའ་རང་འབར་ཞིག་དང་། གཡུ་བ་ནང་ཁོངས་སྐོང་དུ་གསེར་གྱི་སྤྲན་མ་ཡར་མར་དུ་རྒྱུག་པའི་རལ་གྲི་ཞིག། བཀྲ་ཤིས་ལྷུན་པོ་ན། དཔེ་སྤྲུབ་ཁང་ཚན་གྱི་མགོན་ཁང་དུ། སྤྱི་ལོ་ ༡༩༥༨ བར་དུ་ཡོད་པ། ངེད་རང་གིས་དངོས་སུ་མཐོང་བ་ལ་བརྟེན་ནས། གོང་དུ་བྲོས་པའི། གཏམ་བརྒྱུད་དེ་དག་ཕལ་ཆེར་བདེན་པར་སྣང་ངོ་། །

གཞིར་བཏུགས་བགྱིས་པའི་གཞུང་དཔེ་རྣམས་ཀྱི་ཐོ།

བརྗེ་ངག་དབང་ཀུན་དགའ། **རྣལ་འབྱོར་གྱི་དབང་ཕྱུག་ཨོ་ཏི་ཡཱ་ན་པ་ངག་དབང་རྒྱ་མཚོ(སྟག་ཚང་རས་པ)འི་ རྣམ་ཐར་ལེགས་བྲིས་བཻ་ཌཱུརྱ་དཀར་པོའི་རྒྱུད་མང་།** ཕྱི་ལོ་བརྒྱ་རབས་བཅུ་བདུན་པའི་ནང་བརྩམས་པའི་པར་ཤིང་ཧེ་མིའི་དགོན་པའམ་ལྕེ་ལྡེའི་དགོན་པར་བཞུགས།

སྡེ་སྲིད་སངས་རྒྱས་རྒྱ་མཚོ། **དགེ་ལྡན་ཆོས་འབྱུང་བཻ་ཌཱུརྱ་སེར་པོ།** ༡༩༩༡ པར་ཐེངས་གཉིས་པ་བརྒྱབས། །

Cunningham, Alexander, **LADAK, Physical, Statistical & Historical,** 1853, reprint New Delhi, Sagar Publication 1970.

Francke, A. H. **Antiquities of Indian Tibet,** volumes I and II, Calcutta Suprintendent Government Printing India, 1914 and 1926, respectively.

བསོད་ནམས་ཚེ་བརྟན་ཡོ་སེབ། **ལ་དྭགས་རྒྱལ་རབས་འཆི་མེད་གཏེར།** ༡༩༧༦ པར་བརྒྱབས།

Snellgrove, David L, and Skorupski, Tadeusz, **The Cultural Heritage of Ladakh,** Boulder, Prajna Press 1977.

ཀྲང་དབྱི་སུན། **བོད་རྒྱ་ཚིག་མཛོད་ཆེན་མོ།** ༡༩༧༨ ལ་པར་བརྒྱབས།

འགྱུར་མེད་བདེ་ཆེན། **ཐང་སྟོང་རྒྱལ་པོའི་རྣམ་ཐར།** སི་ཁྲོན་མི་རིགས་དཔེ་སྐྲུན་ཁང་། ༡༩༨༣ ལ་པར་བརྒྱབས།

བཀྲ་ཤིས་རབ་རྒྱས། **མར་ཡུལ་ལ་དྭགས་ཀྱི་སྔོན་རབས་ཀུན་གསལ་མེ་ལོང་།** ༡༩༨༩ ལ་པར་བརྒྱབས།

ཡ་ཏན་ཀུང་། **ཧཱུ་ལའི་བླ་མའི་རྣམ་ཐར།** ༡༩༨༦ ལ་པར་བརྒྱབས།

ཐུབ་བསྟན་དཔལ་ལྡན་ས་ཕུད། **མང་ཡུལ་སྐྱེས་ཆེན་དམ་པ་ཀུན་གྱི་རྣམ་ཐར།** ༡༩༨༨ ལ་པར་བརྒྱབས།

Howard, N. F., **East and West, The Development of the Fortressses of Ladakh,** vol. 39. Nos. 1-4(December 1989).

ལ་དྭགས་ཀྱི་སྐད་ཡིག།

རྩོམ་པ་པོ།

འཆི་མེད་རྣམ་རྒྱལ་ལྟེ་བ་པ།

la dwags kyi skad yig

rtsom pa po

chi med rnam rgyal

lte ba pa

LADAKHI LANGUAGE

by

Chhimet Namgyal

District Cottage Industry, Leh, Ladakh.

Summary

The language of Ladakh is Tibetan in origin, both in vocabulary and grammar. A common language does not necessarily mean a common nation on political grounds. The language has got sound symbols, that is an alphabet, and has not got a pictorial or symbolic script like that of China. It is the language of people living not only in Tibet but also in Bhutan, several parts of Nepal, Sikkim, and in India - Lahaul, Spiti, Arunchal etc. We find the traditional five major sciences of Arts and Crafts, Medicine, Logic, Philosophies and Linguistics in it. The five minor branches are Poetry, Astrology, Writing style, Drama, and Synonyms If properly applied this knowledge can be useful for others and through this one is able to attain perfect enlightenment. In addition to the above there are creative works, books on religion and secular histories, biographies etc.

As the language is used in a vast area some differences in pronunciation are bound to appear. If changes are required these should be done carefully and should be implemented with a far sighted consideration. However, Tungkar Lobzang Thinles, a modern leading scholar in Tibet stated that no basic change has been made in the Tibetan Grammar.

1

Chimmet Nyamgyal

ལ་དྭགས་ཀྱི་སྐད་ཡིག།

རྩོམ་པ་པོ། འཆི་མེད་རྣམ་རྒྱལ་ལྷེ་བ་པ།

༄ ཡུལ་གང་འདྲ་ཞིག་ཡིན་རུང་། རང་རང་སོ་སོའི་སྐད་དང་ཡི་གེ་ནི་ཧ་ཅང་རྩད་ཆེ་བ་ཞིག་དང་། དགོས་པ་ཡང་ཆེ་བ་ཡོད་པ་ཞིག་ཡིན་ནོ། འཛིག་རྟེན་གྱི་ཡུལ་ཚང་མ་ལ་རང་རང་གི་སྐད་དང་ཡི་གེ་སོ་སོ་ཡོད་ཅིང་། སྐད་རིགས་ཡོད་ཚད་ཚང་མ་ལ་ནི་ཡི་གེ་མེད། ཡིན་ཀྱང་སྐད་གང་ཞིག་ལ་ཡི་གེ་ཡང་ཡོད་དེ་ནི་སྐད་ཆ་ཚང་ཞིག་ཏུ་བརྩི་བ་ཡིན་ནོ།།

དེ་ལྟར་རང་རེ་ལ་དྭགས་ཀྱི་མི་དམངས་རྣམས་ལ་ཡང་། གཞན་དང་མི་འདྲ་བའི་སྐད་ཡིག་ཆ་ཚང་ཟབ་མོ་ཞིག་ཡོད། འདི་ནི་རང་རེ་ལ་དྭགས་ཀྱི་ས་གཞི་འདི་ལ་ཐོག་མ་ཉིད་ནས་གནས་པའི་མི་རིགས་ཆོས་རིགས་ཡོད་དོ་ཅོག་གི་ཕ་སྐད་ངོ་མ་རང་ཡིན། སྐད་འདི་ཡི་མིང་ལ་བོད་སྐད་དང་ཡི་གེའི་མིང་ལ་བོད་ཡིག་ཞེས་འབོད་སྲོལ་ཡོད། དེ་ཡི་རྒྱུ་མཚན་ནི། དེང་སང་རང་རེ་རྣམས་ཀྱིས་སྨྲ་བའི་སྐད་འདི་ནི། བོད་ཁྲི་སྐོར་བཅུ་གསུམ་གྱི་མི་རྣམས་ཀྱིས་ཐོགམ་ཉིད་ནས་སྨྲ་བའི་སྐད་རང་ཡིན། ཡང་སྐད་འདི་ལ་ཡིག་གཟུགས་མཛད་ནས་ཡི་གེ་སྲོལ་གསར་དུ་གཏོད་མཁན་ནི། བོད་ཀྱི་ལོ་ཙྭ་བ་མཁས་པ་ཆེན་པོ་ཐོན་མི་སམ་བྷོ་ཊ་ཡིན་པས་ན་ཡི་གེ་ལ་བྷོ་ཊ་ཡིག་ཞེས་ཟེར་བ་ཡིན་ནོ།། ཡིན་ཀྱང་སྐད་ཡིག་གཅིག་པ་ཡིན་པས་སྲིད་དབང་གཅིག་པ་ཡིན་པ་ལ་ནི་ཁྱབ་པ་མེད། སྲིད་ཀྱི་ཐོག་ན་བོད་དང་ལ་དྭགས་གཉིས་རང་རང་སོ་སོ་ཡིན་ནོ།།

2

Ladakhi language

སྤྱིར་གཏང་འཛིག་རྟེན་དུ་འདྲ་གཟུགས་དང་སྒྲ་སྦྱོར་ཞེས་ཡི་གེ་ལ་རིགས་གཉིས་ཡོད་པ་ཡིན། རང་རེའི་ཡི་གེ་འདི་ནི་སྒྲ་སྦྱོར་གྱི་ཡི་གེ་ཞིག་ཡིན་པར་བརྟེན། སྒྲ་དག་ཅིང་མིང་ཚིག་སོགས་ཀྱིས་མི་ལྡང་བ་མེད་པ་དང་སྐད་ཡིག་གཞར་ན་ལ་རག་ལས་དགོས་མེད་པ་ཞིག་ཡི། འདི་ནི་ལ་དྭགས་ཙམ་མིན་པར་ གར་ཞྭ། བོད་རིགས། སྦལ་ཏ། གཅིག་སྐན། བོད། བལ་པོ། འབྲུག་སོགས་དང་ ཡང་གོང་གསལ་ཡུལ་ལྗོངས་ཀྱི་མི་རིགས་སོགས་གནས་པའི་འཛིག་རྟེན་གྱི་གཞན་ཡུལ་གྲུ་གཞན་ཀུན་ལ་ཡང་དར་ཡོད་པ་དང་། ད་རུང་དར་གྱིན་འགྲོ་བ་ཞིག་ཀྱང་ཡིན་ཅིང་། དེ་ལྟར་བྱུང་བ་ནི། རང་རེ་རྣམས་ཀྱིས་ཐོན་མི་ཉིད་ཀྱིས་མཛད་པའི་ཧ་སྦྱོད་རིག་པའི་གཞུང་ལུགས་སུམ་རྟགས་ཀྱི་གཞི་མ་བཤིགས་པར་ད་བར་རྒྱུན་འཛིན་བྱས་པ་ལ་བརྟེན་པས་ཡིན་ནོ།།

རང་རེ་སྐད་ཡིག་འདི་ཡི་ནང་ལ་གཞན་དང་མི་འདྲ་བའི་རིག་པའི་གནས་ཆེ་བ་ལྔ། བཟོ། གསོ་བ། ཚད་མ། ནང་དོན། སྒྲ་རིག་པ་དང་། ཆུང་བ་ལྔ། སྙན་ངག། མངོན་བརྗོད། སྡེབ་སྦྱོར། ཟློས་གར། དང་རྩིས་བཅས་བཅུ་ཡོད་པ་ཞིག་ཡིན་ཅིང་། མི་སུ་འདྲ་ཞིག་ཡིན་ཀྱང་རང་རེ་སྐད་ཡིག་འདི་ལེགས་པར་སྦྱང་སྟེ་གོང་གི་རིག་གནས་བཅུ་ལས་རང་གང་འདོད་ཀྱི་རིག་གནས་རེ་ལ་ལག་ལེན་བྱས་ན། ཚེ་འདིར་ལ་བདེ་སྐྱིད་འབྱུང་བའི་རྟེན་གཞི་གདེང་ཁེལ་ཞིག་དང་། ཕྱི་མར་བྱང་ཆུབ་བརྙེས་པའི་ཐབས་བཟང་ཞིག་སྟེར་ཐུབ་པའི་ནུས་པ་ཡོད་པ་ཞིག་ཡིན། རང་རེ་སྐད་ཡིག་འདི་ཡི་ནང་ལ་ལོ་སྟོང་གི་གོང་ནས། བོད་དང་རང་རེའི་ལོ་ཙྭ་བ་མཁས་པ་རྣམས་ཀྱིས་བརྩམས་པ་དང་བསྒྱུར་པའི་དམ་པའི་གསུང་རབ། མཁས་པའི་ལེགས

བཤད། རྒྱལ་རབས་ཆོས་འབྱུང་། ཚིག་མཛོད། སྒྲུང་གཏམ། གཏམ་དཔེ་སྣ་ཚོགས། ལ་སོགས་པ་དང་གཞན་རིག་གཞུང་གི་དཔེ་དེབ་ཏ་ཙང་མང་པོ་ཞིག་ཀྱང་ཡོད་པ་ཡིན་ཅིང་། དེ་ཕྱིར་རང་རེ་གཞོན་ནུ་ཕོ་མོ་རྣམས་ཀྱིས། རང་གི་སྐད་ཡིད་ལེགས་པར་སྦྱངས་ཏེ་ཉམས་མ་བཅུག་པར། ད་རུང་ཡང་ཁྱབ་ཆེ་རུ་གཏོང་བ་ལ་འབད་དགོས་པ་ཤིན་ཏུ་གལ་ཆེ་བ་ཡིན་ནོ།།

དེང་སང་རང་རེ་སྐད་ཡིག་འདི་ལ། དབྱིན་ཇི། འ་རྡུ །དང་ཧིནྡི་ལ་སོགས་པའི་སྐད་ཡིག་གཞན་ལྟ་བུར་ཡིག་སྐད་དང་ཁ་སྐད་དམ་ཕལ་སྐད་གཉིས་གཅིག་འགྱུར་མིན་པར། ཡིག་སྐད་དང་ཕལ་སྐད་ཀྱི་བར་ལ་ཁྱད་པར་ཡོད་པ་ཇི་ལྟར་ཡིན་ཞེས་པ་སོགས་ཀྱི་དྲི་བ་ཡོད་པས། དེ་ནི་གོང་གི་སྐད་ཡིག་ངག་ནི་སློབ་པའི་དུས་སུ་ཐོག་མ་ཉིད་ནས། སྐད་ཀྱི་སྒྲ་གདངས།……སོགས་ཀྱི་ཐོག་ལ་སྣང་དག་ཆེན་པོ་གཏོང་སྲོལ་ཡོད་པ་དང་། རང་རེ་སྐད་ཡིག་ལ་ནི་དེ་ལྟར་མ་བྱུས་པས་ན་ཡིག་སྐད་དང་ཕལ་སྐད་ཀྱི་བར་ལ་ང་རོ་དང་ཚིག་འགའ་རེའི་ཁྱད་པར་ཕྲན་གུ་ཞིག་ཆགས་པ་ཡིན་མ་གཏོགས། དོན་དུ་འགལ་བ་གང་ཡང་མ་ཡིན། མ་ཚད་དབྱིན་སྐད་སོགས་གཞན་ལས་དཔགས་པའི། སྒྲ་གདངས་དག་པའི་ཐོག་ནས་རང་རེ་སྐད་ཡིག་འདི་ལ་ཡོན་ཏན་ཐེ་བས་ཆེ་བར་ཡོད་པ་ནི། རང་རེའི་སྐད་ཡིག་གི་དབྱངས་དང་གསལ་བྱེད་ཚང་མར་ང་རེའི་རྩ་བ། ཨ་དང་། ཏ་དང་། འ་གསུམ་གྱི་ཆ་དང་ལྡན་པས། སྒྲ་གདངས་ཐོན་པར་བྱེད་པའི་རྒྱུ། དབུགས་སྟོབས་ཀྱི་རྩོལ་བ་ཤུགས་ཆེ་ཆུང་གི་ཁྱད་དང་། སྒྲ་གདངས་ཐོན་པའི་གནས་བརྒྱད། ཁོག་པ། མགྲིན་པ། རྐན། སོ། མཆུ། ལྕེ། སྤྱི་བོ་དང་། སྣ་བཅས་ཞིབ་པར་ཕྱེས་ཡོད་པ་དང་། ཕོ་དང། མོ་དང་། མ་ནིང་དང་། ཤིན་ཏུ་མོ་དང་།

མོ་གཤམ་སོགས་ལྷར་བསྟན་པ་དང་། རྐྱང་བརྩེགས་འདོགས་གསུམ་དང་། ད་དྲག་ལ་སོགས་པ་རྣམས་སྒྲ་ཤིན་ཏུ་དག་པར་ཀློག་པའི་ཐབས་ཁྱད་པར་ཅན་མཛད་ཡོད་པ་སོགས་ལས་མངོན་ཐུབ་པ་ཡིན་ནོ།།

ཡིན་ཀྱང་ རང་ རེའི་སྐད་ཡིག་འདི་ལ་ཐོག་མར་སློབ་དུས་ཡི་གེ་སོ་སོའི་སྒྲ་གདངས་ཐོག་དོ་སྣང་ཆེར་མ་བཏང་བའི་རྐྱེན་གྱིས། རིམ་པས་ཡིག་སྐད་ཀྱི་མིང་དེང་སང་ཕན་ཚུན་གླིང་མོལ་བྱེད་སྐབས། ལ་དྭགས། བོད། བལ་པོ། འབྲུག །འབྲས་ལྗོངས། གར་ཞྭ། སོགས་ཀྱི་མི་མང་སོ་སོའི་ཕལ་སྐད་ལ་ཁྱད་པར་ཕྲན་བུ་རེ་ངེས་པར་འབྱུང་གི་ཡོད་པ་ཡིན། གོང་གསལ་ཡུལ་ལྗོངས་ཕན་ཚུན་གྱི་བར་ལ། རང་རེའི་སྐད་ཡིག་འདུས་ཁྱབ་ཅིང་ལོ་སྟོང་ལྷག་ཙམ་གྱི་གོང་ནས་བཟུང་སྐད་ཡིག་གཅིག་འགྱུར་ཞིག་ཆགས་ཡད། དེང་སང་མི་ཤས་ཀྱིས་རང་གི་ཡུལ་དུ་ཁྱབ་ཡོད་པའི་ཕལ་སྐད་དེ་ཡིག་ཐོག་ཏུ་བཀོད་ནས་བརྡ་སྤྲོ་པའི་གཞུང་དང་འགལ་བའི་བསྟན་བཅོས་བརྩམས་སྤེལ་བྱེད་པ་ནི་ལྐུགས་པའི་ལྐུགས་རྟགས་བསྟན་པ་ཡིན། ཁྱབ་ཆེན་པོའི་སྐད་ཡིག་དེ་ཁྱབ་ཚུང་དུ་བཏང་བས་ག་དོག་པའི་ལས་བྱས་པ་ཡིན། ཐོན་མིའི་བརྡ་སྤྲོད་རིག་པའི་གཞུང་སུམ་རྟགས་བཤིགས་ཏེ། ལ་དྭགས་རང་གཅིག་བུའི་ཕྱིར་དུ་སྐད་གསར་ཞིག་བཟོང་བས་ཡིན་ན། དེ་ལ་ཀློ་ལྡན་སུ་ཞིག་གིས་ཀྱང་དགའ་བསུ་ཞུ་མི་སྲིད། བདག་གིས་འདིར་བཤད་པའི་དོན་ནི།རང་རེ་སྐད་ཡིག་ལ་རྩ་བ་ཉིད་ནས་བསྒྱུར་བཅོས་གཏོང་མི་དགོས་ཟེར་བ་ནི་མ་ཡིན་ལ། སྐད་ལ་བསྒྱུར་བཅོས་ངེས་པར་གཏོང་དགོས་པ་ཡིན། སྐད་གང་འདྲ་ཞིག་ཡིན་རུང་། ལོ་ཏ་ལམ་ཞག་ན་སྐད་འགྱུར་འགྲོ་བ་ཡིན། ད་པར་རང་རེའི་སྔོན་བྱོན་ལོ་ཙཱ་བ་རྣམས་དང་མཁས་པ་རྣམས་ཀྱིས་སྐད་ཡིག་ལ་

བསྒྱུར་བཅོས་ཐེངས་ཁ་ཅིག་མཛད་ཆར་ཡོད་དེ་དུས་སྐད་ཡིག་ལྷག་པར་ཁྱབ་ཆེ་བ་ཞིག་དང་། མི་མང་ཕལ་མོ་ཆེ་ཞིག་གིས་གོ་ཐུབ་པ་དང་རྒྱང་རིང་པོ་ཞིག་ལ་དམིགས་ཏེ་བཏང་བ་མ་གཏོགས། སྐད་ཡིག་སྔོན་ལས་ཀྱང་ཁྱབ་ཆུང་དུ་འགྲོ་ཕྱིར་དམིགས་ཏེ་བཏང་བ་ནི་མ་ཡིན་ལ། དེ་ཕྱིར་རང་རེའི་སྔོན་བྱོན་ལོ་ཙཱ་བ་མཁས་པ་རྣམས་ཀྱིས་སྐད་ལ་བསྒྱུར་བཅོས་གཏོང་སྐབས་སྐད་ཡིག་ཁྱབ་ཆེར་གཏོང་ཆེད་དུ་དམིགས་པས། རྩ་བའི་བརྡ་སྤྲོད་རིག་པའི་སུམ་རྟགས་ཀྱི་གཞུང་ལུགས་མ་བཤིག་པར་རྒྱུན་འཛིན་བྱས་ཏེ། ཡི་གེའི་དག་ཆའི་ཐད་སྐབས་དེ་ཡི་ཁ་སྐད་དང་བསྟུན་ནས་བྱས་པ་མ་གཏོགས། ཐོན་མིའི་གསུམ་རྟགས་ཀྱི་གཞུང་ལུགས་བཤིག་སྐྱེ། སྐད་ཡིག་ཁྱབ་ཆུང་བར་གཏོང་བའི་ཡུལ་ལྡོངས་སོ་སོའི་ཕལ་སྐད་སོགས་བཟོས་ཡོད་པའི་དཔེ་མི་སད་པ་ཡིན།

ཐོན་མིའི་སམ་བྷོ་ཊས་རང་རེའི་ཡིག་གཟུགས་མཛད་པ་ནས་ད་བར་ཏ་ལམ་ལོ་ཅིག་སྟོང་གསུམ་བརྒྱ་བཞི་ཙུ་ཙམ་ཕྱིན་པའི་རིང་ལ། བོད་ཀྱི་ལོ་ཙཱ་བ་རྣམས་ཀྱང་རང་རེ་སྐད་ཡིག་འདི་ལ་བཀས་བཅད་ཐེངས་གསུམ་དང་བསྒྱུར་བཅོས་ཐེངས་གཉིས་བཏང་ཆར་བ་ཡིན།

བསྒྱུར་བཅོས་དང་པོ་ནི། ཕྱི་ལོ་བརྒྱ་ཕྲག་དགུ་པའི་མགོ་ཙམ་ལ་མངའ་བདག་ཁྲི་རལ་པ་ཅན་གྱིས་བོད་ཀྱི་སྟོད་ལ་དབང་བསྒྱུར་སྐབས། ལོ་ཆཱ་བ་མཁས་པ་སྐ་ལྕོག་ཞང་གསུམ་སོགས་ཀྱིས་མཛད། དེ་ཡི་རིང་ལ་སྔར་ཡོད་ཐོན་མིའི་སུམ་རྟགས་ཀྱི་གཞུང་ལུགས་མ་བཞིག་པར། ཡི་གེའི་དག་ཆ་སོགས་མང་བར་མཛད་པ་ཡིན། དེ་ལ་བཀའ་བཅད་གཉིས་པ་དང་བསྒྱུར་བཅོས་དང་པོ་ཟེར་བ་ཡིན་ནོ།།

བསྒྱུར་བཅོས་གཉིས་པ་ནི། ཁྲི་ལོ་བརྒྱ་ཕྲག་བཅུ་པའི་མཇུག་ཏུ་མངའ་རིས་ལོ་ཙྭ་བ་རིན་ཆེན་བཟང་པོ་བྱུང་བ་ནས། ཁྲི་ལོ་བརྒྱ་ཕྲག་བཅོ་ལྔ་པའི་མགོ་ཙམ་ལ་ཞྭ་ལུ་ལོ་ཙཱ་བ་ཆོས་སྐྱོང་བཟང་པོ་བྱུང་བའི་པར་ད་མཛད། ལོ་བཞི་བརྒྱ་བདུན་ལྷག་ཙམ་གྱི་རིང་ལ་བོད་དུ་ལོ་ཙྭ་བ་དང་མཁས་པ་བརྒྱ་དང་དྲུག་ཅུ་རེ་བདུན་བྱུང་ཞིང་། དེ་རྣམས་ཀྱིས་ཀྱང་བོད་ཡིག་གི་དག་ཆའི་ཐོག་བཅོས་བསྒྱུར་རིམ་པར་མཛད་དེ་ལ་བཀས་བཅད་གསུམ་པ་དང་བཅོས་བསྒྱུར་གཉིས་པ་ཟེར་བ་ཡིན་ནོ།། བཅོས་བསྒྱུར་དེ་རྣམས་ཀྱི་རིང་དུ། ཕྱར་ཡོད་སུམ་རྟགས་ཀྱི་རིག་པའི་གཞུང་ལུགས་རྒྱུན་འཛིན་བྱས་ཐོག། ཡི་གེའི་དག་ཆའི་ཐད་སྐབས་དེ་ཡི་ཕལ་སྐད་དང་བསྟུན་ནས་བཅོས་བསྒྱུར་བྱས་པ་ཞིག་ཡིན་པ་ལས། རྩ་བའི་བརྡ་སྤྲོད་རིག་པ་ཡིན་པའི་སུམ་རྟགས་ཀྱི་གཞུང་རྩ་གཏོར་བཏང་ནས་རིགས་པའི་གཞུང་ལུགས་གསར་གཏོད་ཟེར་བའི་བསྒྱུར་བཅོས་བྱས་པ་ཞིག་ལོ་རྒྱུས་ཐོག་རྩ་བ་ནས་བྱུང་མྱོང་མེད་ཅེས། མཁས་དབང་དུང་དཀར་བློ་བཟང་འཕྲིན་ལས་ཀྱི་གསུང་རྩོམ་ལས་ཀྱང་གསལ་བ་ཡིན་ནོ།།

དེར་བརྟེན་ལོ་ཆིག་སྟོང་གསུམ་བརྒྱ་བཞི་ཅུ་ལྷག་ཕྱིན་ཚར་བའི་རྗེས་སུ་་དེང་སང་ཡང་། ལ་དྭགས བོད། བལ་བོ། འབྲུག། འབྲས་ལྗོངས། ཨ་རུ་ན་ཅལ གར་ཛ་སོགས་འཛམ་གླིང་གི་ཡུལ་ལྗོངས་མང་པོ་ཞིག་གི་བར་ལ། ཡིག་སྐད་གཅིག་འགྱུར་ཞིག་ཆགས་ཐུབ་པར་བརྟེན། སུམ་རྟགས་དག་པོ་ཡོད་པའི་ཡི་གེ་དང་དཔེ་དེབ་སོགས་ན་ གོང་གི་ཡུལ་ཕན་ཚུན་རྣམས་ཀྱི་བར་ལ་ལེགས་པར་དོན་གོ་ཐུབ་པ་དང་། བཀའ་བསྟན་སོགས་ཀློག་ཐུབ་པ་དང་། དེ་ཡི་དོན་རྣམས་བདེ་བླག་ཏུ་གོ་ཐོབ་པ་བྱུང་བ་ནི། སྔོན་

སྔོན་ལོ་ཙཱ་བ་མཁས་པ་རྣམས་ཀྱིས་སྔོན་མིའི་སུམ་རྟགས་ཀྱི་གཞུང་ལུགས་མ་བཤིག་པར། སྐད་ཡིག་ལ་བསྒྱུར་བཅོས་མཛད་པའི་ཐུགས་བསམ་རྒྱང་རིང་པོ་ལ་བརྟེན་ནས་བྱུང་བ་ཞིག་ཡི་པར་སེམས་སོ།།

ད་རུང་ཡང་གོང་གསལ་ཡུལ་ལྗོངས་རྣམས་ཀྱིས། རང་རང་སོ་སོའི་ཕལ་སྐད་སོགས་བཟོ་དགོས་ཞེས་ཕན་ཚུན་བར་གོ་མི་ཐུབ་པའི་སྐད་གསར་ར་བཟོས་པར། གོང་གསལ་ཡུལ་ལྗོངས་རྣམས་ཀྱི་མཁས་པ་དག་བློ་མཐུན་གཅིག་འགྱུར་གྱིས། སྔོན་མི་ཉིད་ཀྱི་སུམ་རྟགས་ཀྱི་གཞུང་ལུགས་མ་བཤིགས་པར་རྒྱུན་འཛིན་བྱས་ཏེ། ཡིག་སྐད་འདིར་ཡིག་སྐད་ཟེར་བའི་དོན་ཡི་གེ་སྐད་ཡིན་པ་བཀའ་བསྟན་སོགས་བྲིས་པའི་སྐད་ཡིག་ལ་གོ་དགོས་ཤིང་། མིང་ཚིག་སོགས་ཟུར་ཆགས་ཏེ་སོ་སོའི་ཡུལ་ལྗོངས་སུ་ཕལ་སྐད་དུ་འགྱུར་ཉེན་ཡོད་པ་རྣམས་ལ་དག་ཆ་མཛད་དེ། གོང་གསལ་ཡུལ་ལྗོངས་ཐམས་ཅད་ཀྱི་ཕྱིར་སྐད་ཡིག་གཅིག་འགྱུར་ཞིག་ཡོང་ཐུབ་པའི་ཕྱོགས་ལ་འབད་རྩོལ་བྱེད་ན། རང་རེའི་སྐད་ཡིག་འདི་ཡར་རྒྱས་སུ་ཕྱིན་ཏེ། རང་རྒྱལ་ཕྱི་རྒྱལ་གཉིས་སུ་ཁྱབ་ཆེ་བར་འགྱུར་ངེས་པར་འདུག་ལགས།

རྫོགས་སོ།།

འཆམས་ཀྱི་ནད་དོན་མོ་ར་བསྡུས།

དཀོན་མཆོག་ནམ་རྒྱལ།

'chams gyi nad don mo ra bsdus

dkon mchog nam rgyal

THE SIGNIFICANCE OF CHAMS PERFORMANCE

Konchok Namgyal
Central Institute of Buddhist Studies,
Choglamsar, Leh.

Summary: THE SIGNIFICANCE OF CHAMS PERFORMANCE

Konchok Namgyal
Central Institute of Buddhist Studies,
Choglamsar, Leh.

Chams performance is essentially a part of Tantric teachings. It is performed in only those Gompas where the monks do Tantric rituals, and is done in strict observance of the prescribed texts.

In Chams performance the monks wear the costumes and masks of various meditative and protective deities. They hold in their hands articles that are the symbols of the deities. They then come out on to the courtyard accompanied by various musical instruments. They dance around the courtyard with solemn movements of their legs and hands.

Chams performance is characterised by nine dance movements and gestures, and each one has to be performed by every deity:

1. **Gesture of power** - to enable the deity to raise people from Hinyana to the Mahayana level.
2. **Gesture of boldness**-to signify that the deity can transform its physical form to a particular need.
3. **Look of terror** - the power to destroy evil forces.
4. **Mahayana look** - the majesty of the deity.
5. **Look of Horzan** - two types of attachment.
6. **Gesture of readiness** to help others.
7. **Look of compassion** for all sentient beings.
8. **Look of peace** - a calm and abiding nature.
9. **The big wonderful gesture** - the deity has attained shunyata.

The colour of the mask for peaceful deities is white, for merits is yellow, for wrathful is black and for power is red. In the right hand they hold articles like Vajra, Sword, Spear, Hammer, Hook etc. and in the left hand Skull, Urn, Sling etc.

In Tibet the beginning of Chams is traced to the year 811 when Guru Padmasambhava performed the black-hat Chams to conquer the evil spirits who were against him for building Samye Monastery.

1

Chams performance

འཆམས་ཀྱི་ནད་དོན་མོ་ར་བསྡུས།

དཀོན་མཆོག་ནམ་རྒྱལ།

༄། སྤྱིར་འཆམས་ནི་མདོ་དང་སྔགས་གཉིས་ཀྱི་ནང་ནས་སྔགས་ལུགས་ལ་མ་གཏོགས་མེད་པ་ཡིན། དེ་ནས་འཆམས་ནི་གསང་སྔགས་ཀྱི་ཚོགས་ན་ཕྱག་ལེན་བྱེད་པའི་དགོན་པ་རྣམས་སུ་དགེ་འདུན་པ་དག་གིས་ཡི་དམ་རྒྱུར་སྲི་བཞི་ཅེ་རིགས་སྣ་ཚོགས་ཀྱི་ལྷ་དང་རྒྱལ་བའི་བསྟན་བསྲུང་གང་ཡང་རུང་བའི་མངོན་རྟོགས་དང་མཐུན་པའི་ཕྱག་མཚན་དང་ཆས་གོས་སོགས་ཀྱི་བརྒྱན་ཏེ་ལྷ་ཡི་གསལ་སྣང་དང་ལྡན་པའི་སྒོ་ནས་དང་ རྒྱ་གླིང་རོ་མོས་སྔོན་བསུས་ཏེ་འཚུག་ལག་ཁང་གི་ནང་ནས་ཕྱི་རོལ་ཐོན་ནས་འཆམས་རའི་ནང་མི་མང་ཚོགས་པའི་དབུས་སུ་འཁྱིང་འབག་དང་བཅས་ལུས་ཀྱི་གར་སྟབས་སྒྱུར་བ་ལ་འཆམ་ཞེས་བརྗོད་པ་ཡིན།

དེ་བཞིན་ཆས་གོས་ཀྱང་ཞི་རྒྱས་དབང་དྲག་སོ་སོ་ཡོད་པ་ཡིན། དཔེར་ན་ཞལ་འབག་ལ་མཚོན་ན། ཞི་བའི་འབག་དཀར་པོ་ རྒྱས་པ་ལ་སེར་པོ་ དབང་ལ་དམར་པོ་ དྲག་པོའི་རིག་ལ་ནག་པོ་དང་ཁྲོ་ཞལ་ཡོད་པ་ཡིན། དེ་བཞིན་ཕྱག་མཚན གཡས་རྡོ་རྗེ་རལ་གྲི་ མདུང་ ཐོ་བ་ ལྕགས་སྐྱུ་ བེ་ཅན་སོགས་སྣ་ཚོགས་དང་། ཕྱག་གཡས་ན་ ཐོད་པ་ བུམ་པ་ ཞགས་པ་སོགས་མ་ངེས་པ་སྣ་ཚོགས་བསྣམས་ནས་རོལ་མོ་བརྡུང་བའི་སྒྲ་སྙུག་གི་སྒྲ་དང་བསྟུན་ནས་དགམ་པ་གཡས་གཡོན་རྒྱབ་མདུན་ཀུན་ལ་མགྱོགས་འགྲོས་དང་། དལ་བུ་ཅེ་རིགས་སྣ་ཚོགས་ཀྱི་སྒོ་ནས་ཀང་ལག་གི་

ཁྲབ་ཚུལ་མི་འདྲ་བ་དུ་མ་བསྟན་ནས་སྟ་ཡི་སྐུའི་རྣམས་འགྱུར་གཞན་ལ་ཞེས་སུ་འཛུག་པ་དེ་ཡིན།

འཆམས་གི་འཕྱུ་ཁུངས།

སྤྱིར་འཆམས་དང་གར་གཉིས་ལ་འཆམས་རྒྱ་གར་འཕགས་པའི་ཡུལ་དུ་བྱུང་བའི་ལོ་རྒྱུས་གསལ་པོར་མ་མཐོང་ཡང་གར་ནི་རྒྱ་གར་དུ་དུས་འཁོར་སོགས་ཀྱི་སྐབས་མཁའ་འགྲོ་མའི་གར་ཡོད་འདུག། གལ་སྲིད་རྒྱ་གར་དུ་ཡོད་ནའང་ད་ལྟའི་བོད་སོགས་ལ་ཡོད་པ་ལྟ་བུ་མ་ཡིན་པར། གསང་སྔགས་ཀྱི་རྟོགས་པ་མཐོན་པོར་ཐོབ་པའི་རྣལ་འབྱོར་པ་དག་གིས་དགོན་པ་།དུ་ཁང་ནང་ལོག་ལ་གསང་བའི་སྒོ་ནས་ཡོད་སྲིད་ཀྱི་རེད།

བོད་དུ་འཆམས་གི་ཐོག་མ།

བོད་གང་ཅན་དུ་འཆམ་ཐོག་མར་བསམ་ཡས་སུ་བྱུང་བར་བཤད་པ། དུས་རབ་དགུ་པའི་གོར་བོད་ཀྱི་རྒྱལ་པོ་ཁྲི་སྲོང་ལྡེའུ་བཙན་གྱིས་རྒྱ་གར་འཕགས་པའི་ཡུལ་ནས་སློབ་དཔོན་ཆེན་པོ་པདྨ་འབྱུང་གནས་དང་མཁན་ཆེན་ཞི་བ་འཚོ་བོད་དུ་སྤྱན་ལྡངས་ཕྱི་ལོ་ ༨༡༡ ལོར་བསམ་ཡས་མི་འགྱུར་གཙུག་ལག་ཁང་བཞེངས་པར་བཙམས། དེ་དུས་ས་འདུལ་གྱི་ཆེད་སློབ་དཔོན་པདྨ་འབྱུང་གནས་ཀྱི་རྡོ་རྗེ་གུར་གར་འཆམ་མཛད་པ་དེ་ནི་བོད་ཀྱི་ལོ་རྒྱུས་ཐོག་ཆོས་ཕྱོགས་ཀྱི་གར་འཆམས་ཐོག་མར་བྱུང་བར་ངེས། སྐབས་དེར་རྩེ་མ་ར་ལྟ་ཡང་ཐོག་མར་ཕེབས་པར་བཤད། དེའི་རྗེས་ལྷ་ལུ་དཔལ་རྡོར་གྱིས་རྒྱལ་པོ་གླང་དར་མ་བཀུལ་སྐབས་གླང་དར་གྱི་རྔ་པའི་ཇོ་ཁང་མདུ་རྡོ་རིང་ཡི་གེ་སློག་བཞིན་ཡོད་དུས་ལྷ་ལུང་དཔལ་གྱིས་རྡོ་རྗེས་འཆམས་གོས་ཕུ་ཐུང་རིང་མོ་མདངས་བཞུ། ཚུད་པ་ཞིག་བཟོས་ནས་དེ་ནང་

3

Chams performance

མདའ་བཞུ་ཁྲོར་ནས་སླང་དར་ལ་མདའ་འཁེན་བསད་པད་དེ་དུས་ཡང་འཆམས་གོས་ཡོ་འདུན་པན་ཆེན་བསོད་གྲགས་ཀྱི་བཏན་ཆེག་རིན་ཆེན་ཕྲེང་བར་ལྷ་ལྗུང་པལ་གི་རྡོ་རྗེ་ཡིས་ སྙིང་རྗེའི་ལྷུགས་ཀྱི་མདའ་འཕང་སྟེ་སྡིག་ཅན་བཙན་པོ་ལྷ་སར་བསྐུམ་ གསུང་པ་ལྟར་ཡིན། དུས་ཕྱིས་རེམ་གིས་རྩེ་པོ་ཏ་ལ་ ཡུ་རུ་དགོན་པ་བོདད་ཁམ་ འབྲི་གུང་སོགས་ལ་འཆམས་དར་བས་རི་མ་ཀྱིས་ལ་དྭགས་ཀྱི་དགོན་པ་རྣམས་སུ་དར་བ་ཡིན་འདུག།

ཡང་གསུང་རྩལ་གཅིག་ལ་ད་ལྟ་འཆམས་གི་ཐོག་ན་གསང་སྔགས་ཀྱི་ལྷ་ཀུན་མཐལ་ཐུག་ན་ཕྱི་མར་བར་དོའི་གནས་སྐབས་སུ་འཇིག་སྐྲགས་མེད་པ་ལྷ་ངོ་ཤེ་ཐུབ་པར་སོགས་ཀྱི་ཕན་ཡོན་ཆེ་བར་ཡོད་པར་བཤད་སྲོལ་ཡད།

བྱེ་བྲག་ཏུ་མགོན་པོ་འབྲི་གུང་པའི་འཆམས་ནི།

གསར་སྔགས་གསར་མའི་འཆམས་དང་གསང་སྔགས་རྙིང་མའི་འཆམས་གཉིས་ལ་གསར་མ་ནི་རྒྱལ་བ་ཀུན་དགའ་རིན་ཆེན་སྐབས་དང་། གདན་རབ་ཉིད་ལྔ་པ་རྒྱལ་བང་དཀོན་མཆོག་འཕྲིན་ལས་བཟང་པོའི་རྣལ་ལམ་དུ་ཡེ་ཤེས་ཀྱི་དགོན་པོ་སོགས་ ཁོང་གི་དག་སྣང་ལ་བྱུང་བ་སོགས་ཀྱི་མཛད་པ་ཡིན། ཁོང་ནི་ ༡༦༥༦་ནས་༡༧༡༨་བར་བཞུགས། གསང་སྔགས་རྙིང་མའི་འཆམས་ནི་གཏེར་ཆེན་རིན་ཆེན་ཕུན་ཚོགས་སྐབས་ཁོང་གི་དག་སྣང་ལ་བྱུང་བ་དང་ རྗེས་སུ་མཁས་གྲུབ་རིག་འཛིན་ཆོས་གྲགས་པས་གཟངས་དགོན་དཔལ་གྱི་སློབ་དཔོན་ཆེན་པོ་པདྨ་འབྱུང་གནས་ཀྱི་ཞལ་སྟར་སྤྲར་ཡང་དག་ཞུར་མཛད་ཅིང་ནས་གཏན་ལ་ཕབ་པ་དཔལ་ཆེན་ཧེ་རུ་ཀས་གཙོས་ནི་བཀའ་བརྒྱུད་ཏ་ཚོགས་དང་ཞི་ཁྲོ་དམ་པ་རིག་བརྒྱ་ལྷ་ཚོགས་རྣམས་ཞལ་མངོས་སུ་མཐལ་ནས་མཛད་པ་ཡིན། དོན་དུ་འདན་རབ་དས་དྲིན་

ཆེན་ཕུན་ཚོགས་སྐབས་སྙིག་མའི་འཆམས་སྡོ་གཙུག་པ་ཡིན། ཁོང་ནི་ ༡༥༩༥་ནས་ ༡༦༥༩་པར་བཞུགས། གོང་གསལ་འབྲི་གུང་འཆམས་ཕྱོགས་སྒྲིག་པ་ནི་ཕན་གོང་ས་ཞེལ་ཟླ་དྲས་མཛད་པ་ཡིན།

གར་གྱི་ཉམས་དགུ་ནི།

༡ སྒེག་པ་ མཛེས་ཤིང་ཡིད་དུ་འོང་བ།

༢ དྲག་ཤུལ་ ལུས་ངག་ཏུ་ཐོན་པའི་ཁྲོའི་རྣམ་འགྱུར།

༣ དཔའ་བ་ ནུས་པའམ་ཁོད་པ་ གར་ཁུད་ཆེན་པོ་ལྡན་པ

༤ སྙིང་རྗེ་

༥ མི་སྡུག་པ ཡིད་དུ་མི་འོང་བ།

༦ བཞད་གད གད་མོ། བཞད་གར་ཤོར་བ།

༧ རྨད་དུ་བྱུང་བ་ ངོ་མཚར་ཆེ་བ་ ཕུལ་དུ་བྱུང་བ།

༨ འཇིག་སུ་རུང་བ་ འཇག་སྣང་ཆེ་བ།

ལ་དྭགས་སུ་ཡུལ་ལྷར་དམར་ཆོད།

བསོད་ནམས་ཕུན་ཚོགས།

la dwags su yul lhar dmar chod

bsod nams phun tshogs

SACRIFICIAL OFFERINGS TO LOCAL DEITIES IN LADAKH

Sonam Phuntsog
Achinatang, Purig, Ladakh.

Summary

In the beginning Tibetans lived as pastoral nomads near Mt.Kailash. Later they started to cultivate in the valleys, sometimes helped, sometimes harmed by the spirits. To placate these local spirits and deities certain avoidances and sacrificial offerings were practiced among both Ladakhis and Drogpa (Dards settled round Dahanu), and this long survived among the latter. During the last 100 years a succession of rinpoches has repeatedly discouraged these sacrifices and since 1991 they have been abandoned.

See also p.213-214

ལ་དྭགས་ཡུལ་ལྷར་དམར་ཆོད།

སྨན་རིའི་སློབ་ཟུར་བསྟན་འཛིན་རྣམ་དག་གིས་ཕྱོགས་སྒྲིག་མཛད་པའི་སྔ་རབས་བོད་ཀྱི་བྱུང་བ་བརྗོད་པའི་འབེལ་གཏམ་ལས།

ཐོག་མར་བོད་ཡུལ་ཆགས་དུས་གངས་ཏི་སེའི་ཕྱོགས་བཞིར་འཁྱིལ་བའི་མཚོ་བཞིར་གནས་བྱས་ཤིང་གཡའ་རི་གངས་ལ་བརྟེན་ཞིང་འཚོ་བརྟེན་་གཡག། ལུག། ར་གསུམ་ཡིན། སྐབས་དེར་མི་དང་གཉན་མཛའ་བཤེས་རྒྱལ་དུ་གནས་པས་ཡུལ་མིང་གཉན་ཡུལ་ཟེར། དེ་རྗེས་མཚོ་འགྲམ་ཆུ་ཀླུང་ལ་གནས་བྱས་ཤིང་ཀླུ་ཡིས་དབང་བྱས་པས། རྩྭ་ཤིང་ལོ་འབྲས་བསྐྱེད། མི་ཡིས་མནོལ་བཙོག་བྱས་ཚེ་ཀླུས་གནོད་པ་བྱེད། ཡུལ་མིང་ཀླུ་ཡུལ་ན་ར་སེང་སྔོན་ཟེར།

༡ དེ་རྗེས་བཙན་གྱིས་དབང་བྱས། ཛ། བྲག། ཤིང་སོགས་ལ་གནས་ཏེ་མི་ལ་ཕན་གནོད་གཉིས་ཀ་བྱས། དེ་དུས་ཡུལ་ལྷ་བསྙེན་རྒྱལ་ཐོག་མར་དར། ཡུལ་མིང་གདོང་དམར་ཅན་གྱི་ཡུལ་ཞེས་བྱ། འགལ་རྐྱེན་བྱུང་དུས་ཡུལ་ལྷ་དམར་མཆོད་ཀྱིས་གསོལ། འདི་འདྲའི་སྲོལ་ནི་ནང་པའི་ཆོས་དང་འབྲེལ་བའི་ལུགས་གང་ཡང་མིན་པས། ཡུལ་ལུགས་ཞེས་བརྗོད་དགོས་པ་ཡིན། སྲོལ་འདི་རང་བཞིན་ཡུལ་གྱི་གོམས་ལུགས་ཡིན་པས་ལ་དྭགས་སུ་དུས་དེང་སང་བར་ལུས་པ་དེ་རང་ཡིན་ནོ།།

འདི་འདྲའི་སྲོལ་ནི་ལ་དྭགས་དང་འབྲོག་པའི་མི་རིགས་ནང་གཅིག་པ་དར། ཁྲིམ་ཏཚང་ཞིག་ལ་ཕྲུ་གུ་བཙས་སྐབས་ཕ་མ་གཉིས་ཀ་ཟླ་བ་གཅིག་གི་བར་འཛེམ་སྲོལ་ཡོད་དོ།།

༣ འབྲོག་ལྷ་དང་གཞུང་ལྷའི་ཁྱད་ནི། བག་མ་ལེན་སྐབས་ལ་དྭགས་གཞུང་འཁོར་དང་གཞན་གྲོང་གསེབ་རྣམས་ལ་ཡུལ་ལྷ་ཡོད་སར་མཆན་མོ་འགྲོ་དགོས་པ་དང་། འབྲོག་པའི་ཡུལ་ལྷ་ཡོ་སར་ཉིན་མོར་འགྲོ་ཆོག་ཅིང་། ཡུལ་ལྷ་ལ་ལྷ་ཛས་མདུན་བསུས་ཏེ་རྟེད་འཇོ་ཞིག་བཏང་སྟེ། ལྷ་ལ་ཁ་བཏགས་འབུལ་ན་ཆོག་པ་ཡིན། འབྲོག་པས་གཙོ་ལྷ་ཁྲབ་འཛུག་ལ་བསྟེན་ཅིང་། ཡུལ་ལྷ་དང་ལྷ་མོ་རྣམས་ལ་ལོ་གཅིག་ནང་དམར་མཆོད་ཐེངས་ལྔ། ལོ་སར་སྐབས་གཉིས། སྦྱུབ་ལྷ་གཅིག་སྡོ་ལའི་དུས་གཅིག། བོད་ཟླ་བ་བརྒྱད་པའི་ནང་གཅིག། འབྲོག་པས་བ་ལང་དང་སྐྱིན་གཉིས་ལྷ་ལ་བརྩེ་བ་ཡིན་ཟེར་བ་དངོས་འབྲེལ་གྱི་ལོ་རྒྱུས་མ་ཡིན། ཅི་ལ་ཞུ་ན། སྐྱིན་མཐོང་བ་དང་ལྷ་མཉེས་པས། ཞིངས་བཏང་ནས་སྐྱིན་བསད་པའི་རྭ་ཙོ་ལྷ་ལ་ཕུལ་བ་དང་ བ་ལང་གི་ཤ། འོ་མ་ མར་སོགས་ལ་ལྷ་མི་མཉེས་པས་བཀོལ་མི་ཆོག་པ་ཡིན་ནོ།།

༣ འབྲོག་པ་མི་རིགས་ཀྱིས་ཡུལ་ལྷར་བསྟེན་པའི་ལྷ་མོ་སྤུན་བདུན་ནི། ཏེ་ཤུག་ཏུ་ཤུག་པ་ལྷ་མོ། མཁར་རྩེར་བྲག་ནག་ཇོ་མོ། སྐྱིན་གླིང་ཏང་ལ་ཇོ་མོ། ཇོ་མཁར་གཡག་ར་ཇོ་མོ། འུར་བོའུ་ འུར་བོས་ཇོ་མོ་ འདི་སྟག་མ་གཅིག་དང་ལེ་མདོའི་ཡུལ་ལྷ་ཡང་ཡིན། ལྷག་ན་ཇོ་མོ་དང་ཤུ་དཀར་ཇོ་མོ་བཅས་ལ་ཟླ་རེར་དམར་མཆོད་རེ་བྱེད་སྲོལ་ཡོད་པ་ཡིན། ཡུལ་གྱི་ལྷ་མོ་འདི་བདུན་བསྐྱོད་པའི་ལུས་ཡར་དྲུག་ནང་པ་དང་ཏག་ནིས་ཇོ་མོའི་ལུས་ཡར་ཤ་དཀར་དྲག་ཤོས་པའི་མ་ཏ་མད་ཞུ་བ་ཡིན། དེ་བོད་རིགས་ཅིག་ཏན་དང་འབྲོས་ཡུལ་གྱི་ལྷ་པ་ཡིན།

༤ ལ་དྭགས་རྒྱལ་པོ་སོ་དྭག་བསོད་རྣམ་གྱལ་ནས་སྤྱི་ལོ་ ༡༨༩༦ ལོར་བོད་ནས་འབྲུག་པ་རིན་པོ་ཆེ་དང་འབྲི་གུང་ཆུང་ཚང་ཆོས་ཀྱི་བློ་གྲོས་ལ་དྭགས་སུ་ཞུས། ཆུང་ཚང་གཞམ་ཕྱོགས་སྐྱིད་བུ་ཅན་ཐུག་ཕེབས་སྐབས་ཡུལ་ལྷ་ལ་ཟླ་རེས་དམར་མཆོད་བྱེད་པ་ལ་ཐུགས་མི་མཉེས་པ་མཛད། ཕྱིན་ཕེབས་གཡུང་དྲུང་གདོན་དུ་ཕེབས་སྐབས་ལྷག་མ་གཅིག་ནས་ལྷ་པ་འབོད་ནས་ལྷ་ཞུགས་སུ་བཅུག་ནས་བཀའ་འདྲི་གནང་གསལ། ཡུལ་ལྷ་ལ་ལོ་གཅིག་ནང་དམར་མཆོད་ཐེངས་གཅིག་བྱེད་ན་མི་འགྲིག་གམ་གསུངས་པས། ལྷས་ལན་དུ་ ང་ཚོ་ལྷ་ནི་ཤ་ཁྲག་ལ་འཚོ་བ་བྱེད་མཁན་ཞིག་ཡིན། ད་ལན་བླ་མ་ཁྱེད་ཀྱི་བཀའ་བཅག་མི་ཐུབ་ཞུས། དེ་ནས་བཟུང་ཡུལ་ལྷ་ལ་ལོ་གསར་སྐབས་དམར་མཆོད་ཐེངས་གཅིག་བྱས།

སྐབས་དེར་ཆུང་ཚང་ཆོས་ཀྱི་བློ་གྲོས་ཀྱིས་དམར་མཆོད་ཀྱི་ཚབ་ཏུ་བསངས་གཏོང་དགོས་པ་དང་། གསོལ་མཆོད་གཅིག་ཀྱང་བཙམས་ཏེ་བསངས་དང་མཐུད་ནས་ལྷ་ལ་བཤགས་ཞུས་ཀྱི་སྲོལ་གཏད།

སྤྱི་ལོ་ ༡༩༤༣ ལོར་བ་ཀུ་ལ་ཐུབ་བསྟན་མཆོད་ནོར་སློབ་སྦྱོང་ཐོས་བསམ་མཛད་དེ་བོད་ནས་ལ་དྭགས་སུ་ཕེབས་ཆོས་འཆད་མཁན་གྱི་ཕྱག་ལས་མཛད། སྤྱི་ལོ་ ༡༩༤༤ ༤༥ ལོར་གྲོང་གསེབ་སོ་སོར་བཀའ་སློབ་དང་འབྲེལ་ཡུལ་ལྷ་ལ་དམར་གསོལ་མི་ཆོག་པའི་གཀའ་སྒྲུལ། མི་མང་པོ་ཞིག་གིས་ཉན་ཡང་ཐག་རིང་གྲོང་གསེབ་ཁ་ཅིག་ལ་སྲོལ་དེ་ལུས།

སྤྱི་ལོ་ ༡༩༦༠ ལོར་རྟོགས་ལྡན་བསྟན་པའི་རྒྱལ་མཚན་བོད་ནས་ལ་དྭགས་སུ་ཕེབས་ནས་གཞམ་ཕྱོགས་གཡུང་དྲུང་སོགས་ལ་ཕེབས་ཏེ་དམར་མཆོད་བྱེད་མི་ཆོག་པའི་བཀའ་གནང་བས་མང་ཉུང་སྤང་ཐུབ།

དེ་ནས་ཀུང་མང་ཉུང་ལུས།

སྤྱི་ལོ་ ༡༩༧༥ ལོར་སྐབས་མགོན་ཆེ་ཚང་ཀུན་བཟང་འཕྲིན་ལས་ལྷུན་གྲུབ་བོད་ནས་ལ་དྭགས་སུ་ཕེབས། ལན་མང་ འབྲོག་ཡུལ་མདའ། ཧ་ནུ་སོགས་ལ་ཕེབས་སྐབས་དམར་ཆོད་ཡོངས་སུ་སྤང་དགོས་ཀྱི་བཀའ་སློབ་ལ་བརྟེན་སྤྱི་ལོ་ ༡༩༩༡ ལོ་ནས་བཟུང་དམར་མཆོད་སྤངས་ཐུབ་པ་བྱུང་།

བསོད་ནམས་ཕུན་ཚོགས།

ལ་དྭགས་ནང་སོ་ནམ་པའི་ལས།

རྩོམ་པ་པོ

ཚེ་དབང་རིག་འཛིན།

la dwags nang so nam pa'i las

tsom pa po

tshe bang rig 'dzin

FARMING IN LADAKH

by

Tsewang Rigzin

Lagruk, Sankar, Leh

Summary

Ladakhis have been farming for centuries. Most of the soils found in Ladakh are sandy excepting in the villages situated along the Indus river where the soil is finer and dries hard. Only one crop is possible in most of Ladakh, however in the lower areas of Ladakh even two crops are possible in one year. The food grains grown in Ladakh are wheat, barley, peas etc. A variety of fruit and vegetables are also found in abundance in Ladakh. In Ladakh 95% of the population are farmers.

In the past Ladakh was self-sufficient in food grains, and even exported them to the Changthang areas in Tibet. During the long and cold winter, Ladakhis engage themselves in producing domestic clothes and even shoes. Ladakhis are cheerful people by nature and can be heard singing songs for the different occasions of harvesting, sowing and winnowing.

The main problem the Ladakhis face is water scarcity for irrigation and sometimes they are faced with drought situations. Ladakhis store dried grass for animals and dried vegetables for people for food during the winter. Now the green-house is becoming popular.

རྩོམ་པ་པོ

ཚེ་དབང་རིག་འཛིན།

ལ་དྭགས་ནང་སོ་ནམ་པའི་ལས།

ལ་དྭགས་ནང་སོ་ནམ་པའི་ལས་ནི་ལོ་བརྒྱ་ཕྲག་མང་པོའི་སྔོན་དུ་འགོ་ཚུགས་པ་ཡིན་པ་དེ་རང་རེའི་སྔར་ཆགས་ཀྱི་ཞིང་ཀུན་གྱི་ས་སྤྱང་མཐོན་པོ་ཀུན་ལས་ཤིས་ཐུབ། རྒྱ་ཤོད་ཀྱི་ཡུལ་ཁ་ཤས་མིན་པ་ལ་དྭགས་ཀྱི་ཡུལ་མང་ཆེ་བའི་ས་ནི་ཡང་ན་ས་ཕྱེད་བྱེ་མ་ཕྱེད་ཅན་ཡིན།། རྒྱ་ཤོད་ཀྱི་ས་ནི་འཇམ་པོ་དང་པུང་འགོག་ཅན་ཡིན་ཕྱིར་འབད་སྐྱེད་བྱེད་པ་ལ་དཀའ།

ལ་དྭགས་གང་པོ་ས་ཆ་མཐོ་ཤོས་གཅིག་ལ་ཆགས་པས་དབྱར་གྱི་དུས་ནི་ཡུན་ཐུང་ཞིང་འབྲུའི་སྟོན་ཐོག་ལན་གཅིག་མིན་པ་མི་སྨིན། ཡིན་ཀྱང་ལ་དྭགས་གཤམ་ཕྱོགས་ཀྱི་ཡུལ་ཁ་ཤས་ཙུང་དམའ་བར་ཡོད་པས་དབྱར་གཅིག་ལ་སྟོན་ཐོག་གཉིས་ཀྱང་སྨིན། འབྲུའི་རིགས་གྲོ་ ཤེ་རོག་ཡང་མ། སོ་བ། བྲ་བོ། ཆ་དང་སྲན་མའི་རིགས་སྲན་རིལ་ ནག་སྲན་ཀ་རིས། ཀྱེར་ཟེ་དང་རས་མ་སོགས་སྨིན། ཤིང་ཐོག་དང་ཚོད་མའི་རིགས་ཀྱང་གྲང་ཡུལ་ལ་སྨིན་པ་ཚང་མ་འདི་རུ་སྨིན། ལ་དྭགས་ཀྱི་མི་མང་ཀུན་བརྒྱ་ཐོག་ནས་གོ་ལྟ་ཙམ་ས་ཞིང་འབད་མཁན་དང་དུད་འགྲོ་སྲུལ་མཁན་ཡིན་ཅིང་སྔོན་དུས་འབྲུའི་རིགས་ཀུན་རང་འབོས་ཡོད་མཁན་ཞིག་ཡིན་མ་ཚད་བོད་དང་བྱང་ཐང་སོགས་ཕྱི་ལོག་གི་རྒྱལ་ཁབ་ཀུན་ལ་བལ་དང་ཚའི་ཕྱིར་མང་ཉུང་བཀལ་རྒྱུ་ཡོང་བ་ཡིན། ཡང་དུས་མང་ཆེ་བ་སོ་ནམ་གྱི་ལས་མེད་པར་ལག་བཟོའི་རིགས་རང་ལ་དགོས་པའི་གོས་དང་ལྷམ་སོགས་སོ་

སོའི་ཁང་པར་བཟོ་ཞིང་གཞན་ཡུལ་ནས་མང་པོ་ཞིག་འཁྱོང་བའི་སྲོལ་མེད་པ་ཡིན།

སོ་ནམ་པ་ཀུན་གྱི་དཔྱི་དུས་ཞིང་ལས་འགོ་ཚུགས་དུས་དང་སྟོན་དུས་ཡུལ་འཐག་བྱེད་སྐབས་ཞག་བཟང་པོ་རེ་ལ་ལྟ་བའི་སྲོལ་ཡང་ཡོད། ལ་དྭགས་ཀྱི་སོ་ནམ་པ་ཀུན་ཕན་ཚུན་གཅིག་གྲོགས་གཅིག་གིས་བྱེད། དཔེར་ན་སྟོན་དཔྱིད་གཉིས་ས་ལུད་སྐྱེ་སྐབས་མི་དང་བོང་བུའི་རེས། དབྱར་དུས་བ་རེས་དུས་རྒྱུན་དུ་ར་རེས་དང་ཞིང་རྨོ་ལོག་གི་སྐབས་གླང་དེར་སོགས་མཉམ་རོགས་མཉམ་ལས་བྱེད་པའི་སྲོལ་བཟང་པོ་ལ་འབད།དེང་སང་ཡང་སྔོན་སྲོལ་བཟང་པོ་འདི་ཀུན་གླི་དང་ཉེ་འཁོར་མ་གཏོགས་གཞན་ཡུལ་ཚང་མ་ལ་ཡོད། ཡང་ཞིང་ལས་ཅི་ཞིག་བྱེད་ཀྱང་ལས་དེ་དང་མཐུན་པའི་གླུ་དབྱངས་བཏང་ནས་ལས་དེའི་དཀའ་ངལ་བར་དོ་སེལ་བའི་ཐབས་ལ་འབད་ དཔེར་ན་ཞིང་རྨོ་ལོག་གི་དུས་སུ་འཁོར་ཡང་རེ་རེ་ ས་སྔོ་སྐྱེ་དུས་ཡ་ལི་སླ་མོ་ ཁས་བསྐོར་དུས་ཏ་ལོ་བལ་འདུར་སོགས་ཀྱི་དབྱངས་ལེན། སོ་ནམ་པའི་ལས་ཀུན་གྱི་ལག་ཆ་ཚང་མ་ནི་སྔོན་ལོ་མང་པོ་ཞིག་ནས་བཀོལ་ཞིང་ཡོངས་པའི་རང་གི་ཡུལ་དུ་བཟོས་པའི་ལག་ཆ་རྐྱང་ཡིན། འདི་ཀུན་ལས་བྱེད་སྐབས་དཀའ་ངལ་བར་དོ་ཆེ་བའི་ཕྱིར་འགྱུར་བ་མང་ཉུང་འཁྱོང་དགོས་འདུག།

ཡང་སོ་ནམ་པ་ཀུན་གྱི་དཀའ་ངལ་ཆེ་ཤོས་གཅིག་ནི་དུས་དུས་སུ་ས་ཞིང་ཀུན་ལ་ཆུ་མི་ཐོབ་པ་དེ་ཡིན། སྔོན་དུས་ནས་ཆུའི་ཆེར་ཡོད་ཀྱང་ཁ་བ་དང་ཆར་ཆུ་དཀོན་མོ་ཡོད་པའི་ལོ་ཀུན་ལ་ཆུའི་ཕྱིར་ཕན་ཚུན་འཛིང་མོ་དང་སྟོན་ཐོག་བསྐམ་པའི་སྡུག་བསྔལ་འབྱུང་། ཆུའི་ཐོག་ཡར་རྒྱས་ཆ་ན་ད་

ལྷའི་སྟོན་ཐོག་ལ་ཕན་པར་མ་ཆད་ས་སྟོང་མང་པོ་ཞིག་ལ་ས་གཙོག་བྱེད་ཐུབ་ དཔེར་ན་འདིར་དཀོན་མོ་ཡོད་པའོ་ལྷུང་གླིང་དང་རྩྭ་ཕུག་གི་འཐོན་བསྐྱེད་ཀྱང་འཕེལ་བས་ཞིང་དང་མར་གྱི་ཐོག་རང་པོས་ཆ་ཐུབ།

ལ་དྭགས་ལ་དགུན་དུས་གྲང་མོ་ཡོད་ཕྱིར་དུས་རྒྱུན་དུ་སྔོ་ཚོད་སོགས་སྨིན་མི་ཐུབ་པས་ཟླ་བ་མང་པོ་ཞིག་སྔོ་ཚོད་སྐམ་པོ་ཟ་དགོས་འདུག། ཡིན་ཀྱང་ལོ་ཁ་ཤས་ནས་ཤེལ་ལམ་ཤོག་ཤེལ་གྱི་སྔོ་ཚོད་ཁང་ནང་དགུན་དུས་ཀྱང་ཚོད་མ་འབད་པའི་འགོ་ཚུགས་ཡོད།